More praise for

CONFESSIONS

"[A] remarkable memoir about growing up in Mao's China. . . . Mr. Kang serves as an extraordinary guide through an extraordinary period of Chinese history. He lives through the Great Leap forward, the Cultural Revolution, the thaw following Mao's death, the growing democracy movement of the 1980s and the crackdown after the protests at Tiananmen Square. Simply as a documentary record of daily life in China, *Confessions* is a rewarding read, but Mr. Kang, a gifted stylist (well served by his translator, Susan Wilf) has transmuted his struggles into a literary work of high distinction." —William Grimes, *New York Times*

"A haunting, frightening, and ultimately inspiring story." —*Kirkus Reviews*

"Absorbing. . . . Kang's story is a lively, intricate account of communism's panoptic police state. . . . Kang's rugged individualism takes his story beyond the usual narrative of persecution and hardship, making it an incisive, personal critique of a deeply conformist society." —*Publishers Weekly*

"I'll just come right out and say it. This is not only one of the best accounts I've read of life in Communist China, it's a lyrical and compelling read about an imaginative, literary boy trapped in a society hostile to artistic expression." —Andrea Robinson, editor, Book-of-the-Month Club

"Vivid and fluid." —*Booklist*

"The perspective is fresh, the writing fresher, and the analysis, which is built into the stories rather than added afterwards, is freshest of all." —*Library Journal*

"A rich, moving, and unique memoir. Through its honest and intimate language, it attains a kind of universality, vivid, painful, and entirely authentic." —Ha Jin, author of *War Trash* and *Waiting: A Novel*

CONFESSIONS

An Innocent Life in Communist China

KANG ZHENGGUO

TRANSLATED BY SUSAN WILF

W. W. Norton & Company New York · London

Book design by Chris Welch
Production manager: Julia Druskin

Library of Congress Cataloging-in-Publication Data

Kang, Zhengguo.
[Wo de fan dong zhi shu. English]
Confessions : an innocent life in Communist China / Kang, Zhengguo ;
translated by Susan Wilf.
p. cm.
Includes bibliographical references and index.
ISBN-13: 978-0-393-06467-4

1. Kang, Zhengguo. 2. Authors, Chinese—20th century—Biography. I. Title.
PL2869.N565Z47713 2007
895.1'351—dc22
[B]
2006103103

ISBN 978-0-393-33200-1 pbk.

W. W. Norton & Company. Inc., 500 Fifth Avenue, New York, N. Y. 10110
www.wwnorton.com

W. W. Norton & Company Ltd., Castle House, 75/76 Wells Street, London W1T

反者，道之動。

—— 老子 ——

Opposition is the movement of the Dao.
—Laozi

CONTENTS

CONTENTS   ix

LIST OF ILLUSTRATIONS

INTRODUCTION

THIS MAY BE the best account of daily life in Communist China that I have ever read. It stands out not because it recasts the broad outlines of history but because of the extraordinarily lifelike quality of the writing and the credibility of its account of life under Mao. Hundreds of writers of both fiction and nonfiction have given accounts of "the people" (aka "the masses") during China's Mao years, but nearly all use an ideological lens that flattens the perspective and homogenizes the background, indeed starches the clothing, tidies the town square, recolors the sky, and, most important, tells you what to think about a social problem in terms that are usually oversimplified and often grossly false. This account, in contrast, is clear-eyed.

After Mao there was a quick literary reaction against much that Mao had done but not so much against the Maoist style of writing. The scar literature of 1978–80 reversed direction on some key points (Mao's top lieutenants, once infallibly correct, now included the all-evil Gang of Four; the Cultural Revolution was not glorious but violent and bloody; corruption, formerly unmentionable, was acknowledged as a big problem). But the colored lens problem persisted; only some of the colors had changed. Maoist literary style survived as a habit even among writers who consciously sought to pull themselves free from Maoist ideology. For a few who became aware of this problem, the quest for self-extrication itself became a sort of obsession, and this too created problems when they tried to look squarely at history.

Kang Zhengguo, who never bought into Maoism, does not have to tell us how he got out of it. His writing is a powerful indictment of life under Mao but not because he is pushing any alternative ideology. What he gives us is daily experience written from the ground up, as it were, and with a charming transparency that spares no one, including himself; the prose conveys a sense of authenticity that is extremely rare in accounts of life in Communist China. It is startling, when you think of it, that the world has so far had almost no honest accounts of daily experience in a country as large as China over nearly half a century of its modern history. Here, though, we do have one.

Although Kang reveals a great deal about ordinary life in China, his own path is not exactly ordinary. He is by nature an adversative character, a square peg unsuited to the round holes laid out by authorities of any kind, be they his father, his school, his wife, or the Communist Party of China. He thinks for himself and is a bit too quick to assume that if something makes sense to him, it ought to make sense to everybody and therefore be acted upon. His wife says of him, "You always stick your neck out when everybody else has the good sense to lie low." Yet Kang's blunt approach turns out to be an excellent tool for exposing the submerged textures of everything around him. While most of his contemporaries submit to authority, get used to doing so, and eventually regard this as so normal that they become entirely unaware of the patterns that their own lives are observing, Kang does none of this. He trundles his way through life rather like a good-natured rhinoceros, ignoring boundaries, inadvertently dislodging rocks, and occasionally trampling the tails of snakes that spring up to bite him. We follow him from college to brick factory to labor camp to prison and finally into rural exile. The odyssey is revelatory at every stage.

For the social historian, Kang's book opens the door on the mechanics of the Mao-era control system. We get to see, for example, how the use of the official stamp to coerce conformity had a power that went far beyond the particular issue at hand. You want a job? A residence permit? A marriage license? From the point of view of the omnipresent control system, exactly what it is that you want is almost irrelevant. The important point is that I, the official, have the power to withhold it from you, the supplicant, and this power gives me leverage over *every* aspect of your life, whether related to your request or not. You want that marriage license? Behave better at work. You want a job assignment? Submit to authority in your neighborhood. And so on. The "smart" way to handle such pressures is to learn to toady. Kang's way (and he was not alone here; a number of the inmates in the labor camps and prisons are like him in this regard) is to reason on principle, to resist, and in consequence to be snared by the system and labeled a troublemaker in a broad sense that follows one wherever one goes, year after year.

Once snared, miscreants are squeezed. After Kang has been expelled from college and sent home, he finds that his ration coupons have been withheld. He has to impose on the rations of family members, and this makes him feel an increasing pressure to move out. But then he finds—and this pattern repeats itself several times—that the only route *out* is *down*. You can leave home, but only by "volunteering" to live and work at a squalid brick factory. You don't like the factory? You can leave (farther down the social scale) for a rural labor camp. Your counterrevolutionary record is getting the better of you? You can renounce your past, your childhood, your family name, your everything and offer yourself as an adopted son to an elderly bachelor in the countryside. No problem! A few banquets and gifts to grease the wheels, and we in the system can arrange all this for you. The bizarre comes to seem so normal that the simplest of unapproved human expression resembles the derring-do of a spy; an old friend silently passes a note about where to meet, at a later time, for frank talk in a cornfield. Watching Kang spiral downward, the reader is led to muse on the mechanics of social mobility in the other direction. Just what kind of behavior would help one *rise* within a system like this?

Following Kang on his tour of the innards of the Mao years, we come to see the surface impressions of that era quite differently. Take the Great Proletarian Cultural Revolution, for example. How much writing has there been about its radical zeal, its pushing of Communist theory and practice to a new level? Kang does not bother to tell us that this writing is superficial. He just relates what he saw and heard in daily life and in passing makes clear that much of the popular rage that burst forth during the Cultural Revolution was born of recoil from what the Communists had already done, not from a demand that they do more of it. The Cultural Revolution also brought Kang more, not less, access to "bourgeois" pleasures like reading non-Communist books, smoking cigarettes, and chatting with friends.

Kang's supple writing moves seamlessly between his external context and his inner world of thoughts and feelings, thereby showing us not only social patterns but the psychological struts that support them. Fresh insights emerge. In official language, for example, the "collectivism" of the Mao years has always been officially presented as a kind of idealistic group-mindedness, and we do know from other memoirs, such as Liu Binyan's, that elite young people in the 1950s and 1960s did pursue group interests with enthusiasm. But in daily life at many other social levels, the party's power engineering created very nearly the opposite of group-mindedness. It focused sharply on the individual person: *You* are wrong; *you* are alone, *you* need to join the mainstream; and your only route to rejoining it is to submit to *me*, the one who holds power over you. Not just Kang but most of the people in his memoir are actually or potentially trapped by this kind of threat. They are isolated as individuals—or at most in families or small circles of friends—and they perceive the larger society as a majority arrayed against them, while in fact that majority is itself a sea of people who are similarly frightened and isolated. The collective consciousness of the mainstream is an illusion.

One important reason why the illusion can persist is that people fear guilt by association. When one person's political taint becomes known, everyone else keeps a distance. So-and-so is counterrevolutionary? Has a prison record? Stay away! On the surface, the party can claim that this reaction demonstrates collective political will. See? The Chinese people hate counterrevolutionaries! In fact, though, what everybody hates is the possibility that political leprosy will spread to him. Thus each person's calculations about how to survive, when viewed alongside every other person's, produces the surface appearance of unanimous support for the party. The Chinese people were (then as much as now) certainly smart enough to figure all this out and could have done something about it if public discussion and organization had been allowed. But they were not, and everyone knew that anyone who moved to claim these rights was only asking to become yet another political leper. The party further suppressed such thoughts by seeing to it that errant individuals remained intensely aware of their own guilt. After his release from prison, for example, Kang is forced to reimburse the state "for the expense of imprisoning me."

Prohibitions against misbehavior eventually sank in as permanent and unquestioned features of life, as obvious as the rule that you get wet if you go out in the rain. This is why Kang's parents, and later his wife, find his resistance neither admirable nor courageous but simply obtuse. Yet when Kang's fortunes hit rock bottom, he finds (and this has happened with other dissidents) that his spirits get an unexpected lift. When he learns that a friend has burned his diaries, "the thought that I had nothing to lose was strangely calming," Kang writes. The psychological pressure generated by the fear of loss dissipates when little or nothing remains to be lost, or as the Chinese proverb puts it, "Dead pigs do not fear boiling water." Later, after Kang recovers and eventually emigrates—and again comes to feel that he has significant things to lose—he once more is ready to compromise, albeit reluctantly. When he returns to China in 2000, he arranges his itinerary so as not to rile his hometown police during the "sensitive period" of the June 4 anniversary of the Beijing Massacre of 1989.

In the 1970s, when Kang goes to live for several years in the Shaanxi countryside, he arrives there as a cultural outsider and immediately turns into a keen observer of rural life. His book, among its other virtues, presents some excellent anthropology. Other accounts of Mao-era commune life have too often bristled with one or another kind of jargon: either the political cant of Maoism, which paints a superidealized picture that is essentially false or, in more recent times, the puffy academese of certain strains of Western anthropology, whose language can leave the ground and ascend into clouds of splendid uninterpretability.

Kang the anthropologist, in his concrete and lively language, combines an acerbic eye with a good-natured respect for China's folkways. We see how the language of "commune" and "work team" overlay a daily life in which people in fact were acutely aware of private property; no one was in doubt about who owned what tools, grain, animals, or housing, and there was considerable jealousy over who got how many work points. As in pre-Communist China, the boredom of village life put a premium on every small distraction, so that, for example, when someone fell ill, the whole village had an opportunity to drop by, offering "unsolicited advice and expressions of feigned concern." Traditional notions of peasant egalitarianism had been strengthened by Maoist dicta, and villagers, even while coveting their hoes and work points, believed that anyone in the village who got a windfall should be obliged to share some if it. Hence, when Kang's parents in the city pay for a pile of pretty red tiles for Kang to use to put a roof over his head, a stream of villagers drops by to let it be known they would like to "borrow" a few. How to handle these requests and still have enough tiles for the roof became a problem for Kang, who concludes that "a stroke of good luck could be a nuisance in disguise."

The brilliant 1980s short stories of Gao Xiaosheng ("The Money Purse," "Fishing," and others)[1] reveal this same mentality among farmers in another part of China, Jiangsu Province; both Gao and Kang also show how the mental world of Chinese villagers, despite the blandness of daily life (or perhaps *because* of it), could be surprisingly complex and sophisticated. Why, for example, do the people in Kang's village vote for his adoptive father Li Baoyu to be chairman of the Poor and Lower-Middle Peasants' Association? Li had a mixed reputation, "not greedy or dishonest," but often "mulish and stingy" and not very bright, indeed "practically the village idiot." Li's singular credential for office turns out to be that his house is the only one in the village that has no wall in front of it. With no wall, he can hide nothing. Unable to hide things, he will not pilfer from the group. And everybody knows that he is too poor to build a wall. So elect him!

Countryside people are forbidden from moving to the cities, where life is better, and for this reason feel inferior. On the other hand, their envy of urbanites melds into rivalry, so that they sometimes regard urbanites "as

---

[1] *The Broken Betrothal and Other Stories* (Beijing: Panda Books, 1978).

monsters, a different species," just as, Kang wryly notes, "Chinese people in general regarded foreigners."

But for all its good sociology and anthropology, the special virtue of this book is its fine writing. Kang's prose is fluent, lifelike, vivid, graceful. His characters stand up and walk off the page, and his charming turns of phrase are an added treat: The stillness in his village is broken only by "the raucous braying of bored donkeys"; when he is forced to write yet another self-criticism, the blank page "mocked me like a fun house mirror." The credit for capturing Kang's art in English belongs to Susan Wilf, his superb translator. Wilf understands, as many translators of languages as different as Chinese and English do not, that word-for-word reflection of syntax and lexicon can be a pedantic sort of fidelity and that the life and art of a piece are more faithfully served by reading a whole sentence, or several at once, and then contriving to give the reader the fullest and most natural re-creation of the original that one can manage, even if this means completely rethinking the syntax and being "free" with the lexicon.

My field of study is modern Chinese literature, and I have often felt puzzled by the difficulty Chinese writers have had in looking deeply into Maoism and its aftermath. Where is a Chinese Solzhenitsyn, or Vaclav Havel, or Primo Levi? For other modern societies that have endured severe trauma, literature has played a role in facing difficult truths and helping transcend them, but in modern China it's as if a huge reverse magnet lies at the core of the issue. Writers of several kinds have aimed at the heart of Maoism and begun to move toward it but, as they draw near, are deflected in one direction or another.

The scar writers of 1978–80 denounced the Gang of Four and spoke of "ten years of catastrophe." But they told only a fraction of what they knew and felt. They had seen such things as murder, gouged eyes, and parents forced to pay for the bullet that executed their child but wrote only of "unhealthy tendencies." Deng Xiaoping's demand for "stability and unity" blocked their way forward, and most eventually passed from the literary scene after only, as the Chinese idiom puts it, "scratching the itch from the outside of the boot."

A few did persist, in one or another way. Zhang Xianliang, for example, went on to produce a large corpus of fiction and memoirs about labor camps. Zhang is extremely good at describing the psychological consequences of hunger, thirst, sex privation, and captivity, and his insights gain credibility from their congruence with accounts of human beings who have endured extremity elsewhere. Primo Levi's memoir of Hitler's camps, Someth May's account of Pol Pot's, and Ōoka Shōhei's tale of a starving soldier in the wilds of the Philippines,[2] among others, reveal the elemental human nature that Zhang Xianliang finds, in himself and in others, inside China's labor camps. But Zhang, despite all that he achieves, cannot in the end extricate himself from a supplicatory attitude toward the Communist Party of China. Like Wang Meng, Cong Weixi, and many others of the generation of Chinese writers who rode on high hopes for their revolution until the Maoist havoc forced a reappraisal, Zhang emerged from the Mao years "wishing it hadn't been so" and addressing authority, the very authority that had oppressed him, in an almost apologetic attitude. Zhang remains couched in this politically recumbent position even as he records the harshest cruelty of the labor camps. He somehow cannot pull himself free to "live in truth," in Vaclav Havel's phrase, or to transcend to a higher level, as Primo Levi was able to do in his later writing or as Ōe Kenzaburō could do in looking back on the A-bombing of Hiroshima and Nagasaki.

Some of the "modernist" literary works that appeared in China in the late 1980s and the 1990s can also be seen, in part, as posttraumatic symptoms of the Mao years. Worlds filled with murderous toddlers, incestuous fathers, belching grandmothers, horn-blowing deaf-mutes, hoodlums who grin as an electric drill penetrates someone's kneecap, sunlight so hot that it melts the sand underfoot, family history that gets more and more grotesque the deeper one digs, narrative dreaminess that blurs reality and nightmare, and more, all were the creations of a generation of writers who had grown up during late Maoism. However bizarre, these images bear a certain authenticity. Can Xue, whose stories are among the strangest of all, has said that she writes in a sort of trancelike state, allowing, as it were,

[2] See Primo Levi, *The Drowned and the Saved*, trans. Raymond Rosenthal (New York: Summit Books, 1988); Someth May, *Cambodian Witness*, ed. James Fenton (London and Boston: Faber and Faber, 1986); Ōoka Shōhei, *Fires on the Plain*, trans. Ivan Morris (New York: Knopf, 1957).

content to vault from the back of her brain directly onto the paper before her, and then never revises. It may be hard to imagine a more honest way of writing, but for the reader it leaves daunting problems of interpretation. What does she mean by unexplained references to "the man locked up in the hut banging furiously against the door" or "dead moths and dragonflies scattered on the floor"?[3] If such images are one way of looking back at the Maoist disaster, they are yet another kind of oblique expression. They still submit to the power of that giant reverse magnet, the same power that stunted the growth of scar literature and kept writers like Zhang Xianliang locked in supplicatory mode. Twenty years after the death of Mao, after the purge of 1987 and the bloody crackdown in 1989, most Chinese writers had given up fighting the reverse magnet. Many turned around, plunged into the sea of innocuous topics, and, in terms of living standards and fame, found good careers.

We should note in passing that the reluctance to look squarely at the Maoist past is not just a Chinese problem. Westerners have also fallen into self-censorship and have been caught up in a variety of supplicatory poses. These have arisen in part from the same kinds of implicit threats and rewards that affect Chinese people but also in part from the West's old romantic notion that the East is an exotic world and an appropriate receptacle for Western wishful thinking.

Now we have Kang Zhengguo, whose writing is quite free of self-censorship, supplicatory attitude, bizarre modernism, or other deflections of vision of the sorts just reviewed. Kang is free as well from the kind of distortion that, in some writers, grows out of conscious rebellion against such deflection. Kang seems, as he wanders through his memories, completely unaffected by questions of how close he may or may not be coming to politically radioactive turf. He tells us what he saw, heard, and felt and uses the same tone whether or not he happens to be implying that the emperor is naked. For example, when local officials categorize him as "the dregs of society" (a technical term, in Communist jargon) and assign him

[3] These images are taken, almost at random, from Can Xue's story "Hut on the Mountain," Ronald R. Janssen and Jian Wang, *Dialogues in Paradise* (Evanston, Ill.: Northwestern University Press, 1989), p. 47.

to labor, he neither accepts the insult nor turns sarcastic toward it but is almost childlike in his observation of a contradiction in how they have presented things to him: "If labor was so glorious, why did they give all the dirty work to us, the dregs of society, instead of doing it themselves?"

Before the Communist revolution, a few writers, like Xiao Hong in her wonderful *Tales of Hulan River* (1942), were also able to write in this tone of childlike lucidity. But since then examples of the style have been extremely rare in mainland China, where guidelines, "forbidden zones," and required jargon and conceptual categories have driven pre-Communist writing styles deep into the crannies of society, far from the printed page. Pu Ning's *Red in Tooth and Claw*, which Kang Zhengguo admires, is a rare example of writing that somehow survived in one of those crannies. Pu wrote as Wumingshi ("Anonymous"); his account of life in labor camps, which reveals Mao-era realities in unusual depth, reads as if sealed off from both Maoist literary influence and the recoil from it. Kang and Pu are similar in this regard.

It would be wrong, though, not to acknowledge and admire those Chinese writers who at one point did embrace Maoism or were simply engulfed by it and who later consciously sought to pull their writing free from the Mao mentality. This too was done in a variety of ways. Some, such as Zhong Acheng and Wang Zengqi in the 1980s, sought refuge in the language and narrative technique of traditional Chinese fiction and storytelling. In so doing, they drew upon the latent power of Chinese cultural habit, which perdured despite attempts during the Mao years to stomp it out. Other writers, such as the "misty" poets of the late 1970s and early 1980s and some of the modernist fiction writers a decade later, borrowed Western literary form and technique to help with the self-extrication process. In this they had a powerful ally in the widespread assumption in China (whether stated or not) that the West is "advanced." Some writers went, as it were, all the way West-ward in literary terms by adopting Western languages as their very means of expression. Ha Jin writes in English, as, sometimes, does Zha Jianying, while Dai Sijie and Nobel laureate Gao Xingjian have written in French. It may seem odd that a writer's leap "out" of China and into a Western language can leave him or her more free than before to evoke the mood and subtleties of life in China. But this, in a few cases, has indeed been true. I know of no fiction written in Chinese that reveals the mood of Chinese urban life in the 1970s better than does Ha Jin's *Waiting*. Readers of Kang Zhengguo's memoir will note a similarity between it and Ha Jin's prose. Both penetrate daily life in the Communist period very effectively, even as neither carries the slightest hint of Communist literary practice. This is rare.

We might wonder why it is so rare, and has taken so long, for Chinese writing "free of Mao" to appear. At least in one sense the delay is normal. Literary transcendence of major disasters in other modern societies has also taken time. Anne Frank kept a diary during the Holocaust, recording what she saw, heard, and thought in her immediate environment, and after the war some other accounts of pain and suffering appeared soon enough, but it took about forty years before Primo Levi and others had sufficient distance from the catastrophe to be able even to attempt comprehension of it. The literary recoil from Stalin's terror and from the dropping of the atomic bombs on Japan shows a broadly similar pattern. In China the effort to transcend has been more difficult because of the Communist Party's continuing ban on public criticism of Mao. German writers could attack Hitler within months of his death, while Russian writers had to wait about three posthumous years before taking on Stalin. By contrast, Chinese writers, nearly thirty years after Mao's death, still need to tiptoe around his image and pretend to respect certain fundaments of his language and his worldview. Communist Party leaders, fearing that their rule might collapse if its Maoist strut were removed, took steps to ensure that Mao's reputation stayed in place.

These included censorship, which blocks unapproved ideas from publication, and enforced self-censorship, by which a writer withholds or alters his or her expression from fear of some kind of punishment. Both these deterrents have been important in preventing honest literary engagement with China's recent past, and Kang Zhengguo avoids both of them. But he avoids yet another important barrier, which is the controlling power of language itself. This is more subtle and insidious, and it may be worth a short diversion to try to make clear what it is.

To adopt the lingo of people one interacts with is natural, indeed so common that we might call it human nature. It happens even when one does not admire the terms that one's interlocutor uses, as, for example, when I as a professor talk with my registrar about "units" of course work in literature even though I find a metaphor that suggests "measurable lump," like cheese or tofu, to be ridiculous when applied to literature. The pressure to adjust to someone else's terms grows stronger when the other party holds pervasive power over one. During China's Mao years the Communist Party's use of language caused certain patterns of expression to become entrenched within the public so deeply that people took them for granted. Eventually it did not seem strange, but only reasonable, to master the official language in order to protect oneself or to get what one wanted. Public discourse became a sort of language game. In the late 1970s, for example, when it became a national policy to make amends with persecuted intellectuals, professors who wanted better housing did not go to their local party leaders and ask, "Can I have a bigger apartment?" They would say something like "Could the recent policies of Party Central be concretized in my case?"

Eventually, moreover, official language seeped into unofficial contexts where it affected daily-life expression. "Annihilate (*xiaomie*)," for example, was prominent in the Communist lexicon because combat was common in the party's history. Mao Zedong became partial to the word. People who grew up in China in the 1950s through 1970s began to use the word metaphorically in daily-life contexts. When, for example, a bit of food is left on a serving plate at a dinner table and might best be finished off, someone might say, "Let's annihilate it." (The usage is not idiomatic in Taiwan or in overseas Chinese communities.) In 1988 on a public bus in Beijing I heard a little boy say to his mother, "Ma, I gotta pee!" The mother said, "Persevere!," using *jianchi*, a term that had been used for decades for upholding one or another political line but that had come to permeate daily life so thoroughly no one on the bus seemed to find it remarkable.

The seepage of political language into daily life affected literature as well. With the categories and concepts that it entails, political language has done at least as much to impede clear-eyed writing as have editorial censorship and conscious self-censorship. Moreover, its effects have been harder to get rid of because most writers, most of the time, have been unaware of them. Writers in the 1950s were drawn into what Chu

Anping called "the world of the party," in which all public expression observed stylized norms that signaled, regardless of topic and even of viewpoint, "I am part of this partyworld." When Miklós Haraszti observed that Hungarian writers in the 1950s were living inside a "velvet prison,"[4] he was referring not only to the system of material rewards that lured and held them but also to the velvet unreality of official language that cushioned their intellectual work. For China in the late 1950s, in my view, the metaphor of velvet is not quite strong enough. Chinese writers "inside the world of the party" were then more like George Orwell's depiction of Henry Miller, swallowed like Jonah and "inside the whale"—i.e., its stomach—"like a womb big enough for an adult." Orwell invites us to imagine: "the dark, cushioned space that exactly fits you, with yards of blubber between you and reality, able to keep up an attitude of the completest indifference, no matter *what* happens. A storm that would sink all the battleships in the world would hardly reach you as an echo. Even the whale's own movements would probably be imperceptible to you. He might be wallowing among the surface waves or shooting down into the blackness of the middle seas . . . , but you would never know the difference."[5] Were Chinese writers in the 1950s aware of where the great Maoist whale was headed? When the great famine began devouring tens of millions of lives, could they, from their position inside the whale, cushioned by yards of blubber, even begin to describe the sea and the storm? Did the public domain offer them adequate language for such an effort? Twenty years after the great famine, when writers could begin to address what had happened, they were still constricted—by continuing political guidelines and implicit threats but also by language. They spoke of "mistakes," of "prices that were paid," and of how too bad it was, for example, that Mao Zedong had outmaneuvered Peng Dehuai in 1959. Their views were passionate and worth a salute from us, but they still could not say plainly what needed to be said.

[4] Miklós Haraszti, *The Velvet Prison: Artists under State Socialism*, trans. Katalin and Stephen Landesman (New York: Basic Books, 1987).

[5] George Orwell, "Inside the Whale," *A Collection of Essays* (Garden City, N.Y.: Doubleday & Co., 1954), p. 249.

When we read Kang Zhengguo, it can seem oddly striking that we find his outlook so commonsensical. How did such a sense-making approach emerge from such "crazy" times? Moreover, we see that Kang was not alone; we see other ordinary Chinese coping their ways through life, thinking and behaving not like Mao models but in ways that human beings elsewhere in the world can relate to. That human beings in Maoist China were fundamentally the same as human beings elsewhere ought not to count as an insight, and yet given the dearth of honest writing from the period, it does appear as one.

As we read Kang and get deeper and deeper into the nonparty world that it unfolds, the party world seems correspondingly to shrink. It still dominates, to be sure, and is still frightening. But we see more and more that the party world is not coterminous with "China." Since the 1950s the Communist Party of China has always spoken of itself, both internally and to the international world, as if it were China: Nation, state, and party are all one. This rhetorical gesture of course has its political purposes: to suggest that support of the party is support of China, that criticism of the party is criticism of China, that to oppose the party is to be non-Chinese, and so on. Perhaps the most life-affirming fruit of Kang Zhengguo's memoir is that it opens a small space around Kang's daily life and then, as Kang meets others and the space expands, pushes back the hegemonic claim that "party and China are one." The party eventually comes to seem not the whole of the country but a sort of private membership group—albeit a very large one—that rides atop the populace. In 1991 Wan Runnan, the famous chief of the Sitong Company who was obliged to flee China after the Beijing Massacre, commented that "China belongs to the people of China; it is not the private property of the Communist Party." This assertion, obvious in one sense, was unutterable during the Mao years and still sounded radical in 1991. Kang Zhengguo does not repeat the assertion but just assumes it and then tells us how the true owners of China made the best of their lives during difficult times.

—Perry Link
Princeton University
August 2006

自述

CONFESSIONS

1

Liberation

ONE DAY IN the early summer of 1949 Nanny bundled up all her silver jewelry in a piece of blue homespun, grabbed me by the hand, and fled with me out of the Dongguo Gate of Xi'an. Much later I learned that that had been the day of Xi'an's Liberation. "Liberation" was a brand-new word at the time, and I was only five years old, too young to grasp its full meaning. All I remember is that Nanny had been discussing the news with everybody for days: The Nationalist troops were retreating in defeat, and the Communist Eighth Route Army was coming. Nobody could explain exactly what this "army of bumpkins" was, but I could sense the worry in people's faces and tones of voice. The idea of an army, any army, struck terror into Nanny's heart. Her nervousness led me to fear that they were going to sack the city as soon as they arrived. All she had in the world was this bundle of jewelry from her trousseau. Over and over again she took out her silver bracelets, hairpins, and necklaces and then wrapped them up again, as if this would protect them from the marauding hillbillies.

Outside the city gate there was a fork in the country road. One way led south, to Nanny's in-laws' house, and the other side led north, to her parents'.

She had told me her story many times. Her firstborn daughter had died of umbilical tetanus in the year that I was born. Before her milk could dry up, she had hurried off into the city, where she had found a job as my wet nurse. She hated her simpleminded husband and never wanted to go back to her in-laws' house again. She took me with her to visit her parents on holidays, so I could reel off the names of all the villages along the road as fluently as any bus conductor. I remembered where there was a cemetery or temple and where you could buy chilled tea.

On past occasions there had been almost nobody on the road, and the rural scenery had been dull, but this time I saw something different: refugees streaming in both directions, in and out of the city, and bare-chested deserters from the retreating Nationalist Army with red welts on their shoulders from carrying stretchers. I heard the muffled booming of cannons in the distance, and the loud explosion of the great Chan River Bridge being destroyed by the retreating Nationalists. People were lugging all kinds of bundles in their hands, on their shoulders, on carrying poles, and in carts. They were afraid that their personal property would be seized by the passing troops. They feared the retreating army, but they feared the approaching one even more.

We didn't see any armies along the way. But we did see people looting a Nationalist Army base near the road. As soon as the troops evacuated the buildings, a mob surged in and tore them up, making off with wooden beams and sacks of flour, while a group of empty-handed onlookers egged one another on, shouting, "Go for it! Let's get some loot while we can!"

That afternoon we arrived at Nanny's parents' house, a deep, dark earthen cave with a cracked, sooty ceiling, which I was afraid would collapse on us. As I stretched my tired legs on the *kang*,[1] I took a deep breath, enjoying the familiar smell of earth, mildewed straw, and chimney smoke. On the wall there was a shrine to the gods, lit by an oil lamp, with a table of offerings beneath it. Under the table there was a dark pit, which Nanny called a cellar. She climbed down into this cellar and hid her bundle, and then all the neighbors filed in and hid their bundles there too. Finally, the terrifying day passed, and the troops were gone. By the next morning,

---

[1] A heated brick bed used in North China.

when there still had not been any pillaging, the neighbors filed back in to retrieve their hidden bundles, and village life returned to normal.

When Nanny brought me back to our family home in the Dongguan section of Xi'an[2] about ten days later, the Communists had taken over. The whole city was abuzz with the word "liberation," which was emblazoned on posters everywhere. Triumphant songs were popular, and I liked this one:

The sky is blue in the liberated areas,
The people are glad in the liberated areas,
The sun never sets in the liberated areas,
The singing never ends in the liberated areas.

People really did seem as jubilant as the song suggested, as if the mere incantation of this new word, "liberation," could instantly usher out the old and bring in the new. But some things did not change that quickly. Our inner courtyard was still quiet all day; the gray pigeons still cooed on the roof; the big old tree by our door was still half dead, with the same hollow halfway up its trunk; the road from the Dongguo Gate to our house was still pitted; and manure, garbage, and dead cats and dogs were still piled next to the earthen city wall with a sickening stench that reeked from far away.

Once the Communists were in power, there was endless fanfare. Whenever new policies were proclaimed in the streets, parades of teachers and students spilled out of the middle school next door to our house, beating drums and gongs, waving little red and green placards, and shouting slogans. Nanny enjoyed all the festivities. She had always liked going to traditional New Year's parades with our cook, a tall man who would elbow his way through the crowds with me on his shoulders to see all the different costumed characters from various operas. Suspended high in the air from scaffolding cleverly hidden with stage props, they held still, like statues, as the parade marched slowly along. Nanny would point to them and identify them for me.

[2] Near the East Gate of the city.

But this parade was different. Wearing octagonal caps and Lenin costumes or white-towel turbans, the marchers beat on waist drums and danced the *yangge*,[3] twisting and turning, taking a few steps forward, then a few steps backward. From time to time they stopped and stood in a circle to sing and dance for the audience. This new show had nothing to do with the traditional opera, so Nanny could not tell me the names of the characters. The only thing that was the same was the earsplitting banging of the gongs and drums, which reverberated throughout the city so often that most days seemed like New Year's, an audible sign that times had changed.

Of course nobody used the derogatory term "bumpkin Eighth Route Army" anymore. Now it was called the People's Liberation Army. This was its official name, and all others were banned. One evening when a contingent of this army rolled into the Dongguo Gate, we heard someone at our door calling, "Ma'am!" Nanny, who had the typical civilian's ingrained fear of the military, went to answer the door. Later she told Grandmother that her hands had been trembling so hard that it had taken her forever to get the bolt open. That night the troops were quartered in our alley, and they cooked their meals in our kitchen the next day. But people's fears turned out to be groundless. The troops were well disciplined and congenial, and there was no trouble. Nevertheless, the townspeople still called them bumpkins and circulated jokes about them. There was one about a soldier who tried to light his cigarette by holding it up to a lightbulb, and another about some troops who, quartered in a judge's house, dropped to the floor with their guns cocked when they heard a telephone ring.

Once the troops were gone, we were harassed constantly by our new neighborhood police officer, a man in a shabby uniform with a heavy northern Shaanxi accent. We always served him tea in the parlor, but he seemed unaccustomed to smooth cedar chairs, and after sitting for a while, he would shift to a squatting position right on his chair, without even taking off his shoes. The main reason he came was to interrogate Father about his vacuum-tube radio, apparently a forbidden item now. The police seemed to suspect that it was for sending wireless telegrams rather than for receiving broadcasts. Father was summoned repeatedly to the police sta-

[3] A rural folk dance popularized by the Chinese Communists.

tion for questioning. Although they never managed to pin anything on him, he eventually surrendered the radio in exasperation.

Father had gotten his undergraduate degree in water conservancy engineering from the National Northwestern Agricultural Institute and done his graduate work in municipal drainage systems in Chongqing. Then he returned to Xi'an and was hired as head of the Preparatory Department for the new city waterworks. Before the Communist takeover, he had dressed in a suit and tie, parted his hair and styled it with a hair dryer, ridden a motorcycle to work, and entertained in his living room an American engineer from Tennessee, with whom he spoke English. He had also been fond of oatmeal and condensed milk, from boxes labeled in English. When the Communists nationalized all the industries, they retained him as a deputy chief engineer in the new waterworks. Once they sent him to Shanghai to sue the foreign contractors who had built the waterworks before the Communist takeover. After a lengthy stay there he recovered a large sum of money on behalf of the waterworks. But while he was away, our family fell on hard times.

The Kang family, 1945. From the left: Mother and the author, Third Aunt and Cousin Shuren, Cousin Zhengxin, Grandmother, and Father.

The Land Reform campaign had begun, and Grandfather was classified as a landlord. According to the official policy, he was supposed to buy back some real estate that he had recently sold and donate it to the work team to be redistributed to the poor peasants and farmhands. To raise the cash for this, he had to sell our family home in Xi'an at a loss. My parents, who could never afford to buy a house again, rented a place downtown with me and my two younger sisters, Shuzhi and Shuci.

On weekends and holidays we went to visit my grandparents in their garden home next to the ruins of the earthen city wall, not far from the house we had sold. The local people called my grandparents' garden the Kang family cemetery because Grandfather's mother was buried under a stone stupa[4] there. She had been a devout Buddhist all her life, and Grandfather had taken her on a pilgrimage around the mountain temples of South China in the early 1920s, while he was living in Shanghai. Unfortunately, she passed away on the journey. He shipped her coffin back home to Xi'an and buried her by the city wall near our house. His love for her ran especially deep because his father had died long before, and she had raised him and paid for his education single-handedly. At the time of her death he was a leader in local industry, but after her funeral he suddenly decided to set aside all his worldly affairs. After building a two-acre garden around her grave, he moved there to devote himself to the study of Buddhism. Inspired by the Buddhist term "perfect silence," used for the deaths of monks and nuns, he named it Silent Garden.

As far back as I can remember, Grandfather practiced Buddhism in this garden. He hired a craftsman to engrave plates for printing the scriptures,[5] built a guesthouse for visiting Buddhist priests, and organized Buddhist study groups. But he spent most of his time there alone, and family members rarely went to see him. Grandmother and his children and grandchildren lived in their own houses and went about their own business, visiting him only on holidays.

Inside the main gate of Silent Garden there was a round doorway framed by a couplet on a pair of hanging wooden tablets, which I liked to

[4] A Buddhist monument.

[5] A meritorious act in Buddhism.

bang against the wall to scare the lizards into the cracks. Beyond the doorway there was a narrow mossy path through a bamboo grove, blocked by an old trellis of wisteria that had wrapped itself like a boa around a nearby tree. To the left of the trellis there was an artificial mountain and a goldfish pond, and to the right there were some tile-roofed buildings, in front of which a brick path led to the staircase into the main house. Once I passed the brick-floored entryway, I would lift the door curtain and enter Grandfather's inner sanctum, which always smelled of incense. I could usually find him meditating in lotus position, with his flowing white beard and blissful, kindly face, silently counting his *mala*[6] beads.

Father and my uncles always seemed a bit ill at ease in Grandfather's presence. They would hover at the edge of the room and wait for him to tell them to sit down, and then they would sit far away from him, speaking in hushed tones. They were not Buddhists, and I suspected that they were afraid to let Grandfather get a whiff of the meat, tobacco, and alcohol on their breaths since he strictly eschewed these substances. We grandchildren had no such fears of him, however. When I was little, I loved to march right up to him and stroke his beard. If Mother scolded me for it, he would always chuckle. "It's all right; he and I are as close as brothers." Then he would loudly intone the name of Amitabha Buddha,[7] which he had a habit of interjecting into his speech all the time, sometimes in praise, sometimes in regret or even in warning.

I have read Grandfather's autobiography, which he wrote when he was fifty-eight, and listened to parts of his life story. His turbulent era catapulted him to officialdom from humble rural origins. Before he turned to Buddhism, his politics were fairly radical. While still a young student at his home in Lintong[8] during the Qing dynasty,[9] he launched a campaign against foot-binding: He founded an anti–foot-binding association, distributed a song titled "Unbind Your Feet," and let his eldest daughter's feet

[6] Buddhist rosary beads.

[7] Associated with the Pure Land sect of Mahayana Buddhism, Amitabha is said to rule over the Western Paradise.

[8] In rural Shaanxi.

[9] The last imperial dynasty of China (1644–1911).

grow to their natural full size. After he had passed the county-level imperial examinations for the selection of government officials, the Qing government abolished the examination system, and he enrolled at Capital
University[10] as a student of politics and economics. There he joined Sun
Yat-sen's revolutionary party, the Tongmenghui. During the Revolution of
1911, when the Qing dynasty was overthrown, he quit school and
returned to Shaanxi, where he got an important post in the newly established provisional military government. That was when he bought our
grand family house in Xi'an and the large tract of land that later became
his garden. But when Yuan Shikai, the first provisional president of the
new republic, tried to declare himself emperor in 1915, his regime lost
support, and many important officials, including Grandfather, were listed
as wanted men. He hid out in the French Concession[11] of Shanghai for
years, writing articles and publishing a newspaper promoting industry as
China's salvation. He was a leftist who worked with Chen Duxiu, one of
the cofounders of the Chinese Communist Party, and even published a
pamphlet in support of the Bolshevik Revolution. But after he moved into
his Silent Garden in the early 1920s, he abandoned politics and public
office, relying on his real estate as his sole source of income. He became a
prominent local Buddhist, who led local charities, relief work, and education and collected donations to repair dilapidated Buddhist temples.

During the Land Reform campaign for the redistribution of rural property soon after the Communist takeover, the local authorities planned to
attack him and confiscate his garden. Fortunately, the Living Buddha of
Qinghai, a high-ranking Tibetan lama who was prominent in the Northwestern Military Government, shielded him with a special order, sparing
him the brunt of the attack. Although his rural property was seized, he was
allowed to keep the garden where he lived. But deprived of his rental
income, he had to sell his garden bit by bit just to pay his living expenses.
First he sold the piece from the front gate to the wisteria trellis. Next it
was a tract near the back gate, surrounding the shed he used for printing

[10] Later Beijing University.

[11] Concessions were areas of Chinese port cities ceded to the control of foreign powers during
the late Qing dynasty.

the scriptures. On one visit I discovered that the two ends of the garden had been cut off by newly built walls, leaving only the essential central portion.

Grandmother had moved in with him when they sold their house following Liberation, and now she had to follow Grandfather's strict vegetarian diet. In addition, she had to do all the housework herself since they could no longer afford servants. Kitchen chores roughened her pampered hands, which had been accustomed only to playing mah-jongg or holding a water pipe. In the winter her hands cracked from doing the dishes and the laundry, and she covered them with adhesive bandages.

But Grandfather's fortunes improved after a few years. On one of my visits when I was in second or third grade, I noticed that the house had been spruced up in preparation for an important guest. The walls had been whitewashed, and Grandfather had hired a cook to make a vegetarian feast. Later I learned that the guest was an old friend of his, who had become a high-ranking cadre[12] in Beijing and was visiting Xi'an for a meeting. Soon afterward Grandfather was appointed the Buddhist representative on the Municipal Political Consultative Committee, a "united front" organization that included non–Communist Party members.

Now that he had a job he replaced the long Chinese gowns and mandarin jackets he had worn around the house with gray or blue Sun Yat-sen suits.[13] He started to attend meetings and to discuss Communist Party documents with his religious group. He brought home packs of documents and Marxist-Leninist materials to study in addition to his Buddhist texts. The word "study" had taken on a new meaning for him; now it meant changing his old ways and adopting new ones. This was accomplished through meetings, discussions, and poring over documents. It was his job as a committee member to rubber-stamp party policies, to spread propaganda, and to teach people the official lingo. In the political context of the times, to say that an old man from the old society was "studying diligently" meant that he supported the party and the government. Grandfather and the other committee members may have felt constrained by their assignments, but men like him who had worked for the Nationalists must have

[12] A Communist Party official.

[13] Known in the West as Mao suits.

been glad to serve nonetheless. It afforded them some prestige and was far better than being blacklisted or attacked. He even got paid for studying. At the end of each month the committee sent someone over with more than a hundred yuan. They called it a transportation and living subsidy rather than a salary and considered it government support for members of the united front like Grandfather. Since most people earned less than forty or fifty yuan a month in those days, this was very generous treatment indeed. And now that Grandfather had been deprived of his land, this money seemed like manna from heaven.

In the early 1950s landlords all over China were persecuted mercilessly by the poor and lower-middle peasants. When my maternal grandfather and grandmother returned to his hometown in Chang'an County to take care of his aging parents, they were labeled landlords and suffered unspeakable torment at the hands of the villagers. And I shall never forget the anti-landlord struggle session I witnessed on one of my visits to Nanny's parents' village. As soon as we got there, we saw a wrathful mob in front of the school, surrounding a tall, ruddy-faced, mean-looking landlord, whom they called a local tyrant. The villagers had stood two bricks on their sides on the brick pavement, and militiamen wielding red-tasseled spears were forcing him to balance on one foot on the edge of one of the bricks. As soon as he got a trembling foothold, a militiaman would kick the brick out from under him, and he would fall with a heavy thud onto the mossy pavement. The insatiable villagers subjected him to this process repeatedly, while they recited their angry tales of his oppression. His face turned black and blue, and dark red blood streamed from his temples.

Nobody knows how many rural property owners died in the unbridled mob violence of this period. Many of them were much less prosperous than Grandfather. It was only because he had an urban registration card and was chosen to be the Buddhist representative on the committee that he was able to avoid attack, keep his garden, and enjoy a position of respect. If he had still been registered as a resident of Lintong rather than of Xi'an, or if he had not been such a prominent Buddhist, he would have been crushed by the peasants. Thanks to the Buddha and the Bodhisattva Guanyin,[14] the

---

[14] The goddess of mercy, an assistant of Amitabha Buddha's.

fragrance of his Indian sandalwood incense filled his chamber again, and his spare rooms were cleared of tenants and restocked with Buddhist scriptures. Once again he could afford to hire servants to help Grandmother, and gardeners to restore the overgrown garden. Father, using his connections at work, installed running water for him, and he often let me help him plant vegetables and water the flowers. For the time being, Grandfather's ruined garden was back in bloom.

2

Silent Garden

IN THE FALL of 1958 my parents sent me to live with my grandparents and attend Number Two Middle School, which was near Silent Garden and adjacent to the site of our former family house. I still have childhood memories from the yard of that house. Whenever the middle school students sang the national anthem and raised their flag on the playground next door, I used to run to our magnolia tree to hoist the tiny flag that Nanny had made for me. Later, when Grandfather had to sell the house shortly after the Communist takeover, the school converted it into extra classrooms, dormitories, and offices.

In 1958, the year of the Great Leap Forward, the nation became caught up in a frenzy of smelting "backyard steel."[1] It was our "glorious mission" to donate scrap iron to this cause, so our school playground, like most other work units, was heaped with it, along with piles of burned charcoal.

---

[1] The Great Leap Forward (1958) and the First Five Year Plan (1957), intended to industrialize China and communize agriculture as rapidly as possible, included many misguided policies that wrought havoc with the Chinese economy. One of these was the infamous drive requiring citizens to smelt backyard (homemade) steel, which usually turned out to be useless.

Some enthusiasts had tossed in their pots and pans or drawer handles for good measure, even if they were made of copper or tin. The student cafeteria had been temporarily converted into a foundry, equipped with a mighty blower that shook the classrooms with its roar and filled the air with a sooty purplish haze. Nobody seemed to have time for mundane pursuits like eating and sleeping. The upperclassmen manned the furnaces around the clock with holiday spirit, belting out all their new songs and cheering for the molten "steel" as it poured out of the furnaces. Once it congealed into hard black slag, we deemed it a success and swathed it in bright red silk. Then, banging on drums and gongs and carrying big red paper placards that read SURPASS ENGLAND AND CATCH UP TO AMERICA, we marched it triumphantly over to the district party committee.

Classes were canceled more often than not, and even we younger students had to help out at the foundry. When this happened, I began to resent school activities.

My parents had sent me to live with my grandparents because they were too busy with their jobs to take care of me and because they wanted to isolate me from the neighborhood children, whom they regarded as riffraff. Most adults had to work all day and attend mandatory political study sessions and meetings at night, and lacked the time to supervise their children after school. Moreover, few parents could afford to buy their children any toys, musical instruments, or sports gear. So once we had gotten our homework over with, we ran wild in the streets, climbing trees and walls, wrestling and sparring, and even recklessly scaling the city walls.

The city walls of Xi'an were grand and well preserved. The side that faced outward was surfaced with huge bricks, culminating in neat crenellations that loomed impregnably over the city moat, as in ancient times. On the side that faced inward, however, the rammed earth was exposed and weather-beaten. In order to prevent further erosion of the walls, huge brick downspouts had been installed at twenty- or thirty-yard intervals. Slanting along the imposing walls from top to bottom, the spouts protruded like giant skinny ladders. By the late 1950s the municipal government had declared the walls obsolete and closed all the stairways to the top. The only way to get there was to shimmy painstakingly up the narrow spouts, choosing your finger- and toeholds with the utmost of care and never glancing down lest you plummet to the ground below. The climb was nerve-racking and exhausting, and by the time we reached the top all of us were completely worn out. I often returned home from these wild exploits smeared with dirt from head to toe or with torn clothes and bleeding arms and legs.

When I was not indulging in these death-defying pursuits, I loved to read classic swashbuckling fiction. Once I had gotten my first taste of this genre, with Father's copy of *The Water Margin*,[2] I was hooked and proceeded to devour *Journey to the West*, *Roster of the Gods*, *Romance of the Three Kingdoms*, and *Stories of the Tang*. At first I had my parents borrow books for me from their libraries at work; then I borrowed some more from our neighbors. Eventually I started going to bookstalls to rent martial arts tales that I could not find elsewhere. Everything about these stories was fascinating to me, from the terminology for the "eighteen ancient weapons" to the nicknames of all the heroes and swordsmen and the descriptions of the immortals' steeds and magic arts. I recited the battle stories to my playmates, adding gestures and reveling in the formulaic storytellers' language and the marvelous vocabulary I had absorbed from the books. Sometimes I inserted myself and my friends into the stories, imagining myself a martial arts master who was leading the others on a heroic mission. Somewhere far from the city, I dreamed, we would encounter the wonders of ancient times.

When I was thirteen, some of my roughneck friends and I started to save our money for a trip to climb Mount Zhongnan,[3] one of the sacred peaks of China, over summer vacation. Sitting in an abandoned pillbox on the city wall, we planned our expedition and established an explorers' club with me as president. Our first escapade took place when we sneaked out of the mass parades on the May 1 Labor Day and went outside town, where we climbed the walls of a sanitarium for the party elite[4] and got caught by the guards. They called our school, and we were suspended for a day of

[2] Beloved novel, popularized over the centuries by storytellers (and nowadays by television and video games), about a band of Robin Hood–type rebels in the Song period.

[3] Located in the Zhongnan Mountains, a section of the Qinling mountain range, approximately twenty miles south of Xi'an.

[4] This sort of sanitarium was a facility that provided its guests with recreational services, such as professional female dance partners, unavailable to the people at large.

"introspection." Then we had a wall-climbing accident. One boy in our group slipped to the ground from a downspout, broke his leg, and had to spend several months wearing a cast in bed at home. This got us into deep trouble. Several sets of parents complained to the school that their off-spring were being led astray by rabble-rousers. They exposed our plan to climb Mount Zhongnan and named me the ringleader of our group. Claiming that our establishment of the explorers' club without official sanction was a major violation of the rules, the school political director issued a stern warning to our parents.

Father overreacted a bit, especially to the explorers' club, and he admonished me against winding up as a delinquent. Today it was wrestling and climbing walls, he and Mother chided me, but tomorrow I could find myself playing hooky, prowling the streets, and becoming a hooligan. He heartily disapproved of the neighborhood children, who knew they had to scurry out of our house as soon as they heard him coming through the main gate with his bike. That was why he decided to "exile" me to Silent Garden.

My grandparents put me in a room on the west side of the house that they had used as a guest room for visiting monks. It had whitewashed walls, a hardwood floor, and clumsy, old-fashioned furnishings. Tangled wisteria grew on the eaves outside the room, which faced a dense grove of cypress trees. At night the tiny metal bells on the corners of my great-grandmother's tombstone stupa tinkled in the wind, while mice scampered noisily on the floor. I was afraid of the dark, so Grandmother lit a stick of incense by my bed as a night-light and told me to gaze at it while I prayed to the Bodhisattva Guanyin. Grandmother's Bodhisattva Guanyin seemed much more approachable and down-to-earth than Grandfather's Amitabha, who had to do with the future and lived in the faraway Western Paradise, so I began praying to her regularly. Later I found a rusty old sword in a junk pile upstairs, and I spent a few days sharpening and polishing it, along with its sharkskin scabbard, to a gleam. I hung the sword at the head of my bed for reassurance until I had gotten used to being alone in the cavernous room.

This find aroused my interest in ransacking the dusty piles of stuff upstairs and downstairs. I was looking for novels to read, but Grandfather did not have any. Instead, I found ancient, unfamiliar classics, such as the Confucian canon collected in *The Four Books* and *The Five Classics*, the works of the Daoist philosophers Laozi and Zhuangzi, and numerous other compilations of classical philosophy, poetry, and essays. All were antique, large-type woodblock-printed editions, bound in silk thread and written in Classical Chinese, without modern punctuation.

I became fascinated with these musty old books, especially on rainy days when the high humidity kept their dust under control. Sitting on the brick floor in the hall with a stack of them, I wiped them off and pored over them to my heart's content. I read at random, devouring everything I got my hands on. I remember a fantasy novel Grandfather had written, describing a vision of a Buddhist revival, titled *Half a Joss Stick of Reveries*, as well as poetry by the "Eight-Fingered Mendicant," a Buddhist monk who burned off two of his fingers in an avowal of faith. I also enjoyed more Confucian classics in an oversize edition of *The Annotated Thirteen Classics* and *A Shaanxi Miscellany*, a compendium of two thousand years' worth of local literature and history. I discovered documents pressed between the pages of these volumes, such as a letter to Grandfather about Buddhism from the Guomindang leader Dai Jitao and an old newspaper clipping describing a visit to Xi'an by Grandfather's guru, the renowned Buddhist evangelist known as the Master of the Void. Through all this browsing and sorting, my reading skills in Classical Chinese improved as if by osmosis, and by the time I dusted off the entire library, I had plowed through— with varying degrees of understanding—most of the ancient classics.

Those were the most idyllic days of my life. Every day, once my homework was done, I turned to my reading program. I was full of youthful intellectual curiosity and drive and still open-minded and impressionable. Although I often understood my reading only dimly, I found it stimulating and memorable. Later I was deprived of the chance to study for years on end. Even today, more than forty years later, I believe that the reading I did long ago at Silent Garden was the foundation of my intellectual identity and that I have benefited from it all my life. Youth is a golden opportunity to read widely, and people who are denied that opportunity may never get around to making up for it later.

After a while I started to design my own ambitious survey courses in literature and philosophy. When Grandfather's library could no longer satisfy me, I began to frequent bookstores, buying the books I needed with the pocket money my grandparents gave me. Grandmother often let me keep the change when she sent me on errands, and Grandfather liked to reward me with money for good behavior. He was always delighted when I memorized a sacred text, like the *Heart Sutra,* or performed a random act of kindness, such as the time I donated my New Year's money to help a poor classmate pay his tuition. Grandfather rewarded me for my donation with more money than I had given to my classmate. Thanks to their generosity, I usually had enough money for books.

I loved to go to the only secondhand bookstore downtown, where I spent all my savings buying the classics on my reading list. Some of them were for immediate consumption, but I was also avidly building a collection, just as I had accumulated such things as stamps and cigarette cases in my young childhood. My appetite for books was insatiable, and regular bookstore forays became my favorite leisure activity.

Then I discovered that the bookstore also purchased used books, and it dawned on me that I could sell some of Grandfather's useless books on the sly and use the cash to buy the books I needed. I would just be trading one old book for another, I rationalized, and actually renovating the book collection, so nobody could really accuse me of siphoning off family property to line my own pockets. Eventually I managed to quiet my misgivings and try this scheme. Whenever I was short on money, I would choose some of Grandfather's books that I considered worthless, like popular Buddhist reading material and collected works by local authors, and exchange them at the bookstore for the books I wanted. The first time I did this I was conscience-stricken, fearing that Grandfather would suddenly decide to look up something in one of the books I had sold, discover that it was missing, and identify me as the culprit. But it never happened. Actually, except for some rare editions of the Buddhist scriptures and a few big sets of books that Grandfather kept at hand, he did not really know exactly what was on his shelves. I was the only person who was interested in the dusty old tomes, and it had not occurred to anyone that they could be exchanged for money.

Over the course of a few years I replaced all the expendable books in

Grandfather's library with a basic Chinese humanities curriculum, including all the major texts of classical Confucianism, history, philosophy, and belles-lettres. The library at Silent Garden had been fully remade in secret.

My independent study plan consumed all my attention in my teen years. I did not even want to go to school in the mornings, not because I wanted to loaf around the house but because I vastly preferred my own curriculum. School-sponsored activities, both inside and outside the classroom, were becoming increasingly politicized. The highly regimented educational system allowed us very little in the way of course selection, and my teacher's strict enforcement of discipline seemed more appropriate to a correctional institution. I wished that school would provide an environment truly conducive to learning, with more interesting classes. Most of all, I wished that we students would be permitted to relate to one another freely, without being subjected to constant surveillance. In order to prevent my schoolwork from encroaching on my personal study program, I tried to finish all my homework while I was still at school and was satisfied with grades that were average or slightly above.

Grandfather had a friend named Mr. Wang, who often stopped by Silent Garden to borrow books. Knowing that he was an excellent calligrapher, I asked him to make me a copy of a poem that I loved titled "The Year-Round Joy of Reading," written in the heptasyllabic ancient style by the thirteenth-century poet Weng Yipiao. I hung Mr. Wang's artwork on my wall and recited the poem every morning and evening. Grandfather, whose political antennae were more sensitive than mine, was alarmed by my behavior and criticized the message of the poem.

The new government had deliberately gathered a group of Consultative Committee members from all walks of life, Grandfather included, and indoctrinated them until they learned to practice self-censorship and echo the party line. Even though I was young enough to have grown up under the red flag, he was more in tune with the latest political trends than I was. He often told me that I would have been considered an excellent student in the old society. But his praise of my studiousness was tinged with worry that my reading program, which kept drifting farther and farther from the prescribed school curriculum, might accentuate my nonconformist leanings. This was soon after the Antirightist campaign,[5] during which our family was spared direct persecution. Still, Grandfather's constant circumspection made me aware of the insidious political pressure all around me. Even one's choice of private reading material had become a barometer of one's political stance.

Grandfather had begun to sprinkle his speech with newly learned Marxist jargon. For example, since Buddhist doctrine held that the world was created by a chain of cause and effect rather than by an external force, Grandfather seized upon this as proof that Buddhism was "not superstitious" and that it was "compatible with materialism." Unlike other religions, he maintained, Buddhism was basically atheistic.

In 1959, the tenth anniversary of the People's Republic of China, Grandfather toured the Yangzi River Bridge at Wuhan and the construction site of the Sanmen Xia Reservoir[6] with the Consultative Committee. When he came back, he spoke glowingly at committee meetings of what he had seen and even wrote some laudatory poetry. For this he was deemed a truly "red" old person, a glorious appellation in those days. Socialism seemed off to a good start in China, and Grandfather, like many other people, had fallen for Communist propaganda. The promise of the new society, embodied by the major engineering projects he had witnessed on his tour, aroused his sincere patriotic fervor.

Those were the heady days of revolutionary romanticism, and the walls along the alley in front of our school were blazoned with murals and poems exaggerating industrial and agricultural production. There were pictures of cornstalks tall enough to scrape the clouds, mountains of cotton, elephantine pigs, and hens that laid ostrich-size eggs, as well as bold exhortations from Chairman Mao to "Conquer heaven and earth." The city authorities had even deemed it a kind of "production mission" to compose doggerel extolling new achievements, and anyone who penned a few usable lines was hailed as a "poet" overnight.

The walls of Silent Garden created a sanctuary for me from the world

[5] Launched in the spring of 1957 to round up people who had dared speak out during the preceding Hundred Flowers movement, which had encouraged criticism of the party.

[6] Part of the Chinese Communist Party's bold plan to "conquer nature," the Sanmen Xia Dam on the Yellow River contributed to alternating droughts and floods and was eventually torn down.

outside. I ransacked the house for the accoutrements of an elegant scholarly study and used them to decorate my room. I had an inkstone, a brush washer made of shell, a jade paperweight, a bronze incense censer, calligraphy and paintings, and porcelain vases, with my wall hanging of the poem "The Year-Round Joy of Reading" as the finishing touch. But Grandfather, determined to bring me back to earth, wrote a takeoff on this poem titled "The Year-Round Joy of Work and Study" and hung it on my wall. The latest party call was for intellectuals to be both "red and expert." If intellectuals devoted themselves single-mindedly to their professions and book learning, at the expense of political study and manual labor, they were denounced as "white experts." Grandfather's poem, which emphasized that work was as important as study, was a response to this party directive. But I ignored his admonitions, and his poem hung on my wall in vain. In my opinion, its political slogans were just eyesores.

My love of literature was habit-forming, and the more comfortable I was with it, the more I craved it, regardless of the consequences. I had tried my hand at more practical activities, such as playing musical instruments, assembling crystal receiver sets, building model airplanes, and all kinds of athletic endeavors, trying to demonstrate that I could do these things too. But I was clumsy, so I had given up and retreated into my piles of books.

Tasks such as drawing circles or triangles seemed like a nuisance to me, because they demanded the accurate use of a pencil, compass, and ruler. The simple act of choosing my words in writing, however, satisfied me emotionally and intellectually, while requiring only reason and imagination. For me, curling up with a book was the ultimate in relaxation. Father had achieved his goal; I had lost interest forever in the neighborhood children. I was so deeply immersed in my books that I was loath to tear myself away long enough to go visit my parents on weekends. I resisted anything that interfered with my daily study time. This attitude set me at loggerheads with my school.

In those days a "bad student" was one who cut school, brawled, insulted the teachers, and got bad grades. I was not one of them, since I earned decent grades and followed the rules, but I was still never considered a "well-behaved" student. In the politicized language of post-1949

China, the word "behavior," like many others, had added connotations beyond its dictionary definition. "Behaving" meant putting on a deliberate show of allegiance to the authorities. When the teachers and school leadership evaluated your "behavior," they were referring to your politics, and you had to play the game right if you wanted a rating of "well behaved." Behavior ratings were as important as tests and grades since they affected one's class rank, admission to select groups, and future prospects in general. Elementary school students needed good behavior ratings to join the Young Pioneers; middle school students needed them for entrance into the Communist Youth League; and adults needed them too, for party admission.

Good behavior seemed to come naturally to some students, but making a favorable impression on the teachers was not easy for those of us who were not inclined to show off. For example, cleaning up the classroom was a daily chore that we rotated among us. But in that era there was more to the matter than simply maintaining a clean study environment. We actually had cleaning competitions, in which each class competed with all the others in front of the inspection team. So all the students whose turn it was to clean were dragged into the battle, and all vied to demonstrate their good behavior. Compared with the others, I was aimless, clumsy, and antisocial, and the faculty found my recalcitrance irritating.

A corollary of the Red and Expert campaign of 1959 was the Work-Study campaign, which introduced manual labor into the nationwide school curriculum. We middle school students had to take part in several hours a week of productive labor classes, supervised by the head of our school's maintenance and housekeeping department. At the height of the campaign we would be sent to a nearby commune to help with the turnip harvest or to do odd jobs at a small neighborhood factory. If our supervisors could not find any place that needed our help, they assigned us chores on campus that should have been taken care of by the professional maintenance and housekeeping staff.

At home I always helped Grandfather in the garden. In the spring I plowed the ground and planted vegetables, in the summer I carried buckets of water for the flowers, and in the fall I dug up the medicinal knotweed tubers that grew near the wall. I also helped Grandmother gather half-opened honeysuckle blossoms and ripe fruit from the trees. I liked this type of manual labor because it had a clear purpose, and I did it of my own volition. But the manual labor at school was just busywork, designed for the sole purpose of training us to follow orders with feigned enthusiasm. The more the other students showed off, the more I balked, and the time passed with agonizing slowness. I started to dawdle on the job and even to sneak away on my own. My teacher and the cadres filled my record with black marks for these unexcused early departures and absences. Although I was too young to understand politics fully, I was already beginning to develop a dubious political reputation.

自述

3

My Diaries

ONE DAY IN the spring of 1960 Grandmother sent me to buy matches and soap, but all the shops in our neighborhood were sold out. This was a harbinger of a series of shortages, a new experience for me. Next, the street vendors disappeared, and all the restaurants, whether state-operated or partly privatized, ran out of food. During that unusually frigid winter Grandfather was the only one who had a coal-burning stove in his room, and my wing of the house was so cold that my toes froze through my cotton-padded shoes while I was studying at night. My politics teacher told us that serious natural disasters had brought "hard times" on our country.[1]

"Hard times" was the buzzword of the day. Food was rationed, and general belt tightening began. City dwellers were confronted with the unprecedented prospect of hunger, although it was actually more psychological

---

[1] The Great Leap Forward was followed by a deadly three-year famine, which the Communist Party blamed on severe bad weather, although it was mostly created by the misguided agricultural policies of the Great Leap itself. While no exact figures are available, there is a general consensus that this famine led to at least twenty million deaths, most of them in rural areas.

than physical. All urban households were still guaranteed adequate, if minimal, monthly rations, and no one's cupboard was ever completely bare. The people who were really threatened with starvation were the peasants, who, after all, produced the food for the cities. With no guarantees or periodic government distributions to fall back upon, their only option was to flee certain death in the countryside and roam the city streets as beggars.

In a charitable spirit, Grandfather hired one of these refugees, a man from Henan named Mr. Su, to cultivate our vegetable patch and do odd jobs around Silent Garden. Before Grandfather gave him work, he had been alternating between begging and hiring himself out occasionally in the marketplace, but with the money he earned at our house he could fill up on steamed cornbread every day and could even save enough to buy a few ration tickets to send home to his family.

Mr. Su was a taciturn, hardworking man, who told us only the bare minimum about the conditions back where he had come from. He said that there had been an excessively zealous campaign to make everyone eat in mess halls and plant high-yield crops and that the cadres had overreported production, eradicating the savings of all the commune members.[2] His whole village had run out of grain, and people had begun to drop like flies, so he had fled while he could.

I was appalled by his story. Our teacher had told us that the Great Leap Forward had been a big success and had blamed the current grain shortages completely on the "natural disasters" and the Soviet Union's extraction of full repayment of China's old debts. Now I was faced with substantial evidence that he was not telling the whole truth, and I began to agree with the critics of the Three Red Banners[3] policy. No one ever discussed these matters with me, and even Grandfather had no ready answers for my questions. Confused, I recorded Mr. Su's troubles in my diary and wrote a poem depicting him as a trusty, exploited ox that shrank to a mere heap of skin and bones and eventually dropped dead of starvation while tilling a field.

[2] Because the state's tithe was based on the cadres' reports of production.
[3] The General Line for Socialist Construction, the Great Leap Forward, and the People's Communes.

As the food shortages worsened, even cornbread was rationed, and life became tougher for migrant workers like Mr. Su, who was not entitled to an allotment of ration tickets. In the winter malnutrition was rampant. The first symptom was edema, which you could check for by pressing on your forehead or inner calf with your finger each morning to see whether an indentation remained. This finger test became a widespread form of greeting. At first edema sufferers could get doctors' notes to tap into special reserves of soybeans and sugar, but eventually the demand outgrew the supply. Then the party had to call for "combining work and leisure," one of the strange new expressions coined to keep up with the bizarre new developments. This was a policy of reducing people's workloads and proclaiming it everyone's political obligation to minimize calorie expenditure. Since the schools slowed down too, I had much more time to study on my own and write in my diary.

My diary dates back to an evening, during my fifth-grade summer vacation, when I was studying in Father's office as he sipped liquor in a chair opposite mine. On a drunken whim, he staggered over to his desk drawer and pulled out a thick new blank book with a hard blue cover, glossy paper, and color illustrations. Laying it before me in the lamplight, he suggested that I begin keeping a regular diary. This practice, he assured me, would develop both my writing skills and my self-discipline. Eagerly, I flipped the book open to the first page and got started right away.

Father had not told me how to go about keeping a diary, but I was no stranger to the idea. Grandfather had been doing it for decades and had a hundred slender volumes, each labeled according to the year, stacked in the bookcase by his bed. Like old-fashioned account ledgers, they contained running records of mundane affairs, such as the places he went and the people he met or visitors who stopped by and what they said. He also kept track of correspondence with other Buddhists, party lectures and meetings, daily expenses, and seasonal changes in the weather, flora, and fauna. Jotting a few lines in his diary each night, like going upstairs every morning to pray to the Buddha or taking a constitutional around Great-grandmother's grave after every meal, had been Grandfather's habit for many years. His current diary usually lay open on the table for all to see.

The Kang family, 1960. Front row, from the left: Mother, the author's sister Shuci, Grandmother, Grandfather, the author's brother Zhengguan, Father, and the author's sister Shuzhi. Back row, from the left: the author, Cousin Zhengxin, and Cousin Shuren.

But young people like me had a different notion of diaries. My cousin Shuren, who also kept one, maintained that they should be completely private and that it was as unethical to peek at other people's diaries as it was to open their personal letters. Her words impressed me so deeply that I always kept my diary carefully squirreled away.

I admired Grandfather's diaries for their sheer number rather than their content. Remembering Father's injunction to hone my writing skills, I polished my entries every day as if they were personal essays and made sure that my descriptions of events were detailed and comprehensive. I also included a reading journal, consisting of notes on my readings, passages that had caught my attention, and my reactions to books I had read. I lavished more care on my diary every night than I did on my homework, but I was nevertheless embarrassed by my bombastic prose. No doubt many novice writers would have shared my sentiment that one's scribblings should be kept as private as certain parts of one's anatomy. My diary was a burdensome secret, and I worried constantly that someone might discover its immature contents.

The austerity measures created social chaos, which was exhilarating for me. With parents to shield me from the food shortages, I was enjoying the quasi-vacation from school. The cities had been released from the stranglehold of politics, and long-banned merchandise of every description was available again. Free markets, like the one at the renowned Daoist Temple of the Eight Immortals, were bustling. State-run restaurants and grocery stores were deserted, but movie theaters were packed at all hours of the day and night. Billboards announcing new movies were constantly appearing, and we had one foreign film festival after another, featuring the latest from the Soviet Union, Eastern Europe, and even the capitalist West.

That winter I saw huge numbers of foreign films, sometimes sitting through double and triple features. When the lights came on, however, and I got up from my seat and elbowed my way through the crowds, I realized that I was woozy with hunger. Trudging feebly along on the bleak wintry city streets, I was loath to jerk myself back to reality from the dreamworld of the movie screen. I was smitten with the glamour of Europe—cathedrals, palaces, aristocratic manors, high-society balls, prosperous modern cities, and exotic scenery—and couldn't help making invidious comparisons with my own drab surroundings. As soon as I got home, I poured my heart into my diary while my favorite scenes were still fresh in my mind and, too excited to sleep, often kept scribbling until late at night. As my diaries started to pile up, I eyed Grandfather's, aspiring to the day when my stacks would be as tall as, or taller than, his.

Worried about the secrets revealed in my growing stack of diaries, I put a lock on my drawer to protect them from Father and Grandfather, who often visited my room. Since the key was in a nearby unlocked drawer, my lock was actually just for show, but it nonetheless displeased Grandfather and Father. One Sunday, when Father was sneaking a few drinks in my room, he went snooping around, found my diaries, and read them. Infuriated by my private revelations, he gave me a severe tongue-lashing. Maybe he was just grouchy that day from the cheap sweet potato liquor he had been swilling all afternoon, or maybe his frustration with me had been mounting for a long time, and this was the final straw.

Father was an alcoholic, whose daily habit kept him constantly in debt. He was flush on payday, but he frittered away his entire monthly salary within the first week on fancy packaged brands of mao-tai and whiskey. Mother redeemed armloads of empty bottles for a pittance whenever she heard the call of the recycling men outside our gate. After his initial splurge, all Father could afford was rotgut until his next paycheck arrived. "I'm never rich for more than three days or broke for more than a month," was his own wry comment.

He kept sending me out to buy liquor for him even when his money was gone, and I had to stand there and watch him rummage through his pockets for change. Sometimes he even scrounged some from our neighbor Mrs. Li. After he had managed to scrape together a fistful of coins for me, I marched out to the shops with his empty bottle, looking for a refill. If the cheap stuff that he needed was out of stock nearby, I had to keep looking farther and farther afield, and I did so grudgingly, especially since there was rarely a penny left over for me. I have no memories of Father's ever giving us children any spending money, and I was always too embarrassed to ask him for any, even if it was for tuition or school supplies. For that, I always went to Mother.

Father craved the burn of fiery spirits and didn't care for much in the way of food to go with them. He usually sat by himself at a bare table with his glass and bottle, drowning his sorrows in silence. Once in a while he bought a few scarce delicacies, such as peanuts or canned anchovies, and offered me or my sisters a nibble, but he preferred not to seek our company. Far from cheering him up, the liquor plunged him into an ill humor, and he often lost his temper. When his breath reeked of alcohol, I knew enough to stay out of his way. I cannot remember when all this began, but it started to make an impression on me as soon as I was old enough to go out to buy his liquor for him. Instead of eating dinner, he tended to nurse his drink until it killed his appetite. Eventually he made a show of toying with a few bites of food, just so he could say that he had eaten.

Father's wasteful habit was a serious bone of contention between my parents. Our family was considered well off in those days, since he was a highly paid senior engineer and Mother was a middle school teacher. People imagined that we lived extremely well. It was difficult for Mother to tell outsiders how hard up we were because they would not have believed it. When Father got his pay, he gave her a meager allowance for household expenses, reserving the rest to pay back his debts from the previous month and to keep himself supplied with liquor in the coming one. He even asked for her allowance back bit by bit when he had exhausted all his other avenues at the end of the month. Naturally, it infuriated her to see him sitting around the house guzzling liquor.

Mother would serve Father stoically at the beginning of one of his drinking binges, but she lost her patience when he kept postponing dinner. She would snap at him to finish up and try to snatch away his bottle, but he would clutch it tightly, insisting that he needed just one more drink. Eventually she would reheat the evening meal, grumbling under her breath. Then she would erupt at him, dragging out all her old grudges, reciting her grievances against his drinking buddies, and berating him for bringing poverty on the family. At first Father would just sit and drink, letting her accusations roll off his back, as if he had heard everything before and could not be bothered to argue with her. Sometimes, especially if he was drunk, something she said would push him over the edge, and his face would suddenly darken. He would hurl his bottle to the floor, and the sound of its shattering would set him on a rampage. After recklessly smashing everything on the table, he would stagger out the door with his Bluebell brand bicycle to spend the night at the company dormitory.

The cathartic sound of china shattering on the floor snapped Mother out of her bad mood. Some females make a manipulative show of self-pitying tears at the end of a marital tiff, but not Mother. The climax of the fight had provided her with release, and she was ready to turn her full attention to cleaning up the debris. She was the victor for now, having interrupted Father's drinking session and caused him to smash his own bottle and shot glass, and she had recovered her domestic turf. Pleased to have driven him out, she would carefully sweep up the broken shards with her whisk broom and wash the remaining dishes. When all traces of the scuffle had been erased, she would place a couple of teacups, now minus their handles, back onto their tray, as if lining up the last remaining chess-men on a chessboard.

During my years at Silent Garden, Father often visited us on Sunday afternoons. When he was low on cash, he would mooch from Grandmother, who loved to indulge her sons and grandsons. Like a good fairy, she would send her cook out for liquor and some stewed pork wrapped in a lotus leaf and invite Father to enjoy these treats in my room. Once he was safely inside, she would close the door and the door curtain over it and then keep watch in the foyer, puffing on cigarettes and sipping tea. If Grandfather asked her where Father was, she would point at my closed door and whisper, "He's sleeping in there." Grandfather, who never doubted anything Grandmother said, would tiptoe away, clearing his throat and thankfully intoning prayers to the Buddha as he went. Father spent many a peaceful Sunday afternoon this way in Silent Garden.

But he flew into a drunken rage on the Sunday he discovered my diary. He had torn out the two pages that he found particularly objectionable and gave me a severe dressing-down for their contents. The first was the one describing Mr. Su's plight, with its poem comparing him to a trusty old ox. Father warned that I would be criticized for attacking the Three Red Banners if anyone ever found out I had written such a thing. The second was my critique of *The Diary of Lei Feng*,[4] in which I contrasted my diary with his. Mine was a private record, I said, kept solely for the plea-sure inherent in the writing process and in reliving my memories in the future. I did not want anyone else to read my diary, I insisted, since it revealed too many of my scandalous secrets. *The Diary of Lei Feng*, on the other hand, seemed to have been written entirely for show, as if Lei Feng had already arranged for its posthumous publication while he was writing it. I thought it a shame that this young soldier had not written a single word about his love life. Had he ever had a romantic relationship? How could he omit it? That's what diaries were for!

Father was beside himself. He scolded me and ripped the offending

[4] Lei Feng was an altruistic young soldier who died in an accident in 1962, leaving behind a famous diary that all Chinese were made to study when Mao proclaimed the Learn from Lei Feng campaign in 1963.

pages into shreds, then tossed them into my face. In the heat of the moment I protested insolently that he had no right to look at my diary and that it was an illegal "invasion of privacy" to read other people's diaries and letters. This incensed him further, and he slapped me. I raised my arm in self-defense, but this was tantamount to pouring oil on a fire, and he went berserk. Accusing me of trying to strike him, he pulled out his bicycle pump and chased me all around Silent Garden with it, like a policeman brandishing his nightstick. I darted into Grandfather's room, interrupting his meditation and begging for his protection, and in response he rushed out barefoot and whacked Father with his cloth shoe. Father strode away in a huff, muttering about packing me off to a strict boarding school. Grandfather later managed to convince him that it would not look good on my transcript if I switched high schools when I was almost ready to graduate.

Father and I were not on speaking terms for a long time, although we eventually managed to paper over our differences to some extent. I don't know whether he was sorry he had acted on his whim to give me the blank diary in the first place or if he remembered encouraging me to read traditional fiction when he had had a bit too much to drink. I had seen Father get starry-eyed under the influence of liquor, and it was a revelation to me that he could also see through the fog well enough to be a clearheaded, strict censor. From then on he seemed to regret having sent me to Silent Garden to live with my grandparents. His decision that it would be best to isolate me from the delinquent children on our block had backfired unexpectedly. He blamed Grandfather's influence for my habit of indiscriminate reading and writing and thought that I might not have turned out this way if he had not sent me to Silent Garden.

I knew that Father was wrong. Grandfather was such a devout Buddhist that he spent much more time on meditation and prayer than he did on scholarship and seldom read anything other than Buddhist scriptures. He had never been enthusiastic about my grandiose reading plan and in fact had often tried to discourage me from it. Whenever I asked him a random question about some ancient text, he would respond with a gentle putdown, such as "Mere factual knowledge cannot make you a sage." He also loved to repeat the old chestnut "Take action first, and use your leftover energy for book learning."

My love of reading and writing was my own natural inclination. Grandfather was not responsible for it, and Father's vehemence could not dissuade me from it. Something snapped in him on the day of that fight. He seemed to have decided that I was a hopelessly disobedient son and that he should get ready to wash his hands of me. He began this process with the dire prediction that I would have hell to pay in the future unless I heeded his and Mother's advice.

4

Freshman Year

IN THE SPRING of my senior year of high school in 1963, we finished our classes and final examinations early, signed up for college entrance examinations in either the sciences or the humanities, and got busy with our cramming. Father disapproved of my choice of the humanities, which he considered impractical in the China of the day. He often tried to dissuade me from my chosen course of study, claiming that the humanities were rife with dangerous gray areas, while the natural sciences offered the safety of objectivity. Reminding me of the endless ideological campaigns that had plagued the humanities since the Communist takeover, he pointed out that what was deemed politically acceptable one day might soon be denounced as heretical or even reactionary. It was impossible, he warned me anxiously, to build a meaningful career on these shifting sands. In fact, he argued, literature was the most dangerous career I could possibly choose in China, and he hoped I would steer clear of it. He was not alone in his convictions; his mind-set was widespread among intellectuals in those days.

It was not that Father disliked literature. Savoring a volume of classic fiction over a glass of liquor, as if it were a snack, was one of his favorite pastimes. His tastes were limited to a few favorites like the eighteenth-century novel *The Scholars* and the Ming dynasty anthologies *Stories to Teach the World, Stories to Warn the World, Stories to Awaken the World,* and *Striking the Table in Amazement.* I read my first classic novel, *The Water Margin,* on his drunken recommendation. He read unsystematically, constantly revisiting his favorite passages, just as he always returned to his heady, cheap white liquor. In fact he had considerable literary training. He could recite a number of Li Houzhu's[1] short lyrics and had tried his hand at composing old-style poetry. I had read one of his poems in the seven-word regulated form and had been impressed by his mastery of antithesis. He told me that Grandfather had taken him out of school for a year for private tutoring in Classical Chinese and English.

Once when he had had a bit too much to drink, my *Philosophy* magazine caught his eye. Picking up a pen, he scrawled across the back cover, "Philosophy is a useless subject, one that I never want to study." A colleague who came to visit noticed it, and when the next political campaign came along, he used it against Father in a big-character poster, accusing Father of holding "reactionary views." Philosophy was no joking matter in those days. It was practically synonymous with Marxism and Maoism, so that reluctance to study it was suspect. It was no wonder that Father, surrounded by colleagues with such keen political antennae, was leery of sensitive questions in the humanities.

Father tried every possible tack with me, but I simply refused to listen. I disliked mathematics and had no aptitude for it. Even if he had forced me to take the science examination, I probably would have failed. I insisted on studying a subject dear to my heart and refused to spend my life as a drone just for the sake of job security.

"Can't you read the handwriting on the wall?" Father scolded me. "Someday you're going to trip up politically and get us all into trouble. But by then it'll be too late."

The political background check for college admissions in 1963 was the most lenient in years. I had worried that I might be rejected because of my

---

[1] Li Houzhu (936–978 C.E.), otherwise known as Li Yu, was one of the great Chinese poets and emperor of the Southern Tang dynasty.

family's class status or my own personal record, but things went unexpectedly smoothly, and I received an acceptance letter from the Chinese department of Shaanxi Normal University in Xi'an.

Cloth was rationed in the faltering economy of those days, but I was sprouting up like a cornstalk. When relatives saw me on holidays, they joked that I was wasting all of Mother's cloth ration tickets. In fact she did use up our whole family's supply of ration tickets to sew me a new outfit for college. When matriculation day arrived at the end of August, I strode blithely onto campus in my new dark blue jacket and found my way to the reception area for new students in the Chinese department.

"Oh, so you're Kang Zhengguo," the clerk blurted out when I handed him my acceptance letter. I wondered how he knew my name. He shoved the letter back into my hand before I had figured out how to reply. "You can't register yet," he told me. "Secretary Peng has flagged your name and asked me to send you to the department office to talk with him first."

The word "talk" sent chills of conditioned fear down my spine. In my years of experience at school it had never been a good sign when teachers or administrators summoned me to talk. Clutching my acceptance letter, I lingered foolishly at the registration table, unwilling to believe my ears and unable to think of the right thing to say. The clerks ignored me until I finally turned away, bracing myself for my meeting with the unfamiliar secretary. I did not see him in person when I got to the department office but was told that the department was considering revoking my acceptance for some unspecified reason. Crestfallen, I went back home. Father took two days off work, during which he made several trips to the college in his company jeep. Fortunately he had designed the water tower for the college and knew some of the college administrators. They sent some people over to the department to vouch for me, and they eventually succeeded in getting me matriculated.

When I did see Secretary Peng, he revealed that just before the beginning of school, the Chinese department had received a dossier on me from the provincial Student Admissions Office. He gruffly warned me that the Chinese department leaders would never have accepted me in the first place if they had known that my politics were so dubious. Once they had found out, they had considered revoking my admission or sending me for a year of manual labor at the college farm to see if I could prove my worthiness. In consideration of my youth, he continued, switching to a gentler tone of voice, they had decided to admit me on probation, although they wanted me to look deep inside myself and strive for improvement. Then, reverting to his sterner tone, he informed me that the department leaders had assigned me to write a thoughtful confessional essay, which would be the basis of their admission decision. He did not disclose the entire contents of my dossier to me; I was supposed to make a clean breast of things in my essay. He did, however, allow me a glimpse of one piece of the evidence against me.

"Can you identify this?" he asked, smoothing out a wrinkled, desk-size sheet of paper. It was a wall newspaper, and I recognized it. I stood there with a hangdog look, as if at an interrogation.

The previous winter I had created an alternative to the official classroom wall newspaper, *Garden of a Hundred Plants*. I issued my own wall newspaper titled *Pole Star*, for which I wrote the introduction, reviews, poetry, essays, and fiction. I even made a covert trip downtown to commission a friend from another school to design the masthead, a black-and-white picture of chilly stars in a vast night sky that contrasted starkly with the gaudy design of *Garden of a Hundred Plants*.

When my newspaper was ready to release, I got up in the wee hours of the morning and sneaked onto the deserted campus at daybreak with it under my arm. Hastily I strode over to the wall where the class newspaper was posted and tacked mine just above it. Afterward an eyewitness reported to the faculty that she had seen a tall fellow hang the paper there and scurry away. Only a few early birds caught a glimpse of my newspaper because it soon aroused the attention of the political instructor, who sent someone to tear it down immediately. By the time I saw the wall myself, it had been restored to its pristine condition.

The incident had grave consequences. I was easily identified as the culprit and reprimanded over and over by my teacher and my political instructor. It was a violation of school rules, they said, to post a newspaper without official permission, and such an act could be considered illegal publishing. Fortunately they had not found the contents politically objectionable and let the matter go after requiring me to write a confessional essay. But the school administration held my teacher accountable for my actions, causing him to bear a permanent grudge against me. Even after I had given him my essay, he held on to the newspaper as if it were evidence in a criminal case. Several times before graduation I asked him to give it back to me, but he never did. Now I realized that he had rushed it over to Shaanxi Normal University as soon as he heard about my acceptance there.

By the time I handed in my essay and registered at the university, the other students had been on campus for a few days. Mother was grumbling that it had been an uphill battle to get me admitted and that I had disgraced the Kang family by being asked to hand in a confessional essay before I had even started. I was discouraged too, and when I walked into the dormitory with my bedroll on my back and saw my roommates for the first time, I worried about how I was going to survive the next four years there.

The class monitor's bed was right next to mine, so that he could keep an eye on me. He was an adult with a wife back home in the countryside, and he had just been transferred from the army. He lorded it over us in his faded army green, a reminder of his prestigious background. Maintaining military discipline at all times, he strutted around grimly with his dossier on all of us under his arm. I suspected that he had not been brought to Shaanxi Normal University purely for the sake of getting an education, but rather for his expertise in assembling a class and lining it up for roll call.

Since school began just before National Day, October 1, we were sent out onto the field to rehearse marching in step for a parade across the new city square, where we would be reviewed by the provincial and municipal leaders from the rostrum. The administration regarded this as an ideal opportunity to instill some discipline in us. Thanks to our class monitor's zeal, we rehearsed much more than any of the other classes and were still at it long after they had gone back indoors. His swagger was even more pronounced when he was putting us through our drills as if we were new recruits in boot camp. Constantly tooting on his earsplitting whistle, he called out slogans for us to echo in chorus.

Now that I was living on campus, I had no convenient escape from group activities. Moreover, I had promised the department before matriculation that I would be on my best behavior, and I dared not step out of line. I remembered all the tantalizing college brochures I had seen posted on the bulletin board when I was finishing high school. I had sweetly imagined that campus life in an institution of higher education would be idyllic, as it was in the movies, and had pictured myself studying under the trees in the mornings and evenings, with light music wafting through the air. Who would have thought that I would be put under surveillance as soon as I arrived? Every Monday I started counting the days until the weekend, and I rushed home on the bus the moment the Saturday afternoon cleaning was over with. But I had to get back in time for study hall on Sunday evenings, knowing that our ever-punctual class monitor was going to walk into the classroom with his dossier as soon as the bell rang to take attendance.

The students at Shaanxi Normal University came from all over the province. Most were peasants, and many were Communist Youth League members. I stuck out like a sore thumb among this upwardly mobile crowd, all concerned with making a good showing. The students who had already been accepted into the Communist Youth League were jockeying for admission into the party, and practically everyone else was trying to get into the Youth League. If all you wanted was to lie low and stay out of trouble, trouble would seek you out. As the saying goes, "The tree craves peace, but the wind keeps blowing." The class struggle outside the campus reached its long arm into our midst.

I was immersed in biographies of famous men, among them a life of Napoleon. When my literary theory professor saw me carrying it around, he started to grill me about why I was reading it. An up-and-coming junior faculty member, he had the most political acumen of any of my professors, along with the knack of penning adroit political essays and the ability to adopt a stern expression on his fat, swarthy face when necessary. He insinuated that my interest in Napoleon implied that I cherished dubious political ambitions, which he was duty-bound to bring to light.

On another occasion someone reported me to the political instructor for reciting Hamlet's "To be or not to be" soliloquy in the dormitory. He summoned me to his office, demanded to know if I was depressed, and accused me of having suicidal intentions. I was shocked and struck by the absurdity of all the snooping. Whenever I entered a room and noticed my classmates and professors eyeing me, my head promptly started to throb. I tried to avoid group activities. As soon as classes were over for the day, I would hide out in a corner of the library reading room with a stack of books until dinner. Afterward I would go sit there again until closing time, studying or penning diary entries and letters to high school classmates. When the lights went out, I would grope my way back to my bed in the dark, take my diary out of my book bag, and stash it under my mattress.

In the last semester of high school some of my classmates and I had formed a study group to cram for the college entrance examinations. We often met at Silent Garden. One member of our group was a young man named Li Zhimin, who was also planning to study Chinese literature. He liked to write poetry and had been the editor in chief of the official class wall newspaper, *Garden of a Hundred Plants*. He had admired my rival paper, *Pole Star*, and written a poem in my honor, and we had become good friends. When the college examination results were posted, we found out that I was going to stay in Xi'an to attend Shaanxi Normal University, while he had been accepted at a more prestigious out-of-town school. On our parting day we agreed to stay in touch throughout our college years, to support each other, and to read each other's manuscripts.

Once he had arrived at his school, he wrote me a long, lyrical letter, using beautiful language, calligraphy, and stationery. I replied enthusiastically in kind, and thus began our regular biweekly exchange of missives, which were meticulously crafted in every detail, including the penmanship on the envelopes. We wrote to vent our feelings of alienation and depression in our new surroundings and to complain about irksome people and situations. Although we were fully aware that it was unwise, even risky to put such negative feelings into writing, we somehow imagined that our personal correspondence would remain inviolate.

In one of his letters Li told me that he was sitting on the top floor of his college library, which was built in the style of the Kremlin, and that the Yellow River was visible in the distance. I replied that I too was sitting in my college library, a palatial building with a huge roof, which had a magnificent view of the Great Wild Goose Pagoda.[2] We both threw our-

---

[2] A major landmark of Xi'an, built in the Tang dynasty.

selves wholeheartedly into our letter writing. Whenever I got one of his letters and sat down to reply in my corner of the reading room, I imagined our correspondence as an exchange of telegrams, every stroke of my pen analogous to the dots and dashes of Morse code. Our epistolary game heated up as we went along, lulling us into a false sense of security. But his constant letters and their eye-catching envelopes had already been noticed on my campus. There was a letter box in the mailroom for every class, and one student was designated to get the mail. After a while I sensed that he was suspicious about the fat, decorative envelopes from Li Zhimin and that his glance was aggressively prying.

The feeling grew on me that Father had been right: Before 1949 it would have been appropriate to enroll in a Chinese department for the sheer love of literature, but such a choice now was folly. I started to regret having chosen the humanities and having come to this intellectual backwater. Very few of my classmates had any talent or background in literature. In an era when most of the smart students chose science, the Chinese department tended to attract the weaker individuals and even those of poor moral character. For the most part the faculty was mediocre too. The professors who were old enough to have suffered during the Antirightist campaign carried their prudence to the point of idiocy, while the younger ones merely trumpeted the literary policies of the day.

School had been exciting during the opening days, when my books and lecture handouts had still been brand-new, but after a few weeks our classes settled into a tedious routine. When my mind started to wander, I amused myself by doodling in the margins of my handouts or notebooks, jotting down bits of poetry, disjointed ideas, or isolated words and phrases. Other students did the same. If anyone had been interested in collecting these surrealistic fragments of "automatic" stream of consciousness, they might have discovered something of literary merit or put together a valuable anthology of classroom literature.

Unfortunately such literary games were off-limits to Chinese college students of 1963. I had once read that spies sifted through people's trash for information. Some of my fellow students stooped to such behavior, searching for evidence of other people's "reactionary" views. One day in politics class, when the professor was railing against the Soviet Union's revisionist policy of a World of Three "No's"[3] from his podium, something possessed me to doodle: "Three 'No's': No Party Members, No Communist Youth League Members, and No Classroom Cadres." After class I rashly tossed my notebook into my desk, without stopping to worry about if anybody had been reading over my shoulder. I did not realize the gravity of my error until the political instructor summoned me to his office.

Despite their title, political "instructors" did not teach any classes but were stationed in the dormitories as eyes and ears for the police. They were supposed to spy on us, keep the dorm clean, conduct political study sessions, listen to our thought confessions, and write reports about our behavior. They had a say in our admission to the party or the Communist Youth League, as well as our postgraduation job assignments. Like many young political instructors, ours had been militant during the Antirightist campaign. As a reward he had been invited to stay on at the college after graduation instead of being sent back to his native village in southern Shaanxi. Moreover, he had been hired as a political cadre, in the most upwardly mobile position on campus. He always looked as if he had pinkeye, with bloodshot eyes and gummy eyelids that he could barely keep open.

I entered his office and stood in front of his desk. Flashing a piece of paper at me, he asked me if it was mine, and I acknowledged that it had been torn from my notebook.

"It's a good thing you admitted it," he said. "Are you aware that you would have been charged with writing a reactionary slogan if this piece of paper had fallen into the wrong hands?" His words hammered at me like a cudgel. I inspected the incriminating piece of paper more closely, to ascertain that it was indeed mine. Widening his gummy eyelids to reveal his beady eyes, he accused me of making a brazen attack on the party and of holding a grudge against party members, league members, and student cadres. He insinuated that by tearing out the offending page and giving it to him, my classmate had saved me from being arrested as an active counterrevolutionary. My slipup was an active breach of the rules, he blustered.

---

[3] In the early 1960s Nikita Khrushchev advocated a world with no war, no nuclear weapons, and no class struggle, an idea that the Chinese Communists denounced as the "revisionist" theory of a World of Three "No's."

He had reported it to the party, and Secretary Peng was going to announce it to the whole department. I was soon put through a series of "talks," with the secretary of the departmental party branch and the section chiefs for student affairs and campus security, each of whom required me to write a confessional essay.

The rainy, dreary autumn of my first semester at college finally passed, and winter vacation arrived, affording a temporary respite from the smothering pressure of school life.

5

A Glib Confession

AT THE BEGINNING of the spring semester of 1964 I was recruited onto the men's basketball team. Coach Qin, who was also our physical education instructor, handpicked me because I was the tallest student on campus. He took me under his wing and was the only faculty member who showed me consistent kindness while I was at Shaanxi Normal University. I enjoyed training with the team, eating my fill on athlete's rations, and traveling in school vans to games at other colleges. As the spring weather turned balmy, bringing the flowers into bloom, I had finally found an escape from my meddlesome classmates. This was the only pleasant interlude I had in college.

One day, as I was sitting in a window seat on the van to an off-campus game, a member of the women's team happened to sit down next to me. She had close-cropped hair, a cheery manner, and a refreshing disregard of the usual barriers between the sexes. Before long we had struck up a friendly conversation. The lurching motion of the speeding van bumped us against each other, and we inched closer together without realizing it. Her hair fluttered in my face, blown by the breeze from the open windows. Taking out a handkerchief that gave off a girlish, soapy scent, she flicked off a speck of dirt that had landed on my shoulder.

She was a sophomore in the mathematics department. The next day in the cafeteria she asked me to recommend some foreign novels, and we agreed to meet in the library after study hall. From then on the landing in the southwestern stairwell of the library became our regular meeting place. When the weather turned hot, we went out onto the terrace, where we would lean on the railing and gaze toward the south. I was fascinated with a brightly lit complex that I could see in the distance and composed for her a poem about it in which I compared the cluster of lights to falling stars. As our relationship progressed, we took walks off campus, went to the movies on weekends, and rode our bikes together on the outskirts of town. Our relationship blossomed throughout the spring semester.

All male visitors to the fortresslike women's dormitory had to undergo cross-examinations by the gatekeeper and then register in the visitors' log before they could enter. This unpleasant procedure, and my aversion to prying eyes, kept me away from her desolate little courtyard. Consequently, she took the lead in our relationship, often stopping by the men's dormitory to ask me out on the weekends.

Shaanxi Normal University was such a conservative backwater that some people jokingly dubbed it the Shaanxi Bumpkin Institute. During orientation the administration had announced that it was against the rules for students to date, but they never drew a clear line between dating and friendship. Female students, who were in the minority, usually sought one another's company rather than associate with males. By appearing openly as a couple all around campus, we were exposing ourselves to charges of violating the antidating rule. With my nosy, narrow-minded classmates buzzing behind my back, I felt both awkward and powerless.

The political instructor got wind of the situation before long. Jumping to conclusions, he called me to his office.

"I've never seen you do any good deeds, like Lei Feng, and you always seem to be the first to disobey the party," he said. "You smoke in the dorm, and you're dating a girl on campus. You arrived here with a history of serious ideological problems, and now you've started breaking school rules. I learned from your dossier that you wrote love poetry to a girl in high school and that she turned you in to the teacher. You've been corrupted all your life by bourgeois hedonism! Now it's been reported to me that you and your girlfriend from the mathematics department were drinking wine together on campus on the Dragon Boat Festival and that your conduct was unwholesome." He paused to wipe his bloodshot eyes with his handkerchief. "I shudder to think where all this is leading," he continued. "I'm warning you: Don't forget what you promised Secretary Peng in writing at the beginning of school. You can be expelled at any time for unsatisfactory behavior."

I listened politely, without saying a word in my own defense. In fact plenty of my classmates had girlfriends or boyfriends but managed to stay out of trouble at school by behaving themselves on campus, while slipping out for trysts at the botanical garden nearby. My girlfriend and I were not good fakers, believing that we had nothing to hide. We made no secret of our relationship and were surprised when we got into trouble.

At the beginning of the fall semester Coach Qin summoned my girlfriend and me to his office. Poker-faced, he asked us to return our uniforms, meaning that we had been kicked off our teams. I had no regrets, aware that I was not much of a basketball player and that I would never have amounted to much more than a benchwarmer. However, I did feel sorry to have let Coach Qin down, especially since he had even given me some of his own cigarette ration tickets to encourage me to practice basketball.

This crackdown spelled the end of our romance. She had never experienced unexplained discrimination before, and it made her uneasy. Meanwhile I soon got into worse trouble and had no time for love. Our relationship had been my only fleeting taste of friendship during my brief sojourn at college. There were many unpleasant days to follow.

The fall semester was dominated by campus-wide political drives. First we criticized *Early Spring in February*, a romantic film about two small-town teachers, and then we attacked the theory of "middle characters."[1] After that came the divisive campaign to study the "nine polemics," a series of

[1] The theory, advanced by the literary critic Shao Quanlin, held that peasants should be depicted in literature as ordinary people with human failings rather than as purely heroic, revolutionary figures.

open letters from the Chinese Communist Party to the Soviet Communist Party. We sat through endless meetings and were constantly required to profess our innermost thoughts to the party. We were urged to speak our minds, but this was merely a ruse to smoke dissenters out of hiding. The campaign was targeted for the most part at students who came from undesirable class backgrounds or who had not made good showings of themselves politically. Sickened by the sight of people abasing themselves and their families in public, I kept my own mouth shut.

I had done my best to behave myself in my freshman year and had imagined that once I had shed my bad high school reputation, I might be able to finish college uneventfully and land a job somewhere. My girlfriend had tried to prod me gently onto the right course politically by helping me draft an application to the Communist Youth League, but I was sure I would be making a fool of myself by submitting it. I failed to follow through with her suggestions and never managed to join another Communist organization once I had set aside my red Young Pioneer scarf at age fifteen. Now, as I sensed my situation deteriorating, I saw no point in trying anymore. Yearning for escape from this stifling "bumpkin institute," I began to consider dropping out.

The authorities required most students to speechify in public as a matter of routine, like a hand-washing campaign. However, they were trying to mount a serious case against me, so I had special private sessions with the political instructor while my classmates attended their meetings. Everyone knew that I loved to write and had several notebooks filled with my reading journals. The political instructor told me that the authorities wanted to see them. Realizing that they held all the cards and confident that my journals were beyond reproach, I blithely handed them in.

The political instructor soon returned them to me, not having found much of interest, and I thought the crisis was over. But then he suddenly turned up at my dormitory just as I was leaving for town one Saturday afternoon late in the fall. Gruffly he informed me that the party had confined me to campus for the weekend to write a penetrating confession and warned me not to take the assignment lightly.

The next day was Grandfather's birthday, the most festive time of year at Silent Garden. The chrysanthemums were in full bloom and the persimmon trees were laden with ripe fruit. Well-wishers would come bearing gifts, including the famed Fire Crystal persimmons that our relatives always brought from Grandfather's hometown of Lintong. Each of these small, glowing red orbs had a stem end that came out like a plug when the fruit was ripe, so that you could pour the luscious persimmon flesh directly down your throat. Miserable over being kept from the vegetarian birthday banquet, I hunched over my blank sheet of paper in the library.

My mind ran through a gamut of conflicting emotions. By then I was an old hand at the confessional essay format. I would string together a series of exaggerated clichés, glossing over offenses wherever possible. Then I would attach meaningless labels to the misdeeds that I could not sidestep and conclude with a self-reproach and a promise to do better. I always padded my essays, figuring that a lengthy piece would be more likely to create a sincere impression and get me off the hook. Over time I had come to understand that the higher-ups already believed the worst about me and would allow me no peace until I wrote something that persuaded them of my contrition.

Still, human beings have a sense of dignity and honor. What gave the political instructor and the party secretary the right to treat students like criminals awaiting trial? Whom were they referring to when they said that "the party" required something? As far as I knew, the now-ubiquitous practice of extracting confessional essays from people was unprecedented in Chinese history, unknown even in the "bad old days" of Nationalist rule. The practice had begun as a tactic for discipline within the Communist Party before 1949. According to party history, Mao Zedong had been criticized and compelled to write such an essay for the party leadership in his early years, and he had later forced numerous high party officials to produce essays for him. During the constant political campaigns since 1949, public figures and highly placed intellectuals had vied to make confessions to the party; in fact the public forum pages of the newspapers had been flooded with their essays, which were held up for emulation as models of thought reform. By now the confessional essay had become a routine punishment—and a cruel exercise in shameless hypocrisy—for everyone in China, including immature students like me, whose time should have been better spent.

Angrily I tossed my pen aside and stalked out onto the balcony to gaze at the view to the south. The severity of this attack distinguished it from all previous ones. The political instructor had told me that I should make a clean breast of my grave wrongdoing and that the party was giving me a chance to earn lenient treatment by confessing voluntarily. He wanted me to trace my problem to its roots in my class origin and especially to Grandfather's influence on me. I suspected that this time they had some kind of case against me, which would make it hard to get by with my usual perfunctory formulas. But I had no idea what I was supposed to confess. I was a good student and had done no wrong. It was unfair to ask me to bear false witness against myself or anyone else. I could craft a beautiful essay, but it would be useless unless I could second-guess them.

I sat chain-smoking the pack of fancy cigarettes I had bought to console myself while I churned out the essay. I had nothing but the deepest love and respect for Grandfather, even though the party had castigated him as a landlord, and I had always refused to denounce him just to get myself into the party's good books. The party exhorted young people like me to "disassociate ourselves from our class origins" or to be "saved through education," but I found these slogans offensive and could not bring myself to follow them.

In truth Grandfather was more in tune with the Communists than I was, and I had gotten into many arguments with him over the years by turning a deaf ear to his lectures about party policy. Purely from the standpoint of the party, which ostensibly sought to enlist the support of fellow travelers, I thought that he deserved praise rather than blame. After all, he had served faithfully on the Municipal Political Consultative Committee.

Racking my brains for the nature of the accusations against Grandfather, I finally stumbled on a possible answer. The year before, he had protested the disbanding of the Society for the Dissemination of Buddhism, which he had created single-handedly and run for more than thirty years. It had been located in a large compound on East Boulevard and had boasted an auditorium, a reading room, and a guest sitting room. Grandfather had held meetings there on Sundays, sometimes inviting a Buddhist master to deliver a sermon. After 1949 the society had donated most of its land to a public elementary school but had not managed to appease the government, which had ultimately dissolved it and seized the rest of its land. At the time I had appreciated neither the significance of the society nor the blow to Grandfather's spirits when it was disbanded. It was not until many years after these events that I came to understand the true nature of its mission: to proselytize Buddhism.

Just after 1949 Grandfather had attended retreats at the monasteries on Mount Lingyan[2] and Mount Zhongnan and had decided to become a monk. Unfortunately for him, he had been compelled instead to return home, where he was classed as a landlord and placed on the Municipal Political Consultative Committee. Hoping to find some roundabout way to adhere to his mission under the new regime, he had tried to be flexible about adapting Buddhism to Marxism. I remembered hearing him quote a remark Lenin had made to a gathering of religious leaders to the effect that they were free to practice their religions in the Soviet Union but that he was also free to campaign for atheism. Although Lenin was a master of sophistry, Grandfather clung to this distortion of the truth as a talisman against inevitable policy reversals. The party tolerated the members of Buddhist orders as an advertisement of its pretense of religious freedom and also because the orders maintained the historic temples, which were tourist attractions. But it objected to true grassroots organizations like Grandfather's society of lay Buddhists, whose community outreach work—sponsoring study sessions, publishing, and other activities—infringed on the turf of official propaganda. The very nature of the Society for the Dissemination of Buddhism was taboo under communism.

I considered the usual epithets the party might apply to Grandfather and decided that it would be entirely inappropriate to label him as a believer in the "decadent ideology of the feudal landlord class" or "poisonous religious superstition." And even if he had been somewhat "exploitative" in the sense that he had owned real estate, there was no denying his pre-1949 contributions to relief work, charity, and local education. When I was a child, I had often heard Nanny talk about the disastrous North China drought and famine of 1929, during which people had consumed all the available grass and tree bark and even swallowed toxic white clay. Leafing

---

[2] Near Suzhou, in Jiangsu Province.

through the stacks of old books at Silent Garden years later, I had discovered printed records of Grandfather's famine relief work, such as a "Report on the Calamity in Shaanxi," printed by his Society for the Dissemination of Buddhism, which contained photographs of the stricken areas and appeals to the nation for famine relief. He had also helped establish schools and soup kitchens for famine victims, as well as orphanages that offered a basic education along with ethical, Buddhist training. Such activities were prohibited now, since the current regime denied the occurrence of famines at all. During the "hard times" that we had just survived, for example, no one was allowed to breathe a word about hunger, and the news media were forbidden to report the deaths by starvation. With such an attitude, the government could not allow a grassroots organization to engage in relief work. In order to maintain its iron grip and to seal off all alternative sources of information, it had to clamp down on organizations like the Society for the Dissemination of Buddhism.

All I could remember was how Grandfather had tried to edify me. Before I learned how to read, he had shown me *Paintings to Protect Life* by Feng Zikai[3] and had demonstrated to me that charity meant respect for the sanctity of life. He treated his plants with the same reverential attitude that he maintained in his altar room upstairs, subjecting us children to all kinds of taboos. He never let me pick flowers when we were strolling in the rear gardens and would slap my hand and scold me if I happened to break off a branch of the Chinese ilex in passing. Sometimes he seemed to carry his values to the point of absurdity. For example, he would not touch a flyswatter, preferring instead to whisk insect intruders back outdoors. Powerless to stop the frenzy of killing during the nationwide campaign to exterminate all sparrows, he had prayed at home around the clock.

Grandfather always tried to convert his visitors to vegetarianism, maintaining that carnivores were endangering their own health in addition to treating animals cruelly. He earnestly pointed out that animals howled and shed horrified tears as they struggled under the knife and that their anger chemically contaminated their blood. To bolster his argument, he repeated a provegetarian tale that he had heard from Master Buddhist Radiance,

[3] A Buddhist writer and artist particularly famous for his cartoon art in the 1920s and 1930s.

about a wet nurse who had quarreled with her master shortly before nursing her charge. After the baby had drunk her milk, his face turned purple, and he died. The doctor's diagnosis had been that the wet nurse's anger had contaminated her milk. According to Grandfather, this story proved his point about meat.

Grandfather also taught me the value of manual labor. "Rise at dawn, sweep the courtyard, and maintain cleanliness within and without," he reminded me daily, quoting from the Ming dynasty Neo-Confucianist Zhu Bolu's *Maxims for Managing the Home.* Grandfather was a sincere, peace-loving old man, whose tireless repetition of moral platitudes often struck young people as pedantic and ridiculous. I could not see any way in which he had been a bad influence on me. I had learned the basic academic skills in school, but I had him to thank for my ethical upbringing. I sat with my pen poised over the blank sheet of paper, head throbbing, and chain-smoking furiously.

I finally decided to resort to my usual evasive tactics and concocted a wordy document full of hot air about my exploiting class mind-set of laziness and disdain for honest labor. I also "confessed" that I shared the dream of the Soviet revisionist writers, to be "white and expert," to establish my reputation as an intellectual authority, and to enjoy a villa, a car, and a decadent bourgeois lifestyle. I went on to admit that I looked down on the poor and lower-middle peasants and that I bore grudges against the student cadres and the party and Communist Youth League members.

Wondering what to use for a conclusion, I remembered a four-line poem that one of Father's classmates had written in his graduation yearbook. The author had inscribed the poem in beautiful brushwork on the pink yearbook page, near a photo of herself in the upper right corner. With a stylish hairdo and dress, she stood with her hands clasped behind her, against a studio backdrop of billowing seas. I had liked the ring of this inscription and had committed it to memory, so I inserted it into the end of my confession:

The past is a beautiful memory,
The present a hazy symbol,
The future a daunting mirage,
There is no certainty in life.

My conclusion was that this poem expressed my mood, a reflection of the negative worldview of the declining landlord class. This was the standard jargon, but I went a step further, vilifying myself as a dutiful descendant of the landlord class, a pampered son of the bourgeoisie, and a Soviet revisionist sympathizer. To embellish these hollow-sounding clichés, I wove in some remorseful-sounding phrases in the style of late-nineteenth-century European fiction. Some passages that I was rather pleased with set a tone of bizarre self-pity. But I stopped short of betraying myself completely. While playing up criticism of my gloomy decadence, I scrupulously avoided inflammatory terms like "antiparty" and "antisocialist."

I filled several pages and personally delivered them to the political instructor before dark. I had no choice, knowing that worse things were in store for me if I failed to comply. Within bounds, I figured, self-calumny was analogous to a smallpox vaccination. Maybe a small dose of the toxin now would save my life someday.

6

Emergency Transfer

I HEARD NOTHING FOR a long time after I had turned in my long self-critical essay and, assuming that this crisis would pass just like all the rest, I eventually relaxed. Before I knew it, winter had arrived. As I was on my way back to the dormitory one evening after dinner, the branch secretary of the Communist Youth League approached me breathlessly and told me to find a secluded place where he could give me some urgent news. In the failing light I ducked into a grove of trees with him right behind me. The departmental authorities had decided to confiscate my diaries and letters, he said, and there was a plan to take me to my house under departmental escort the next day to collect them. This news was still top secret, he continued, and he should not be leaking it to me, but he had my best interests at heart. He added that he would try to get our political instructor to include him in the trip to my house to get the documents and warned me to start thinking now about which of my private documents I should destroy before they could be seized. I could not see his face clearly in the gloom, but I could hear the agitation in his voice. "It's a breach of party discipline for me to tip you off like this. You mustn't breathe a word of this to anyone for as long as you live. If the department leadership hears about it, they'll throw the book at me."

In addition to the branch secretary, we had one other party member in our class, the class monitor. Although he was at heart a plainspoken person, in those politically charged times he adopted an affected, militaristic pose, a harsh manner, and a radical leftist attitude. Still, he and I developed a special bond: We were the only smokers in our class, and we often shared our cigarettes and smoked together in the dormitory. As our smoke wafted in the air and the nicotine took effect, we unwound and forgot about politics for a while. So I managed to coexist peacefully with him at times, even if he reassumed his dogmatic military demeanor afterward.

The branch secretary, who had started out as a party functionary in a county seat in northern Shaanxi, was more congenial than the class monitor, and his manner was not at all stiff or formal. With his northern Shaanxi drawl, he was as soft-spoken as an old lady and in fact had a slightly effeminate manner, which was probably the influence of his hometown folkways. He was worldlier than the class monitor, and also more complex. Behind the principled facade he cultivated as branch secretary lurked hidden interests in taboo subjects like superstition and sex. Whenever our political instructor sent him around to try to indoctrinate me, he felt safe in revealing these interests to me, a "backward"[1] student, instead of doing his job.

Once he brought over a copy of *Mayi Physiognomy* and interpreted my facial features for me, saying that I had two ill-omened moles under my right eye called teardrop moles. But he added right away that their location fortunately meant only that I might have some setbacks in my youth. Had they been on the lower part of my cheek, my whole life would have been ill starred. I picked up the mirror and examined my face, paying special attention to the area under my eye. There really were two faint little black spots on my skin, which was not particularly white to begin with, so they were as easy to miss as dim stars in the night sky.

I found his interpretation troubling. It reminded me of an ominous fortune I had once gotten, and I told him about it. Grandfather had a set of

---

[1] Someone who does not adhere strictly to Communist doctrine.

ivory dominoes and a booklet titled *Divination with Dominoes*. After casting the dominoes three times, you could tally your scores and look up your fortune in the booklet. "Augury should be reserved for momentous decisions," Grandfather admonished me. He refrained from dabbling with the dominoes, claiming that overuse would exhaust their magical powers. Still, I pestered him to tell my fortune all the time, not because I needed to but because I loved to puzzle over the cryptic rhymes in the booklet.

After we had finished our three-day-long college entrance examinations, many of my classmates went to consult the oracle at the Temple of the Eight Immortals, while I went home and told my own fortune with Grandfather's dominoes. It turned out to be unpropitious, with a conclusion that read:

Seventy-two battles, none lost.
With songs from Chu, a smashing defeat.

This was an allusion to the ancient story of the king of Chu's defeat by the king of Han in the third century B.C.E., and it did not bode well for me. I was disappointed, but I did not really believe in fortune-telling anyway, so I put it out of my mind.

The branch secretary also let me in on his secret obsession with sex. Once he brought me a few volumes of a lithographed edition of the erotic novel *The Golden Lotus* and asked me to tell him if it was unexpurgated. I told him I had never laid eyes on this masterpiece. My specialty was classical literature, and I knew little about the popular or the erotic fiction of the Ming and Qing dynasties. Whenever he broached the topic of sex, he would stammer evasively but then ask me leading questions, hoping I would share some of my juicy secrets. At first I was on my guard, suspecting him of baiting me to get me into trouble, but I quickly dismissed this possibility. It was just that his was a repressed personality, and he felt safe venting in my presence.

In those days Chinese people existed in a narrow-minded world where they had to repress their emotions and hold their tongues. Driven by survival instincts, people kept their antennae out and lived in constant fear that someone might betray them. Thus, for any thinking individual, the

chance to complain or to speak freely about prohibited topics was as satisfying as a taste of forbidden fruit. I sensed that everyone, attackers and
victims alike, had repressed urges to step out of line. For this reason I was
sympathetic to the branch secretary's eccentricity.

During winter vacation of freshman year I had received a letter from
him in northern Shaanxi describing his personal depression and the
squalor in the villages. His gloomy tone had been entirely inappropriate
for a party member. I remember feeling gratified to discover through this
letter that there were kindred spirits to mine within the party. In fact he
was much braver about speaking his mind than I was, since he had had the
courage to put his ideas in a letter to me, while I had only dared mutter to
myself in my diaries. Well aware that he would get into trouble if word got
around about the letter, I had hidden it in a suitcase in my house. Later he
seemed to regret having written it and hinted repeatedly that he would like
to have it back, but I had not had a chance to retrieve it for him yet, and
now the authorities were planning to seize my papers. I figured that the
main reason he had taken the risk of tipping me off was that he was afraid
our political instructor would get his hands on the letter.

On the evening that he put me on the alert, I went to the library to
write in my diary as usual. As I opened it, the heading, "Volume Thirty-
six," caught my eye. "Thirty-six volumes already!" I sighed to myself, pat-
ting it as I imagined all the other volumes stacked in my bookcase at home.
How much smaller was my stack than Grandfather's? I wondered. And if I
kept making entries until I reached Grandfather's present age, how much
bigger would my stack be than his was now? But the departmental authorities were going to confiscate all my papers the next day. What should I
do? My first overriding impulse was that surrendering my treasures would
be unbearable. Once the authorities got their hands on them, they would
become mere black marks in my dossier, like the *Pole Star* wall newspaper I
had edited in high school, and I would never have access to them again.
Then again, I thought, maybe I should hand them over. My indecision was
giving me a splitting headache.

I even indulged a fleeting fantasy that I would abscond with my suitcase
of letters and diaries and take my friend the young woman basketball
player with me. Like characters in the movies, we would go to the station

and hop onto a train, and the two of us would huddle together and watch through the window as this hateful city and its telephone poles receded into the distance. At this point in my daydream I resolved not to relinquish any of my papers, even if it meant expulsion from college. I was really fed up with college anyway. Sometimes I even wished they would just hurry up and expel me.

I knew that it would be ruinous to turn in my diaries. I had not forgotten the case of Cai Guanglan, a senior at the college, who had been expelled. The departmental leadership had culled his reactionary views from his confiscated diaries and had made them into a special exhibit constituting evidence of his crimes. They had learned from his diaries that he had even stolen some books. People would have felt sorry for him if he had merely been charged with reactionary thinking, but nobody pitied a thief. His example struck terror into my heart.

I had so many diaries that they could find plenty of reactionary views if they wanted to, to say nothing of my secrets, especially romantic ones. The thought of all the ramifications made me feel flushed and weak-kneed. My mind was finally made up. I was not going to betray myself.

The next morning it started snowing, and I went to my morning classes as if nothing had happened. Then, after bolting down a quick lunch, I sneaked off campus while everyone was still in the cafeteria, hopped onto the Number Fifteen bus, and made it home without any difficulty. Opening my suitcase, I started to sort through its contents: all thirty-six volumes of my diary, including the volume I had brought back with me from campus; the huge sheaf of all the letters I had received over the past few years, still in their stamped envelopes; and all the poetry I had written, along with a lot of other manuscripts. Without taking the time to sort things carefully, I emerged onto the street a few minutes later, suitcase in hand.

The snow was falling heavily now. There was a big demonstration in town that day against the American bombing of Vietnam, and the streets were mobbed with marching demonstrators carrying noisy bullhorns and chanting, "Down with American imperialism." Not wanting to take any chances, I decided to splurge on a pedicab. "Take me to the Dongguan section of town as fast as you can," I instructed the cabbie. Sitting inside the dark curtained cab with my suitcase, as if I were in a sedan chair, I felt nervous but exhilarated. To bolster my courage, I imagined myself the hero of a movie. Instead of Xi'an, this was a city in the "white areas"[2] before Liberation, and instead of diaries, my suitcase contained classified party documents, which I was delivering to a comrade.

In this grandiose, self-pitying frenzy, I turned up at my old girlfriend's house with my suitcase. She had been a member of our cram study group for the college entrance examinations. Although she had not passed, she was prettier than all the girls who had. I had just started sneaking cigarettes back then, and she had pilfered pack after pack from her father for me, since they were rationed at the time. I admired the way adults looked when they smoked, and I liked to strike foppish poses. Holding the cigarette between my fingers, I would tilt my face upward to take a puff, then spit out a leisurely chain of smoke rings. While I rehearsed my poses, she learned to light my cigarettes gracefully, like a hostess attending to her guest. I also envied the nicotine stains on Father's fingers, which came from years of smoking. In order to speed up the process of acquiring these stains myself, I used to squeeze my cigarette butts as I dragged on them and soon, the nails and fingertips of my right hand were tinged with brown too.

"How do you like this color?" I asked, showing her my hand.

She grabbed it and sniffed. "It smells wonderful. Just how a man ought to smell."

Through this contact I discovered how warm and smooth her skin was. And she had tiny dimples on the backs of her hands. From then on we found excuses to touch each other. When we were tired of studying, I challenged her to arm-wrestle me, but she refused, putting her arms behind her back and protesting that a girl could never beat a boy. With my promise to let her use both hands and start with an advantage, however, she consented, and we sat down across a table. As she tried to pull my right arm down with both her hands, I observed her furrowed brow, clenched lips, and flushed cheeks. To gain leverage, she kept inching her arms closer to her chest. I yielded on purpose, letting her pull me toward her chest until it was almost touching our clenched hands, and I could feel her heart beat-

---

[2] Areas still under Nationalist control.

ing. But my arm stayed put. All I wanted was to prolong the contest so that I could keep squeezing her hands. Eventually she started to weaken, but instead of pinning her arm down right away, I started to pinch the most sensitive spot on her hand. Her flesh was as tender and soft as if she had no bones. She yelped in pain and almost lost her temper at me.

She seemed bright, so I could not understand why she was such a poor student. During our group study sessions she seemed to be studying and learning the material but somehow could never remember it later. She had actually joined our group just for the fun of it, and her presence livened up our sessions quite a bit for me. Although we were the same age, she seemed precocious and careworn. Sometimes she closed her book and softly recited the material she was trying to memorize, but then she would pause, lost in reverie.

She claimed that the hot weather ruined her appetite and that she was afraid of gaining weight. I assured her that I thought her weight was perfect and complimented her on being as voluptuous as a peony.

"How do you know?" she asked, pleased but skeptical.

"Well, then, let's see how heavy you are," I replied, spreading my arms to pick her up.

She agreed, pressing against me. I picked her up, held her in the air long enough to estimate her weight, and pronounced her not at all heavy.

Through these playful intimacies, we exchanged some electric touches. But with hindsight, the electricity was feeble, like a vague, ineffable yearning. After the examination results had been posted, everyone in our study group was admitted to college except for her, so she had to stay at home. Too embarrassed to see anyone, she cut off relations with all of us.

I went to visit her, but she just burst into tears and gazed at me with her brimming, wistful dark eyes. With the passing of summer, the somberness of our preparations for the college entrance examinations had vanished, and everything had returned to normal. It was as if she and I had put on new faces and had never played those flirtatious games. I tried to find a few comforting words for her, but they came out sounding forced.

Now that I was in danger, I thought of hiding my incriminating suitcase in Grandfather's garden, but on the way I decided it would not be safe there. Instead, I made a desperate shift in course to her house, the safest place I could think of. She was the only one of my old classmates who was still living at home, so I had no need to worry about her college authorities coming to snoop around. When I got out of the pedicab, I finally recovered my senses, and as my urgent footsteps crunched in the snow, my imaginary movie scenario and dreamlike reminiscences vanished without a trace. I knocked hesitantly on her door and tried, in the gentlest tone of voice I could manage, to ease her concern upon seeing me so suddenly. Then I filled her in quickly on my situation, begging her to let me store my suitcase in her house for a few days until the emergency was over. She caught on quickly and readily agreed to keep it for me. She even teased me by asking if I was afraid she might peek inside the suitcase and find out my secrets. I replied that if there were any secrets, they were all ones she shared with me, so if she wanted to peek, she could.

Unable to agonize over every detail in the heat of the moment, I left the suitcase with her and rushed back to campus. But I dared not go back to the dormitory, where people would be looking for me. Instead, I hid in my usual corner of the library, but I had to skip my nightly diary entry for the first time in years. The tension and exhilaration of the day had faded, and real terror was now descending on me like a giant shadow. As it approached, I shrank into my corner. The lights-out bell rang for the last time. The library was closing, so I stood up and went downstairs. The streetlights cast a dim glow in the deep, dark night. I was on the brink of a nightmare, with nowhere to hide.

7

Expulsion

I HAD JUST GONE to bed when my political instructor burst into my room and hustled me out to Campus Security. Once there I was interrogated by a couple of officers and cadres from my department about where I had been that day and where I had hidden my diaries. I insisted that I had gone nowhere but the library and that I had no diaries other than the reading journals that my political instructor had already seen. Ignoring my protestations, they encircled me under a set of glaring lights and took turns trying to squeeze information out of me. At first they alternated between bluster and wheedling, but when that failed, they started to browbeat me, banging on the table and stool for emphasis. Unless I came clean, they threatened, they would turn my case over to the Great Wild Goose Pagoda Precinct police station the next day. They kept questioning me until I grew bleary-eyed in the wee hours of the night.

But they did not let me go back to my own room. When I opened my eyes the next morning, I found myself in a different room, on the second floor. A single lightbulb dangled from a short cord near the ceiling, the window was bolted shut, and I had new roommates. I was not even allowed to go to the toilet unescorted.

My political instructor stopped by and announced that my departmental party branch and Campus Security had jointly decided to sequester me for formal investigation. Campus Security, which was an arm of the police, apparently had the power to detain students and had already sequestered several from my department since the beginning of the Nine Polemics campaign. A few weeks earlier, while walking down the hall with a classmate named Zheng Liang, I had noticed people sitting on stools outside certain rooms. Zheng Liang had informed me that they were guarding students who had been locked up. At the time I had no idea that similar misfortune would soon befall me.

Now Zheng Liang was one of my student guards, and he and the other, whose name was Fu Cang, escorted me to the cafeteria for breakfast. My political instructor had laid down the law: I was not allowed to walk around by myself, have personal contact with anyone, leave the dormitory without permission, or go home. Since there was insufficient reading light in the room, I asked Zheng Liang why the bulb was so near the ceiling. He told me that this, along with locking the windows, was a measure to prevent me from attempting suicide. Campus Security had even removed everyone's personal scissors from the room.

After breakfast my political instructor and class monitor took me to my house to look for my diaries and letters. They had been there the day before, after they had discovered my suspicious absence from campus, but had come away empty-handed. This time they discovered a heap of ashes near the wall beneath a window, and a wastebasket full of torn-off notebook covers. Their suspicions aroused, they summoned my sister Shuzhi back from her classroom at Xi'an High School for questioning. She asserted truthfully that the papers she had burned had been her own, not mine, but they were unsatisfied with her reply. Even if the papers were her own, they warned her, she did not have the freedom to burn them at will. Moreover, they threatened, no one in our family would be above suspicion as long as my papers were unaccounted for. My political instructor barked that she needed to correct her attitude and that they would report her to her school's party committee unless she made a clean breast of things. Unable to pry any information out of her, they ultimately concluded that the burned papers had been mine.

My political instructor calmed down a bit once he had given up hope of finding my papers. Patiently he extracted from me the names and addresses of people I knew or corresponded with and wrote down everything I said. I thanked my lucky stars that he had not asked about my old girlfriend, figuring that he must not know I had hidden my suitcase at her house. Wondering if she was aware of what had befallen me, I fretted that she might be scared into surrendering my papers. As my anxiety level rose, I longed to sneak out for a quick rendezvous with her.

I had been daydreaming about her for the last few days in the dormitory. Like the spotlight on a stage, my mind's eye had been trained on her image, revisiting old memories.

On last year's Dragon Boat Festival she had come to see me alone, without the other members of our cram group. As she entered the main gate, she had called out that she had brought a pack of mung bean cakes for our family. Once she was in the foyer, I had detected a refreshing herbal fragrance that had reminded me of a traditional Chinese pharmacy or the incense at Grandfather's altar.

"You smell marvelous," I had commented, sniffing her all over.

"It's here," she had replied, dodging me. Opening the top button of her short-sleeved blouse, she had loosened the collar a bit to reveal a tiny peach-colored sachet atop her tight chemise. When I put my nose there, she had shoved me aside, promising to take the sachet off for me later so that I could sniff it to my fill. I had grabbed her wrist, which was bound with a colorful silk thread bracelet that dug into her plump, voluptuous forearm.

"Didn't you want to see Grandfather's altar room?" I had asked. "It's especially beautiful up there today, so let's go see."

Slowly I had led her by the hand up the dark staircase, which creaked with every step. The dingy corridor upstairs was festooned with cobwebs full of dust balls and mouse dung, but sunlight streamed in the windows of the altar room, reflecting our images in the polished surface of the red lacquer incense table. Gilded statues of the Three Buddhas of the Western Paradise stood solemnly in their niche, surrounded by a Buddhist pantheon and a pair of glass-encased metal reliquary stupas enshrining the precious remains of Master of the Void and Master Buddhist Radiance. A choking cloud of incense poured out of the censer. Giddily she had leaned her shoulder toward me as if inviting me to remove her sachet.

My reverie faded, and my thoughts drifted back to the present. That evening the authorities cross-examined me again about the location of my diaries. This time they set me a brutal deadline: Hand in the diaries the next day, or they would turn my case over to the police. I wondered if they would really stoop to such a thing.

As I lay dozing in bed late that night, my body seemed to float back to Grandfather's altar room. The censer was still pouring out smoke, but the table had somehow risen. Smiling like a bodhisattva, my girlfriend perched on the edge of the table with her legs dangling down and began to unbutton her blouse. Maroon sparks flashed from the sachet on her bosom. Then her facial features blurred, and she inclined her bare breast toward me as if offering to nurse a baby. When I tried to pluck off her fiery sachet, it remained just out of reach, and I grabbed her nipple instead. Then the altar room burst into flames.

Awakening with a start, I realized that my vision had been only a jumbled dream. With my roommates snoozing soundly, I lay in the dark, worrying about her and my diaries, and decided to sneak out to her house again.

I slipped off campus during lunch break the next day. Changing buses on the way, I was even more jittery than I had been on my first trip. Then, just as I was making a mad dash from the last bus stop to her front gate, I saw my political instructor and his henchmen closing in on me from behind on their bicycles. They had given me plenty of rope, and I had hanged myself. How stupid of me to lead them here!

The consequences were utterly disastrous. Alarmed by the news that I was under investigation, she had burned the contents of my suitcase furtively in her backyard the night before. The college authorities alerted the neighborhood police, searched her premises, and found a pile of ashes next to the outhouse wall. Then they extracted the whole story from her, recorded her deposition, and forced her to sign it. However, the only evidence they got was the empty suitcase. She was seriously implicated in my scandal, and she and her parents hated me forever as a result.

She avoided me whenever I ran into her on the street, and eventually our paths diverged completely.

The mockery of the empty suitcase drove my political instructor and his henchmen into a violent rage, and they seemed on the verge of kicking the daylights out of me. I realized that things had reached rock bottom and found the idea that I had nothing to lose strangely calming. After a while they grudgingly returned the suitcase to me, along with a volley of curses. "You're a flagrant reactionary!" they fumed. "How dare you destroy the evidence?"

Zheng Liang told me that the burning of my diaries had been deemed a criminal act. Denied access to this trove, the authorities were planning to build their case against me based on my day-to-day conduct.

The interrogations were basically finished. Zheng Liang and Fu Cang escorted me to some of my classes and stayed with me in the dormitory the rest of the time. The class monitor also moved into our room to keep an eye on me. Now, however, he had made a clean break with me, and we no longer shared cigarettes. His militaristic posturing was more pronounced, and he always seemed to be hurrying out with my political instructor, carrying a dossier under his arm.

According to Zheng Liang, the department was "gathering information" on me. When I asked him what that meant, he explained that all my old friends and classmates were being asked to denounce me in writing. The week before, the authorities had collected denunciations from my whole class, and now they were looking outside the college. Fu Cang told me that at a party meeting the class monitor had accused the Youth League branch secretary of condoning my reactionary behavior. As a result, the branch secretary had been deprived of the opportunity to go out to dig up the dirt on me. Meanwhile, the class monitor, his old enemy, had risen to the top.

From time to time my political instructor summoned me to corroborate the reactionary views that were being attributed to me. In some cases the views were indeed mine. In others my accusers had distorted my original meaning, but I admitted to having said something similar. Sometimes, however, people were simply putting words into my mouth. With the bold inexperience of youth, I readily admitted to any remarks that I remembered having made, bearing the brunt of my actions as intrepidly as a newborn calf might face a tiger.

For example, I was charged with repeating the following facetious comment by H. G. Wells: "About two-thirds of the face of Marx is beard. . . . It is exactly like *Das Kapital* in its inane abundance. . . . [I have] a gnawing desire . . . to see Karl Marx shaved. Some day, if I am spared, I will take up shears and a razor against *Das Kapital*; I will write *The Shaving of Karl Marx*."[*]

I remembered having said this to a fellow student who, like me, had a bad class background. On one occasion he and I had been singled out for confinement to the dormitory during a party in honor of a group of Albanian visitors, an experience that I had found highly insulting. Eager to have his name removed from the blacklist, he had reported me, completely out of context, for quoting Wells. This was the basis for later charges against me of "slandering the patriarchs of the revolution."

One of my friends from middle school had reported me for something I had said to a peasant food vendor at a free market who had jacked up his prices during the shortages after the Great Leap Forward. He was charging a whole yuan for a roasted sweet potato. Protesting this exorbitant price, I had turned and walked away.

"Wait a minute, comrade," the peasant had called.

"We're not comrades!" I had retorted.

My old classmate had quite a memory, dredging up such a trifle. I knew that my middle school classmates were all very innocent and had probably not meant to bad-mouth me. My political instructor must have put them up to it.

"The landlord class might show its true colors anytime," I imagined him saying. "Even when he was just walking down the street, Kang Zhengguo might have shown his hatred of the poor and lower-middle peasants. Think about the times you've spent with him. Have you ever seen him insult a poor or lower-middle peasant?"

The charges against me had already been drafted, like subheadings in

[*] H. G. Wells, *Russia in the Shadows* (London: Hodder and Stoughton, 1920), pp. 69–70.

an essay, and my political instructor was merely collecting examples for each one. Sticking to his interpretation of the anecdotes that he had extracted from people, he turned a deaf ear to my explanations of extenuating circumstances. All he wanted from me was an acknowledgment of each allegation so that he could bring formal charges against me.

Zheng Liang and Fu Cang, both decent young men from poor peasant families, remained straightforward in all their dealings with me. If they thought that I was being treated unfairly, they would say so. I lent Zheng Liang my stylish new blue jacket because he was embarrassed to wear his shabby, old-fashioned homespun when visiting friends at other schools on weekends. I also shared my thermos of hot water for face washing with Fu Cang, who had chilblains on his hands, and he often gratefully went down to the boiler room to refill it for me. A few busybodies smeared my two guards for political wavering on account of such minor slips, but they steadfastly continued to behave as they saw fit.

My political instructor stopped summoning me once he had confirmed all the trumped-up charges. I knew that this was the lull before the storm and that I would be punished as soon as the verdict came down from above. One day when Fu Cang, Zheng Liang, and I were alone in the room, Fu Cang opened the door and peered out into the corridor, then shut the door again.

"The college has approved your expulsion," he said earnestly. "I'm just warning you so that you can brace yourself for what's coming."

"Tomorrow morning there's going to be a struggle session against you," Zheng Liang added. "You'll be expelled, but nothing worse. Remember this so that you can get through the session without losing your cool." I appreciated their moral support.

At breakfast the next morning Fu Cang and Zheng Liang were replaced by new student guards, a pair of hard-liners whom I had always disliked. They hustled me into the struggle session, which was in a huge lecture hall packed with college administrators, faculty members, and all the Chinese department sophomores. The walls were plastered with combative signs, like NEVER FORGET CLASS STRUGGLE. I was shocked to see a poster with the words CRIMINAL LANDLORD ELEMENT beside Grandfather's name. I had been confined here for only forty days. What had been happening outside? No wonder my political instructor had been so intent on making me denounce Grandfather's influence.

Thanks to Zheng Liang's warning, I managed to sit calmly throughout the pro forma abuse. The struggle session was scripted, beginning with the administration's announcement of my expulsion and proceeding through a series of faculty and student diatribes against me from the podium. Each speaker was required to vilify me to fan the flames of class struggle. I had seen it all before: the decor of the lecture hall, the order of the program, the posturing and cadence of the speakers, and the pep rally–style chanting of hostile slogans.

But this time I was the victim. They had even tossed in a gratuitous sideshow act about the "bad old days," featuring a female student who recited a well-rehearsed monologue about the grief that a landlord had caused her family. She sobbed when she got to the sad parts of her litany, which stimulated new rounds of earsplitting slogan shouting from below. An amused smile flitted across my face as I watched these histrionics, and this angered some of the militants.

"Stand up!" they bellowed.

The crowd picked up the chant. "Stand up, stand up!"

"Down with Kang Zhengguo's swaggering!" someone yelled, brandishing a fist. The crowd echoed him.

Their hoarse, threatening cries struck terror into my heart but somehow elevated me at the same time. I was amazed that I, at the tender age of twenty, had done something worthy of such large-scale vituperation. My two guards prodded me to my feet, and I woodenly faced the sea of raised fists and the din of shouted slogans. As my gaze moved from one familiar face to the next, I wondered why everyone seemed so angry. Was I seeing real hatred, or was it artificial? I had done no one any harm. I wished I could explain that I was just a scapegoat and not a real reactionary. Some poor wretch had to play the villain in every campaign, and the role had unluckily fallen to me this time.

After the struggle session I was taken to my political instructor's office for the last time. The formalities were very simple. He handed me the official ruling of my expulsion, saying that I was being sent home imme-

Kang Zhengguo following his release from detention, 1965.

diately. It was January 5, 1965, although the written decision was dated December 26, 1964. With a strong sense of relief, I strode out of the campus gates in the piercing winter wind. Fu Cang and I took the bus into town, while my political instructor and the class monitor followed on their bicycles with my bags, which they had packed for me. They were also carrying my residence permit and ration tickets, saying that they wanted to hand me over in person to my neighborhood police.

8

The Dregs of Society

M Y ESCORTS DUTIFULLY delivered me and my dossier to the police station. I was headed home to my parents' house, but now that I no longer qualified for student status, I had to settle the problem of my domicile registration[1] with Officer Hua, our neighborhood policeman. I watched as my political instructor handed him my residence permit and food ration tickets and then stepped into an adjoining room with him to go over my dossier. After my escorts had left, Officer Hua berated me, ordering me to wait at home on my best behavior until he could let me know what the next step would be. He kept my permit and ration tickets without mentioning how I could get them reissued.

The reissue should have been a simple matter, since I had never left Xi'an, but Officer Hua was determined to make me suffer for my expulsion from college. When I went back to see him, he just rolled his eyes and told me to write an essay. I brought him the essay the next day, but he brushed me off with a vague promise to "look into the matter" and

---

[1] All Chinese were required by law to have residence permits, which officially specified one's domicile and had to be reissued if one wished to move.

instructed me to wait until the following week. Then, when I went the next week, his colleagues told me nonchalantly that he was out of town on a long business trip. Without my residence permit I could not get my rations, and without my rations there was no way I could pull my own weight in the family.

Now that I was out of work and school, the official term for me was "social youth," which meant that I was not employed in a state-run enterprise. It may seem strange that the word "social" could assume negative connotations in a self-proclaimed socialist society like China. In fact "social youth" was not necessarily a derogatory term since it often referred to young people awaiting matriculation or employment. The police had even worse terms for us. If they were trying to be polite, we were "miscellaneous personnel," but if they were not, we were "the dregs of society."

Officer Hua had warned me to stay away from other dregs of society, mentioning some of my old friends by name, including Li Zhimin. Baffled, I asked around and learned that Li had been expelled and sent home before I had. I stole out to his house to see him, but his parents stopped me at the door, adamantly refusing to let me in. When I got home, I found Fu Cang, my college classmate, waiting for me there. Explaining that my political instructor had sent him to return some things I had left in the dormitory, he took me out for a meal at the lakeside restaurant in Xingqing Park, where he revealed why our department had suddenly decided to confiscate my diaries and letters. He said it had all started with some letters I had written to a friend at a college out of town, which was also conducting the Nine Polemics campaign. The campus police there had found my friend's diaries and letters in one of his storage trunks, including some letters mailed from the Chinese department at Shaanxi Normal University, so they had turned them all over to our departmental party branch. This meant that my department had already had my letters on that autumn weekend when my political instructor suddenly made me write my self-critical essay. According to Fu Cang, my stubborn refusal to volunteer any information about my relationship with this friend had aroused departmental suspicions that I was concealing a serious thought crime, and the department had expected to find more clues in my diaries and letters. Now everything was clear. Li Zhimin's surrender of my letters to the authorities had set this chain of events in motion. No wonder that I had not heard from him, or that his parents had not let me see him.

But Fu Cang seemed to have an ulterior motive for his visit. He told me that after my expulsion a rumor had been circulating that the branch secretary of the Communist Youth League had written me a letter. Our class monitor had been pointing the finger at the secretary during party meetings, and the departmental leadership was investigating his relationship with me. Fu Cang seemed to be trying to worm something out of me, but I did not tell him anything. I had to watch what I said to him now. Maybe he was just gossiping and simply wanted to bring me up-to-date, but it was also possible that the department had sent him to snoop around, or that he was sounding me out on behalf of the worried branch secretary. No matter what, I was determined not to say anything that could incriminate the branch secretary. After all, he had taken a considerable personal risk to tip me off about the departmental plans to seize my documents.

When Fu Cang saw that I was not responding to his probe about the branch secretary, he changed the subject. After the investigation had begun, he said, the cloud of suspicion had extended to my friend the young woman basketball player, and her departmental leadership was still forcing her to write self-critical essays accounting for her relationship with me. Listening to Fu Cang's news, I felt free as a bird. Let them have their class struggle on campus! I was not going back there anyway, so none of it made any difference to me.

My biggest headache right now was my lack of a residence permit, for which I had to put up with the constant silent reproach on my parents' faces, to say nothing of Officer Hua's scorn. But he had something up his sleeve. First he procrastinated for more than a month, until my parents and I were desperate. Then he suddenly turned up on our doorstep, sounding downright friendly and well intentioned, with the news that he had found a job for me as a worker at a construction materials plant just south of town. Handing me a form to fill out, he assured me that I would get my residence permit and ration tickets if I accepted the job and filled out the form.

"Why are the police finding work for you? They're not supposed to do that. The borough is," Father commented suspiciously when he came home and heard the news. He told me that the form was not to be taken lightly and that I should wait until he had done some asking around before I handed it in. He was right. As it turned out, the "construction materials plant" was the infamous Number Two Brickyard, which everybody in Xi'an called the labor camp kilns.[2]

With the forced closing of many state-run enterprises during the famine after the Great Leap Forward, the state had given this labor camp brickyard, one of two in Xi'an, to the municipal Security Bureau. It had transferred all the prisoners out and manned it with "conscript labor," which was a new term at the time. Starving migrants from the countryside had flocked to the cities, the streets of which were already filled with laid-off workers from defunct state-run enterprises. The opening of the free markets[3] attracted these vagrants to business activities, some of them illegal, such as trading in food ration tickets or other coupons with floating values, a practice that the authorities called scalping. There would have been no need for such scalping in a society where goods were plentiful and trade was fully legal. The problem was that people were caught unawares as government policies toward the free markets blew alternately hot and cold. The Security Bureau rounded up all the scalpers periodically for investigation but only sent them to the labor camps in the rare cases involving serious "crimes." Most of them were detained temporarily as conscript laborers until they could be proved innocent and released.

By the spring of 1965, when I was confronting my decision, the economy had improved. The Security Bureau had spruced up the image of the labor camp kilns with a new sign at the entrance of the Number Two Brickyard that read JIAN'AN CONSTRUCTION MATERIALS PLANT OF XI'AN and had started to "recruit" people like me, the unemployed dregs of society, to work there in addition to the conscript laborers. The official jargon for us was "resettled workers," a term that also applied to freed prisoners and conscript laborers whose original work units did not want them back. In

[2] "Labor camp" is used throughout this book as a loose translation of the Chinese terms *laogai* and *laojiao*, literally "labor reform" and "labor reeducation," referring to the entire Chinese penal system, which is analogous to the Soviet gulag.

[3] Markets that were not owned by the state.

resettlement facilities like the Number Two Brickyard, which the Communist Party established specially for us next door to the prisons, we had to continue our "reeducation." A jail term was finite, but the reeducation process of a resettled worker was not.

I could read the handwriting on the wall. Officer Hua was determined to steamroller me into going to the brickyard whether I wanted to or not. But Father was still hoping to save me and was running around, trying to pull strings on my behalf. His plan was for me to delay as long as possible, until the Security Bureau's recruiting drive was over, and then figure out some other way to get my residence permit. Father had no illusions about what kind of place the Number Two Brickyard was. He had always tried to shelter me from the bad influence of riffraff in our neighborhood. Now his worst fears had come true. The job that Officer Hua was foisting on me was going to land me, a "reactionary" college student, in a den of thieves. Father was afraid that I might be permanently corrupted if I was exposed to such bad influences while still so young.

I understood his misgivings, but I was at the end of my tether. His constant gloom and Mother's nagging were getting on my nerves. Even worse was the shame I felt sitting around the house all day, stuffing my face with food rations that rightly belonged to my parents, brother, and sisters. I decided that I would rather be at the brickyard, despite its unsavory reputation, backbreaking work, and low pay. I was not going there as a convict, I figured, so I would be able to go out freely in my spare time. All in all, it would be a rare opportunity for me to get a glimpse of the lowest rungs of society. As a child I had read the biographies of Communist Party heroes who had languished in Nationalist jails, such as *Comrade Wang Ruofei in Prison*, and their romantic, revolutionary stories had planted seeds in my mind that were starting to sprout now. Father thought I would be plunging into an inferno, but I imagined a swashbuckling adventure and had even developed something of a martyr complex. Despite Father's insistence that I was making a momentous decision, I thought it was child's play, foolishly imagining that I might meet some Robin Hood types among the criminals who had been released from the labor camps.

Officer Hua kept dropping in to pressure me, and Father kept putting him off. Meanwhile, I became convinced that I could not go on living in our multifamily compound, with its dreary courtyard full of clotheslines. I had come to dread the sight of Officer Hua's long dark face. One day I got fed up and took out the form that he had given me. Before Father could get home from work, I filled it out and rushed it to the police station. I had accepted an invitation from hell.

9

The Gates of Hell

IN MARCH 1965 I became a resettled worker at the Jian'an Construction Materials Plant of Xi'an. Resettled workers received salaries and certain benefits, but they had to perform manual labor under strict supervision, without freedom of speech or movement, and were forbidden to quit their jobs or to apply for a change of domicile. If they went AWOL, the wardens were empowered to round them up and drag them back in handcuffs, as if they were escaped prisoners. Thus, although the party line claimed that resettlement was a social service and an example of socialism at its best, from the workers' point of view, it amounted to incarceration or to being treated as trash for recycling.

Even though I was aware of these drawbacks, I walked into the trap on my own two feet. After I got my residence permit and ration tickets back from Officer Hua on that fateful day, I packed up my college textbooks—*Ancient Chinese, An Anthology of Chinese Literature*, and *College Russian*—intending to finish my education in my spare time. Then I slung my student bedroll across my back and took the Number Fifteen bus three stops south of the college to the street just outside the brick-

The walls and watchtowers of the Number Two Brickyard.

yard gates. First I noticed the high enclosing walls, studded with watchtowers. Then, as I got closer, I saw the electrified netting on top of the walls and the sentries in the towers. There were armed guards and wardens at the gate, but they paid little attention to people coming in, reserving their scrutiny instead for people on the way out and even inspecting the chassis of every truck loaded with bricks that left the facility.

Upon my arrival I reported to the wardens' office, handed in my residence permit and ration tickets, and received a little red plastic booklet stamped "Entry and Exit Permit for Resettled Personnel," containing my photo ID. These permits were nothing like the work IDs that state employees had. They were valid only inside the compound, where they distinguished us from the conscript laborers beneath us and the cadres above us. Their primary purpose was to restrict our freedom of movement. In this sense they functioned like the magical metal headband that the Tang priest used on the Monkey King.[1] We had to carry the permits at all times, and we were forbidden to leave the brickyard if we lost them or if the wardens confiscated them, as they could do whenever they pleased. In fact all they had to do was call the gatekeepers and tell them that our exit privileges had been revoked, and we were grounded. In general, the only time we could try to leave the site was after work on Saturday afternoons anyway, since we had compulsory political study most weeknights.

The wardens had a rationale for treating us like this. As they revealed in their constant pep talks, they assumed that most of us were thieves. "We're keeping you off the streets for your own good," they assured us. "For every one of you that stays here instead of stepping out, there'll be one less missing wallet in town. Besides, you can't really get into too much trouble around here. So just stay here and behave yourselves. You'll get rehabilitated faster and help us keep law and order in town." I thought this was preposterous the first time I heard it. After all, those of us who were not pickpockets were being stigmatized unfairly. But the wardens took professional pride in these repeated harangues; as far as they were concerned, we were all dregs of society and deserved heavy-handed treatment whether we were thieves or not.

One young newcomer refused to submit to such rigid regimentation. When something urgent came up at home one day, he went to the main gate after work but had the bad luck to arrive at a moment when the gatekeepers were not letting anyone out. His arguments fell on deaf ears, so he just walked out without permission. The gatekeepers called the authorities right away, and before he even got to the bus stop, he was intercepted by a motorcycle and hauled back to the brickyard, where he was clapped into the conscript labor brigade. "This is an arm of the dictatorship of the proletariat, not a nursery school," the wardens constantly reminded us. "Like it or not, we're going to train you to heel, lie down, and roll over on command." Their favorite threat was: "The conscript labor brigade is right on

[1] An allusion to the classic Chinese novel *Journey to the West*, in which Xuanzang, a Tang dynasty Buddhist priest on a pilgrimage to India, disciplines his assistant, the mischievous Monkey King, with a metal headband that shrinks on command. See *Monkey*, trans. Arthur Waley (New York: Grove Weidenfeld, 1943).

the other side of that wall. It's easy enough for us to transfer you from this side to that one. All we have to do is assign you a place to sleep over there."

There was little real difference between the two sides. One of the first things I saw when I arrived at our barracks was the list of "Regulations for Resettled Personnel" on the wall. Its authoritarian tone sent chills down my spine, and the sight of the miserable resettled workers all around me was enough to dispel any romantic illusions I had ever cherished about places like this. In fact our barracks had originally been a cellblock, with rows of makeshift bunks along the walls, each equipped with paper-thin bedding. I could tell from the mousy gray hue of the bedding, which matched the conscript laborers' uniforms I had seen, that my roommates had served time next door.

Choosing an unoccupied space, I unrolled my bedding, piled my books by my pillow, and lay down. I tried to console myself with the thought that I should try to make the best of things for now and that I could always try to quit later if I could not stand it. At least I had cafeteria meal coupons worth fifty pounds of grain per month, a brickyard worker's ration. Every day I cashed them in for meals, which I enjoyed alone, leaning against a wall in the sun. Being self-sufficient, no matter how much I had to suffer otherwise, was vastly preferable to depleting my parents' rations.

In the cafeteria I bumped into Ermao, an old neighbor from my elementary school. He had been admitted to technical school, but soon afterward the technical schools had all been disbanded. Then he had tried to make a living hustling on the free market and had somehow ended up here. He told me that Officer Hua had summoned him to the police station for questioning one day two years ago and had clapped him into the conscript labor brigade. But he had taught himself how to fire the kiln and was now a resettled worker on the kiln operating squad.

Ermao took me up on top of the east kilns, where he gave me an orientation to brickyard life. From this vantage point we could see the whole brick manufacturing area, with its rows of unbaked bricks and heaps of yellow dirt. He told me that the workers had made all the bricks by hand until recently, when the brickyard had acquired a mechanical brick press. At the moment this huge monster was noisily gobbling up dirt as fast as a brigade of men with pickaxes and shovels could empty their cartloads into the giant chute behind it. Meanwhile, the press was spitting out bricks in front, and another brigade was carting them off to an area where a third brigade was stacking them to dry. "There aren't any cushy jobs down there," Ermao informed me. "Every one of those unbaked bricks weighs a dozen pounds. An eight-hour shift will do you in unless the press has a breakdown." He said that operating the kiln was the best job. With three squads of three men each, and each squad at its own kiln, you had more freedom and privacy than the workers who had to keep up with the brick press.

Father had been correct in his prediction that heavy physical labor was in store for me after my expulsion from college. All new arrivals at the brick-yard were assigned to the brick manufacturing area since the work there required nothing more than sheer brute strength. I was a soft, inexperienced youth of twenty, and my hands blistered up right away. This job was much tougher than the days of "volunteer work" I had put in as a student, when all we usually had to do was to look busy. Now that I had to toil in earnest for eight hours every day, I was getting my first real taste of manual labor and was discovering that in fact its worst discomfort was not the fatigue but the constant surveillance. Even though resettled workers were supposedly different from conscript laborers, we still had brigade leaders and foremen riding herd on us, and they abused us as if we were merely beasts of burden.

Mother had packed me some canvas work gloves, but they were little use. The only way to develop a workingman's hands was to let my blisters bleed and form scabs and then to let the scabs break open and heal again, until they turned into tough calluses. As long as the brick press was operating, I had to keep feeding dirt into the giant chute behind it. When I got tired, I would lean on my shovel for a moment and lubricate my palms with my own spit, as I saw the other workers doing. Then I would grab my shovel again and keep going. This initial period at the brickyard was the hardest for me. Later there was an opening for a kiln operator, and I got the job, thanks to Ermao's recommendation to Brigade Chief Liu.

Ermao, the head kiln operator, and his assistant, Changhai, were in charge of building the range. As their helper I was supposed to seal off the kiln opening with discarded bricks and paste it shut from the outside with mashed wheat straw. The kiln was like a giant pot half buried in the earth, with a vented dome reaching two or three stories above the submerged

The remains of the east kilns in 2004.

floor. Once it was filled to its capacity of two hundred thousand bricks, we would split up to make the preparations for the firing. We wended our way through a system of tunnels to get to our underground work space, which was pitch-dark inside when the lights were off and shaped like a northern Shaanxi peasant's cave with a vaulted brick ceiling. When the fire was lit, Ermao and Changhai tended it, using a special shovel to spread the dampened coal evenly. My job was to keep them supplied with fuel, and I did that by mixing coal powder evenly with water and piling it beside the kiln. Once this was taken care of, I had little else to do for the first few days of the ten-day firing cycle, while the kiln baked at low temperature. But the going got rougher when the heat was turned up, with the kiln burning more coal and more cinders to clean up. We were a dozen yards underground, and we had to use a winch to load all the cinders into baskets for hauling up to the top and shipping to a special faraway dump site.

Although the job was grueling and sooty, we still found plenty of time in the eight-hour workday just to sit drinking tea, smoking cigarettes, and chatting. We could even cook campfire style. Sometimes men from the other squads dropped by for lively little get-togethers. But if we were tired, each of us would take a turn standing watch so the others could nap. Down inside the tunnels, oblivious of the time of day and sheltered from the weather, we were free to do as we pleased in our leisure moments, as long as we kept an eye out for our supervisor.

I got nothing but blank stares when I told people that my crime had been to keep diaries. "Why'd you do a thing like that? You think you're another Lei Feng or something?" scoffed Changhai, who also teased me whenever he saw me studying in my spare time. None of the men who worked in the bowels of the kiln shared my interest in literature. Most of them were serving time for theft or racketeering. Naturally their conversation did not stray far from their profession. There was a man from Shanxi nicknamed Robin Hood, renowned for his pickpocketing skills, who brought back Peony brand cigarettes for everybody whenever he went into town. Instead of taking it easy down underground, he used all his spare time to hone his skills by dropping a slippery piece of soap into a vat of hot water and retrieving it as quickly as he could with two fingers. Changhai had grown up in a gang in the notorious Second Street slums and was a veteran of the labor camps. Word had it that he too had started out as a thief but lacked the necessary skills, so he had established a racket, sending kids out to do the dirty work and taking a cut of their proceeds in return for his protection.

Robin Hood and Changhai were irrepressible, blustery fellows, but most of the rest of the several hundred resettled workers at the brickyard preferred to lie low and bide their time until they were released. Some of them labored in earnest and renounced their lives of crime, but others managed to outwit the wardens and keep up their activities on the sly. Their motto was "Catch me if you can," and a couple of them eventually got what was coming to them. One of them went AWOL one day, and the next day we heard that the police station downtown had called to ask the brickyard to send someone to pick him up. Since he seemed like a hardworking, clean-cut young man, nobody had suspected that he was a pickpocket. We heard that he had been caught red-handed in the train station, dragged back to the brickyard, and clapped into the conscript labor brigade.

Brigade Chief Liu was a lax supervisor, so we could get away with working sporadically and having perfunctory political meetings. He had been there a long time and preferred to keep a low profile and to look the other way when it came to details, as long as his wards got their work done and kept their noses clean. The paternalistic mixture of kindness and intimidation that he used on us reminded me of the way the bosses in old-fashioned shops treated their clerks. He would bawl people out just for show, and they would go through the motions of their jobs with smirks on their faces, doing their best only occasionally. Somehow a kiln load of bricks would eventually get finished and another would be lit, so that the twenty-four kilns that lined the east side of the manufacturing area, like a row of castles, spewed smoke around the clock.

When the bricks were almost finished baking, our final task was to build an earthen moat around the top of each kiln, which we filled with water once the fires were extinguished. This job was called watering the kilns. As the water seeped down inside onto the red-hot bricks, they slowly cooled and developed a bluish tinge. While we worked, the kilns emitted clouds of scalding vapor, like giant steamers, and heated the ground underfoot until it scorched us through the soles of our shoes.

Once I discovered that a faucet near one of the kilns had hot water. This was a stroke of luck for me, since the brickyard had no bathing facilities, and we usually just dabbed ourselves off with the water we heated when we were underground. I started visiting the faucet regularly to wash up after work. Tossing my grubby uniform onto the ground, I would stand there naked in the broad daylight, regardless of the weather, and shower to my heart's content. The faucet was on the southeast corner of the compound, facing a big empty field and the heavily guarded high surrounding wall, which nobody ever approached. The armed sentries in the watchtowers were probably the only people who could see me.

At around four o'clock every afternoon when I got off work, I would wash up and then go sit in the shade on top of one of the old, abandoned kilns to watch the activity in the manufacturing area below. At this time of day the flat work surface was as hot as a griddle, with the broiling late-afternoon sun directly overhead and the steam seething underground, and the resettled workers and conscript laborers were sweating as they struggled to keep up with the mechanical brick press. Many of them were bare-chested, with straw hats on their heads and towels around their necks to dry themselves off. The conscript laborers had the toughest jobs. On their backs they wore cattle hide mesh sacks for lugging bricks around, protecting their skin with a layer of burlap scraps. Under the watchful eyes of the sentries, they loaded the dried bricks into the kilns for firing, hauled the smoldering finished bricks out again, and stacked them up to be packed onto the big trucks that came in. Unloading the kilns was an especially onerous task, since they belched foul sulfuric fumes and eye-stinging cinders. Even with huge fans roaring at the mouths of the kilns, the bricks were still searing hot. The workers on this shift toiled in the blazing sun every afternoon from two o'clock until six. Occasionally one of them would reel with exhaustion, accidentally letting the bricks on his back crash to the ground, and the brigade leader would curse him even if his legs and feet were bleeding. I secretly thanked the Bodhisattva Guanyin for protecting me from such a dreadful job.

My old friend Li Zhimin also turned up as a resettled worker. I had heard that Officer Hua had been trying to get him locked up here and that his mother had been resisting, but Officer Hua had somehow prevailed. Both our parents had forbidden us to have any further contact, and he was obviously avoiding me. I wanted to ask him to explain how his school had managed to confiscate my letters, but I never got a chance to speak to him. Adopting exemplary behavior from the moment he arrived, he transformed himself completely during the course of six months. With his frayed work uniform and shaved head, he looked penitent and hardworking. Eventually he was put in charge of a squad of conscript laborers and quickly mastered the stern, scolding manner that petty prison foremen adopted toward their subordinates. I heard that he was the brigade chief's stooge and was being paid forty yuan a month, unlike most of the new arrivals, myself included, who got only thirty.

One day, as I watched his squad coming back from work at the manufacturing area, I was shocked to see how much he had changed. He looked more robust, and his once-delicate facial features had coarsened and assumed a cruel, malicious cast. He pretended not to recognize me, as if he had obliterated our shared past from his memory. Human relationships are impermanent, and politics can destroy even the closest of friendships. Baffled, I wondered if his zeal was merely a pretense to ease his lot or if he sincerely believed he had committed a crime and was determined to reform and claw his way to the top in this inferno.

I could see no point in keeping my nose to the grindstone there. I never fell for the phony pep talks we got from the leadership of the brickyard about settling down in the brickyard and regarding it as our home. If labor was so glorious, why did they give all the dirty work to us, the dregs of society, instead of doing it themselves? From my first day there I had known that it constituted penal servitude. There was no glory in it. Its purpose was to fatigue us and to break our spirits. To the leadership, reform meant driving us so hard that we had no mental energy left for other pursuits. I had detested meaningless drudgery ever since my first manual labor classes in high school and had resisted it ever since as a form of enslavement.

As a resettled worker I followed the strategy of taking it easy whenever I could. I admired the work habits of carnivorous animals like lions, which were free to loll around all day once they had finished capturing their prey and wolfing down their fill. How different they were from cows and sheep, which spent all their time in docile grazing! My job firing the kiln demanded bursts of grueling, sweaty exertion, after which I could smoke and think quietly for hours with nobody looking over my shoulder. I treasured laziness and sought opportunities for it as my means of self-preservation. I had no intention of undergoing a transformation like Li Zhimin's, nor could I fathom why he seemed so eager to perform slave labor.

When the day's work was done, some people walked over to the military barracks next door to watch propaganda movies under the stars, but I preferred to sit alone on top of an abandoned kiln enjoying the sunset. I watched as the silhouette of the Zhongnan Mountains grew murky, evening fell on the empty fields, and the lights gradually came on all around me. The brickyard was only three bus stops from Shaanxi Normal University, and in the light of the setting sun I could clearly make out the huge roof of the palatial library. As the sky darkened, the lights in the reading room on the top floor came on, with the pale, peaceful fluorescent glow that I knew so well. Ever since my expulsion I had been having a recurring dream that I had been reinstated at the university and was studying again at my old desk in the corner of the reading room, surrounded by all my old books. My dream was so vivid that I could even hear the humming of the fluorescent lights, and I would wake up full of joy, which soon turned to dejection as I lay wide-eyed in the dark.

Once night had fallen, I looked back at our walled compound. The contrast was stark. Dim, evenly spaced lights dotted the electrified netting atop the high walls, rising from north to south along with the contours of the land. Parallel rows of dreary streetlamps lit up the huge manufacturing area between the east and west kilns. Thinking back to the library, I suddenly understood "where I was."[2] This was the sea of lights that I had seen from the campus. At dusk I used to gaze to the south from the top floor of the library, and the lights coming on in the distance had inspired me to compose poetry. I had noticed that the outer ring of lights varied in height, while the inner ones seemed denser and brighter. Their twinkling in the misty night was the stuff of dreams. Wondering whether the illuminated area was a public square, a street market, or a village, I had recited my poetry softly, comparing the distant lights with falling stars. Now I realized that my poetry had been an absurd prophecy. Glancing at the lights of the enclosed compound once more, I wiped away a few hot tears with the back of my hand.

[2] An allusion to a famous line of poetry by the Song dynasty woman poet Li Qingzhao, describing her feeling of alienation at dusk one evening while she was far from home.

10

Disaster Strikes

ONE DAY IN the autumn of 1965 Shuzhi announced that she had seen Grandfather plodding slowly past our house, looking as if he had sustained a back injury. He had not paused or even seemed to hear her when she ran after him, calling his name. Then our maid Caixia revealed that earlier in the day she had escorted him to the Sleeping Dragon Temple, where he had been the victim of a struggle session conducted by a new ad hoc committee of the Bureau of Religious Affairs. The Sleeping Dragon Temple was in the same alley as my parents' house, and I had gone there to play as a child. Grandfather had founded the Buddhist library and supported the abbot there, who was known as Master of Light. How could they defile such a holy place with struggle sessions? Caixia said she had not been allowed inside, so she had stood eavesdropping in the courtyard. She had been able to overhear the rise and fall of the voices of the monks and lay Buddhists as they had made speeches against Grandfather, punctuated by the sounds of a scuffle. Grandfather, a white-bearded old gentleman in his mid-eighties, was being beaten.

The Chinese Communist regime did not allow any organizations to exist

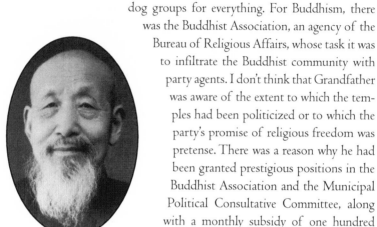

Grandfather.

independently of its control, and it had special watch-dog groups for everything. For Buddhism, there was the Buddhist Association, an agency of the Bureau of Religious Affairs, whose task it was to infiltrate the Buddhist community with party agents. I don't think that Grandfather was aware of the extent to which the temples had been politicized or to which the party's promise of religious freedom was pretense. There was a reason why he had been granted prestigious positions in the Buddhist Association and the Municipal Political Consultative Committee, along with a monthly subsidy of one hundred yuan. As a prominent Buddhist spokesman for official policies he was an unwitting figurehead for the party's united front policy of the political assimilation of nonparty members. In the comparatively relaxed climate of the past few years he had fallen for a host of false promises. Imagining that he could promote Buddhism as he had before the Communists, he had continued to advocate religious reform. Unfortunately his proposals—to hold gatherings to celebrate Buddhism, for example, and to require temples to enforce religious discipline—had aroused the ire both of the party and of the monastic community. Maybe even at the bitter end he still failed to understand that his religious zeal exceeded the limits tolerated by the authorities, who saw the latest political campaign as an opportunity to attack him.

After living peacefully under communism for sixteen years, Grandfather was getting a taste of the party's sinister tactic of turning people against one another. He was bewildered by the virulence of the attacks on him by monks, nuns, and lay Buddhists, who had always treated him with respect but now seemed even crueler than the cadres in charge. He never realized that the party agents within the monastic community had been informing on him all along and that the party had been keeping a dossier on him, lying in wait as he incriminated himself.

After his repudiation by fellow Buddhists, Grandfather was charged with the crime of attacking the party's religious policy. Then he was stripped of all his religious posts and expelled from the Municipal Political Consultative Committee. His hundred-yuan subsidy was cut off, and he and Grandmother started to have trouble making ends meet, just as they had when their property had first been confiscated shortly after 1949. He started to sell his books, which were his only remaining valuable possessions: rare compendiums, official dynastic histories, local chronicles, and photolithographs of Song dynasty editions of the Buddhist scriptures. These were heirlooms that I had long coveted, but they were carted away, along with the trunks and cabinets that held them, by secondhand-book dealers.

Then came a more serious blow. One evening shortly after Grandfather's expulsion from the Consultative Committee, the police burst into Silent Garden with an arrest warrant, snapped a mug shot of him, and started to ransack the house. They ripped up his bedroom floor and Grandmother's *kang* but found nothing. If they had found any of the stuff of propaganda movies and fiction—a ham radio, firearms, or records of old assets and debts to be hauled out in case the Communists were overthrown—they would have arrested him on the spot as a counterrevolutionary. But such things happen only in movies and fiction. Instead, they seized all "reactionary" items: his diaries, his entire pre-1949 photo collection, anything to do with Guomindang leaders he had known, such as calligraphy by Yang Hucheng and Yu Youren, and all his correspondence with Dai Jitao, whom the Communists had declared a war criminal. They stuffed everything into burlap bags and took it away. They also officially declared Grandfather a criminal landlord element and placed him under the surveillance of the local police station. From then on he was subjected to legal persecution. He was put under house arrest and had to submit regular written reports of his personal ideological "reform" to the police.

Things kept getting worse. By the fall of 1965 the Socialist Education campaign, with its emphasis on class struggle, was in full swing across the nation. It included the Four Cleanups campaign, in which special work teams assigned class status to landlords and rich peasants who had escaped classification during the Land Reform campaign, so that their property could be confiscated.

Grandfather was not as lucky this time as he had been during Land Reform. Whipped up by the work team, a peasant named Cao from the commune next door accused Grandfather of encroaching on his land to build Silent Garden. His family had made this baseless accusation back during Land Reform, but their attack had fizzled out because Grandfather had been shielded by the higher-ups. Now that the authorities had targeted Grandfather, however, they reopened the worn-out case, which resulted in heavy criminal charges against him. The commune had held a grudge against him for the last fifteen years, maintaining that his property should have been redistributed to it. Now, finally, the current campaign was providing an opportunity for reparations. Disregarding his status as an urban resident, which should have protected him from being treated like a peasant, the commune took possession of everything but the rooms that he and Grandmother were currently occupying. This included all his land and even the room that I had occupied as a child.

Times of crisis reveal inexplicable variations in the moral fiber of different individuals. Grandfather had many descendants, some of whom lost no time in denouncing him to save their own skins as soon as he was declared a criminal landlord element. But others, such as Father, my cousin Zhengxin, and Third Uncle, who helped my grandparents after they were deprived of their normal income, were more generous.

One weekend later that winter, having just received my meager pay from the brickyard, I went to visit my grandparents at Silent Garden. On my way to their house I recalled how Grandmother had liked to stash food in the drawers of the red lacquer table on the *kang* in her bedroom, a small room curtained off from Grandfather's inner sanctum. She never seemed particularly eager to consume the food and often seemed to forget that it was there. She also never seemed to mind if I pilfered it. Grandfather rarely poked his nose into her affairs and did not go into her room casually. I was the only family member who did that, and whenever I did, I would rummage through her drawers for treats. When my brother and sisters came to play on holidays, I would sneak them into her room, and we would open her drawers and gobble everything up. Grandmother never mentioned her missing goodies, as if she had put them there just for us.

Grandmother had been in her seventies back then. Since she had spent so much money on me over the years, she often held up her fingers for me to count on, asking me to try to figure out when I would graduate from college and get a job, how old she would be by then, and whether she would live to see the day when I could buy things for her. Now, although I had not graduated from college, I did have a job, for better or worse, and so I could finally treat her. Her patience had not been in vain. I bought a couple of my grandparents' favorite sweets, miniature persimmon pies with candied osmanthus blossoms and special "southern candy" from a shop near the Drum Tower. Adding in a small sum of money, I went to pay my respects.

I was shocked by the change in Silent Garden. Except for my grandparents' rooms and the outdoor passageways, the commune had sealed off all the rooms with strips of paper. It had marked the good furniture for confiscation, including the red lacquer table where Grandmother had stashed her food. The maid, Caixia, had quit her job, meaning that Grandmother was back to cooking three meals a day. Grandfather's voice was raspy, his conversation no longer punctuated with hearty laughter. He seemed reluctant to confide in me about his plight and spent most of his time in seated meditation with his eyes closed, his face gaunt and wizened, as if the only thing that still belonged to him in his inner sanctum was his own frail skeleton.

Insisting that the Constitution guaranteed religious freedom, Grandfather defended himself to any visitors who stopped by. "Why can't we burn incense and pray to the Buddha?" he pleaded. "There's nothing superstitious or feudal* about such things, and it's a complete distortion to say there is." The commune demanded that he surrender his statues of the Buddha, but he remained adamant. "I won't give up my statues and my religion," he snapped, "until you get the Constitution amended." The commune mem-

---

*Religion is often denounced in the atheistic culture of Communist China as superstitious, and "feudal" is a term used relatively loosely to refer to aspects of pre-1949 society that are considered backward or oppressive.

bers were peasants, who still held the gods somewhat in awe. They were mainly concerned with Grandfather's property, so they carted off some furniture but left his panoply of Buddhas in the family shrine upstairs.

Despite Grandfather's haggard appearance, his spirit was not completely broken. He kept meditating, burning his incense, and counting his rosary beads. And he still made nightly diary entries in a pocket-size notebook by his bed. At times he closed his eyes serenely and muttered, "They're predicting that Buddhism is going to die out, but they're wrong. Buddhism has been around for more than two thousand years, and has survived all the attempts of rulers throughout the ages to wipe it out. This onslaught is sure to fail, and so are any future ones. Buddhism is eternal."

11

Dreams of Freedom

IT WAS A midwinter Sunday, and the brick manufacturing area was deserted. With the wardens off for the day, everyone got a break. All was still, except for the smoke puffing out of one of the kilns. Some of my energetic coworkers had gone downtown, leaving a few lazybones napping on their bunks. The barracks reeked of sweaty feet, greasy hair, and unwashed bedding. Craving fresh air, I strolled out of the brickyard and into the neighboring countryside, a desolate checkerboard of withered brown fields and dull patches of green. After I had climbed down one hill and up another on a rough dirt path, a group of bicyclists with rifles on their backs whizzed by, scouring the landscape for wild rabbits. Then I passed an old man gleaning leftover corncobs from a heap of dried-up cornstalks by the roadside. With no particular destination in mind, I meandered along, hoping that the exercise would lift me out of the doldrums.

The city was so close that I could see the ancient Bell Tower, a major Xi'an landmark, from my hilltop, but I might as well have been in another world. I had been completely cut off from all my former classmates since the day of my expulsion. They shunned me if they saw me on the street, and I self-consciously averted my gaze and hurried by. I knew that I was under surveillance and that it would have been unreasonable to expect anyone to take the risk of having contact with me.

I was worried about my family, who found it necessary to cover up my embarrassing plight. Conversation was awkward whenever visitors came, because I found myself tongue-tied when people asked me ordinary questions like "Where do you go to school?" and "What do you do?" The truth was problematic, yet I could not lie and say that I was still at Shaanxi Normal University. I never knew where to start or what tone to adopt. I needed to deflect such conversations or to avoid them altogether. Deeply ashamed to be such a burden to my parents, I often stayed at the brickyard, where I belonged, on Sundays.

Life at the brickyard also weighed heavily on my mind. Our squad leader, whose name was Mr. Fu, was cast in the same mold as my class monitor at Shaanxi Normal University; China's social system seems to breed such bullies, who fawn on their superiors while abusing those beneath them. He was originally a skilled worker from Xi'an, who was sentenced to the labor camps on trumped-up charges of counterrevolutionary conspiracy. Although he had been an intelligent, competent young man to start with, his three-year stint in the camps transformed him prematurely into a wily old prisoner. During the lean years after the Great Leap Forward, he had returned to the city, where he had made some money "racketeering" on the free market and been tossed into the conscript labor brigade at the brickyard. Eventually he had been promoted to the status of resettled worker, and then to squad leader.

When the brigade leader was away, Mr. Fu was the boss, and he behaved like a servant who dons the master's clothes and struts around in front of the mirror when the master is out. A shameless, gifted mimic, he delivered perfect facsimiles of the brigade leader's harangues whenever he led political study sessions, carrying his model's tone of voice and mannerisms to their extreme. His lectures were unbearably long-winded. He would start by introducing a general principle, then proceed to single out a few people in the group for criticism. Raising his voice, he would rebuke his targets, invoking Chairman Mao's teachings about the dictatorship of the proletariat. Then he would prod the accused to their feet, demanding that they stand up and account for their crimes.

"Shall we punish them?" he would yell.

"Yeah, let's get the bastards!" replied the yes-men in the audience.

What had started out as a lecture would turn into a miniature struggle session, as the ostracized workers rose and faced the audience. Some sincerely addressed their wrongdoings, while others maintained a stubborn silence or loudly defended themselves. Certain sadistic onlookers often leaped up and punched the victims to satisfy their own violent cravings.

As I continued my meditative stroll in the hills, I started to regret my rash decision to sign up at the brickyard. The place was simply a vipers' pit and completely lacked the Robin Hood types and thrilling adventures that my favorite prison novels had led me to expect.

After my expulsion Father had ominously predicted, "You'll never get anywhere in this world until you can clear your name." Now there were rumors suggesting that the political climate might have relaxed enough to make this possible. I had heard that some college campuses were retrenching a bit from the excesses of the Nine Polemics campaign and that a victimized student had leaped to his death from the Great Wild Goose Pagoda, shocking the provincial party committee. There were also reports that the Shaanxi region of the Northwest Bureau of the Central Committee[1] had a new, enlightened leader, the former general secretary of the Communist Youth League. Emboldened by these bits of hearsay, I sent several letters of appeal to the provincial party committee and to the Northwest Bureau of the Central Committee, hoping against hope that they would issue an order to reopen my case or rehabilitate me, but all my letters disappeared into the void.

Doggedly, I began to explore possibilities for transfer out of the brickyard. I was willing to go anywhere. When it was time for the army's annual recruiting drive, a few of my coworkers and I tried to enlist. Despite the personal statements of resolve that we handed in along with our applications, we all were rejected outright. I told Ermao what had happened, and he called me a fool.

[1] The highest Communist Party authority in the northwest administrative area, which included Shaanxi, Gansu, Qinghai, Ningxia, and Xinjiang.

"You're just kidding yourself!" he snorted. "Haven't you ever seen the poster that says, 'An army member brings glory on the whole family'? Even people with spotless credentials have to go through a strict background check and a competitive selection process. Such good luck is not for the likes of us! There's plenty of manpower in China. We're not even good enough to serve as cannon fodder."

With the army out of the question, I turned to the next best option. Word had it that jobless young people were being recruited for permanent relocation to a reforestation corps in the barren hills of northern Shaanxi. I told Changhai that I was thinking about signing up.

"I wouldn't go even if I was offered a ride there in a deluxe sedan chair," he exclaimed, "because it would mean giving up my urban residence permit. No matter how awful this place is, at least you're still registered in Xi'an. Your residence permit is really a treasure! If you lose it, it'll be harder to get back to the city than it would be to get into heaven."

But unlike Changhai, I had my heart set on getting out of the brickyard, no matter where it took me. After the unpopular reforestation corps rejected my enthusiastic application, I applied to move to the countryside with the first batch of young people to do so. But when our neighborhood clerk said I was not the kind of person they wanted, I had to accept reality. Officer Hua had closed off all my alternatives in Xi'an, and the only way out of the brickyard was down: to the labor camps.

Concluding my walk in the hills, I hiked back to the road, boarded the Number Fifteen bus, and took it to the end of the line, the town of Weiqu, in Chang'an County on the outskirts of Xi'an. There I continued my aimless wandering. Trucks and horse carts were parked all along the main street, which boasted a few shops and restaurants. This was a place where some of my coworkers came on their days off, instead of going all the way into downtown Xi'an.

The town of Weiqu seemed embroiled in some kind of public event that day. The street was plastered with slogans and mobbed with pedestrians. I made my way toward the shrill sound systems that were blasting from the middle school playing field, where I found a huge crowd. I had stumbled into a county-wide tribunal, and verdicts were being read out from a faraway stage against landlords charged with "class retaliation,"[2] county-level leaders arrested for "sabotaging the Socialist Education campaign," and a bunch of common criminals. The Central Committee had designated Chang'an County as a spearhead of the Socialist Education campaign and given its work teams carte blanche here.

As I stood in the dense crowd listening to the scathing invective from the stage, the rising din of slogan shouting enveloped me like a whirlwind. Terror-stricken, I fled and made my way quickly along the road south.

I strode briskly away from the swarming crowds, looking for a lofty vista point in the mountains. Meanwhile, the sky clouded over, and snow started to fall. I ascended Shaoling Plateau, where I found the Du Gong Temple[3] on the edge of a cliff, and stood outside the locked gate contemplating the view below. By that time the air was so thick with swirling snow that I could not see a thing. The white flakes teemed down from the heavens, as if to fill every nook and cranny on earth.

Invigorated by the majestic view, I felt a warm current coursing through my body. I stood my ground valiantly, allowing the snow to coat me as it had the trees, rocks, and buildings. As I stood there, I had a vision of the blizzard enshrouding the brick manufacturing area, the east and west kilns, and the entire brickyard and then going on to freeze the residence permits and files at all the police stations and personnel departments in China, burying them forever. Someday we would awaken to find that our dossiers were blank, as pure as the driven snow.

---

[2] Injuring someone from a good class background, such as a poor peasant. The criminal justice system was weighted against people with bad class backgrounds—i.e., the formerly wealthy.

[3] Du Gong is an honorific title for the eighth-century poet Du Fu, China's greatest, who once lived on Shaoling Plateau. The temple is a popular vista point. Visiting a scenic historical site to muse about one's troubles in comparison with those of the ancients is a classic motif in Chinese literature.

12

Unwelcome Guests

ONE SUMMER DAY in 1966 I passed the Northwest Bureau of the Central Committee on my way back to the brickyard from town and remembered how I had hoped that the authorities there might exonerate me. But now, to my surprise, I discovered that the once-powerful bureau had come down in the world. Although the People's Liberation Army still guarded the gate, the walls were plastered with big-character posters attacking the bureau, and I elbowed my way into the crowds of people reading them.

Students with red armbands were making speeches on every street corner, demanding radical changes in leadership. At first their strange attire— straw sandals and army uniforms—led me to mistake them for actors, perhaps fresh from a performance of a revolutionary drama about the early Chinese Soviet Republic.[1]

The violent acrimony that accompanied the birth of the Cultural Revolution was unprecedented in recent memory. People who had been sup-

---

[1] The Chinese Communists established the Chinese Soviet Republic, otherwise known as the Jiangxi Soviet, in Ruijin in 1929; they were driven from it by the Nationalists in 1934.

pressed since the Antirightist campaign of almost a decade before had recovered their voices and were taking bold potshots at their party committees. I wondered where they, and the students, got their nerve. Confined to the bowels of the brickyard, I heard only the standard party line. I was disconcerted by the sudden reversals in the world beyond but, as always, found the mayhem exciting.

As the storm raged outside the brickyard gates, the leaders reined us in even more tightly. At an assembly they announced that participation in mass campaigns was forbidden to inmates of the public security system and that we were not allowed to do anything but study the documents assigned to us.

"You guys are all monsters and demons,"[2] Brigade Chief Liu told Ermao, Changhai, and me one day in the tunnel. "The Cultural Revolution is going to revolutionize you."

His comment made me uneasy, but he insisted that he meant well. We were safer inside the brickyard than out, he explained, and we should stay on the premises and behave ourselves instead of running around downtown.

One young fellow, who had joined the brickyard as a resettled worker at about the same time as I had, received summary justice for demanding to participate in the action. At lunchtime one day he hung up a big-character poster accusing the brickyard leaders of "suppressing the masses," and they put him behind bars that very afternoon. A few days later they announced at a brickyard-wide assembly that he had been sentenced to three years in the labor camps, and he was whisked away to a work farm in northern Shaanxi. His example served its purpose of scaring the rest of us into submission. Meanwhile, the mechanical brick press kept humming, and the kilns never stopped spewing smoke. Mr. Fu's lectures at our stepped-up evening political study sessions grew even more long-winded, and gate security was visibly increased.

Having heard rumors about Red Guard raids on people's houses in Beijing, I spent a few Sundays at my parents' house sorting my book collection, which I had transferred there from Silent Garden. My books were my most prized possessions, despite their low cash value. Although some had

[2] Class enemies.

come from Grandfather's shelves, I had paid for many of them myself. Sometimes I even squeezed a little book money out of my monthly salary, which was a mere thirty yuan minus whatever I spent at the mess hall. Like a librarian, I had cataloged each volume and imprinted it with my personalized ex libris stamp.

In my early days at college I had had no inkling that my private correspondence and diaries would be confiscated. Likewise, I now failed to recognize that my personal library might be in danger until I heard that the Red Guards were coming. But once the news had reached me, I quickly understood that I would have to dispose of my forbidden books. In Communist China one must keep one's ear to the ground and protect oneself whenever a new political campaign rears its head.

That fall, as the Red Guard campaign against the "four olds"[3] rippled across Xi'an, contingents from the local middle school raided some of the homes in our neighborhood. Apparently the police and the neighborhood committees chose the targets and whipped up the students, who then ransacked the designated properties for hidden weapons, records of pre-1949 assets and debts, or buried treasure.

One day on the way home I witnessed the Red Guard desecration of the Sleeping Dragon Temple. The gate was hung with a big sign purporting to be a "legal order," listing the monks' crimes, and the following revolutionary couplet framed the red-lacquered temple door:

> Smash the clay idols! Tear down the temples! Wipe out superstition!
> Old monks and young nuns—get back to the laity!

Inside, students were vandalizing the main hall with hammers and paint. They had broken off the limbs of the giant gilt statues of the Three Buddhas of the Western Paradise, exposing their innards of pottery stuffed with straw. They had also tossed piles of sutras out into the yard to fuel a raging bonfire and forced all the monks to kneel around it in a circle, as if it were a campfire.

The abbot of the temple, a portly gentleman called Master of Light,

---

[3] Old ideas, culture, customs, and habits.

was kneeling there too, his face flushed as he stared goggle-eyed at the burning books. When a Red Guard tried to snatch the rosary beads around his neck, he clutched them protectively, as if he would rather die than give them up. At this the enraged "little revolutionary generals" started to beat him, smacking him right on his bald pate with their leather belts until they drew blood. Unable to watch anymore, I turned and beat a hasty retreat. Master of Light had told me on an earlier occasion that this rosary, a string of 108 lustrous, marble-size amber beads, was a treasured souvenir of a group pilgrimage to Burma, which he always wore when he went out. Later I heard that the Red Guards had confiscated it and beaten him to a pulp. Deeply distraught, he had hanged himself that night.

My parents awaited the arrival of the Red Guards with relative composure, knowing that there was little of value in the house. Thanks to Father's long-standing drinking habit, we had no cash, gold, or silver, and Mother had never owned any jewelry. In fact my parents could barely afford an ordinary wristwatch. Their only fear was that the Red Guards would find books condemned as "poisonous weeds" on my shelf and that Father would be held accountable. He was already in trouble at his work unit, where big-character posters, viciously denouncing him as a "bourgeois reactionary academic authority," had popped up.

My parents had been cowed ever since the crackdown on me. Now they feared that the Red Guards had an explicit list of banned books and that we would be charged with earth-shattering crimes if they found any. It was on their advice that I took a preemptive strike at my own library. I pulled out all the books that had been denounced since the campaign against *Notes from a Three-Family Village*,[4] along with anything by writers who had been criticized in the media. After careful consideration of my selection, I tied up my "poisonous weeds" into two big bundles and went out and sold them as scrap paper. I spent the money on some fresh red dates to share

[4] This 1966 campaign marked the beginning of the Cultural Revolution. It was an attack on Wu Han (mayor of Beijing), Deng Tuo (secretary of the Beijing Party Committee), and Liao Mosha (member of the Beijing Party Committee) for publishing *Notes from a Three-Family Village*, a volume of essays criticizing Mao's policies.

with my sisters and brother. My heart ached as we devoured them, but I consoled myself with the thought that my remaining books might now be spared. In a state of high alert our whole family settled down to wait for the Red Guards' arrival.

My youngest sister Shuci's middle school, which was near the Northwest Bureau, was full of children of high officials, who formed some of the most destructive Red Guard contingents in town. But Shuci was excluded from the Red Guards and harassed at school because of her relationship to Grandfather (a criminal landlord element), Father (a bourgeois reactionary academic authority), and me (a notorious diary burner). Her reaction was to strike an ultrarevolutionary pose at home, where she went on the rampage against the "four olds," like a self-appointed Red Guard for our family. She vented her pent-up aggressions on me by making scathing remarks and burning some of my vintage books.

One day she went with my cousin Zhengxin to Silent Garden and incinerated a pile of Buddhist sutras there, then came home and torched several of my traditional thread-bound Chinese books, including a splendid edition of *The Complete Works of Zhang Taiyan*[5] in a custom-made wooden case. Discovering her mischief when I came home, I realized that although I would normally have challenged her, I would have to bite my tongue in the current political climate. Then the Red Guards at Father's work unit ordered him to surrender all the old books in our house. He himself had none, so he took some of mine and handed them in. Even though I was unhappy about my sacrifice, I could not begrudge him this small favor.

After these preliminary forays against my collection, only a few traditional thread-bound volumes remained. With books disappearing whenever I turned my back, I began to fret helplessly about the ones that were still arranged on my shelves. I wished I could store them all somewhere else, but where? No house was safe in this turmoil, and no one would dare accept them. Besides, I might get caught while I was transporting them or even just carrying them out of our front gate. I knew that somebody was probably spying on every move made by our family, which had been rele-

[5] A renowned late–Qing dynasty scholar and revolutionary.

gated to the "five black categories."[6] The end of the world seemed nigh, and there was not much I could do about it, except take a few more useless precautions at home. I buried my *Selections of Refined Literature*[7] in the rice crock and stuffed a fine edition of *Romance of the Western Chamber*, annotated by Jin Shengtan,[8] into some bedding in the wardrobe. Then I stashed more of my favorites, including some rare editions, in a few pitiful hiding places around the house. Somewhat comforted, I abandoned the rest of my collection and returned to the brickyard with my fingers crossed.

On my next visit home I discovered that Red Guards from Father's work unit had stormed through our house, which was strewn with debris. Mutilated books, denuded of their covers, were scattered all over the floor, and my bookcase was almost completely empty. *The Complete Works of Lu Xun*,[9] however, were intact, as were all of the studies of classical Chinese literature by Wen Yiduo.[10] It seemed that the raiders had been somewhat informed about literature or at least aware that Mao had praised Lu Xun and Wen Yiduo. But my well-thumbed copy of *Lyrics of the Tang and Song Dynasties* had vanished, as had the first volume of my fine edition of the fifth-century classic *The Literary Mind and the Carving of Dragons*. The second volume was fortunately still on the floor, although the Red Guards had ripped off its cover and stomped on it. In a daze, I stood before the half-empty bookcase, remembering the books that had stood in the gaps.

My brother, Zhengguan, told me that the Red Guards had come equipped with spades and a big truck. Right away they had located all the

[6] In Mao's China, people were divided into the "five red categories" (workers, peasants, soldiers, revolutionary martyrs, and party cadres), and the "five black categories" (landlords, rich peasants, rightists, counterrevolutionaries, and bad elements).

[7] The sixth-century collection *Wen Xuan*, regarded as the most important anthology of classical Chinese literature.

[8] Beloved ancient drama of star-crossed lovers. Jin Shengtan, a renowned seventeenth-century scholar, was denounced in Communist China.

[9] Revered by Mao, the great twentieth-century writer Lu Xun (died 1936) was virtually the only pre-1949 Chinese author whose works were not banned during the Cultural Revolution.

[10] Twentieth-century Chinese poet, assassinated in 1946 and honored as a martyr in Communist China.

books that I thought I had concealed so cleverly. Then, after rapping on the floors and walls without discovering anything suspicious, they had rummaged through Mother's two big wooden trunks for precious metals or bankbooks but had found only a ten-yuan bond. This they had confiscated, along with a couple of "reactionary" old newspapers from the Nationalist period that had been used to line one of the trunks. They had also objected to Father's collection of old gramophone records from the 1930s and 1940s, which included albums by the Shanghai pop star Zhou Xuan and the Beijing opera singer Ma Lianliang. They had smashed some of the records and loaded the rest onto their truck, leaving none behind. Unable to find anything of real value, they had carted off some of the better furniture, including an old leather sofa set and the dressing table from Mother's trousseau. Still, along with a huge stack of books from my room, they had managed to fill only half of their truck.

Silent Garden was plundered too, on a drizzly day in early winter, by the neighboring commune and the Red Guards from the local middle school. The commune announced its plans to seize the entire house and dispatched its members to cart away my grandparents' few remaining worn-out possessions. Then it evicted my grandparents, who were eventually relocated into a cramped flat that the commune had confiscated from another landlord.

My grandparents had plenty of offspring, but everyone except for Zhengguan and Zhengxin was either too busy or too timid to help them in their hour of need. With all the schools closed from 1966 to 1976, the duration of the Cultural Revolution, Zhengguan was as free as a bird. He went all the way to the Dongguan section of town every day to check on my grandparents and to help Zhengxin with chores like fetching water and shopping for food.

One overcast Sunday Zhengguan took me to my grandparents' flat, which consisted of a single room, with a kitchen on one side of a wooden divider and a one-hundred-square-foot living area on the other. There was a *kang* along the northern wall, opposite Grandfather's bed. The tiny space between the bed and the *kang* was filled up with a table and two stools, so that Zhengguan and I barely had enough room to turn around. The dilapidated paper panes in the old-fashioned windows whistled in the icy wind.

The only source of heat was a coal-burning kitchen stove, which was barely warm to the touch. All their belongings, even Grandfather's set of divination dominoes, were gone. Grandmother had pitched them into the well in panicky preparation for the coming Red Guard raid.

On the day of our visit I found Grandfather lying in bed, groaning weakly, with a bandage on his forehead and a sallow cast to his cheeks. Grandmother told me that the Red Guards had marched him through the streets, prodding him from behind to move faster, until he had fallen flat on his face and cut his forehead. Fortunately he was physically fit for a man of his years and had not broken anything.

The commune appropriated Silent Garden in its entirety and burned Grandfather's books and his wooden blocks for printing Buddhist sutras. It also smashed the altar room and swept away its furnishings, including the small stupas containing the relics of Master of the Void and Master Buddhist Radiance, along with all remaining traces of my grandparents.

In China, where most people made do with humble, cramped quarters, anyone who lived in comfort was seen as fair game for leveling in the name of justice. People turned to looting whenever law and order broke down, even stooping to grave robbing. Back in the days of Land Reform the neighboring poor and lower-middle peasants had spread rumors that there was treasure in Great-grandmother's grave and that one of her maids had been buried alive with her. In those days Grandfather had enjoyed government protection, so the peasants had not been able to act on their suspicions. Now their moment had come. They demolished Great-grandmother's tombstone stupa, hammered her engraved stele to bits, and used it as scrap for their foundry. They did not stop there. Next they dug up her entire grave and exhumed her coffin, yet their search, like the Red Guard incursion into our house, proved fruitless. Instead of buried treasure or the remains of the maid who was supposed to have been sacrificed so horribly, they found only four crude pottery teacups and an oil lamp. All they could do at that point was transfer the coffin to the commune graveyard and raze the empty plot.

13

Runaway

As I was browsing the big-character posters on the street on a wintry day in 1966, it dawned on me that people everywhere were jumping onto the Cultural Revolution bandwagon to try to better their own lots, and I sensed their pent-up rage spilling out like water roiling over a dam. Temporary factory workers were calling for permanent status; youths who had been sent to the countryside wanted to return to the cities; victims of the wave of layoffs a few years back were demanding reinstatement. All the posters adhered to a similar formula. After paying lip service to Chairman Mao's revolutionary line, which conveniently proclaimed the right to rebel, the aggrieved parties blamed all their problems indiscriminately on the bourgeois reactionary line. Now that the leaders had been pronounced fair game, nobody was afraid to lash out at them anymore.

One day, when we had a few moments to chat just after firing up a kiln load of bricks, Changhai excitedly shared some news with us. On his trip to town that day he had seen posters calling for the dismantling of the public security system.

"Our days in this hellhole are numbered," he predicted, with his characteristic optimism.

Ermao, who was something of a spoilsport, disagreed. Watching me thrash about recklessly for escape from the brickyard, he had always counseled me to wait patiently instead. He believed that the brickyard's function as a resettlement facility was only temporary and that someday the authorities would take it over from the Security Bureau and turn it back into a prison. When that day came, he maintained, the police would make us leave even if we wanted to stay, but for now personal protests would be counterproductive. "There's no point in rushing headlong into things," he warned me. "You'll see."

Given this predisposition, he was quick to put a damper on Changhai's eagerness to join the fray. "Don't kid yourself," he said. "As long as the police control this joint, not even a revolution can do us much good. We'd better just hunker down and do our best here and have some fun with our hard-earned money in town whenever we can."

The author's sisters, Shuci and Shuzhi, brother, Zhengguan, and a classmate on their "Long March" to Yan'an in the winter of 1966.

Changhai, always voluble, was undeterred. Spluttering and gesticulating wildly, he informed us that workers were not allowed casual access to the office anymore because it was full of big-character posters attacking the brickyard leadership and the Security Bureau party committee.

"So what?" countered Ermao. "Cadres wrote all the posters, and it's their business, not ours, if they decide to rebel against their party committee. There's nothing in it for us."

Still fired up, Changhai added that some of the resettled workers were organizing to demand better treatment. I knew that it would not do me any good to join them. Everyone who had been forced to come here had a bad police record, which doomed their cause. Besides, my case was different from theirs. My only hope lay in the cancellation of my expulsion and the restoration of my student status. Mindful of these issues, I had always carefully kept my distance from mutinous plots.

This time, however, I took my cue from the appeals that I saw popping up all around me. I had heard that many victims of persecution had gone to Beijing to petition for redress and that the State Council had set up a special reception center for them. At any rate, it was not against the law to try my luck. Even if my application came to nothing, at least I would be able to say that I had not missed the unique opportunity provided by the Cultural Revolution to see Beijing, the hotbed of revolution.

One freezing day in late December my friend Mao Zhiyi and I sat huddled over a small fire in a sheltered spot atop one of the kilns, plotting a trip to Beijing. The brick manufacturing area had been deserted for days on end because the cadres, who had divided into two warring factions, were too busy to supervise us.

Mao Zhiyi dressed like a student from the classic movies about the youth revolution of May 4, 1919, with thick glasses, a traditional Chinese tunic, and a scarf neatly hanging down his chest. He was several years older than I was and had graduated from college while I was still in high school, during the lean years following the Great Leap Forward. Unemployed after graduation, he had made a foolhardy attempt to escape from China after hearing a rumor that Chinese refugees were being allowed to cross from Shenzhen into Hong Kong. Hopping a train to Guangzhou, he had found a hotel and started to make inquiries. Unfortunately the Security Bureau had gotten wind of his plans, arrested him, and sent him back to Beijing, after which he had done a two-year stint in the labor camps for his crime. Then he had returned to his parents' home in Xi'an, where his local police officer had, like mine, browbeaten him into rashly agreeing to commit himself to the brickyard as a resettled worker. From then on he had shown admirable courage, insight, and legal aptitude by filing repeated demands for freedom at the Security Bureau. Soon after we met, he had announced his plans to sneak away to Beijing to appeal his case, and I had decided to go with him.

Under cover of darkness that very night, we groped our way through a hole in the compound wall, slunk to the train station via a back route, and boarded a night train to Beijing.

In those days Red Guards and rebels from all over the country were surging into Beijing, and the economy-class car of the train was so tightly packed with students traveling to "exchange revolutionary experiences"[1] that we had to shimmy in through the window. The aisles, luggage racks, and toilets were stuffed with people. Since the conductors could not thread their way through the crowded train, no one was punching tickets or providing any services. There was no heat or drinking water, and I was faint with the lack of fresh air. Still, all the passengers were in high spirits, belting out revolutionary songs and chanting quotations from Chairman Mao. Their fervor was infectious. Ordinarily I loathed displays of whipped-up mass sentiment, which often struck me as vulgar. I tended to remain unmoved even in surroundings that most people found inspirational, such as the fanfare of the National Day parades. But this time I was drawn into the boisterous singing on the train despite myself and felt my blood begin to pulsate swiftly through my veins as I shouted at the top of my lungs. Momentarily starry-eyed, I pretended I was a revolutionary, forgetting my blacklisted status.

Mother had always opposed any political activism on my part. In the current upheaval, she insisted, malcontents like me had better lie low for

---

[1] During the fall of 1966 schools were closed and train tickets were free of charge for young people who wished to travel around the country in response to Mao's call for young people to "exchange revolutionary experiences."

safety's sake. She maintained that someone with a dubious political record like mine would be called to task for sticking his neck out during a campaign, even if others might be able to do so with impunity. She had objected to my going to Beijing to petition my case, but I had not heeded her advice. Helplessly she had warned me that I would worsen my own predicament unless I started to exhibit some self-control.

This had been Mother's constant refrain, and the more she nagged, the more I resisted. I was no longer content to keep slaving away in the bowels of the kiln while millions of students, including my younger sisters and brother, were gallivanting around the country, enjoying free food and lodging wherever they went.

I had just translated the narrative poem "The Novice" by Mikhail Lermontov,[2] and it had aroused my impetuosity. It told of a young Georgian man who was captured by a Russian general, imprisoned in a monastery, and then mortally wounded by a leopard during an escape attempt. I was intoxicated by his daredevil quest for freedom, his passionate deathbed soliloquy, his evocation of the natural grandeur of the Caucasus, and most of all by his hyperbole: "A taste of honey is worth the price of death."[3]

Toiling away underground at the brickyard, I had often dreamed of escape. Now I was finally taking some action and found myself carried away by my unusual, inspiring surroundings. Appealing my case was in part simply an excuse to get away from the brickyard and enjoy a glimpse of the world outside, however brief. Like Lermontov's hero, I was willing to accept any consequences, even arrest or death. The rebellion beckoned me like sunlight outside a closed window, and I could not bear to spend any more time indoors in the gloom.

The train arrived in Beijing in the middle of the night. Before dawn we made our way down Chang'an Boulevard to the registration facility that the State Council had set up for petitioners, but the clerk there did not even understand what we meant when we described ourselves as resettled workers. Seeing that our work IDs said "Jian'an Construction Materials

---

[2] Russian Romantic poet (1814–1841).

[3] An allusion to the Bible, I Samuel 14:43.

Plant of Xi'an," he sent us to stay at the reception center managed by the Department of Construction Materials.

It turned out to be a big empty meeting room, with reed mats spread on the floor for sleeping. Everyone was issued a woolen blanket, although the heat was turned up so high that it took your breath away and dried out your skin. I sat on my mat and got to work on my application for rehabilitation, drawing carefully chosen quotations from the four-volume *Selected Works of Mao Zedong* that I had brought along especially for this purpose. I described myself as a victim of the bourgeois academic line, naively believing that all I needed was a persuasive application peppered with appropriate quotes from Chairman Mao.

The capital was festooned with big-character posters, which I browsed like outdoor newspapers as I strolled along the buildings and streets where they hung. They dealt with everything under the sun, but I was most interested in the personal appeals, which gave me an opportunity to compare other people's grievances with mine and to study their rhetorical styles as a model.

Once my appeal was written, I wondered how to submit it. Fortunately Mao Zhiyi had been to school in Beijing and knew his way around. He took me to the main gates of the Communist Party central headquarters at Zhongnanhai[4] and the Diaoyutai State Guesthouse to wait for an opportune moment. We braved the piercing January wind all day, stamping our feet to keep warm and hoping that Premier Zhou Enlai or a member of the Cultural Revolution Leadership Group would emerge. As we stood there, we heard propaganda trucks with blaring loudspeakers endlessly circling the city and watched streetcars emblazoned with slogans race by us like strange beasts. Shreds of torn posters floated by on the wind and skittered away across the pavement, like dirty, discarded rags or used bits of toilet paper. Eventually the daylight faded, the streetlights came on with a feeble glow, and our fervent hopes began to cool.

My big opportunity finally arrived on January 5, 1967, when Zhou Enlai and the Cultural Revolution Leadership Group met rebel worker factions from around the nation at Capital Stadium. I squeezed my way to

---

[4] A group of buildings near the Forbidden City.

a railing between two sets of bleachers near the rostrum and got ready to toss my petition at the dignitaries seated there. When a round of thunderous cheering broke out, and the entire stadium was a sea of waving "little red books," I balled up my document and threw it at the rostrum, right into the lap of one of the dignitaries. I could not see his face well enough under his army cap to tell who he was: Wang Li, Qi Benyu, or Guan Feng.[5] At any rate, I saw him pick up my petition, glance at it, and stuff it into the pocket of his army overcoat.

I was relieved now that my mission was accomplished, but Mao Zhiyi and I still had to take measures to protect ourselves after our return to the brickyard. The State Council reception center had a special official form letter for this purpose, which proclaimed that the government supported petitioners and instructed work unit leaders to do the same. In those heady days the reception clerks stood ready to grant almost any request of the petitioners. They listened to our story, then filled in our names and the name of the brickyard on the form letter, added their supportive comments and signatures, and finished it off with a big vermilion stamp. We accepted the precious letter from them as if it were a sacred edict, and Mao Zhiyi slipped it into his pocket for safekeeping. Our qualms assuaged, we went out and took the streetcar to go sightseeing at Beihai Park and the Summer Palace.

After enjoying the mayhem in the capital for a couple of weeks, we boldly reappeared at the brickyard. Presented with the official letter from the State Council, the bosses had to accept our story, but they seemed somewhat dubious and said that they would need to give the matter especially careful consideration. They had to proceed cautiously in that era of constant political reversals. Our sole punishment was a few weeks' confinement to the brickyard.

We had picked the right two weeks to be absent. Ermao told me that while we had been away, some of the resettled workers had joined a citywide group of rebels in a sit-in at the gates of the Security Bureau. For this they were being severely punished, and several of the ringleaders had been apprehended. They included Changhai, who was being held in detention

---

[5] Three members of the Cultural Revolution Leadership Group.

at the Security Bureau. They had been accused of being active counter-revolutionaries, which was a felony.

Down underground again, I missed Changhai's booming voice and found that he had been replaced with a Muslim fellow who went by the nickname Pimple Ma. As I fired one load of bricks after another, my petition occasionally seemed to offer a brief glimmer of hope in my otherwise bleak future. But that hope was quickly veiled in obscurity again, as if blocked by a dark curtain.

My petition had vanished without a trace, like a pebble tossed into the sea. Common sense told me not to expect a response. The Cultural Revolution Leadership Group had so many affairs of state to deal with that it could not possibly have time for my paltry problems. Instead of giving up, however, I pinned my hopes anew on the Cultural Revolution at Shaanxi Normal University.

I decided to return to campus for the first time since my expulsion. With a pounding heart and flushed cheeks, I approached the gates and hesitated before gathering the courage to enter. The campus evoked ripples of nostalgia. My early trials and tribulations had not yet eroded my youthful sensitivity.

Thanks to the rebellious mood of the day, several former classmates greeted me warmly and supplied me with a writing brush, ink, and paper when I told them that I wanted to make some big-character posters. Continuing in the same vein as the petition I had written in Beijing, I painted myself as a victim of the bourgeois academic line and forced the connection between my demands and the aims of the Cultural Revolution. But even I was dubious of my own rhetoric. As I stood and reread the posters after I had hung them up, my self-confidence waned, and I began to suspect that my efforts would be futile. Were my posters an exposé of the powers that be or of myself? Or had I muddled the two? My reasoning began to strike me as fallacious, and my accusatory tone seemed inappropriate in a plea for leniency. I was grasping at straws. If I found my own self-defense unconvincing, surely no one else would be persuaded. Maybe I was just risking further humiliation by plunging into the maelstrom at this point.

Sheepishly, I turned to leave, scanning the other big-character posters along my way. To my amazement, the rebels were excoriating the college president, Secretary Peng, and my political instructor for criminally "lax treatment and protection of the reactionary student Kang Zhengguo," at the same time I was claiming that they had persecuted me! The posters also implied that the rebels were planning to drag me back to campus to be pilloried along with their bigwig targets.

Chants of "Beat the drowning dog"[6] thundered in my ears, as I imagined a mob of students approaching me with fists raised to administer the coup de grâce. Like a smack on the face, the posters had brought me to my senses and undermined my blind, superstitious faith in the power of the written word. What had I been thinking? I should have known better than to make such a fool of myself, digging myself even deeper into trouble. Crestfallen, I glanced around me and beat a hasty retreat from the campus.

---

[6] A famous quotation from the twentieth-century writer Lu Xun, used during the Cultural Revolution to encourage people to crush their defeated enemies completely.

自述

14

Dr. Zhivago

P IMPLE MA'S FACE and neck were riddled with acne, and even his pudgy shoulders and back, which he revealed when he stripped off his shirt to stoke the kiln, were horribly blemished. During breaks he peered into a pocket mirror and squeezed his pimples until his skin was bruised. Cigarette smoking forged the bond between us. On my thirty yuan a month, I could not afford fancy cigarettes, but I was not a heavy smoker and needed no more than half a pack a day of the ordinary kind. Pimple Ma, however, frittered his money away on luxury brands and suffered nicotine cravings when he was broke. At such times he turned into a shameless mooch, and I was the only person who always supplied him cheerfully. I liked his happy-go-lucky attitude and knew that despite his wheeling and dealing, he was basically a man of his word.

His singing is what attracted me initially. Although his voice was untrained, he had practiced humming along with the soundtrack of *The Vagabond** and

---

* *Awara*, the great Indian director Raj Kapoor's 1951 film about a vagabond named Raj, was beloved by Chairman Mao and a smash hit in China, especially for its title song. See http://www.uiowa.edu/~incinema/awara.html.

could belt out a fair rendition of "Raj's Song." He had a powerful, if raspy, bass and brought his performance to life with a convincing, although somewhat crude, imitation of Raj. He would always sing for me after I had plied him with cigarettes, or I would thrust them on him after his performances.

Barely literate, Pimple Ma was scornful of education. Whenever he saw me reading, he would poke my book and scoff, "Get down to business." But his idea of "business" was completely alien to me. All he wanted was to earn a little extra cash for food, drink, and fun, while I was an incurable bookworm.

Those were inflammatory times. Armed struggle reached its peak in the summer of 1967, and many work units were paralyzed. Production at the brickyard had come to a virtual halt. The police had dismantled their own party committee, and the conscript laborers were idling in their cells. Even the interrogations had ceased. But while the militants made revolution, the rest of us loafed quietly on the sidelines, still drawing our state salaries. People like us were known as the footloose and fancy free. As a resettled worker I was still required to show up for my shift, but after the mandatory newspaper study session I was basically free to do as I pleased. I figured out how to wheedle permission slips for sick leave out of the medics, and spent many weeks at home. There I devoted myself to my old pursuits of study and translation, having abandoned any dreams of rehabilitation or participation in the Cultural Revolution after my discouraging visit to Shaanxi Normal University.

A few volumes of my Russian literature collection, mostly the works of Lermontov and Turgenev, had survived the Red Guard raids on our house. Equipped with my Russian-Chinese dictionary, I delved into the original texts, with their rich, unfamiliar vocabulary, and honed my translating skills. I had a deep respect for translators and the service that they performed, having enjoyed many foreign classics in their Chinese renditions. In fact the impetus for my study of Russian was to translate my favorite pieces into Chinese. Shuzhi's Russian teacher, who had an impeccable record and a good class background and had even served as an army translator, had been immune from the Red Guard raids, and I often went to his house to browse in his still-intact Russian literature collection.

According to folk wisdom, our minds blank out several times a day, as if possessed by a demon. In modern terms, this demon may be our genetic predisposition for error, as mistakes that appear to be accidental usually have subtle, mysterious causes. All of us harbor demons in the deepest recesses of our consciousness, and everyone is prone to devilish ideas and disastrous misbehavior at times. Perhaps this explains what I did next.

Shuzhi's teacher's Russian literature collection was outdated and left me unsatisfied. He had none of the contemporary works I wanted to read, especially the trailblazing monuments of thaw literature such as Yevtushenko's poetry, Solzhenitsyn's fiction, and especially Pasternak's *Dr. Zhivago*. I knew that Pasternak had been awarded the Nobel Prize for literature, but I had no access to information about him or his novel. I longed to obtain these new Russian books and translate some of them, just as I had recently been obsessed with the impulse to run away. My mind was an agitated jumble of the political constraints of the era, the restlessness of youth, the thirst for knowledge, and the urge to write. It suddenly occurred to me that there must be a way to get the books I wanted directly from the Soviet Union.

I was secretly infected with the mood of two poems by Lermontov that I translated at the time. One was "I Want to Live," in which he asks:

What sea
is not roiled by storms?
What poet
has lived without suffering?

In the other, "The Sail," he says:

Restlessly it seeks the storms,
As if only storms could offer peace!

Consciously or subconsciously I was flirting with danger.

I had feared that life at the brickyard, with its grinding rhythm of daily toil and nightly political study, might dull my mind and my interest in literature and that I might end up completely transformed into a manual laborer like the old-timers there. But the Cultural Revolution gave me an unexpected opportunity to resume my intellectual activities. I had not forgotten the warnings of my elders, nor was I unaware of the dangers of literary pursuits. I simply had nothing better to do with my time and found that literature kept me happily occupied.

One day in May 1967 *People's Daily* carried a harsh critique of the Soviet revisionists for publishing *Dr. Zhivago*. Branding Pasternak a renegade author and *Dr. Zhivago* a counterrevolutionary novel, the article claimed that the publication of this book was proof of the ideological decadence of the Brezhnev revisionist clique. The article itself was a piece of hack writing, but it piqued my curiosity. During political crackdowns an attack on a book in the press could become its claim to fame. The negative publicity simply functioned as an advertisement. After I read the article, I became obsessed with the notion of getting a copy of *Dr. Zhivago* to read and translate.

Now, many years later, when I tell people what I did after reading *People's Daily* that day, they shake their heads at my folly. As soon as I put down the paper, I dashed off a letter in Russian to the Moscow University Library, explaining that I was an avid fan of Soviet literature and requesting a loan of *Dr. Zhivago* by mail. I remember going to the post office and calmly asking the price of an airmail stamp to the Soviet Union. Then I affixed the stamp, inserted the letter carefully into the mailbox slot, and went home, expecting prompt results.

From then on I had something to look forward to in my otherwise drab existence. But with the passage of time I began to feel the way one does when trolling in vain for fish. Day after day the mailman arrived without my book. Gradually I lost interest in waiting for it, and my restless yearnings focused elsewhere.

15

Underground in Xi'an

PIMPLE MA HAD clearly struck it rich. He started to supply me with cigarettes, bought himself a stylish outfit to wear into town after work, and sported a succession of shiny new watches. While he dodged the nosy people who grabbed his wrist, trying to peek at the brand names, he trusted me enough to show them to me when we were alone, and all of them were big-name Swiss imports like Omega and Enicar. Unfortunately I had never had a passion for watches, so the value of his collection was lost on me. I did know, however, that saving up enough money for a watch was a priority for many people in those days. In China of the 1950s and 1960s watches were luxury items that were beyond even my parents' reach, to say nothing of mine.

Pimple Ma, who was doing time for fraud, called himself a watch dealer and claimed that all the watches were part of his inventory. He kept offering to take me out on the town, but I was worried about being seen in public with such a shady character, and he was also somewhat leery of me. One day in the summer of 1967, when work had come to a standstill at the brickyard, and I had abandoned any hope of rehabilitation, we took a bus downtown to Mr. Sun's House of Mutton on East Boulevard for a bowl of its famed mutton soup.

As we sipped our tea and slowly tore our wheat cakes into bits to sop up the fragrant broth, Pimple Ma coached me in the secret lingo of the Muslim street world. Eventually our conversation drifted to his watch dealing. It turned out that his "Swiss" watches were counterfeits, worthless old mechanisms refurbished with new faces and crystals, which he unloaded on unwitting travelers at the Xi'an train station. As he explained to me, he would approach a likely target in the crowd and try to strike up a conversation. If his target seemed receptive, he would confide that he was desperate for cash because he had lost his wallet or because of a family emergency. Then he would slip the watch off his wrist and offer to sell it at a loss. Not everyone fell for his story, but some bargain hunter always did. Once the deal was concluded, a departing train would whisk the dupe so far away that later regret would be useless. Pimple Ma commented astutely that if he found one sucker per day at the train station, there would be enough to last him a lifetime.

After our meal we strolled over to the Bell Tower neighborhood, where he ducked into a clock and watch repair shop, took a newly reconditioned watch out of a pigeonhole, and strapped it on. Then he announced that he was going to the train station to sell it, hopped onto a streetcar, and waved good-bye to me.

Although the Cultural Revolution was ostensibly a campaign to eradicate "bourgeois" pastimes, it actually fueled their revival by providing plenty of leisure time to those of us who were not embroiled in the infighting. Some people assembled transistor radios, while others practiced musical instruments. Still others enjoyed cultivating a fashionable dietary supplement called black tea fungus. They let the fungus cultures mature in dishes of tea until they were about the size of jellyfish, then scooped out the fermented liquid and drank it sweetened with sugar. People rolled their own cigarettes with simple gadgets when the shops ran out. Couples who had been trapped in commuting marriages were reunited when their work units halted production, and pregnant women paraded the streets in unprecedented numbers.

The Red Guards themselves released some of the spoils of their campaign against the "four olds," and I quietly obtained a variety of private reading materials. Among them were quite a few masterpieces, including an unexpurgated edition of the erotic classic *The Golden Lotus*, minus a few key pages. One day Pimple Ma took me to the Great Mosque in the Muslim quarter, where some of his Red Guard friends were storing their booty. There we found piles of phonograph records, which the Red Guards offered to let us take home, and I chose some famous dance tunes and Russian folk songs. For the people I knew, this period was a miniature renaissance, a touch of spring on the cultural wasteland.

The ice was broken between Pimple Ma and me. Although he disdained reading, he asked me to teach him the elements of music so that he could show off in front of his friends, and he took me downtown whenever he was feeling flush. After a meal of mutton soup, we attended various gatherings where people danced to the oldies, smoked, and sipped tea. The dancers, whose skills probably dated back to the political relaxation after the Great Leap Forward, had gotten a bit rusty during the subsequent political campaigns, but now the strains of Strauss's "Blue Danube" or the Russian folk song "Blossoming Red Elder" had loosened them up, just as a screwdriver might unfasten a screw.

I did not fit into this crowd of fun seekers, who were a few years older than I was and appeared to be seasoned veterans of affairs of the heart. I suspected that I was the only person there who was still as inexperienced as Rastignac, the young protagonist of Balzac's *Le Père Goriot*. Fortunately Pimple Ma stayed at my elbow, although I had to endure his gibes at my ignorance. Assuming the role of Vautrin, Rastignac's corrupter, he kept foisting women on me and providing slick demonstrations of how to handle them.

The music also brought back my memories of dancing. After the Great Leap Forward, when I was still in high school, I had noticed the dances at the Sino-Soviet Friendship Association Building on my way to the movies at Northwest Theater. The sound of the music and the sight of the stylishly dressed dancers had been tantalizing, but I had lacked both ticket and partner, to say nothing of decent clothes. A few times I had ventured just inside the doorway to watch, but I had slipped away again quickly for fear that people would laugh at me. Once a classmate we called Towhead had taken me inside, and I had made a clumsy attempt to learn a couple of dance moves. Later, when I was in college, I had gone to the 1964 New Year's dance at the Institute of Foreign Languages, where I took a few turns around the floor with a young woman from the English department. After that, dances had been formally banned as examples of revisionist decadence.

In 1967 Pimple Ma and I frequently wended our way through narrow lanes reeking of mutton in the Muslim neighborhoods of Xi'an to join in various private parties, held in cramped rooms and attended by the local "idle crowd." The music and dancing were just a cover for the real reason people went to these get-togethers, which was to mingle with the opposite sex. This was particularly true of me, since the stigma of the brickyard prevented me from courting anyone formally. Everyone knew that it was a quasi-labor camp, and any woman who was in the market for a serious boyfriend would have been scared off if I had breathed a word about working there. Before I started going to parties with Pimple Ma, I had never sought romance beyond my immediate circles. Now, however, I was discovering that I could dally with perfect strangers in a public setting.

Pimple Ma dismissed my prior relationships with female classmates as juvenile and goaded me into a state of angst regarding my lack of sexual experience. The reason why I was still a virgin in my early twenties, he taunted, was that I was a bungling, brain-dead "bookworm." I burned with feelings of inadequacy and humiliation whenever he and his friends bragged about their amorous conquests, and I resolved to remedy the situation as soon as possible. Seizing on his opportunity to lord it over me, the uneducated Pimple Ma declared himself my coach in the realm of love and devised a plan to introduce me to various women he knew. He assured me that they would be glad to oblige me as long as I played my cards right.

At one dance Pimple Ma introduced me to a Muslim girl with doll-like eyelashes. "Xiuying, come on over here and dance with my friend the college student," he called. She smiled at me with perfect composure.

There was no room on the crowded makeshift dance floor, but we embraced lightly and went for a brief whirl to get acquainted. It would have been awkward for me to visit her afterward because she was embroiled in divorce proceedings, so Pimple Ma arranged for her to come to my house to borrow some books, and I supplied my address. Although she and I both seemed to agree tacitly to our ultimate goal, Pimple Ma recommended that I move slowly, wooing her with sweet talk and dates to movies and restaurants before I made any advances.

She stopped by on the appointed day, setting in motion a chain of events that seemed almost scripted. Dolled up like a glamorous Shanghai lady instead of the Xi'an Muslim that she was, she sat down across from me and struck the aloof pose of some beauty in a famous painting. Her body language was standoffish, and when she did utter a few words in her Xi'an Muslim twang, she sounded jaded and indifferent. I froze up during the lapses in our conversation, and we sat there in awkward silence. Finally she got up, looked through my half-empty bookcase, chose a foreign novel, and left, her ostensible mission accomplished.

I told Pimple Ma that things were not going smoothly, suggesting that she and I might not be cut out for each other. But he blamed the problem on my bumbling rather than a lack of interest on her part. In love affairs, he instructed me, the man had to take the lead, as on the dance floor. If the man asserted himself, the woman would follow; however, even a seasoned woman could not display her dancing prowess with a hesitant man. He encouraged me to "go for it," without fear of rejection.

But I was truly incapable of leading this "dance." When she was ready to return the book, she arranged to meet me at a secluded spot in town. I never did follow up on Pimple Ma's suggestion to invite her to restaurants and movies, simply because I could not afford it, and our relationship stalled. Pimple Ma ascribed my failure to my poverty.

"It's no use just to advertise the fact that you're a college student. You can't get a girl without shelling out some cash."

He concluded that a gold digger like Xiuying was an inappropriate match for a humble scholar like me and advised me to forget about her.

Before long, he offered to introduce me to someone else, a music teacher who, he claimed, was much nicer than Xiuying, although not as pretty. He was sure we would like each other. This time he introduced us formally at a teahouse, where we sat in lounge chairs on a carpet of fragrant fallen blossoms under a shady mimosa tree. The music teacher turned out to be good-natured and vivacious, and our conversation ranged from music to literature to our own personal experiences. With Pimple Ma as comic relief, she and I seemed off to a good start.

By the time fall rolled around, however, we had exhausted all possible conversation topics, a fact that we discovered one evening as we sat in a dessert bar, sipping a hot brew of fermented sweet rice. I had not forgotten my goal, but despite my apparent intimacy with her, I seemed to have delayed beyond the point of no return. I was still a beginner, and although I was drooling over her, something always held me back. Pimple Ma, who devoured women as voraciously as he consumed mutton soup, called me a chicken.

"I'm sure she likes you. It's your fault for not trying hard enough," he commented pointedly.

Frustrated, I realized that there had been something wrong from the start. Neither Xiuying nor the music teacher had swept me off my feet. It was not merely a question of faulty technique, as Pimple Ma asserted. I had simply never developed the requisite chemistry with the women he had appointed as my coaches in the realm of love.

Pimple Ma had complimented me on my initial progress with the music teacher, but when I failed to press my advantage, he sneered that I was hopeless as a ladies' man. The women he had helped me meet, he pointed out, had plenty of suitors and were not impressed by a "stinking egghead." He reserved his sharpest barbs for my stinginess.

"You can't expect to get something for nothing. Lots of guys have blown a fortune on Xiuying without getting their hands on her. If you think a skinflint like you can have his way with women, they're always going to be pie in the sky for you." He even offered to lend me money to spend on the music teacher.

This was more than I could bear. Besides, I had come to doubt that he was in sole possession of the gospel when it came to women. I was fed up with being under his wing and told him so. It was time to strike out on my own.

16

A Chance Encounter

I SPENT PART OF the summer of 1968 working at the brickyard and the rest at home on sick leave. By then I had figured out how to meet women without Pimple Ma.

One day we got off work as soon as we finished reading the newspaper in our political study session, and I went downtown early. Following my usual routine, I got off the bus at the Bell Tower and ambled past the Post Office Building to scan the big-character posters on the wall outside the New China Bookstore. Just as I was about to cross the street at Peace Market, I noticed a familiar female figure slowly wending her way past me on a bicycle. She glanced back at me, as if considering slowing down but afraid of attracting attention. I racked my brains for her name.

"Shen Rong!" I managed to call out just as I was losing sight of her. She turned around and headed back toward me.

I had met her at a party the night before. Hearing repeated loud sighs during a melancholy song, I had looked up and met her misty gaze across the crowded, dimly lit room. I had not been able to talk to her during the party but had fortunately managed to ask her name as we were leaving. Otherwise I would have had to watch helplessly as she rode past me just now.

Pleased to have run into each other, we strolled along together and started to get acquainted. I divulged that I was a resettled worker at the brickyard, and she mentioned somewhat vaguely that she worked at a vocational school on the western outskirts of town. She accompanied me through the back streets to my house.

We had just arrived in my cramped room when Pimple Ma suddenly knocked on the door and barged in, stepping on Shen Rong's foot. She recoiled peevishly and then moved to a different seat, waving her fan as if to shoo him out of the room. I was about to reprove him when I realized that the two of them knew each other well and that Pimple Ma had stepped on her foot in jest.

"Fancy meeting you here!" he snickered, trying to get a rise out of her, but she refused to break her sulky silence. I shared her obvious wish that he would make a tactful exit, but he did not seem to have any intention of doing so. After a while she left in frustration.

"Her name is not Shen Rong!" Pimple Ma snorted when I started to talk about her. "Everybody on the dance floor knows her, and her name is Shen Mengxia. How did you manage to hook up with her?"

"You haven't seen me in a while," I replied. "I've figured out how to stand on my own two feet now, so maybe I deserve a little more respect."

After complimenting me profusely on my progress, Pimple Ma launched into a diatribe against Shen Mengxia. Admitting that he had stomped on her foot just to annoy her, he explained that she had been the queen of the dance floor a few years back and that he had wasted a great deal of time and money pursuing her. Not only was Shen Rong a fake name, he asserted, but she also did not work at a vocational school and was a disgraceful tease and a slippery character in general. I shouldn't take anything she said at face value, he advised, and I had better watch out or she would try to use me. Reserving judgment, I replied that I did not care what her name was or where she worked and that I had nothing to lose because I was penniless anyway.

When I went downtown after work the next day, she was standing at the same spot where we had met before, as if waiting for me, and we walked together to my house and went to my room. Embarrassed by the events of the previous day, she started to bad-mouth Pimple Ma, calling him a con artist, and expressed surprise that I would associate with the likes of him. Just at that moment he burst into the room again, whereupon she frowned and scurried out the door. I ran to catch up with her. She said that she wanted to get together with me again later and would either return to my house or meet me at a designated spot. She had heard that I was a writer, she confided, and hoped I would help her draft a document to help resolve a crisis. She begged me not to get the wrong idea about her or to believe anything that Pimple Ma said behind her back. Turning her misty gaze on me, she mounted her bicycle and rode away.

Expecting her to return at any moment, I hoped Pimple Ma would take his leave soon. But he did not move, nor was he the least bit apologetic. Disregarding my agitation, he sat in my room until nightfall, unburdening himself to me. Word had leaked out about his watch business, he said, and he thought the cadres might have found some evidence against him. The brigade leader had summoned him for a talk, and he had stayed away from the brickyard since yesterday, afraid that if he showed his face there, they would confiscate his exit permit or slap him back into the conscript labor brigade. He wanted to know if I would run away with him. If my answer was yes, we could take a train to Zhengzhou, where his watch business was based.

I rejected the idea out of hand because it violated the governing principle of my social interactions at the brickyard. I was willing to work side by side with petty criminals, to go out on the town with them, and even to make friends with them, as I had with Pimple Ma. However, despite my need for money, I drew the line at joining in their scams. No matter how much I longed for freedom, I knew better than to trail Pimple Ma around in his life of crime. Besides, I was not in trouble with the brigade leader, as he was, so it made no sense for me to run away with him. In any case, I was sure the police would catch us.

Career criminals like him spent their lives popping in and out of jail and went back to their old tricks as soon as they were released. For them, a few years behind bars meant no more than a temporary suspension of business as usual. My case, however, was entirely different. I was convinced that I would someday be absolved of my thought crimes, as long as I did not stoop to criminal behavior. But if I did, then my name would be sullied forever, as if it had been dragged through the murky waters of the Yellow River.

With this in mind, I reminded Pimple Ma that I did not have the makings of an outlaw. I would only get in his way, I warned him, and having me along might make it easier for the police to nab him again. Nothing I said could shake his determination to run away, but I needed him to understand that I was incapable of mastering his profession, even if I wanted to. It takes talent to commit fraud, and I was incapable of uttering so much as a little white lie. Where would I find the skills to hawk counterfeit watches at train stations?

After a meal at Mr. Sun's House of Mutton we went our separate ways in the muggy summer night. The city street, with its grimy big-character posters and fetid sewer drains, seemed squalid in the yellowish glare of the streetlamps. I followed Pimple Ma with my eyes, as if watching from the shore while a tiny boat, pitching on the waves, vanished over the horizon.

17

Love in an Abandoned Temple

S HEN RONG HAD promised to meet me at one o'clock at the Post
Office Building, and I arrived on time, but she was not there. Not
being the sort of person to wait in such circumstances, I left after
a few minutes. A week later she turned up at my house with an attractive
new hairdo, two pigtails that brightened her rather ill-starred features, and
sidled up to me with a grin. She offered no apology. After a bit of small
talk she finally mentioned her oversight, needling me with the claim that
she had arrived a bit late that day, waited "for ages," and left in frustration.
Then she explained that she had not come to see me sooner because she
had spent the last week "out of town with a friend." Her words, and especially her mention of a mysterious friend, stung a bit. She kept glancing
around uneasily, as if worried about more interruptions, but I assured her
that Pimple Ma had left town. Nonetheless, she insisted that I take her out
somewhere and hinted that it would be worth my while.

We went to the Xingshan Temple, on the southern outskirts of town,
which had been closed during the campaign against the "four olds." All the
monks were gone, and the main hall was boarded up. Now the grounds
had a new name, Red Kerchief Park, and a ticket booth at the entrance.

Millions of proper names were "revolutionized" during the Cultural Revolution. For example, the Foreign Languages Institute became the Anti-imperialist Antirevisionist University, the Institute of Politics and Law was renamed the Dictatorship of the Proletariat University, and Shaanxi Normal University was called the People's Normal University. An alley known as Scholar Lu's Alley became Reed Marsh Alley, to avoid honoring a scholar who had passed the imperial examinations. There were no marshes there; the curious new name was a gratuitous allusion to the revolutionary model opera[1] *Shajiabang*, which centers on a Communist hideout in the marshes in the 1940s.

Although Red Kerchief Park was a playground, few mothers dared bring their children to such a desolate, remote location. However, it was a convenient destination for dating couples and the best lovers' lane in town.

We strolled over to the brand-new deserted swing set. She stood on a swing and swung back and forth a bit, then complained that she was dizzy, so I got on and faced her protectively. When we started to move, the upward motion of the swing pressed our bodies together. I leaned down toward her, and she tilted her face up. Our lips brushed lightly for a moment, setting us on fire like the stroke of a match. The heat of the moment was fueled by all the obstacles, intentional or not, that we had encountered since the night when I had first been drawn by her misty gaze.

She said she felt weak-kneed and was afraid of falling. Sensing a warm stirring in my loins, I was also eager to abandon the swing. Experience suggested that I had better carry this playful beginning to its logical conclusion, or else this relationship would fizzle just like all the others. Wordlessly we got off the swing and found our way to the rear of the park, looking for an appropriate spot.

We ended up in a small courtyard behind the main hall of the temple, on a slate terrace strewn with fallen red mimosa blossoms that gave off a faint medicinal aroma in the cool breeze. There was no one in sight; we were probably the only people in the park. Now that we were on solid ground, I was free to scoop her up in a bear hug, taking her breath away,

[1] During the Cultural Revolution only eight "model works," consisting of revolutionary opera or ballet, were allowed in the mass media.

and we melted into a long French kiss. My awkward, impetuous advances rumpled her hair, a few strands of which caught on my button, yanking her scalp, and she scoffed at my clumsiness. She removed my hand from her breast, complaining that I was wrinkling her blouse, and proceeded to unbutton it herself. After demonstrating how to unfasten her bra, she offered me her bare breasts. I ushered her to a spot beneath a mimosa tree and pressed her back against the tree trunk. She held still and let me fondle her breasts, but firmly stopped my other hand from fumbling inside her pants.

"Have you had enough?" she asked, smoothing her clothes when I came up for air.

Tongue-tied with embarrassment, I did not reply. She smiled archly, looking somewhat titillated and gratified by my display of boyish desire. Extracting my hand from her pants, she wiped my fingers with her handkerchief and told me that she had her period. If I would just cool off for a couple of days, she promised, it would pass, and I would have plenty of opportunities to take liberties with her.

She had perked up since her arrival at my house earlier that day, as if her batteries had been recharged. I, on the other hand, felt worn out and strangely uneasy.

"What's the matter with you?" she snapped, noticing my distraction. "Do you want to run home to your mommy?"

Concerned that certain rumors might have diminished my respect for her, she asked me what Pimple Ma had said about her. To tell the truth, I was not the least bit interested in her past. At that moment I had a one-track mind and was in no mood for irrelevant conversation. I told her what Pimple Ma had said, holding back some of the details to avoid embarrassing her. Heaping abuse on him, she demanded that I stop associating with him. She admitted that Mengxia had been her name but claimed to have changed it formally to Shen Rong, not as part of the Cultural Revolution mania for name changing,[2] but in order to make a clean break with her past. Then she launched into her story.

During the heyday of the dance parties after the Great Leap Forward,

[2] *Rong* means "glory."

she said, she had been a physically precocious schoolgirl of fifteen or six-teen. She made a point of boasting to me about the bluish tinge in her eyes, which she claimed had been even brighter in those days. Turning to me, she instructed me to look at the whites of her eyes, and I noticed that they did indeed have a slight bluish cast, which nicely offset her moist dark lashes. Examining them inflamed my desire again, and I felt myself melt-ing. Her coquettish, triumphant gaze bound me like an unbreakable strand of silk, until I was overwhelmed and had to avert my eyes. Then we fell into each other's arms again, and I allowed my hands to roam boldly over her body until she collapsed under the tree with her eyes closed. Putting one hand behind my neck, she placed the other on my chest, saying that she wanted to feel my heartbeat. A moment later she removed it, chided me for my apparent lack of passion, and told me to feel her heart, which was thumping like a drum.

"Well? Do you admit that your heart isn't racing like mine?" she demanded. "You're a faker. Now I think you're just fooling around with me."

I admitted that my response was not as strong as hers but maintained that one's heart rate had more to do with individual physiology than with love. "People have different blood types," I countered. "Your pulse doesn't prove anything. Is your hand some kind of lie detector from the CIA?" To end the bickering, I urged her to get on with her story.

Like me, she had been an outsider at the dances who had gradually been drawn in by the lights and music. Young and vain, she had been eager to flaunt her charms in such glittery surroundings. But hedonism is riskier for a woman than it is for a clod like me, ill equipped as I was to seduce anyone with my shabby clothes and empty wallet. A loose woman, by con-trast, is an easy target for a predatory man with the means to ensnare her in a web of small favors.

Although her tale of woe tugged at my heartstrings, it was the familiar story of countless innocent girls who, like moths attracted to a flame, let men transform them into women during one-night stands. At a fateful party she had danced with the womanizing scion of a lofty official family. An inexperienced middle school girl, she had allowed her head to be turned by his status and had fallen for him during a few whirls around the dance floor. After the party he had taken her to his mansion and robbed her of her virginity as effortlessly as a child blows a bubble with bubble gum. As she departed on that cold January night, he had cloaked her in a stylish new overcoat, as if paying off a courtesan with a gift. All he, a married man, had wanted was the novelty of deflowering her, and he had dropped her as soon as he made his conquest.

The consequences had been disastrous. Pregnant, she had been expelled from her middle school in disgrace and had found a job as a temporary construction worker. The privileged young man had been apprehended, convicted of a string of previous similar crimes, and sent to jail. From then on she had been saddled with a terrible reputation. She had found another boyfriend, but he had abandoned her because of her history. Then she had married someone else, but they had soon separated, and she had been living with her parents ever since.

"Well, are you going to hold this against me?" she asked, gazing at me mistily after a brief silence.

I hesitated, at a loss for words. Actually I was feeling guilty because I had already heard most of her story from Pimple Ma and realized that her pathetic history was exactly what made her approachable. I had searched far and wide for a loose woman. What right did I have to stand in judgment of her? As long as she did not disapprove of my reputation as a reactionary student and a resettled worker, I was satisfied.

"I was expelled from my school too," I replied after a while. "I was labeled a reactionary, and have been a resettled worker ever since, so my past is even more checkered than yours. Let's forget about the past, since we hadn't even met each other in those days."

This brought a smile to her face. Standing in the lengthening shadow of the tree, she put her arm around my neck, tilted her face up, and gave me a long kiss. With renewed ardor, we resumed our endless petting, until the cawing of the crows at nightfall reminded us to leave the park.

18

Lessons from a Goddess of Love

ONE DAY IN the summer of 1968 Shen Rong came to visit me, but I was on my way to Silent Garden with Zhengguan to take care of Grandfather, who was seriously ill. He and Grandmother had spent the winter of 1966–67 in the cramped apartment the Red Guards had forced them into after evicting them from Silent Garden. Then, during an official campaign to correct some of the Red Guards' injustices, the owner of the apartment had asked for it back. With great difficulty, Zhengxin had gotten permission from the commune for my grandparents to return to Silent Garden.

The commune had taken over the whole house by that time and had put a partition in the foyer, which confined my grandparents to only three of the rooms they had occupied before. Although Father and Zhengxin had also fallen upon hard times, they were supporting my grandparents. Zhengxin was poorly paid, and Father's salary had been reduced to a meager living allowance now that he had been deemed a bourgeois reactionary academic authority. In order to defray my grandparents' living expenses, they even had to pawn the few ramshackle pieces of furniture that had survived the Red Guards' pillaging.

Both my grandparents had always enjoyed good health, and we had taken it for granted that they would live to a ripe old age. But the continuous attacks on them, combined with the reduction in their living standard, drove them both to an early grave. Grandmother died first, in the fall of 1967, and Grandfather developed a terminal illness immediately afterward, before he had even finished the prescribed period of chanting prayers for her. Because Father and Third Uncle were imprisoned in the "cow pens"[1] under the "dictatorship of the masses," Zhengxin, Zhengguan, and I were the only ones left to take care of Grandfather.

On that summer day in 1968 the three of us, accompanied by Shen Rong, pulled Grandfather to the hospital in a handcart borrowed from the commune. Once there, Zhengxin took care of the paperwork and consulted with the doctors, while Zhengguan and I lugged Grandfather around on a stretcher from one examining room to another. Shen Rong played the part of loving granddaughter-in-law and sat by his bed, fanning him, mopping his brow, giving him sips of water, and shooing away flies. He was covered with grapelike clusters of blisters, which kept bursting, oozing foul yellow pus, and spreading, leaving a trail of festering red scabs. Looking as if he had been scalded from head to toe with boiling water, he lay naked in the sweltering summer heat, covered only by his sheet and gauze bandages. It must have been deeply humiliating for a man who was entirely lucid, as he was, to lie as still and helpless as a child, exposing his hideous disfigurement to everyone in the room while the doctor casually manipulated his most private parts.

Grandfather was in full possession of his mental faculties and was determined to use every last breath in his body to pray silently for his next incarnation. I, however, found the doctrine of karma baffling and preposterous. It seemed to me that after devoting the latter half his life to Buddhism, Grandfather should have accumulated enough merit to have been spared such a gruesome death. Was there really such a thing as bad karma from a previous incarnation, as Grandfather believed? I remained skeptical. Nonetheless, I could offer no better explanation for the mysterious workings of fate.

---

[1] Makeshift prisons set up at work units during the Cultural Revolution.

He had been diagnosed with lymphoma. The doctor told us that since it had metastasized, we might as well take him home and prepare for his funeral. Grandfather was not covered by the public health system, and we were strapped for cash. In an era when people were being beaten to death every day, human life had lost its value. We carted him home, carried him into his room, and laid him on the *kang* where Grandmother had breathed her last. Mrs. Wang, the aide we had hired for him, bustled around, expertly dressing his blisters. An old woman with bound feet, she was alone in the world and supported herself with temporary jobs of this sort. Thanks to her, we were spared the burden of caring for Grandfather around the clock. Moreover, since she was a poor peasant, her impeccable political credentials entitled her to haggle with the commune leaders on our behalf. She drove a hard bargain and often came out on top.

Mrs. Wang clucked over Grandfather as her deft hands worked unflinchingly to clean off the pus that had oozed from his blisters on the way home from the hospital. Shen Rong sat beside her, handing her medicated cotton balls. Then Zhengxin and Zhengguan left, but Shen Rong and I stayed, planning to enjoy the seclusion of the garden. Shen Rong slipped Mrs. Wang a sheaf of ration tickets, and she got the hint. After dinner she made up the bed on the *kang* in the outer room and invited us to spend the night there.

Silent Garden was completely ruined. Most of the plants and trees had been cleared away, and the yard was coated in soot from the commune foundry. I could hardly bear to look around carefully. It was getting dark, and the foundry was closed for the night, so Shen Rong and I had the place to ourselves. I led her to the courtyard in the rear, which was near the city wall and relatively private with the gate closed. We climbed a few steps up onto a raised brick terrace and stopped beside a stone table and bench. The tall willows cast swaying shadows in the evening breeze. I remembered how our family had sat on this terrace to cool off in the summer heat and how Grandmother had lit incense and set out moon cakes and fruit on the stone table at moonrise on the Mid-Autumn Festival. Now the table was so filthy that there wasn't even a place to sit down.

Shen Rong made a trip to the toilet and came back whispering that her period had ended. To hurry it along, she said, she had been guzzling popsicles and cold drinks for the last few days. She reached into her pants, pulled out a clean sanitary napkin, and showed it to me, then tossed it into the bushes. In the still of the night the moonlight illuminated the terrace as brightly as a stage, with a shadowy plot of dead weeds in place of an audience. Now that Shen Rong had removed the last obstacle, she looked at me invitingly, as if to say, "Let's get on with it."

We stripped off our clothes, she deftly and seductively, while I was awkward and embarrassed. Like an actor who has forgotten his lines, I hesitated momentarily as we faced each other naked. Then I took her in my arms, and we felt the thrill of flesh pressed against flesh. Fondling each other through our clothes for the last couple of days had whetted our appetites for more. Surrendering to my instincts, I pressed her close to me. The night air was cool and damp. Watery moonlight streamed down from the sky, and the trees cast shadows that swirled beneath us like seaweed. Our murky silhouettes writhed and bobbed, as if we were merman and mermaid embracing undersea.

It was very late by the time we went to bed on the *kang*, but we continued our insatiable caresses throughout the night. Shedding my inhibitions in the darkness, I let her be my guide in repeated explorations of her pleasure.

She had always taken the lead in our relationship, but I knew that we were at cross purposes. Fully aware of my naiveté, she hoped to use sex to ensnare me in a long-term relationship, which was exactly what I feared most. All I had wanted was to satisfy my curiosity about sex, and I had been using her for this purpose all along. Maybe I was as reprehensible as the cad who had robbed her of her virginity, but perhaps not. She was at a different stage in her life now, and this time she was the initiator. If she had not made the first move, I might never have mustered the courage to do so.

Now that I had achieved my goal, I would have had no regrets if she had simply left me. At the very least, there was something to boast about if I ran into Pimple Ma. Now I knew what sex was all about; this in itself was reason enough for what I had done.

"So, how was it last night?" she cooed the next morning, glancing at me as she combed her hair.

I was tongue-tied. It goes against my nature to try to butter people up by finding the words they want to hear. Even if I know what I ought to say, I usually can't bring myself to say it. The events of the night before had blurred in my mind like a half-remembered dream, and I really hadn't felt any unusual passion. So I replied noncommittally that I hadn't been swept off my feet as I'd imagined I would. Naturally this wounded her feelings, and she accused me of coldness and insensitivity.

"Maybe you'd like a virgin better, so why don't you go find one?" she scoffed, and started to pester me the same way she had at the Xingshan Temple. Hastily I explained that I had simply been telling the truth. This was just a beginning for me, and we were still unfamiliar with each other's bodies. Once our relationship had deepened, I would probably have some special feelings to report to her. At this her face softened. Peering into the mirror, she rumpled her neatly combed hair and pulled a few stray wisps down over her forehead and temples.

"Let's stay here again tonight then," she suggested brightly. "I'll make sure you enjoy it this time."

Grandfather was lying on his *kang* with his eyes closed, intoning his mantras and counting his rosary beads. He seemed oblivious of his surroundings.

Shen Rong and I walked to Xingqing Park and sat in a grove of trees to wait for nightfall. The sultry summer day seemed interminable, the grove was airless, and my mouth was parched. I had not been home or to work for two days in a row. Glancing at my strange surroundings, I suddenly felt as nervous as an elementary school student playing hooky. The mere sight of familiar-looking passersby made me uneasy.

We were sitting on a hill built of dirt reclaimed from a lake bottom, just beyond the rear wall of Silent Garden. Between the trees, I could see the terrace in our rear courtyard, which the blinding midday sun illuminated like a spotlight. The thought popped into my mind that the previous night's rendezvous was like an episode from *Strange Tales from the Liaozhai Studio*,[2]

---

[2] A well-known collection of short stories by the seventeenth-century author Pu Songling, which often feature romantic encounters between scholarly young men and beautiful female fox fairies or ghosts.

which had been one of my favorite books when I lived in Silent Garden as a high school student. In those days I had sat on the terrace many a night praying for romance and concocting stories like the ones in the book, but featuring myself as the hero. In each one I foolishly imagined a fox fairy or female ghost suddenly emerging from the darkness and alighting on the terrace.

"What are you thinking about?" She punctured my reverie by poking me with her finger.

"Nothing," I replied.

"What's the matter with you? Are you done with me now that you've gotten what you wanted?" Silence made her uncomfortable, especially if I seemed withdrawn, and when she couldn't stand it anymore, she would slyly try to get a rise out of me. "Tell me the truth. Do you love me or not?" she demanded, turning her most alluring gaze on me.

"Our actions speak for themselves. Do I really have to put things into words?" I parried.

"Yes, I want an answer. I want to know what's on your mind." She put her hand on my chest to feel my heartbeat.

"I really wasn't thinking anything," I answered after a moment's hesitation.

"And you'd just sleep with me without thinking?" Her face fell.

"You didn't ask me before we did it. Why didn't you make me swear my love to you before we went to bed together?" I took a hard line with her, trying to steer her away from a formal discussion of the word "love." There was no way I could tell her that I loved her. As far as I was concerned, "I love you" was a storybook phrase, and it would have been absurd to inject it into the present conversation.

I am the kind of person who always balks at having words extracted from me, no matter whether they are about politics or my personal feelings or whether the demands come from a powerful organization or an intimate individual. In fact I dislike declaring my feelings at all, especially if it involves false posturing.

Sensing my reluctance to speak, she nestled close to me and wheedled, "Is sex all you want?"

"You can think that if you want to," I muttered.

She took this as an admission of guilt, and her face darkened. "You scum!" she exclaimed.

I sensed that I had lost the argument, and my ears started to burn. I was well aware that she was a girl with a pathetic history and that I had taken advantage of her. But then she switched to a gentler tack and nestled against me again, pressing her cheeks against the stubble of my beard until her face was flushed. After a while she resumed her relentless interrogation, concluding with a proposal of marriage. When I remained tight-lipped, she remarked lightly that she had been "just asking" and told me to calm down. But then she demanded sternly that I give the matter serious thought and let her know one way or the other by the next day.

The afternoon passed in tiresome questioning. I couldn't tell whether she was seriously exploring our future together or just flirting, appearing to take the moral high ground so that she would feel better about what had happened between us. The more she tried to elicit promises from me, the more I resented her, and I began to regret having gotten involved with her so rashly in the first place. The night loomed ahead, and I started to dread going back to Silent Garden. Tonight would not be as romantic as last night. I was almost ready to break off our relationship.

We returned to Silent Garden and went to bed on the *kang*, rocking each other smoothly all night in the dark. From time to time we heard Grandfather calling Mrs. Wang. People exist in isolated worlds, and it is impossible to suffer in another person's place. Even when someone is dying, life goes on for the rest of us. Shen Rong lay sweetly in my arms, her spontaneous moans of pleasure drowning out Grandfather's groans from the other side of the wall.

自述

19

Arrested

ONE DAY THAT fall I went to visit Grandfather. His blisters had shrunk with the fading summer heat, but he had shriveled up like a piece of dried fruit. Noticing a small notebook by his pillow, I opened it and found that he was still keeping a diary, an attempt to make sense of his final days on earth. Although all his Buddhist sutras had been confiscated, a fellow Buddhist had supplied him with two more, which he kept at his bedside and read constantly. He had not abandoned his prayers and kept fingering his rosary beads slowly, in rhythm with his lethargic pulse, as his spirit feebly prepared to slough off his body like a cicada skin.

In a gravelly, gasping voice, he inquired about Shen Rong, whom he remembered from her visit during the summer. I had long since broken up with her, but I decided to spare him the details.

"She's too busy to come see you today, Grandfather, but she sends her best regards," I lied. Then I showed him some food that I had bought for him, pretending that it was a gift from her. Soothed, he closed his eyes and offered thanks to the Buddha. Like most old folks, he used his own experience as a frame of reference for understanding the affairs of the younger generation, which often resulted in displays of misplaced concern.

Shen Rong had stayed with me at Silent Garden for three nights in a row. As I was walking her back to her parents' house on the last morning, she had pressured me to marry her.

I had emitted a huge smoke screen, cautioning her that tying the knot with me would bring her inconceivable annoyance. The brickyard cadres had a way of sabotaging the workers' marriage plans. Believing that only trickery could net a "stinking" resettled worker a wife from outside, the cadres demanded a certificate from the woman's work unit before they would issue the paperwork authorizing a marriage license. However, even if you complied, they visited the woman's work unit, ostensibly to investigate but actually to expose your bad record. Claiming that it was their duty to prevent you from concealing shameful secrets, they would reveal to her that you were a thief or a sex offender. Needless to say, such meddling had broken up many a loving couple.

Unfazed by my warning, Shen Rong had offered to bring the certificate from her work unit in person to the brickyard cadres and demand face-to-face that they issue the paperwork. I had tried to put her off with one more excuse, that there was no decent housing for resettled workers at the brickyard, but she had countered that she would be happy to rent a place in a village nearby. Having run out of excuses, I had been forced to admit that I did not want to get married right then.

"Well," she had replied, rolling her eyes. "Then let's forget the whole thing. Why didn't you just say so from the start? Anyway, I know what's wrong: You're afraid my bad reputation will rub off on you."

We sparred verbally in this tiresome manner for several weeks, until we finally split up. For a long time afterward I was not sure what had happened. I did not know whether my rebuff had hurt her feelings or if she had been planning to break up and had used the proposal of marriage to give me cold feet. Or perhaps she had merely been teasing, to spice up our relationship. At any rate, I was loath to marry her; that had never been my aim. In fact I was too depressed and anxious in those days to consider marrying anyone.

One brooding, rainy autumn evening, when I was alone on duty in the shed on top of the kiln, I composed a poem, a new set of lyrics to the ancient tune "A Sprig of Plum Blossoms":

Awakening from a dream of losing you
One stormy autumn night,
I see the clepsydra has almost run dry.
With hours to kill before morning,
I step outside to a desolate scene
Of forlorn crickets chirping
And fields choked with weeds.

Across the river, among reeds cloaked in frosty dew,
A lone goose stands.
Above, in her cassia-scented moon palace,
Chang E pines away.
As I yearn for the morning light,
A lovely lady appears
Her stockinged feet drenched with chilly dew.

Overcome with foreboding, I stuck my gloomy poem between the pages of the antique book I was reading. What could I say to Grandfather about my relationship with Shen Rong? Flat on his back in bed, he was incapable of understanding me, especially since my current friends and interests were so far beyond the limits of his experience. After four long years at the brickyard I was no longer the boy student who had lived with him at Silent Garden. When I was small, Father had been afraid that I would learn delinquent behavior from the neighborhood children, but now I had sunk to depths that he could never have envisioned back then. I was somewhat comforted by the thought that Grandmother had survived long enough to enjoy gifts of food from me, purchased with my own hard-earned money, but I regretted that Grandfather was going to die before my wedding day and would never meet his future granddaughter-in-law.

During my visit he asked for some eight-treasure rice pudding from a restaurant in town, and I promised to buy it for him on the following

---

* Chang E stole the elixir of immortality from her husband and absconded to the moon, where she became the lonely "moon goddess."

Thursday, when a fresh batch would be available. Alas, I never managed to keep my word. I was arrested that Tuesday afternoon.

I was on the second shift that fateful day and had punched in at four o'clock. Changhai, Ermao, and I were stoking the kiln, which we had just lit. Changhai had returned from six months in the Xi'an Detention Center, commonly known as Department Five, and often regaled us with tales of his experiences there. During the big crackdown that had netted him, he said, the place had been chock-full; the bunks were so crowded that if you wanted to turn over in the night, you had to call out, "One, two, three," so that everyone would roll over in unison. If you got up to go to the bathroom, your place would be gone by the time you got back.

That afternoon I had some Diamond brand cigarettes from Albania, which I shared with Changhai and Ermao before lighting one myself. Just as Changhai was launching into one of his stories, our squad leader suddenly arrived with the message that the brigade leader wanted to see me. I snuffed out my newly lit cigarette, jammed it back into the package, and followed the squad leader to the office.

The brigade leader was standing beside a table where a stranger, a peasant wearing an old-fashioned jacket, was seated. He told me to sit down across from him. Then the brigade leader introduced him as Sheriff Cong from the Security Bureau, and the two of them exchanged glances.

"Kang Zhengguo, please rise!" the brigade leader suddenly barked.

"I have an announcement," said the sheriff, pulling a sheet of paper from his briefcase and starting to recite in a droning voice. I could not make head or tail of what he was saying, except for his final words: that I was "being detained in accordance with the law."

Events unfolded swiftly after that. Before I knew it, the brigade leader had clapped a set of handcuffs on me. Then he and the sheriff hustled me back to the barracks for a search, beginning by inspecting my person. Opening my package of Albanian cigarettes, the sheriff carefully squeezed each one between his fingers, like a hero in the movies searching a captured American-trained Guomindang spy for microfilm. Then they ransacked my bunk too and discovered my disrespectful use of the thick second volume of Mao's *Selected Works* instead of a brick to prop up one of its wobbly legs. They found the antique book containing my poem and confiscated both.

They rolled up my bedding, escorted me back to the office to complete the paperwork for my exit from the brickyard, shoved me into a jeep, and pushed me into the middle of a spare tire in the rear. Then they strapped the huge bedroll onto my back; it was so heavy that I could barely sit up.

Finally I had left the brickyard. Little had I known that I would leave the same way as everyone else, transferred to somewhere worse instead of returning to normal life. The official jargon for this kind of transfer was "handover to a higher authority."

We pulled out of the brickyard in a drenching downpour, the raindrops splattering when they hit the ground. The speeding jeep made countless turns, finally delivering me to a high-security detention center. Noting the spire of the Small Wild Goose Pagoda nearby, I realized that I had arrived at Department Five of the Xi'an Security Bureau, the place that Changhai had described so often.

It was September 19, 1968, a day I shall never forget as long as I live.

20

Prisoner Number Two

A SWARTHY GUARD USHERED me down a long brick-walled walkway with watchtowers at each end and a strip of exposed sky overhead. My belt and shoelaces had been confiscated during the search earlier that day, along with my wallet and the suspicious pack of cigarettes, so I had to shuffle along in my unlaced sneakers, hitching my pants up with my hand and lugging my bedroll on my back. We eventually turned left into the fourth row of cells on the east side of the prison and stopped in front of Cell Number Five. The guard turned his key in the huge lock on the massive door and pushed it open.

"You counterrevolutionary bastard," he blustered, brandishing his heavy key ring at me, "if you don't behave yourself, you'll never get out of here." I had been half expecting him to shove me into the cell as they do in the movies, but it didn't happen. I walked in quite normally, under my own power.

During my entry procedures I had been given a long list of prison taboos, including discussing my case with anyone or revealing my real name. Now the guard reminded me that while I was in jail I would be known only by my serial number, Number Two.

As soon as the door clanged shut and the guard's footsteps receded into the distance, my new cellmates clustered around me. Upon learning that I had come from no less a place than the Number Two Brickyard, which qualified me as a veteran jailbird, one of my cellmates, a Muslim who introduced himself as Number Fourteen, took the lead in welcoming me. My other cellmates followed suit and began to pump me for information about the outside world. A couple of them, who seemed like professional scalpers, were particularly interested in the price of grain ration tickets and black market conditions in general.

When they heard that I had missed dinner, they advised me to ask for something to eat. But I was still in a state of shock, and food was the farthest thing from my mind. In fact, although they seemed to mean well, their urging gave me the sense that they were more interested in the food I might get than in my personal needs. Although I had little appetite, I finally let them goad me into yelling a few times, "Reporting! New arrival Number Two has not had dinner." Number Fourteen chimed in at the top of his lungs too, but our cries met with dead silence. I gave up, and my cellmates' hopeful faces fell along with the darkness of evening.

I glanced around the cell. Bunks extended the length of both side walls from front to back, leaving only a narrow space to walk between them. The door was at the front of the cell, and there was a urinal in the back corner. The best place to sleep was near the door, since the farther back you went, the closer you were to the urinal. Such matters were decided on the basis of seniority, with the new arrivals starting at the back and moving up as inmates departed and vacated their bunks. Luckily, however, the cell was not filled to capacity, so the picture was not as grim as the one Changhai had painted for me.

Number One, who had been there for four or five years, occupied the prime spot by the door. He was a "historical counterrevolutionary"[1] whose case was still pending. Number Three was a physics professor from Shaanxi Normal University who had been rounded up during the Socialist Education campaign and had languished without an interrogation for several

---

[1] A person who served the Guomindang government or army in an official capacity before 1949.

years. Number Six was a fierce-looking robber with bloodshot, shifty eyes, who spent most of his time sitting cross-legged on his bunk. Number Seven came from a textile mill on the eastern outskirts of town and seemed to have committed some sort of financial crime. He never discussed his case with us but sat lost in mental calculations all day with a frown on his face. Number Nine was a peasant from nearby Chang'an County who had been a member of a gang of thieves that stole precious irrigation motors. Number Fourteen, called Fourteen for short, was a hooligan whom the Red Guards had caught in the act of gang-raping a girl from Sichuan. Number Three, the cell chief, assigned me the bunk next to Fourteen's. A dim lightbulb hung from the ceiling overhead, and in the southeast corner of the cell there was a window covered with iron bars, previously only the stuff of fiction as far as I was concerned. It had been simply one more ordinary day for my cellmates, all of whom had now drifted off to sleep, but for me, as I lay there in the dark, the agony was just beginning.

I still had no idea why I had been arrested, and I needed to figure it out and devise a defense to use at my interrogation. During my stay at the brickyard I had learned the difference between formal arrest and mere detention. The police had the right to detain suspects whenever they wanted, without filing formal charges against them in court, but they also sometimes released them if they were unable to build watertight cases. Like many new detainees, I foolishly tried to comfort myself with wishful thinking. Maybe they would discover that I was not the man they wanted. Or maybe I was being detained because of some political campaign that would blow over, and I would be released on parole in a few months. I simply could not imagine what crime I had committed to deserve this treatment. It was true that I had gone to Beijing to seek redress, but I had not broken any laws, and the denial of my request had been enough punishment in itself. And none of my dealings with Pimple Ma and Shen Rong had been illegal. What else could it be? The way that they had searched me suggested that my case had to do with something I had written. They had been terribly suspicious of everything on my person, even inspecting my cigarettes one by one. But I was innocent. Why had Sheriff Cong selected such a small-time target when there were so many hardened criminals at the brickyard?

Eager to get my interrogation over with, I asked my cellmates when they thought it might take place. Number Three, whom I called Professor Liu once I found out his real name, warned me that it might take a couple of weeks before the authorities got around to it and advised me to settle down and get used to prison life. He explained that it was standard prison routine to make you wait for your interrogation while they softened you up a bit both mentally and physically. By keeping you locked up without any explanation, while at the same time starving you slowly into submission, they could raise your anxiety level and weaken you to the point where it would be easier for them to squeeze the truth out of you.

As a newcomer I had more reserves of body fat than anyone else in the cell and did not even finish the first breakfast they served me. Although I was still hungry, I simply could not choke down another bite of the unappetizing salty corn gruel mixed with bitter cabbage leaves. My cellmates, however, all wanted my leftovers, most of which I gave to Fourteen. I did not finish my gruel the second day either, thinking it reminded me of pig fodder, but after a few days it started to taste good to me. I cleaned my bowl and even wished for seconds. Except for holidays, however, half a ladle full each morning was all we got.

Two inmates had the job of serving breakfast first thing in the morning. One carried in a big basin of gruel, while the other brought a bucket of boiled drinking water. Getting the food was a highly stressful process. When the guards arrived with breakfast, they shouted just outside each of the seven cell doors along our row, and the pair on duty scrambled out to get the food. If their timing was off, the annoyed guards would skimp on the portions, so they had to be ready and waiting to sprint to the door as soon as they heard the call for Cell Number Five. Then they had to hold the basin in the most convenient position for the guards, so that they would be inclined to generosity. There was an art to catching the watery gruel. The faster the guards ladled it, the more solids it contained, but if they had to pause and wait with their ladles in the air, while the inmates adjusted their basin, some might be lost. Since the skill of the inmates on breakfast duty directly affected the well-being of everyone in the cell, we all gave them plenty of moral support at food-serving time. If they came back in with the basin saying that today's gruel was thick, or that the ladles had been full, or that they had gotten some doughy clumps, our faces lit up with joy. If they had not done a good job that day, we would sigh with regret.

On my first day it was Number Nine and Number Fourteen's turn to get breakfast. They returned with average pickings and started to distribute them to us. Our bowls were lined up and ready, and all eyes were upon Fourteen as he doled the food out spoonful by spoonful, down to the last drop. But there was another step to the process. In order to prevent the server from giving anything extra to himself or to his buddies, Professor Liu had prepared a sack of cardboard chits with all of our serial numbers on them so that we could draw lots to see who would get first pick among the bowls. After the day's winner had chosen his bowl, the rest of the inmates would choose according to seniority. This meant that even though you had your own bowl, you never knew which bowl you would get.

The only advantage to being a server was that you could clean the basin, scraping any remaining specks of gruel into your bowl. Even though this was a pitiful reward for serving the food, everyone was eager to take on the job. After dividing the gruel as fairly as if they had used a kitchen scale, the servers finished cleaning the basin, not wasting a morsel. I lacked the patience for this and never scraped the basin when it was my turn for breakfast duty. In fact I was reluctant to shoulder the huge responsibility of breakfast duty at all or to find myself face-to-face with the swarthy guard, so I often let Fourteen go in my place, relinquishing my precious basin-scraping rights to him. In a cell full of men listless with hunger, worldly-wise Fourteen stood out as a hardworking, optimistic fellow. He did not take advantage of anyone but earned every drop of extra gruel that he got.

Department Five was Xi'an's largest detention facility and was said to be better managed than the others. Imprisonment is nothing to rejoice about, but I am thankful to the Bodhisattva Guanyin that I was assigned directly to Department Five rather than some branch facility and was put into a cell where people got along with one another reasonably well. Fortunately I never encountered the kinds of bullies that Liao Yiwu and Liu Qing[2] describe in

---

[2] Liao Yiwu and Liu Qing are well-known dissidents, veterans of the Chinese gulag, and authors of memoirs describing the brutality of Chinese prison life. Liu Qing has served as head of the New York–based organization Human Rights in China.

their prison memoirs. I cannot speculate here about whether this is because I was simply lucky or because jails and their occupants degenerated between my day in the 1960s and theirs in the 1980s and 1990s; all I know is that I was spared the kind of terror that they experienced.

We were forbidden to doze on our bunks during the day. According to the rules, after breakfast we were supposed to sit quietly and reflect on our errors, study Mao's works, or read the single copy of *People's Daily*. However, we did not always obey the rules. By about two o'clock, when the morning's watery gruel had passed right through us and we were famished again, we could smell the aroma of the preparations for that day's dinner, although we still had to wait until four o'clock for it. Standing on a pile of quilts, Number Nine craned his neck to look out the tiny window at the chimney smoke and predict what we would get. He pointed to the three chimneys on the kitchen roof and said that since the second one was belching smoke, dinner would be steamed buns. This verdict was based on long experience, and sure enough, at dinner we each got a brownish wheat bun and a bowl of slightly watery vegetable soup. The bitter boiled turnips tasted good to me, and the salty broth, flecked with a few drops of oil, impressed me as a perfect balance of color, fragrance, and flavor. Alternating bites of vegetable and bun, I polished off all the food at my normal speed and then filled up the gaps in my stomach with drinking water. After that I tried to find a way to forget my remaining hunger until the next meal.

Some of my cellmates had unusual eating habits. Number Nine seemed to derive spiritual sustenance from keeping one steamed bun in reserve at all times. He always waited until he got a fresh bun before eating the old one he had saved and then hoarded the new one in a special bag that he hung on the wall. I could not imagine why he bothered to do this. He got no more food than the rest of us and always had to eat cold, stale buns. Perhaps the momentary illusion that he had an extra bun was comforting. Number Seven was a very particular diner. After spreading a clean handkerchief in front of himself, he julienned his bun painstakingly with a piece of string, which he called his bun cutter. Then he set the strips of bun out on his handkerchief like a heap of french fries and used a tiny stick to spear each one into his mouth and chew it slowly. After the rest of us had gobbled up all our food, he would still be savoring his sumptuous feast of bun strips.

Everyone was supposed to receive fourteen ounces of grain a day, but in fact we got less than that. Our vegetables were old and wilted, and the cooks never bothered to trim off the roots and yellow leaves. They always put in too much salt, then sprinkled in a few drops of soy sauce and oil to make the food seem more satisfying. Our starving bodies avidly absorbed this meager fare, leaving almost nothing to be excreted, so we rarely had bowel movements. At first my bowels still functioned normally since I had some reserves of lubrication, but as time passed, I developed the serious constipation that was endemic in the jail and could move my bowels only every few days. We were not allowed to heed the call of nature but had to go to the toilet during our "airing," an extremely tense five minutes when we were taken outside, cell by cell, once a day. If one cell took too long, it would cut into the next cell's time and keep the guards on the job longer, so they were always yelling at us to hurry up. As soon as they unlocked our door, we would make a beeline for the toilet, where we would strain, holding our breath, until our intestines were about to split, but we only managed to excrete tiny, rock-hard lumps, and our rectums cracked and bled. Sometimes, just when we were about to succeed in moving our bowels, the guard would yell at us from outside, and we had to pull up our pants, scurry back into the cell, and hold the bowel movement in until our next airing. I noticed that Professor Liu often came back from the toilet looking pained and clutching his belly. With his gray, sunken cheeks twitching, he would flop down on his bunk to recuperate. He was so severely constipated that he had to pry his bowel movements out with his hand. Every trip to the toilet was like a surgical operation for him, during which he held his breath and strained so hard that he collapsed, half dead, once he got back to the cell.

As I sat on my bunk, I often recalled the term "airing" from the prison novels I had loved as a child, about Communists incarcerated by the Guomindang. In these novels, the airing was always an opportunity for clandestine contact, when the revolutionaries could touch bases with one another, exchange books, letters, maps, and party instructions, and plot jailbreaks or riots. The passages describing the airings were always the most exciting parts of the books; in them, the yard seemed like an open-air club for the prisoners, where they could relax together briefly every day.

The revolutionary romanticism of these novels had thrilled me so much that I had even developed a vague yearning to go to jail myself, so that I could join in these heroic exploits. Now, as I recalled these naive sentiments, I felt that fate was mocking me. Maybe this reading material had somehow led me into my current predicament, and I had now been granted my secret childhood wishes. Unfortunately, however, I was not in a fictional Guomindang prison but in a Communist one, under the dictatorship of the proletariat. Completely lacking in the drama I had dreamed of, post-1949 prisons were grim and forbidding, and the Communists had sealed up—as if with reinforced concrete—all the loopholes through which the Guomindang had formerly let its prisoners slip.

As the guards said, "If being in jail was a picnic, wouldn't everybody want to come? A little bit of hunger and suffering will teach you who's boss."

21

Interrogation

INTERROGATION WAS OUR only diversion. As the sunlight streamed into the cell every morning after breakfast, we sat there hoping the guards would call for us. I got my first opportunity to go about ten days after my arrest. Just as I was leaving, Fourteen reminded me to pick up as many cigarette butts as I could for everybody, tinging the outing with a bit of excitement. After being cooped up for so long, I was finally getting my chance for some mischief, and I was ready for action.

As soon as I stepped into the long corridor, however, my heart sank. This was, after all, an interrogation, not a scavenger hunt. I tried to guess what they already knew about me and to plan what I should say, but I kept drawing blanks. Although I could be cocky when risk taking was called for, I tended to get hopelessly flustered in any serious match of wits. I was venturing blindfolded into the unknown. I knew I had to steel myself.

The floor of the interrogation chamber was indeed littered with cigarette butts. Sheriff Cong, the man who had arrested me, was in charge of the proceedings. He had a young recording clerk at his side. When I sat down in my designated seat, I was puzzled to find that it was attached to the floor. Then I remembered how Li Yuhe, the hero of the model opera

The Red Lantern, had fought his Japanese captors by flipping over a table, and I understood that the chair had been nailed down to prevent me from using it as a weapon. My interrogators were certainly not taking any chances. I glanced from their faces to the cigarette butts on the floor, but this was not the moment to stoop over and snatch them.

Sheriff Cong began with a verification of routine facts: name, place of birth, class status, etc. He then turned to the same tactic that my political instructor and party secretary had used on me at Shaanxi Normal University. Instead of telling me why I was being detained or charging me with a specific crime and asking me to confess, he told me to make my deposition first. As if the reason for my arrest were a riddle to which only he knew the answer, he had turned the interrogation into a guessing game.

From the point of view of the authorities, the more I revealed the better. The much-touted official policy was: "Lenience for confessors— severity for resisters." I had grown up believing that a person was guilty until proved innocent and had, over time, become a master of beating around the bush whenever I was required to make a self-criticism. By confessing to the most trifling offenses that I could, I thought, I would obtain the clemency promised in the slogan. Having the right to remain silent was a concept I could never have imagined at that time.

On the other hand, since resisters were punished severely, it was unthinkable to stonewall an interrogator. I knew that my captors might resort to beating me because the system lacked even the most minimal legal safeguards. I believed that I had developed the internal resources for dealing with such a beating if necessary and was prepared to take whatever they dished out. Nonetheless, I preferred to try to dodge their blows if I could.

With all this in mind, I launched into my confession, starting with how I had gone to Beijing to seek redress and how I had put up big-character posters at Shaanxi Normal University. But Sheriff Cong, obviously uninterested in such peccadilloes, cut me off. Then he started to grill me about a mimeographed journal titled *People Today*, which had been officially deemed a "reactionary" underground publication. Its chief editor, a former student, was now a resettled worker at the Number Two Brickyard, but his assistant, a middle school teacher, had been arrested, charged with conspiracy, and executed a few years earlier as an active counterrevolutionary.

I had once owned a thick volume of *People Today* and thought that the term "reactionary" was an exaggeration, since it was an apolitical journal filled with romantic, sentimental poetry and essays.* Still, it had met with surprisingly ruthless suppression. While I had been detained at Shaanxi Normal University, the authorities had sent some people to my house to confiscate my copy. My terrified sister had managed to thwart them by quickly dumping it in the trash, although they entered a black mark in my dossier nonetheless. But that case was ancient history. What was the point of rehashing it now? I decided that Sheriff Cong was merely using it as a red herring, intended to unnerve me.

Then he changed his tack and asked me if I'd been a member of the workers' literary club at the Number Two Brickyard. Immediately I went on guard, as if he'd jolted me with an electric shock. I was well aware that association with any suspicious clubs could result in charges of counter-revolutionary conspiracy. I remembered an evening of poetry and wine with some former cultural propaganda workers who had been consigned to the brickyard. I had composed a poem on the occasion, containing the following couplet:

Standing on high, I survey the enclosure;
Cup lifted, I sink into drunken despair.

Alarmed, I wondered if one of the other fellows had gotten into trouble. But Sheriff Cong's mention of the so-called literary club had sounded tentative. I realized that he was just probing at random, hoping to extract some information from me, and decided to stonewall him.

But then he suddenly asked me what Russian books I had read and what I had translated. Now the answer to the riddle was rearing its ugly head. As I had feared, the charges against me stemmed from the letter requesting a copy of *Dr. Zhivago* that I had mailed to the Moscow University Library. I confessed to having written the letter.

"Did they send you the book?" Sheriff Cong pressed, suddenly interested.

* The Cultural Revolution was an exceptionally puritanical period, during which depictions of romance between the sexes were essentially banned from literature and art.

"No, they never did."

He ended the interrogation session at that point, ordering me to reproduce the contents of my letter from memory, both in the original Russian and in Chinese translation. While he and his assistant waited outside for me to complete my task, I seized my chance to scoop up all the cigarette butts on the floor. Once I had written the required document, I was escorted back to my cell.

A few days later I was interrogated again, primarily for the purpose of checking my deposition. Back in my middle school days the Communist Youth League had come into our Russian class and given us Soviet pen pals. I had been assigned a girl from Novosibirsk named Lyuda, who had sent a photo of herself sitting on a park bench in a nice dress with her hair in pigtails and a handbag on her knees. This early correspondence had later inspired me to write to Moscow University.

In my own defense, I claimed that I had not been aware that there was anything wrong with writing a letter to the Soviet Union. After all, such correspondence had been encouraged in my middle school; in fact it had been sponsored by the Communist Youth League as an expression of Sino-Soviet friendship. Sheriff Cong was unconvinced. I could tell by his tone of voice that he suspected me of more far-reaching motives than merely borrowing a novel. But what on earth was I being accused of? The authorities could speculate as they wished and charge me with whatever they pleased. Their goal for now, however, was to get me to confess to having written the letter so that they could trump up their charges against me.

I talked my case over with Professor Liu and Fourteen, who tried to comfort me with the assurance that such a trifling offense did not deserve a sentence. In their opinion, I would probably be released during the customary amnesties around the Western and Chinese New Year. But Number One was still reserving judgment. An old hand at this, he admonished me against indulging in wishful thinking. While acknowledging that my letter was indeed a trifle, he reminded me that the authorities had free rein when it came to deciding what charges to bring against me.

"Now we're supposed to call the Soviets revisionists or social-imperialists, instead of the friendly big brothers they used to be. They've become China's number one enemy," he said. "Why didn't the police come for you when they intercepted your letter more than a year ago? Why did they wait until now, when the Soviet revisionists have occupied Czechoslovakia? Your case is heavily political, so they might decide to make a mountain out of a molehill."

His analysis was going way over my head. "If they charge you with collusion with a foreign country," he explained, "you'll have to serve some time." He added that once the police got their hands on you, they were going to keep you in their grasp, even if they knew it was an injustice. If they let you off too lightly, they might as well be slapping themselves on the face.

"It's easy to land in the slammer but hard to get out," he sighed. "That's the way it goes around here. Get with it, man! They'll let you know soon enough."

22

Food Fantasies

OURTEEN ROLLED A couple of cigarettes with the tobacco from the butts I had gleaned, and I watched as Number Six and Number Nine took on the challenge of lighting them without matches. First, Number Nine extracted some cotton stuffing from my mattress, snapped a few sorghum bristles off our whisk broom, twisted a wad of cotton around each bristle, and laid them on the bunk. Then Number Six rubbed a brick rapidly back and forth on top of them until we smelled smoke. Ripping off a wad of fuming cotton, he coaxed out a few precious sparks by fanning it in the air and blowing gently. It was child's play to produce smoke, but generating sparks was tricky, as the cotton would not ignite if you waited too long or blew too hard. We discarded a heap of singed cotton and broom bristles before getting it right. Professor Liu watched in trepidation from the sidelines as we played with the forbidden fire, but he did not try to stop us.

In the throes of nicotine withdrawal, I thought wistfully of my confiscated pack of Diamond brand cigarettes. People often said that a postmeal cigarette was heaven on earth, and this was true for me as long as I was well nourished. But I soon learned that smoking while subsisting on scanty rations of corn gruel was an entirely different matter. Once Number Six had lit a cigarette, he handed it to me, and I greedily inhaled a couple of drags of smoke. To my surprise, I was overcome with nausea rather than pleasure. With head reeling and hands tingling, I started to retch and had to lie down on my bunk to recuperate.

My cellmates whiled away the hours with an ingenious, if primitive, form of textile manufacture. Although I never tried my hand at this enterprise, I let them help themselves freely to the generous stuffing in the thick new mattress my mother had just brought me for the winter. Holding a homemade spindle in one hand and spinning it with the other, they would coax a fiber out of a wad of cotton and twist it into a thread with their fingers. Then they would intertwine several of these threads into a strand thick enough to be woven into cloth. Among other things, they made me a pair of sock protectors, cozy covers we wore over our socks to spare them the wear and tear of scuttling around on our wooden bunks all day.

They also cleverly contrived makeshift pencils from empty tin toothpaste tubes. First they cut off the stiff ends of the tubes, which contained the raw material for the pencil "lead." After beating the chopped-up tin into a thin, cylindrical shape with their rice bowls, they attached it to a whittled stick, and presto!, a pencil.

It was against prison regulations for inmates to have pencils. Even if the authorities assigned you to write an essay in the cell, they always collected all the pencils again as soon as they could. I understood that certain items posed a risk for inmates inclined to attempt suicide or jailbreak, but I simply could not imagine why we were forbidden to have pencils, which hardly seemed like lethal instruments.

Fortunately I had my cellmates' homemade pencils and a supply of blank paper from home, which I used to record Fourteen's mouthwatering descriptions of imaginary culinary tours of Xi'an. Whenever he felt hunger pangs, he reminisced lovingly about the delicacies at all the famous restaurants along the four main thoroughfares inside the Xi'an city wall, from the East Gate to the central Bell Tower and out to the West Gate, and from the South Gate to the Bell Tower and beyond, to the North Gate. I wrote down the name of each restaurant and its specialty, as well as his detailed recipes for Xi'an Muslim dishes, such as cured lamb, mutton soup with flatbread, pancakes stuffed with baked lamb, and honeyed sticky rice wrapped in bamboo leaves.

Fourteen's descriptions reminded me of treats I had enjoyed as a child, and I jotted down some of my fondest memories too. There were street markets galore in Xi'an in the early 1950s, before private enterprise was swallowed up by the state during the Great Leap Forward. We had an endless variety of food right in Kaitong Lane, where I lived, with plenty of restaurants, street stalls, and door-to-door peddlers with carrying poles. Most of the food was cheap, often costing only a few pennies. For example, at the gates of my school on chilly winter mornings, vendors sold hot, steaming bowls of creamy date soup or almond-scented wheat porridge. For a few cents more, I could add a twisted cruller to dunk in my porridge or a sesame flatbread sandwich filled with comb-shaped fried wontons.

Food rationing was still unheard of in those days, and the street markets were as colorful and earthy as they had been before the Communist takeover. People used leaves of lotus or bamboo to package takeout orders of cured pork or sticky rice with red beans or dates. One popular stall on Luoma Street sold sweet, clear rice liquor, heated in a dark bronze kettle, sprinkled with fragrant yellow laurel, and served in a crude pottery bowl decorated with blue flowers. Another vendor had shallow black china bowlfuls of cool white bean jelly cubes, flavored with hot pepper oil, garlic, and perfectly mixed mustard sauce. One bite of this pungent concoction, slurped with red chopsticks, was spicy enough to make customers' eyes water. On the way home from a show on a cold winter night, people could sit on the benches at the stalls near the entrances to the small lanes and feast on hot sour mung bean meatball soup for a dime. The steamed dumplings for sale outside the East Gate were as puffy as steamed buns, and rich but not greasy, while the vendors along West Boulevard served numbingly spicy steamed mutton with raw garlic. Roast chicken glistened with oil in the streetlights there, beside wheelbarrows piled with chopped lamb scrap meat tinged with red food coloring. Inside specially shaped, lidded wooden basins, smoked pork hearts, lungs, and intestines were arranged as they had been in the pig's belly. This was called bang bang pork, named after the tapping rhythms the vendors beat on their wooden basins to attract customers.

Alas, all these regional specialties disappeared after the Great Leap Forward.

With Grandfather at Silent Garden, I learned to appreciate the simple pleasures of Buddhist vegetarian cuisine. In the spring Grandmother plucked the succulent reddish green leaves of the Chinese toon tree in the south corner of the garden for her cold tofu salad with sesame oil; they were faintly bitter but left a sweet, grassy aftertaste. In the summer we sent pleasant chills down our spines with hot sour noodle soup, seasoned with a leafy twig of red Sichuan peppercorns picked fresh from the tree in our rear courtyard. In the late fall we harvested overripe, frostbitten pumpkins, which we could steam until they were mealy and sweet, or braise in soy sauce, so that they tasted like hot roasted chestnuts, or mince with five-spice powder for a dumpling filling that rivaled any meat. Every day in the winter we had carrots, diced and cooked with soy sauce and MSG or tossed with white cabbage in a colorful chilled salad to accompany our red bean porridge. Grandfather's name for carrots was mini-ginseng roots, and he told us they were very nutritious.

Grandmother had a special recipe for a cool, refreshing summertime drink that was supposed to have a detoxifying effect. First, she sun-dried her fresh-picked young bamboo leaves, honeysuckle buds, and pink mimosa petals. Then she steeped them in boiling water, producing a golden herb tea that she sweetened with a pinch of sugar. Grandfather's favorite drink was longevity tea, brewed from knotweed tubers; this was the legendary drink of the He family of ancient times, who were supposed to have lived to a ripe old age without going gray thanks to the knotweed growing in their well. We had knotweed vines on the walls of our side courtyard, and Grandfather said that the white portions of the tubers nourished your qi, or inner energy, while the red ones enriched your blood. Every fall I dug up the sweet potato–size tubers, washed and dried them, sliced them with a bronze knife, and mixed them with black beans. Then I steamed this concoction nine times, drying it in the sun each time, eventually resulting in a black paste, like herbal medicine in a Chinese pharmacy.

I wondered how Grandfather was. I had been in detention for more than a month, and he was probably still waiting for me to bring him the eight-treasure rice pudding I had promised. I had no idea how much longer I would be held in custody and was afraid that he might not live to see the day of my release.

In addition to keeping food memoirs, I used the homemade pencils to work on my English. Professor Liu had taught English before the Communist takeover and still remembered it even though he had been behind bars for many years. He made me a vocabulary list on the blank pages of my copy of Mao's *Selected Works*, which I memorized to while away the seemingly interminable hours between meals. I also studied English translations of Mao's quotations and poetry, which my parents had sent me upon request. Since Mao was the sole author we were permitted to read, these were my only English textbooks.

Number One, an excellent calligrapher, also agreed to give me some lessons. Our homemade pencils were inadequate to the task, however, so Fourteen and Number Nine offered to improvise a writing brush and ink for us. They fashioned the brush handle with ease from our whisk broom, but the brush head was a tall order. Fourteen extracted a tuft of black wool from his overcoat, but it was too soft and unwieldy, so I let him yank out a bunch of my hair, which was rather wiry, and he bundled it together with the wool to stiffen it. Number Nine figured out how to make ink. He had a pair of black homespun trousers, dyed with natural vegetable coloring, which bled heavily in the wash. He soaked them in a basin for a few days, allowing the inky sediment to settle to the bottom, and then poured off the clear top layer of water, leaving a thick black residue. After repeating this process several times, he scooped the resulting black liquid into a soap dish and put it on the windowsill to evaporate and thicken for a week.

When the ink was ready, Number One spread a sheet of paper on my bunk and inscribed some model characters for me to copy. Despite the makeshift brush and watery ink, he managed to produce deft, powerful brushstrokes, which nicely fleshed out his upright block lettering. Lacking a continuous supply of ink and paper, however, I was unable to practice until Professor Liu had a brainstorm. The wooden surfaces of our bunks had been burnished with the sweat and friction of many inmates over the years. Suggesting that I paint characters with water on this glossy surface, Professor Liu got a bowl of water, dipped the brush into it, and demonstrated. I followed his lead and began to practice, wiping off the wood each time I had filled it up.

My day was full of lessons. After breakfast I memorized English vocabulary words, practiced my spelling, and recited quotations from Chairman Mao or had dictation practice with Professor Liu. At midday I filled a bowl of water to practice my calligraphy. After the weather turned cold, it was too chilly in the cell to sit still on the bunk all day long, but I lacked the energy for vigorous exercise. Sometimes Fourteen and I did a bit of ballroom dancing in the space between the bunk and the wall, just to get our legs moving. I sang all the songs I remembered from my *Two Hundred Famous Songs from Foreign Lands* as we waltzed languorously back and forth between the door and the urinal.

We all ran out of steam in the afternoons. Prolonged semistarvation had taken its toll on our health. Professor Liu sat ashen-faced on his bunk, leaning limply against the wall and groaning softly; his stomach tied itself in painful knots when it was empty. Number One, who had adapted to life in jail, sat cross-legged on his bunk all the time, conserving energy with his eyes closed. Although he was gaunt, his skin was tawny, and he still had some pep. Number Seven and Number Nine kept busy with their weaving, using up the new stuffing in my mattress.

Fourteen was the liveliest occupant of the cell and a great raconteur, whose vivid tales of his youthful pre-1949 escapades took my mind off my growling stomach. He had been a playboy, patron of numerous prostitutes, and had done time in a Guomindang prison for street fighting in the Muslim quarter. As he reminisced, he crooned the popular songs from the brothels and dance halls of those days and described their former locations in detail. I mentally followed his verbal map as he guided me through all the red-light districts of the city, from Chrysanthemum Garden to the Kaiyuan Temple.

Number Six, a rather antisocial man, was a thief who had been in and out of jail countless times. This time he had been caught digging through the wall of a bank. When he heard I was from the Number Two Brickyard, he embraced me as a soul mate and regaled me with accounts of his experiences at Camp Willow, part of the Malan Farms labor camp complex in northern Shaanxi. He had fond memories of the abundance of local potatoes and apples there when they were in season. His descriptions moved me to fantasize about Malan Farms and even to imagine that such a destination might be a desirable outcome for me. Pathetically I had begun to focus on obtaining lenient treatment, as my hopes of release waned with each passing day.

The harmony in our cell proved fragile, however. I provoked a fight that completely shattered the peaceful little world we had built so painstakingly. There was a long-standing rift between Fourteen and Number Six. I had learned this on my first day in the cell, when Fourteen cautioned me to beware of Number Six, calling him a hoodlum and a fink.

Number Six used prison-issue bedding. His quilt was stuffed with a sparse layer of low-grade cotton that had clumped together inside its cover, leaving numerous bare patches. It was freezing in the cell, and his request for a new quilt had been ignored. Every night he slept huddled up into a ball inside his thin quilt. At bedtime he always wanted to shut our tiny window, which was our only source of fresh air. But if he did, the stale odor of the urinal and unwashed bedding was overpowering. Since I had a warm quilt, I always opened the window after he had shut it. We bickered constantly and gradually became enemies. Professor Liu counseled me not to squabble with Number Six about the window, urging me to show some compassion. But Fourteen egged me on.

"It's against the rules for him to climb up on the windowsill the way he does," he said, "so you won't get in trouble even if you beat him up." Standing on my tiptoes, I could open the window, which was near the ceiling in the northeast corner of the cell, but Number Six, who was a short man, practically had to clamber onto the windowsill to close it again.

One evening we got into a scuffle. I kept opening the window, and he kept slamming it shut. Finally, he lost his temper. The blood rushed to his cheeks, and his neck bulged.

"You counterrevolutionary!" he snarled.

This incensed me, and I pounced on him. We started to grapple on a bunk, making a ruckus in the night that brought the security guard and warden rushing into our cell.

"Why don't you pick on somebody your own size?" barked the warden, noticing how tall I was compared with Number Six.

"He hit me first," I protested. "I was just trying to stop him from climbing up on the windowsill at night."

"Why were you doing that?" the warden demanded, turning fiercely on Number Six.

Number Six, normally rather taciturn, stammered out a vague reply.

"You son of a bitch!" yelled the warden. "You've been plotting a jailbreak!" Then he questioned everyone in the cell about Number Six's behavior.

Fourteen seized the opportunity to stab Number Six in the back, asserting that he climbed onto the windowsill and gazed outside on a regular basis. Taking a huge nail and some rope made of knotted cloth strips out from under Number Six's bunk, he handed them to the warden. In fact Number Six had saved the nail, which he had extracted from a loose spot under his bunk, for innocent purposes, and the rope was for tying up his luggage. But it was against the rules for him to possess such things at all, to say nothing of climbing onto the windowsill. Now he was in a bind; the warden had both witnesses and incriminating evidence.

Realizing that it would be impossible to vindicate himself at this point, Number Six vented all his fury on Fourteen, bypassing me. For a long time he had been watching Fourteen's every move and storing up evidence against him. He took out the small knife that Fourteen kept hidden under his bunk and gave it to the warden, reporting Fourteen at the same time for rolling cigarettes. Fourteen retaliated by telling how Number Six had made fire. Now desperate, Number Six blabbed about everything he could think of, no matter how trivial. First he took my calligraphy materials out of my bag and told the warden about our homemade writing brush and ink and my calligraphy lessons. Then he squealed on Fourteen and me for dancing in the cell and on the others for spinning thread and weaving cloth. Between the two of them, they spilled all our secrets.

The next morning after breakfast the door clanked open, and several wardens came in to conduct an inspection of our cell. They confiscated my pencil and writing brush, our spinning and weaving equipment, and all our homemade products and handcuffed Fourteen and Number Six with their hands behind their backs. Number Six's crime was "plotting a jailbreak," while Fourteen's was "instigating illicit activities." Number One and Professor Liu were also accused of covering up for us.

The warden rattled a pair of handcuffs in my face. "It'll be your turn next unless you start behaving."

Now two of our little group of seven were handicapped, and we all suffered along with them. Their wrists swelled and turned black and blue, the pain of the constricting handcuffs hampering all movement. Everyone was too angry at Number Six to help him eat, so his food sat untouched in his bowl. He stonily refused to ask for help, until Professor Liu finally took mercy on him and spooned the cold gruel into his mouth. I waited on Fourteen, taking charge not only of his feeding but also of his entire process of urination. The torture was the worst at night; the handcuffs made it impossible for the victims to find a comfortable sleeping position or even to lie down and get up without help. Number Six passed out on the third day, and we yelled for the warden, who came and unshackled both men. Applying a traditional acupressure technique, Number One pinched Number Six's philtrum until he recovered consciousness.

I blamed myself for their suffering. Knowing that I was bigger than Number Six, I had gotten carried away. But it had been a mistake to antagonize a thug like him. The quality of prison life depends in large measure upon the relations between cellmates, and the pointless discord that I had instigated had negated all our industrious pursuits.

When I was first locked up, a few green leaves had been clinging to the tree outside our tiny cell window, but they all had turned yellow and fallen off by now, leaving the branches bare. Two months had passed, and it was late November. At around eight o'clock one evening we got word that someone was going to be released. It was customary to do this after dark, in order to preserve the city's image of respectability by keeping the prisoners out of sight.

When we heard the news, each of us promised that if freed, we would visit the family of someone who had been left behind. I agreed to do this for Professor Liu, who was extremely worried about his wife and children, having heard nothing from them since the raid on his house more than two years earlier. Although he lived near the South Gate, a ten-minute walk from the detention center, he might as well have been buried alive.

Then Fourteen resumed his tales of restaurant hopping and had gotten as far as the intersection of Duanlümen Street and East Boulevard. He had entered the China Café across the street from the Northwest Theater and had just ordered a bowl of hot fermented sweet rice seasoned with yellow laurel when the cell door burst open.

"Number Two, get your bags ready. Pack your bag, and make it snappy," barked the warder from the doorway.

Elated, Fourteen turned to me. "You're a free man, brother," he informed me fondly. "You'll even be in time for a bowl of fermented sweet rice at the China Café tonight!"

Everyone congratulated me and pitched in to help me pack. Believing that I was on my way home, I bequeathed my thick mattress to Fourteen, so that my former cellmates could continue to weave cloth from its stuffing.

After the door had clanked shut behind me, I heard the muffled sound of Fourteen's excited voice: "He's going to taste fermented sweet rice tonight!"

自述

23

The Verdict

LADEN WITH MY huge backpack, I followed the warden down the main walkway, out the heavily guarded main gate, and into a spacious office. To my surprise, I did not see any cadres from the Number Two Brickyard there. That did not bode well since it was standard practice for correctional institutions to return freed prisoners to their original work units. My heart sank as I realized that I might not be released. Sheriff Cong, my interrogator, and a young, unfamiliar cadre were waiting for me in armchairs. They approached me as I came in, and the young cadre announced that I was going to receive lenient treatment, thanks to the relatively clean confession I had made. I breathed a sigh of relief, thinking that maybe I was going to be released after all. Then he took out a printed document and launched into a rapid-fire reading. As I stood there, dazed in the glare of the lamps, my mind kept wandering at critical moments, and I was unable to absorb most of what he said. When he had finished, he handed the document to me in triplicate and told me to sign it. I skimmed it and deduced that what he had meant by "lenient" treatment was three years in the labor camps.

The nature of the criminal charges and the description of the "facts" of the case rankled me. "I can't sign this," I said. "It's full of mistakes."

"So, you're refusing to sign, are you?" he replied darkly. "If you want a battle of wills, let's have one tonight. We have all the time in the world. But you'll end up the worse off for it."

I held my ground.

"Don't take this signature business too seriously, though," he admonished me. "The prisoner's signature is just a formality. The verdict takes effect whether you sign or not. But I'm warning you, if you keep making trouble, you'll be accused of denying the charges and obstructing justice, and you'll get slapped with a longer sentence."

I knew I was defeated. I signed the verdict, took my copy, and followed the warden to the holding cell for convicted criminals, which was in the second row of cells on the east side of the building.

At that moment I realized how shortsighted I had been to leave my mattress behind for my cellmates. Without it, I would have to sleep on a bare wooden plank tonight and every night for the foreseeable future. I told the warden that I had forgotten the mattress, and he sent one of my new cellmates to retrieve it for me. I wondered what Fourteen and the others were saying about me now. Were they still fantasizing about me enjoying a treat at the China Café? This new cell was my only "café," and the printed verdict was my "treat," a treat so bitter that it took me all night to swallow and digest it.

For the first time in my life I lay sleepless until morning. In a stupor I stared at the dusty lightbulb, which shone all night long, until my eyes burned and my neck ached. Then I took out the verdict and studied it, milking it for every shred of information I could find. Each word stung like a pinprick to my scalp.

I had earnestly quoted Chairman Mao in the petition for redress that I had written in Beijing, believing that apt quotes from Mao, whose words were regarded as "supreme directives," would win my case for me. But now, in an ironic twist, the Military Control Commission of the Xi'an Security Bureau was invoking Mao as its authority, and theoretical underpinning, for my sentence. Following the obligatory format of the times, the verdict opened with a quotation from his "little red book":

Supreme Directive

Our state is a people's democratic dictatorship led by the working class and based on the worker-peasant alliance. What is this dictatorship for? Its first function is to suppress the reactionary classes and elements and those exploiters in our country who resist the socialist revolution . . . or in other words, to resolve the internal contradictions between ourselves and the enemy.[1]

The verdict itself was headed: *"Decision Regarding the Labor Reeducation of the Criminal Reactionary Element Kang Zhengguo."* The charge that I was a criminal reactionary element, which harked back to Mao's quote, was an escalation. Shaanxi Normal University had expelled me as a "reactionary student," preserving my status as "one of the people" despite my alleged thought crimes. Now, however, I was being categorized as an "enemy of the people" according to Mao's framework.

I read on. The first paragraph summarized my reactionary history and reactionary family background:

> Kang Zhengguo, male, twenty-four years of age, of Huwang Village, Huaqing Commune, Lintong County, Shaanxi Province, Han nationality, landlord class background, a student, college dropout, current resident of 80 Kaitong Lane, Xi'an. Grandfather, Kang Jiyao: a criminal landlord element. Father, Kang Shensheng: a criminal, once sentenced to labor reform, later released and employed at the municipal waterworks, now in custody of the masses. The criminal, Kang Zhengguo, attended Kaitong Lane Elementary School and No. 8 and No. 2 Middle Schools from September 1951 to July 1963 and the Chinese Department of Shaanxi Normal University from September 1963 until his expulsion on December 25, 1964, for reactionary thought crimes. In March 1965 he became a laborer at the Jian'an Construction Materials Plant of Xi'an. In detention since September 19, 1968.

---

[1] *Quotations from Chairman Mao Tse-tung* (Beijing: Foreign Languages Press, 1967), pp. 37–38.

I believe that one should be held accountable for one's own crimes, which have nothing to do with one's family. But the Communists believe in visiting the sins of the fathers on their children in the name of class struggle and that reactionary traits are inherited. There was a popular saying during the Cultural Revolution: "If the father is a reactionary, the son is a bad egg." By starting off with my "reactionary pedigree," my verdict implied that Father's and Grandfather's criminal statuses somehow justified my punishment.

However, the facts in the verdict were grossly distorted. Shortly after 1949 Father's work unit had committed him briefly to a detoxification facility to cure him of his opium habit, but he had never been convicted of a crime. Asserting that he was a criminal was an intentional smear to create the illusion that Grandfather, Father, and I, three generations of reactionaries, represented what Mao regarded as a criminal reactionary class, which the state dictatorship had to suppress.

The second paragraph described my crimes:

> Investigation has revealed that after being expelled from college and becoming a resettled worker at the construction materials plant, the criminal Kang Zhengguo continued to behave as a diehard reactionary. He took advantage of the Cultural Revolution to try to reverse the correct verdict against him. Worst of all, on May 12, 1967, using the pseudonym of Kang Zhen'guo[2] and the false return address of the Xi'an Foreign Languages Institute, he sent a letter to the Moscow University Library in the revisionist Soviet Union. He was seeking a copy of the counterrevolutionary novel *Dr. Zhivago* by the traitor Pasternak, which had just been denounced in *People's Daily* the day before. The said criminal also took the opportunity to attack China's criticism of this reactionary novel and to plot collusion with the enemy in counterrevolutionary activities. In accordance with the directive "Regulations for Increasing Public Security in the Cultural Revolution," it is hereby decided that he shall spend three years in labor reeducation for reactionary thought crimes and scheming to

[2] In written Chinese, "Zhen'guo" looks entirely different from "Zhengguo."

collude with the enemy. His term, which began on September 19, 1968, will terminate on September 18, 1971.

Military Control Commission of the Xi'an Security Bureau
November 16, 1968

I was being sentenced to three years in the labor camps merely because I had written to the Moscow University Library to borrow a novel. But the verdict delved into my past and twisted the facts to make it seem as if this act had been an outgrowth of my ingrained reactionary stance rather than simply an isolated whim. It occurred to me that my trip to Beijing might have led to my current predicament. Maybe the petition I had submitted to the Cultural Revolution Leadership Group had found its way back to the brickyard and provoked the authorities into having me apprehended.

I could see from the detailed description of my letter that the police had my original letter to Moscow, and I wondered how they had gotten it. Had they learned about it from my confession, or had they known beforehand? I had written it in Russian and, thinking myself clever, had indeed used the Xi'an Foreign Languages Institute as the return address on the envelope, although I had given my real address on the letter inside. The accusation that I had used a pseudonym was false, however. I had signed my name in Russian, which the Chinese censors had retranslated back into Chinese as Kang Zhen'guo. I decided that they must have intercepted the letter before my arrest.

As I pursued this line of thought, it finally dawned on me that the police probably censored all letters to and from foreign countries. What a fool I had been! I had never even dreamed that my letter would be plucked from the mailbox before it was sent out, inspected by the police, and easily traced back to me. But why had they waited more than a year to prosecute me?

It made no sense to charge me with collusion with the enemy. Although Sino-Soviet relations had deteriorated to the point where "enemy" was an accurate designation, I certainly had not colluded with the Soviets. The charge implied that I had exchanged sensitive information with them, threatening China's national security. After all, the release of *Dr. Zhivago* had been announced in *People's Daily* and was hardly a state secret.

The error of my ways was finally becoming clear to me. The first time around, I had been expelled from college and sent to the brickyard for writing letters to Li Zhimin. Now I had been branded a criminal reactionary element and sentenced to three years in the camps, again because of a letter. I lay on my bunk, overcome with wave after wave of remorse. My heart ached as my parents' repeated admonitions echoed in my ears.

"You got yourself into this mess by studying foreign languages to become a translator," I said to myself, facing the wall. "None of this would have happened if you hadn't known Russian!" I leaped up, grabbed the English and Russian translations of *Quotations from Chairman Mao* beside my bunk, and stuffed them into my backpack. Fear of being prosecuted for desecrating Mao's works was the only thing that stopped me from tearing them into shreds and pitching them into the urinal.

"I'll never read another foreign book or study a foreign language again for as long as I live!" I vowed.

24

The Holding Cell

THE HOLDING CELL was a crowded limbo for transient prisoners, ranging from condemned criminals to people on their way to the labor camps. New arrivals like me streamed in, clutching their verdicts, and sat poring over them dazedly. Some complained vociferously, while others merely sighed to themselves or sat in the corner muttering in desperation.

Pathetically, my cellmates envied my "light" punishment. In their opinion, I was lucky to have been sentenced to labor reeducation, treatment usually considered too gentle for "enemies of the people," rather than bona fide prison. This was the party line, and I had heard it before but had not swallowed it, as my cellmates had. Frankly, I did not think it made much difference and did not feel that I had special privileges during my time in the holding cell.

With its Antirightist campaign of 1957, the party created about five hundred thousand rightists and had to establish the labor reeducation system as a legal rubric under which to send them to the camps along with common criminals. The law authorizing this innovation was signed by Premier Zhou Enlai himself. Even though people were still being stripped of their rights and freedom, the newspeak term—"labor reeducation" instead of "labor reform"—cloaked the system in humanitarianism and created the illusion that it was designed for the edification of the younger generation.

Since labor reeducation was not considered a true prison sentence, in the early years people were not told how long they would be behind bars. Once you had seen the error of your ways, the party promised, you would be released. The drawback of this for the Communists was the economic burden of supporting large numbers of prisoners indefinitely, which became unfeasible during the waves of famine and depression that followed the Great Leap Forward. Unable to afford their upkeep during this period, the government released a number of such prisoners and began to limit people's sentences.

Labor reeducation was capped at three years, the main reason it was seen as a lighter punishment than labor reform. However, because it was regarded as a light punishment, the police had the authority to sentence people without the kind of due process, however perfunctory, that was still required for labor reform. If you offended your boss, for example, he or she could, with a single phone call to the police, arrange to have you sentenced to labor reeducation on vague charges of "troublemaking."

Shrill radio news broadcasts wafted into our cell all day long from the nearby main office. It was late 1968, a period of political campaigns and crackdowns. The prisons swelled with new arrivals, and a number of people landed in our cell for "vicious attacks on the Great Leader Chairman Mao."

One of them was a scrawny middle-aged administrator from a defense factory on the eastern outskirts of town. During a political study session, he told us, he had aimlessly picked up a pin and poked a few holes in the *Guangming Daily News* on his desk. When he went out to the bathroom, one of his colleagues had leafed through the newspaper and discovered that the pinpricks had penetrated to Mao's picture on the back page. The colleague had reported his find to the party. The poor administrator, now deemed an active counterrevolutionary, had been charged with a "vicious attack on the Great Leader" and locked up in a cow pen, where he had endured savage beatings. Then he had been turned over to the police, sentenced to four years, and transferred to our holding cell.

Another man, a worker at a commune-run factory in the city, had carelessly shattered a plaster figurine of Mao while dusting a table. Aware of the dire consequences of his error, he had furtively wrapped the fragments in newspaper and sneaked them into the trash. Unluckily for him, however, this act had not escaped the eagle eyes of the chairwoman of the neighborhood committee, who was always on high alert for sabotage by class enemies. She had extracted the fragments from the trash and handed them over to the police, who had apprehended him, charged him with deliberately and viciously trashing Mao's image, and sentenced him to six years.

There was also a teenage boy from the backcountry, with the slurred speech of mild mental retardation, who had received a seven-year sentence for writing counterrevolutionary slogans. A local counterrevolutionary group had apparently crowned him as its figurehead "emperor" and egged him into scrawling "Down with Mao Zedong" and "Down with Lin Biao" on the school blackboard. He did not know what had become of the group of conspirators, but he had fortunately been tried as a minor and had the advantage of his poor peasant origins. If he had been an adult or a member of a landowning family, he could easily have gotten the death penalty and a summary execution. He and I exchanged mementos when he left the cell. I gave him my enamel mug, and he presented me with me a lovely big bowl made of woven wheat stalks coated with black shellac. Although the shellac was smelly, the bowl was light and durable and came in handy later in the camps.

One evening the door suddenly opened, and a new convict came in. His bedroll was disheveled, and he seemed completely beside himself. He stood muttering unintelligibly in the space between the bunks, where I was pacing back and forth until the sight of him stopped me in my tracks. We stared at each other in astonished recognition.

"Guozi?" he asked, using my childhood nickname. "What are you doing here?"

"Mr. Wang!" I exclaimed. "What are you in here for?"

"Never mind," he replied bitterly, stamping his foot and shaking his head.

Relieving him of his bedroll, I encouraged him to sit down. Before launching into his tale of woe, he fished out a depleted pack of Peony brand cigarettes and handed them around cordially.

"These are left over from my daughter's wedding," he told us. "She and my new son-in-law just came back from Kunming, and he brought them to me in the cow pens. The guards took away my whole carton during their search, but luckily I had one more pack stashed away." He took out his lighter and lit our cigarettes. Not daring to inhale deeply, I puffed lightly instead, savoring the rare treat. The tips of our cigarettes glowed amid swirls of smoke in the glare of the bare lightbulb. A pleasurable sensation suffused my limbs; I felt giddy, as if riding on a cloud.

Mr. Wang was one of the old drivers from the city waterworks, an authentic member of the proletariat who had been a chauffeur for various capitalists before 1949 and had been employed at the waterworks ever since the purchase of its first jeep. He knew my family well because he often drove Father to and from work. Father had told me that he had been a staunch conservative at the beginning of the Cultural Revolution and had antagonized the rebels by opposing their defiance of the entrenched party committee. The rebels had started trying to frame him as soon as they seized power and had gotten their chance one day when he had unfortunately blurted out, "Down with Chairman Mao," instead of "Down with Liu Shaoqi," while teaching his children to shout slogans. Even though he was an old proletarian, he had been branded a counterrevolutionary and slapped with a five-year sentence. As he told his story, he reminded us indignantly that he had always been a faithful servant of the party.

I inquired about Father and the rest of my family. Mr. Wang told me that he had been in the cow pens with Father, and Father was fine. He was popular at work, and since he had neither enemies nor significant blots on his record, he had merely been required to do his share of routine manual labor. However, Grandfather had passed away shortly after my arrest and had died asking his aide why I had not brought him the eight-treasure rice. Shuzhi was working on a farm, waiting for a job assignment from her school, and Shuci had followed Mao's call for youth to settle in the countryside. Mother was doing manual labor far from home with her colleagues and students. Zhengguan was home alone with no school to attend and had recently stopped by to visit Father at the cow pens, bringing a cough syrup bottle full of liquor. Father had shared the liquor with him, Mr. Wang told me cheerfully, and then he started to hum a few bars of Shaanxi opera. I remembered that he was an opera buff, who had sung in many amateur performances at the waterworks. His verdict listed his fondness for opera as one of his crimes, accusing him of singing "old operas that glorified feudal emperors, kings, generals, and ministers." The rebels had apparently felt the need to pad the flimsy criminal charges against him with whatever nonsense they could dredge up.

By then I had seen quite a few verdicts, and all were travesties of justice.

Mao's image had become a monstrous totem and a convenient outlet for people's aggressions. At the same time, the nation had gone paranoid, endlessly pillorying people on trumped-up charges of attacks on Mao. Suddenly the copies of Mao's works in my backpack seemed like time bombs. Terror gripped me as I thought of the English vocabulary lists Professor Liu had inscribed for me on the blank pages. I wished I could erase them, but I could not imagine where to find an eraser.

Mr. Wang was soon sent off to the labor camps, and one mid-December morning I found out that my turn was next. Mindful that I was being banished to a faraway place, I packed my precious possessions with the utmost care. I had recovered my wallet, which still contained cash and ration tickets, and as I stuffed it into my pocket, I wished I could run out and buy a couple of sesame seed cakes. Inside my old pack of Diamond brand cigarettes I found my remaining seventeen cigarettes, plus the half-smoked butt left over from the day of my arrest. I quickly polished off the butt while the clerks were taking care of my exit paperwork in the office. They soon emerged, one carrying a bulging briefcase; the other strapped my bedroll onto my shoulders and handcuffed me. Thus encumbered, I would not have been able to run far, even if the opportunity had arisen. I was told that I was going to be marched to the He Family Temple Provincial Labor Reeducation Detention Center and that I must obey the rules on the way: to stay near my guards and not to talk to anyone I met.

The leaden sky threatened snow. Winter cabbages lay in piles in the fields and shop doorways, while gusts of nippy wind stirred up the dirt and fallen leaves on the ground. I trudged along, sandwiched between two police officers, my bedroll constantly slipping off my shoulders. Most passersby stepped skittishly aside when they caught sight of the fearsome manacles on my wrists.

When Lin Chong[1] was tattooed and marched into exile in a cangue,[2] his buddies held a farewell banquet for him and watched over him during his journey. Xia Minghan, the Communist whose final, shackled march to his execution is immortalized in *Poetry of Revolutionary Martyrs*, secured his place in history by leaving behind impassioned verse. But at that moment I cut a wretched and ridiculous figure rather than a grand or tragic one, and I was mortified to think I might run into someone I knew.

When we passed a restaurant at the main intersection of Yellow Goose Village, I asked permission to stop and buy some sesame seed cakes, but my request was denied. I plopped down onto the ground, claiming that I was too weak to take another step, and my escorts started to prod me. This attracted a small crowd of onlookers, in front of whom I insisted loudly that I would not be able to continue without buying some food. Most of them eyed me scornfully, but one middle-aged woman was moved to pity and begged my guards to let her buy me the sesame seed cakes. They flew into a rage, shooed the crowd away, and cantankerously shoved me to my feet.

The corn gruel I had eaten for breakfast had done little to stave off hunger, and my bedroll seemed heavier with each step I took. I began to fear that I might collapse by the frozen wayside. But people have a hidden reserve of endurance that they can squeeze out if necessary, like the last drop of moisture in a sponge. Gritting my teeth, I forged ahead until I finally reached the He Family Temple Detention Center.

---

[1] An outlaw hero similar to Robin Hood, from the classic Chinese novel *The Water Margin*.

[2] A heavy wooden yoke worn by prisoners in imperial China.

25

Induction

T HE DETENTION CENTER was a gathering point for convicts from all over Shaanxi on their way to the labor reeducation camps at Malan Farms. There we received a humiliating initiation while we waited for a large batch of us to accumulate so that we could finish our journey.

Instead of cramped cells, we all lived in one huge barracks, which we kept spick-and-span, military style, neatly folding our quilts on our wooden plank bunks every morning. The door was unlocked, but there was a watchtower above us, manned by a squad leader around the clock. When we needed to go out to the toilet, we had to call out for his permission and wait for his response.

All day long we sat on our bunks with bowed heads, poring over the newspapers and Mao's works, reflecting on our errors and writing confessional essays, while the cadres dropped in constantly for spot checks and impromptu struggle sessions. At the first one of these sessions that I witnessed, a couple of pickpockets who were waiting to be shipped back to Malan Farms after a thwarted escape attempt were forced to stand up and confess their crimes. The audience pressed them to acknowledge any additional crimes they had committed while at large, but they insisted that their only violation of the law had been the robbery for which they had been arrested.

At subsequent struggle sessions, everyone was forced to stand up and confess to the group. Since we all were new arrivals, and none of us knew the others, this was a form of self-introduction. The confessions were supposed to be thorough, dredging up the so-called root causes of the crime and including revelations of further, previously undisclosed offenses. At the end of each session the cadres handed out paper for additional confessions, warning us that this was our last chance to earn lenient treatment through cooperation and that our sentences would be doubled if we withheld information that came to light later. "Lenience for confessors—severity for resisters," was their slogan, but only greenhorns fell for it. The hardened criminals, on the other hand, had a comeback:

"Lenience for confessors"
Means a sentence toting bricks.
"Severity for resisters"
Free at New Year's——get home quick!

The veteran criminals, like the two pickpockets, claimed to have learned this principle from bitter experience. Knowing better than to confess to anything unless they had been caught red-handed, they stuck to the motto "If a thief has left no trail, he should stay as tough as nails." Thus we had one blustery struggle session after another, but no one ever confessed anything important.

The head of our group, a former army platoon leader, strutted around in a spiffy green uniform, although he was an inmate himself. Early in his career he had seemed poised for a bright future in the army. But tragedy had struck when he had divorced his peasant wife, who had then leaped to her death from the train on which he was taking her back to her village. Blamed for her suicide, he had been expelled from the party and sentenced to three years of labor reeducation.

His style of dress, and his swaggering, reminded me of my class monitor at Shaanxi Normal University. Basking in the faded glory symbolized by his old uniform, he seemed to revel in the power granted him by the party to conduct struggle sessions. They were supposed to be merely pro forma, but he infused them with vitriol, hauling out his quota of wretches for attack every day. Starting at the brickyard, I had attended countless struggle sessions without ever having had the misfortune of being victimized at one. But now I felt that the possibility was uncomfortably close. Nervously I hoped we would leave for Malan Farms before my turn arose, sensing that the group leader had his eye on me and had put me on his blacklist.

Luckily a bizarre episode provided some unexpected cover. During one particularly scathing struggle session a ruddy-faced guard came in and called me aside. Alarmed, I left the struggle session with him, wondering what I had done wrong. He ushered me into an empty room, closed the door, and told me to sit down. Then he went out and peered around the corridor before starting to speak. His unease suggested that he might be planning to use the pretext of chastising me to request a favor in private. I remembered him from the day of my arrival, when he had been one of the guards who had demanded to see my written verdict. I had noticed him because after reading it, he had exclaimed to his colleagues, "Wow, a college student!" His name was Squad Leader Yang.

Alone in the room with me now, he launched into an official interrogation but then suddenly shifted gears.

"Do you know how to write poetry?" he asked out of the blue.

"You've come to the right person," I replied in surprise. "I write old-style classical poetry."

Pleased, he handed me some papers. "Read these poems and comment on them," he commanded tersely, as if assigning me to write a confessional essay.

Despite his peremptory tone, I could see that he wanted me to polish the poems for him. He shut me in the empty room like a student taking a test, while he paced back and forth outside the door, pretending to guard me and masking his nervousness with a deadpan expression. This was after all a prison, and guards were forbidden to relate to inmates on a personal level.

Mao's poems, which were tremendously popular, had spawned many inferior imitations. Young readers untrained in Classical Chinese had no appreciation of the technical subtlety of Mao's craft. They seemed to think that composing poetry was a simple matter of stringing together hollow, fine-sounding phrases with seven syllables per line. They deemed their four-line poems "truncated verse" and their eight-line ones "regulated verse," but they seemed blissfully ignorant of the complicated rules for tonal patterns, antithesis, and allusion.

Squad Leader Yang's poetry fitted into this category. His diction was choppy, and his vocabulary impoverished. His verse was mere doggerel, dashed off according to formula and crammed with hackneyed phrases and slang. I had little appetite for polishing such compositions, but I was moved when I realized that they were love poems dedicated to a peasant woman named Hongmei, who seemed to be the author's fiancée. A guard who could develop even a crude literary sensibility in the barbarous surroundings of the detention center was certainly a cut above his oafish colleagues, who did nothing but stuff their faces and harass the inmates. The poems needed a thorough revamping, so I adopted Squad Leader Yang's poetic voice and poured out love lyrics, addressed to Hongmei, that turned out to be quite a departure from his original. When he came back into the room, I gave him a frank explanation of the flaws in his poetry to justify my revisions. To my surprise he accepted everything gladly, took the poems, and stuffed them into his pocket, but I did notice that his face was even redder than usual.

From then on, he kept churning out poetry for me to polish. One snowy day, when he was monitoring one of our struggle sessions from his watchtower, he shouted down to me to come outside. The flurries in the air seemed to have stirred some crude poetic impulse in him. Weighting a piece of paper with a clod of dirt, he threw it down to me. It was a writing assignment. He wanted me to compose a spin-off of Mao's 1936 poem "Snow," which describes a "northern landscape" enveloped in "ten thousand miles of whirling snow."

Infected by his enthusiasm, I returned to the struggle session, where I tuned out the ugly shouting all around me and scribbled a poem for him. When it was finished, I wrapped it around a clod of dirt and lobbed it back up to him. He caught it and opened it. I could see his lips moving atop the tower as he recited it with apparent pleasure.

The poetry I wrote for Squad Leader Yang was nothing more than an exercise for me. It was not heartfelt, and I dismissed it from my mind as soon as I wrote it. But I thanked my lucky stars that my uniformed group leader seemed to have no inkling of what Squad Leader Yang and I had been doing, although I doubted whether he, with his convict status, would have dared confront Squad Leader Yang. At any rate, the days passed, and I managed to avoid being victimized at a struggle session.

One day after New Year's 1969, Squad Leader Yang tipped me off that we were soon to be transferred to Malan Farms and offered to help me mail a letter to my family from outside the detention center. I thanked him from the bottom of my heart and gave him my letter that afternoon.

At the crack of dawn the next morning the brigade leader ordered us to get up and pack for the trip to Malan Farms, and he read out the rules for the journey. After breakfast we lined up in the yard, where we were frisked and each issued a big steamed bun, our lunch for the road. Unable to wait until lunchtime, I wolfed it down right away. During this period of semi-starvation I always gobbled up food as soon as I got my hands on it, without worrying about hoarding it or stretching it out.

We were herded like cattle onto a big truck and handcuffed together in pairs, the left hand of one person shackled to the right hand of the other. An armed guard stood in each of the four corners of the open truck, and more guards with terrifying machine guns were poised for action in the driver's cabin in front. The wintry morning mist obscured my view of the route we took out of Xi'an. As the truck gathered speed, the biting wind whistled by, until I felt as if I had been doused from head to toe with ice water and had turned into a chunk of frozen meat.

When we finally completed our 125-mile journey to Malan Farms headquarters that afternoon, I gradually thawed out, gingerly wiggling all my stiff extremities until they recovered some sensation.

26

A Shattered Dream

I FIRST HEARD TELL of Malan Farms from Zhao Yi, a distant relative of mine.

Until his arrest during the Antirightist campaign, he had been on the Shaanxi Party Committee, where he was the secretary's favorite aide. Then he had been banished to labor reeducation at Camp Jiangnan in the Malan Farms complex, along with many eminent rightists. Sent home to Xi'an during the famines after the Great Leap Forward, he had found work mixing cement and hauling bricks on a construction site. Eventually the leaders of the party committee had decided to offer him his old job back, on the condition that he write a self-critical essay. This he had obdurately refused to do. As if determined to be an embarrassment to the committee, he had responded to his old boss's call for a meeting in bare feet and dirty work clothes. Upon his arrival he had picked a fight with the gatekeeper, who had denied him entry to the building, and his old boss had had to retract his offer of employment. After drifting around town for some time, Zhao had decided to relinquish his urban residence permit, leave his wife and children with her parents in the city, and move back to the countryside in Lintong to take care of his aging mother. There he had become a commune member.

His wealthy in-laws, who owned a secluded single-family house in a back alley of Xi'an, had been a natural target for the Red Guard raids of the fall of 1966, but they had been spared by a stroke of luck. The marauding Red Guards, as unfamiliar with the terrain as out-of-town bandits might be, had relied on tips from the local neighborhood committee regarding which houses should be ransacked. The committee had marked the gates of all targeted houses, including Zhao's, with paper signs. Frightened, the whole family had cowered behind locked doors awaiting disaster. But a gale had blown away the sign one night, and the Red Guards had missed their house. By this miracle, Zhao's enormous library had remained intact. I lived nearby, so I often visited him to borrow books after mine had been confiscated.

As a misfit in the educational system I had studied alone in my youth and had never been able to find a teacher or even an adequate conversation partner. My chats with Zhao, whom I met as a young adult, were my first tastes of the pleasures of conversation as a learning experience. Whenever I heard that he was coming to town for a visit, I went to his house, where he plied me with tea and cigarettes deep into the night as I listened to his edifying opinions on a wide range of topics. Unlike the other elders in my life, who tried to toe the political line, Zhao never wagged his finger at me, and I felt that I could speak my mind frankly to him. Whenever I did, he would peer at me with a twinkle in his eyes and launch into a diatribe that made my ideas seem tame by comparison. He could discourse intelligently on all my interests: classical Confucianism, history, philosophy, poetry, painting, calligraphy, and even twentieth-century literature and the Western classics.

I was his match when it came to Chinese or Western humanities, but I had to shut my mouth when he held forth about the Chinese revolution or Marxism. His understanding of Chinese Communist Party history, the Comintern, and the works of Marx and Engels was eye-opening for me. He could trace his party lineage back to the original northern Shaanxi branch and was a Soviet fellow traveler and classical Marxist. He had read Marx, including *The German Ideology*. From the very beginning of the Cultural Revolution, he had suspected Mao's motives and recognized that it was a farce; he recommended that I read two of Marx's works, *The Eigh-*

teenth Brumaire of Louis Bonaparte and *The Civil War in France*, to shed light on current events.

Zhao won my heart with his outspoken opposition to Mao, whom he disliked both politically and personally. Although I had been called a reactionary student, I was hardly worthy of the label. My aversion to Mao was merely a superficial objection to his cult of personality, and I knew little about intraparty power struggles, purges, or the revolution. Zhao, however, was an insider. Before 1949 he had been a leftist student who had run away to Mao's base area in Yan'an. Later, as an aide to the secretary of the Shaanxi Party Committee, he had witnessed the inner workings of the Communist Party. He had determined that Mao was a despot shortly after 1949, after hearing some of Mao's outrageous speeches to party cadres, as summarized by Wang Zhen.[1] Wang had quoted Mao as saying, "The cadres' job is to rule six hundred million Chinese people, and I am the Red Emperor!" Mao had also said, "Leadership boils down to intervention. You must control everything," and, "China has no true minorities, only different ethnic groups. There's nothing wrong with Han chauvinism! Han people make up ninety-four percent of the population, including plenty of proletarians."

I have Zhao to thank for prodding me into looking beyond my own personal dissatisfaction to see my problems in the larger context of the mistakes of the Chinese Communist Party. The only one of his beliefs that I found unconvincing, although I was not knowledgeable enough to critique it intelligently, was his blind conviction that the Soviet Union was a model of socialism and that the Soviets could do no wrong. Still, he was an immensely satisfying conversation partner, and when his visits to town were too infrequent, I would start to feel terribly bottled up.

He reserved his most devastating criticism of Mao for late at night behind closed doors. His interpretations of Mao's poetry were hilarious. My favorite was his reading of Mao's 1961 quatrain "The Fairy Cavern," ostensibly a description of a scenic cave on Mount Lu in Jiangxi, as an erotic poem. Zhao claimed quite convincingly that the "sturdy pine in the gathering dusk" in the first line of the poem was a metaphor for Mao him-

---

[1] A veteran Chinese Communist, born in 1908, who served as vice-premier of China from 1988 until his death in 1993.

self, while the "heavenly" Fairy Cavern stood for his wife, Jiang Qing. Zhao's hobby was traditional Chinese medicine, and he had studied *The Medical Classic of the Yellow Emperor* and a number of ancient sex manuals. He asserted that in such texts "sturdy pine" and "fairy cavern" were standard metaphors for the male and female genitalia and that he had it on good authority, a high cadre in the Northwest Bureau of the Central Committee, that the senior Communist leader Kang Sheng had procured heaps of pornographic reading material for Mao back in the Yan'an days.

Zhao also wrote old-style poetry, and we exchanged a number of poems. He particularly admired a couplet in one of the poems I composed for him, which went as follows:

> How can I escape to Peach Blossom Springs?[2]
> If only I could smuggle a sledgehammer to Bolang.[3]

He called me a "promising young man,"[4] but in fact my poem was sheer bombast, and I had no intention of taking such radical action against the despotic regime.

Sometimes we even frightened ourselves with our talk, and Zhao would step outside and peer into the yard before returning to our conversation. In those days there was no telling when someone might be eavesdropping, but Zhao's single-family house provided us with the privacy we needed. We talked until we were exhausted and Zhao, who had bronchitis, started to cough uncontrollably. Then his wife would emerge to quiet us down, and I would get up and slink out in embarrassment. As soon as I stepped out into the night, I was terrified that someone might have overheard us, and could not help anxiously looking back to make sure no one was following me.

Zhao, a self-taught practitioner of Chinese medicine, was an expert on

---

[2] An allusion to a poem, by the fourth-century poet Tao Yuanming, describing a Shangri-la where a group of people had hidden for several centuries from the tyranny of the Qin dynasty.

[3] An allusion to an unsuccessful attempt by Zhang Liang to assassinate the Qin emperor (a despot to whom Mao is often likened) in the third century B.C.E. at a place called Bolang. Zhang later became the strategist for Liu Bang, founder of the Han dynasty, which replaced the Qin.

[4] Another allusion to Zhang Liang.

the pulse, acupuncture, and moxibustion.[5] He tinkered boldly with his prescriptions and had cured some stubborn illnesses gratis for family and friends. From him I gained valuable exposure to the classic texts of Chinese medicine and the rudiments of its practice, and he presented me with a set of acupuncture needles as a gift. Since natural science texts were the only books other than Mao's works that were allowed at Malan Farms, while I was at the detention center in Xi'an I had asked Zhengguan to bring me the Chinese medical handbooks and acupuncture needles I had gotten from Zhao. Following his example, I took them with me to the labor camp, where I thought they might come in handy.

Zhao's stories fueled my romantic fantasies about Malan Farms. We human beings are weak, pathetic creatures; in desperate circumstances, we compromise and lower our expectations. During my time at the detention center, as it dawned on me that release was out of the question, I started to look forward to going to Malan Farms. According to Zhao, there was a huge library at Camp Jiangnan, and many famous writers and professors were gathered there. Ridiculous bookworm that I was, in my imagination Malan Farms took on a poetic luster. I likened my banishment to that of the Russian Decembrists, who had managed to sustain their intellectual pursuits in their Siberian exile. I expected that the inmates at Malan Farms would be extraordinary and would include plenty of people like Zhao.

After my arrival, I discovered that I had been right to bring my medical equipment, but that my fantasies about Malan Farms had been sheer indulgence in my old habit of foolish, melodramatic daydreaming. After the Antirightist campaign, Malan Farms had operated several labor reeducation camps set up along a river, but later, as the rightists were gradually released, these camps had filled up with common criminals instead. By the time our group arrived in 1969, more than a decade after the Antirightist campaign, only Camp Willow, where I was sent, was still used for labor reeducation, but few rightists remained. Now it was full of juvenile delinquents, mere boys serving sentences for petty crimes. When we lined up to go out for work, I stuck out like a tall, slim white poplar tree in a clump of bushes.

[5] A traditional Chinese medical treatment involving the transdermal application of smoldering *moxa* (the herb mugwort) to the patient.

In the yard at Camp Willow I found that I recognized 20 or 30 percent of the inmates as veterans of the Number Two Brickyard, and most of them were thieves. They had a standing joke that the brickyard was their alma mater, as if they had been graduates of the same school and had been promoted to Malan Farms. I thought that the term "alma mater" was especially applicable to my experience, as the brickyard had in fact been my "prep school" for the labor camps. In addition to initiating me into prison life, it had given me an opportunity to network with a wide variety of jail-birds, so that from then on I saw familiar faces everywhere I went.

I had arrived too late. The extraordinary individuals I had hoped to hobnob with had either died or vanished. There was no one at Malan Farms I could learn from, unless I wanted to become a career criminal after my release.

27

An Overdose of Potatoes

ON OUR WAY to Camp Willow, the mountain outpost of Malan Farms, we stopped at general headquarters, which was down in the plains, to get warm and grab a bite to eat, and then we lined up behind our brigade leaders for the arduous four-mile climb. My backpack was overloaded with the books and clothes my parents had sent, and I, like everyone else, was debilitated from my long confinement in the detention center. We had to stop constantly to catch our breaths, and all of us were completely worn out by the time we had crossed a couple of ridges. Fortunately the cadres from Camp Willow had sent some seasoned prisoners down to meet us halfway and cart our luggage to the top. Otherwise we would never have made it, even if we had kept trudging until midnight.

Most newcomers, along with anyone else who might conceivably run away, lived within a walled compound in a large brigade, which was divided into small groups for all activities. Our group, which was formed upon our arrival, attended daily political study with Instructor Lu, who kept up the process of humbling us that had begun at the detention center by organizing constant struggle sessions, some large and some small.

At mealtimes, when everyone reported to the main yard in groups, our pale faces distinguished us from the veteran prisoners. Now that we were laborers, we were eligible for increased rations of fifty pounds of grain per month, much more than we had received at the detention center. Day in and day out we were fed cornmeal produced on the premises, receiving rice or steamed buns made of white flour only on holidays. Breakfast was usually a bowl of corn gruel and a small cornmeal bun, and lunch and dinner consisted of a large cornmeal bun and a bowl of vegetables. Although no one felt well nourished, the longtime prisoners managed to subsist on these rations. But we insatiable, scrawny newcomers from the detention center kept sniffing around the yard between meals like wild dogs, looking for scraps of food.

Some people tried to ingratiate themselves with the prisoners who staffed the kitchen. If they greased the right palms with cigarettes, they were rewarded with the privilege of helping with the cleanup and nibbling some of the pot scrapings while they were at it. One young newcomer named Wang Jianzhong, who came from a high-ranking military family and had been arrested as a hooligan, was particularly adept at this practice. He also begged shamelessly for people's leftovers, enabling him to recover faster than anyone else in our group, and his cheeks started to fill out visibly soon after our arrival.

Other newcomers bartered their clothing for cornmeal buns, often trading with the outside laborers. These were prisoners whose jobs as herdsmen, drivers, or stable workers required them to live beyond the compound walls, freeing them to come and go as they pleased. They had so many opportunities to forage on their own that they hardly needed their official rations and were in a position to prey upon the half-starved newcomers by trading their rations for the goods the newcomers had brought. Having swapped their leftover cornmeal buns for nice clothes, they then exchanged the clothes with local peasants for more food to bring back to the camp, which they used to fleece the newcomers some more. One day soon after my arrival a sentry caught one of these outside laborers leaving the compound with a bagful of clothes after a meal. An official investigation revealed that he had gotten all of them in exchange for his leftover cornmeal buns. The clothes were confiscated, and he was stripped of his outside work privileges and clapped back into the brigade.

Some of the younger, more effeminate newcomers granted sexual favors to the homosexual prisoners in exchange for food. In our group there was a dainty young fellow from a song and dance troupe who walked with a wiggle, made eyes at all the men, and deliberately let a few wisps of hair straggle out from under the brim of his army cap. He smoothed his skin with perfumed face cream, leaving a fragrant trail in the air when he walked by. Soon after his arrival he was dubbed Second Little Sister and got catcalls wherever he went. Some of the men took liberties with him and even stroked his cheeks or slapped his bottom in public. He accumulated throngs of admirers, who kept him well fed. At mealtimes the servers even dished him out bigger helpings than they gave other people.

Then there were the charlatans like Liu Zhiyuan, who hoodwinked people into giving him food. He was a former conscript laborer from the Number Two Brickyard, whom I had first met at the He Family Temple Detention Center. I got along well with him because he had an educated manner of speaking and showed an interest in my handbooks of traditional Chinese medicine. Duped by his endless bragging, I planned to join him in his exploits after my release from the camp and lent him my acupuncture needles and medical handbooks.

Later, during a struggle session against him, I found out that he was a brazen, ignorant quack and that he had been using my equipment to treat prisoners' illnesses in exchange for their leftover cornmeal buns. He had ultimately taken his hoax too far, talking his way into the camp headquarters, where he had taken the cadres' pulses and written herbal prescriptions for them. When they had gone to the traditional Chinese pharmacy to fill the prescriptions, the pharmacist had spotted some errors, which had been verified by the camp medical staff. Furious, the cadres organized a struggle session against Liu and threw him into the maximum security brigade, where they beat him into submission. Then they bawled me out for lending him my equipment, which I eventually retrieved from him.

With the mountains blanketed in snow, we were cooped up every day for meetings, political study, and struggle sessions, where the cadres made us report one another for two infractions I'd never heard of before—unauthorized food consumption and profiteering—which referred to our transactions with the outside laborers. The camp was rife with such activities, despite the campaign from above to stop them, since we had few other ways to supplement our meager rations of three servings of coarse grain a day. We were so closely supervised that we had virtually no opportunities to do anything on our own. Our group lived together in the same barracks and shared a bucket of food at each meal. Every morning after breakfast we assembled our ranks for roll call before following the brigade leader into the fields, under the watchful eyes of armed sentries. At the end of our shift we returned as a group, after which we had roll call again. Trusty inmates guarded the main gate and every corner of the compound around the clock.

The plowing group, which consisted of prisoners who had almost completed their sentences, existed in a sort of halfway house. Considered at low risk for running away, these men went outside independently on various assignments, although they still lived within the compound. Now, during the idle winter months, it was their job to gather firewood to heat the rooms for our meetings and political study sessions. While they were out, they were free to visit peasants in the mountains or to go into the town of Malan, order meat at restaurants, and bring things back for other people.

The plowing group kept all the best firewood in its barracks. On our day off every Sunday I went there to visit friends and bask in the glowing embers of the oak wood fire, which gave off a baking heat that dried out my eyelids and almost scorched the knees of my padded cotton trousers. One of my friends there was Heizi, a former conscript laborer from the Number Two Brickyard, who was kind to me because we both had known Ermao. Whenever I dropped in, he took out a leftover cornmeal bun and used his sickle to cut it into thin slices, which he sprinkled with salt and red pepper, toasted over the fire, and gave to me. Informing me that newcomers were usually released from the brigade at some point, he predicted that I would be transferred to the orchard group in the spring. Supervision was much more lax there, since the orchard group was full of ordinary citizens assigned to manual labor, including students and workers from Xi'an. In his opinion, as long as I could be trusted not to run away, the cadres would not keep a former student like me under strict surveillance forever.

Heizi offered to go shopping for me when he went out to gather wood, so I gave him my secret supply of cash and ration tickets and asked him to get me some food. When we first arrived at Camp Willow, the cadres had told us to exchange all our cash for scrip, promising that we would have the chance to purchase what we needed from a traveling vendor who visited the camp periodically. They did not permit us to keep cash and warned us that anyone who did so risked blacklisting as a potential runaway. But I had heard long before my arrival that it was a good idea to keep some cash and ration tickets, so I had hidden my supply in the insoles of my cotton-padded, rubber-soled shoes. Heizi helped me make secret purchases of white flour steamed buns, snacks, and cooked meat, which took the edge off my cravings and greatly relieved the misery of my early days in the camp.

Heizi also helped me smuggle my first letter home through the post office in the town of Malan. We were not allowed to seal the letters we mailed from camp, since they were censored by the brigade leader. It was forbidden to mention hardship or despair or even to ask our families to send food. We had to confine ourselves to platitudes like "The government is treating us well" and "Everything's fine here" or "I'm trying to reform myself and turn over a new leaf as quickly as I can." When letters failed to meet these guidelines, the brigade leader confiscated them or returned them to their authors for rewriting. Most people were willing to take the risk of smuggling letters out, so that they could speak their minds.

At the same time that hunger was eroding our pride, it was also accentuating our selfishness. Obsessed with food, I sent home endless greedy requests to my parents to mail me things, without stopping to consider the hardships I might be creating for them. Drooling at the sight of the treats that the other prisoners from Xi'an received in their packages from home, I made long, detailed shopping lists for my parents: thin egg noodles, flour fried in beef fat, meat jerky, hot pepper sauce, and so on.

My family responded promptly with packages containing most of the provisions I craved. One night, someone stole the meat jerky Shuzhi had sent me, so I bartered some of my clothes for a small wooden chest where I could lock up my stash. My new riches cheered me up and gained me prestige, along with entry into the clique of prisoners who got regular shipments from Xi'an. On Sundays we huddled over a small stove to share our goodies. At one of these feasts I opened my mouth and declared, "Every cell of my body yearns for food." This turn of phrase hit the nail on the head for everyone. Years later I bumped into one of these former fellow inmates on the streets of Xi'an. Recalling my pithy remark, he took me out to a fancy restaurant to reminisce over dinner.

But there were also plenty of have-nots, who had to make do with their meager rations because they had no cash, ration tickets, extra clothes to barter, or packages from home. Knowing they were on their own, they somehow found the courage to endure hunger. One of these fellows, whose name was Chen Kejian, slept in the bunk next to mine. After the Sunday meal he yanked his quilt over his head and tried to sleep. Although he was aware of our feasts, he pretended not to be and never seemed jealous. If I offered him some tidbit, he always refused politely, accepting only if I insisted and then not without excessive displays of deep gratitude. Like me, he had come from the Number Two Brickyard, but I had never met him before because he had worked on the west side while I had been on the east. He told me that he was the unwanted child of a broken home. His father, a former officer in the Guomindang army, had perished in a labor camp shortly after the Communist takeover. His mother had remarried quickly, abandoning him to his impoverished grandmother, and he had dropped out of middle school and run away. Later he had been picked up for stealing and sent to the Number Two Brickyard for two years. After completing his sentence, he had stayed on for a time as a resettled worker but eventually returned to a life of vagrancy. Then he had been sentenced to three years in the labor camps and arrived in my group.

As my old cellmate Number Six had predicted, we often ate potatoes at Camp Willow, since they grew plentifully on-site. They were large, with purple skins and starchy, mealy flesh that stuck in your throat. Despite their abundance, I never got my fill of them during my first winter there because they were being kept in reserve for spring planting. In a clearing on the side of the mountain, at a higher elevation than our prison yard, was camp headquarters, which consisted of storage caves and houses for the cadres and guards. Above that was a row of potato cellars, which appeared as narrow openings in the grass. During the slack winter season the potatoes were sorted daily, and the few that were slightly spoiled were delivered to the kitchen, where the cooks pared away the mold and boiled the edible portions for us. Since only a few rotten potatoes were available each day, all we got was diluted potato slop, the color of dirty dishwater. As the weather warmed up, the cooks culled more potatoes from the cellars, and our soup got richer, reaching its peak during the spring planting, which required only the eyes of the potatoes. After the prisoners had excised the eyes with their sickles, mixed them with ashes, and sent them to the fields, the remaining potato flesh went to the kitchen, where the cooks rinsed it, chopped it up, and simmered it for us in huge cauldrons. At mealtimes everybody got a big bowl full of potato chunks, and there were plenty of leftovers. I was finally able to enjoy the abundance that Number Six had described for me. There was enough to satisfy anyone's appetite, no matter how voracious.

During the spring planting season a group of newcomers arrived from the detention center in Xi'an, their pale faces chapped and peeling from exposure to the sun and wind. After a few months in the camp I was becoming a seasoned prisoner, and the sight of the newcomers made me realize that I too must have looked like a hungry ghost at first. Unlike me, however, this group arrived during the once-yearly glut of food, which triggered an eating binge in one of the famished young newcomers. First he gobbled down his own potatoes, and then he polished off everyone else's leftovers until he ended up writhing on the ground in agony. There was nothing the doctors could do for him, and he died of a gastrointestinal obstruction. He had actually stuffed himself to death.

Such behavior was beyond my personal experience, but I had heard of it in an old nursery rhyme. When I was a child in Xi'an, flocks of crows would fly into town in the evenings and sit cawing on the trees, and we would stand beneath them and chant:

Fly away home, old crow, old crow,
Cook some beans for your ma, and cook 'em just so.
Your bowl makes one, and mine makes a pair,
Stuff her to death for all I care.

Stuffing oneself to death is animal behavior. In the spring we occasionally found bits of lamb in our bowls of potatoes because the shepherds were sending dead lambs over to the kitchen. As soon as the weather warmed up and the grass started to grow, the hungry sheep started gorging to make up for their long winter's deprivation. Some of the lambs ate uncontrollably, with deadly consequences. I had seen their carcasses, and their bellies were bloated like balloons.

It took our ancient forebears centuries to develop the concept of table manners, a significant marker of civilized human conduct. But prisons, especially Communist ones, tortured people with hunger, reducing them to subhuman behavior.

The day after the young man's death the cadres assigned me and one other fellow to prepare his corpse for burial. We found him in one of the caves near the potato cellars, next to a flimsy makeshift coffin. He reeked of fermentation. The decomposing potatoes in his belly had swelled him up until he was as round and stiff as a cylinder made of stone. We could not pull a clean pair of pants up over the bulge in his middle no matter how hard we tried, so we had to bury him with his pants down.

From that day on, the sight of the potatoes in our food buckets, with their pale greenish sprouts, always reminded me of the young man's distended belly and ghastly green face. Whenever I picked up my bowl of potatoes, I got a funny taste in my mouth, while the haunting nursery rhyme from my childhood kept ringing in my ears:

Your bowl makes one, and mine makes a pair,
Stuff her to death for all I care.

28

Sisyphean Labors

A S HEIZI HAD predicted, after a few weeks of indoctrination I was transferred to orchard duty along with a number of other new prisoners from Xi'an. There were four big orchards at Camp Willow, full of apple trees along with a few peaches and pears. Orchards One and Two were on the mountain near headquarters, while Orchard Three, to the southwest, and Beiyang Orchard, to the north, were on remote peaks. The hike uphill to the orchards from the barracks wore us out before we even started our hard labor at the top. The slightly increased rations at Camp Willow had bolstered my physical strength somewhat, but the endless, grueling labor still took its toll. Although I had suffered semi-starvation in my former prison cell, at least I had been allowed to spend most of my time loafing on my bunk. But now my tools felt like instruments of torture, and I was expected to work as unflaggingly as a machine, drawing upon hidden reserves of strength. No one ever dared rest unless our leader, Brigade Chief Yang, called a break.

We had two main chores in the orchards while the fruit was ripening: coating the tree trunks with limewash to repel insects in the early spring before the buds came out and spraying diluted pesticides on the branches and leaves once the trees had begun to bloom and bear fruit. We needed large quantities of water to mix the limewash and dilute the pesticides, but the area was so barren that we barely had enough to drink, to say nothing of maintaining the orchards. We had to haul the water on carrying poles from springs at the bottom of the ravine, all the way up to the orchards on their high mountain terraces. This task was usually given to able-bodied young men, unless the brigade chief assigned it to some troublemakers as punishment.

Brigade Chief Yang selected the water bearers on our first day in Orchard One. Since I was the tallest in the brigade, he chose me first. Next was Wang Jianzhong, who was also young and tall and looked well fed, with greasy skin and a hefty build. My pompous former group leader from the detention center, another brawny man, was chosen too. If he was unhappy about his assignment, he had only himself to blame for advertising his stalwartness by sporting his eye-catching army uniform. A few experienced water bearers rounded out the team, which was headed by the leader of the orchard group, Fu Xiangrong.

Brigade Chief Yang, an agricultural school graduate and a professional cadre, spoke with the broad accent of the central Shaanxi plains and was an impatient, stubborn man. He detested the wily prisoners and always chose good men, who led by example, to be his underlings. Fu Xiangrong, a worker with a booming voice from the Xi'an East Wind Instrument Factory, was a salaried inmate. This meant that he was guaranteed the right to return to his factory after his release from the camp and that he was regarded as more trustworthy than the rest of us. Unlike so many blustery jailers who enjoy hazing new prisoners, he was upstanding and kind and always ready to lend us a hand. He told me that the buckets were all roughly the same size, so there was no need to choose carefully, but it was important to have a good carrying pole. He selected a light, slightly curved one for me to try, then led us down to the bottom of the ravine.

The rugged, winding path to the bottom snaked through boulders and withered grass. It had been pounded out by my predecessors, who had left behind footholds or makeshift stone staircases in some of the steepest spots. After many trips I learned to switch my pole to my left shoulder during the easy descent, when the buckets were empty. This relieved my swollen, burning right shoulder, which I always used to carry the full buckets up the hill. I took my time on the way down, breathing deeply through my nose and trying to muster strength for the imminent upward climb, which I knew would be both strenuous and risky. One misstep, and I would fall flat on my back.

After I had filled my buckets, I would head for the top. At first the loaded pole did not feel very heavy, but my right shoulder soon started to ache. The discomfort increased until I began to fear that my shoulder joint was going to dislocate or fracture or that I might collapse on the spot. All I could do was try to alleviate the agony by boosting the pole up with my right hand. The discipline of the convict labor gang allowed no rest; moreover, there were no level spots where I could set my buckets down for a moment. No matter how long the path was, once I had shouldered the pole I had to make it to the top without pausing. Just as Sisyphus had been unable to relax even momentarily, for fear that his boulder would roll back down and crush him, I could not put my buckets down or their contents would spill.

Fu Xiangrong taught me that carrying water involved a certain degree of skill even though it was a menial task. The first technique I needed to practice, he said, was learning to carry the pole on either shoulder. The first time I tried to use my left side, the pain was excruciating and I could hardly keep my balance. But once I had shouldered the pole, I had to press on. Over time I built up my left side until it was as strong as the right. The swelling in my right shoulder subsided, and I noticed that I was developing muscles and calluses. Now my left shoulder was inflamed, but eventually that healed too, and the skin toughened up. Eventually I became as adept as Fu Xiangrong at the art of changing shoulders.

Next, Fu Xiangrong taught me some fancy footwork to prevent the pole from cutting into my shoulder like a deadweight. Keeping my shoulders rigid as I walked, he explained, would only make things worse. Observing his gait, I discovered that he swung his body to jiggle the pole with each short, powerful stride that he took. This jiggling motion relieved the pressure on the shoulder momentarily. Walking behind him and imitating his footwork, I managed to establish a rhythm and provide my shoulder with an ephemeral respite each time I jiggled the pole. During that precious moment the shoulder revived itself slightly. But that was not the only advantage to this technique. Jiggling the pole also helped keep the water from spilling. If I plodded woodenly to the top, the buckets would slosh, and I would lose a certain amount of water by the time I emptied it into the vat. Then Brigade Chief Yang would bawl me out or even force me to do some extra runs as punishment.

The former army man was worn out after a few days on the job. His ruddy complexion had gone sallow, and his furrowed brow had collapsed, so that he no longer looked preoccupied. He simply lacked the requisite physical strength. He thought that the brigade chief would give him an easier assignment if he kept writing essays about Mao's works. This trick might have worked in another group, such as that of Instructor Lu, who was concerned with ideology and indoctrination and would have taken his special military background into consideration. But Brigade Chief Yang was a practical man who did not set much store by political bombast.

One day the former army man turned up for work clutching his waist and groaning. Opening his shirt, he showed Brigade Chief Yang that he had strapped a piece of broken tile over his liver, which he said was inflamed. He had gotten the idea from a well-known newspaper story about a deceased hero, a zealous Maoist, who had used this home remedy for liver pain so that he could keep working despite a severe case of hepatitis. To the army man's surprise, Brigade Chief Yang was totally unmoved by his performance and even held it against him. He refused to relieve him of his water-bearing duties, and at the end of the workday he called an impromptu meeting and ordered him to stand up and confess to malingering. Yanking off the man's army cap, Brigade Chief Yang pushed his head down and swore that he was going to "cure him of his pigheadedness." But this fellow probably did deserve milder treatment than the rest of us "enemies of the people." He had been an army officer and a party member, and his crime had been somewhat accidental. Eventually Instructor Lu intervened on his behalf, and Brigade Chief Yang transferred him to an easier job on the pruning team.

Orchard One was the farthest from its water source, but the climb was gradual. I took this path at a measured pace, counting every step and breathing slowly through my nose to keep my heart rate down. If I allowed myself to pant, my throat would start to burn, and I would tire out very quickly. Sometimes I thought I was about to collapse by the wayside, but I managed to avoid having an accident by concentrating on counting the steps that I took and keeping my feet moving one after the other. People's legs often buckled beneath them on this job, and they stumbled and fell, spilling the contents of their buckets. They got themselves wet, but even worse, they made the path slippery, annoying the other water bearers.

Since I am a tall man, I dislike stooping and need to protect my back. I sewed together several layers of soft blue cloth to fashion myself a back brace such as those worn by athletes, moving men, and stevedores. It supported my waist like magic, and whenever I thought that I could not carry my pole any farther, I could always squeeze out one last drop of strength by tightening it a notch.

The spring for Beiyang Orchard was deep in the valley, a steep, sweaty climb up a long staircase carved in the hillside. Hidden in a gloomy stone hollow, the spring emitted a faint white vapor and was littered with dead butterflies. The place gave me the shivers, as if it were the netherworld, and I never lingered there longer than it took me to fill my buckets. The climb was so steep that I could not swing my pole as I usually did but had to reach out to grab the handles of my buckets and hoist them up with my hands. Every time I had to set out for that eerie spring, the mere thought of climbing back up those 250 steps was enough to give me a stitch in my side.

As arduous as the job was, I preferred it to the easier one of spraying insecticide because sprayers worked in teams under the watchful eyes of the brigade chief and the group leader and had little autonomy. As a water bearer I worked alone, accountable to no one but myself, and could often set my own pace. Even better, I could take it easy sometimes, as long as I had filled my quota. We water bearers often hurried through our work and then lay down on the hillside to stretch our limbs in the sun. Although the job was physically grueling, it was relatively carefree.

29

The Rope of the Law

ONCE THE PESTICIDE applications were complete, Brigade Chief Yang sent most of our group to help with the summer harvest, leaving only a few of us behind to guard the ripening fruit. I was assigned to watch over Beiyang Orchard, maybe because I had proved myself trustworthy as a water bearer by then. My main task was not so much to protect the fruit from potential thieves, who were rare in those barren hills, as to scare away marauding crows.

I lived in a thatched hut above the road, overlooking terraced fields planted with an early-ripening variety of crisp, juicy pears with a sweet melonlike flavor. Brigade Chief Yang had not given me much equipment for my job. All I had was a few firecrackers, a plaited hemp whip, and my basin and enamel rice bowl. When crows alighted on the trees, I could crack the whip, beat on my basin and bowl, or set off a firecracker, but usually it was enough just to charge down into the orchard, shouting and brandishing my whip.

My first days there were idyllic. Some of the pears were already golden ripe, and I devoured most of them. The few crows that approached the orchard were easily shooed away. I whiled away the days lolling on a sheet of plastic under a shady tree, nibbling pears, puffing on cigarettes, resting my worn-out limbs, and reading. I had gotten out my field guide to Chinese herbal medicines, planning to learn to identify some of the species that grew wild in the area.

From the doorway of my hut I could see the sunny slope of Tortoise Shell Peak, which was planted with wheat. Heizi, who had been forced to labor in the harvest there, had described lugging prickly hundred-pound bundles of wheat down the steep mountainside in the scorching sun, assailed constantly by tenacious horseflies. He told me that the job had destroyed an entire layer of his skin.

Heizi had been released and sent home, but I still had to endure two more autumn harvest seasons in the camp. It is frightening and depressing for prisoners to contemplate their sentences; the remaining time always seems interminable. Cracking my whip and shouting at the crows, I gazed pensively at the wheat fields until my reverie was interrupted by a stinging sensation in my arm. It was a huge horsefly, a species native to the Malan region. As I smacked it, I noticed that it had drawn blood and thanked my lucky stars that I was not toting the harvest down from Tortoise Shell Peak, in which case I would not even have had a free hand to use in self-defense.

Before long, my brief respite came to an end. The pears ripened, and crows flocked to the orchard. From dawn to dusk they attacked in droves, like American bombers over Vietnam in the movies, and I had to charge back and forth among the trees to scare them off. As soon as I drove them from one spot, they gathered in another, and as I chased them, damaged pears kept dropping to the ground. I made a slingshot but kept missing the crows and knocking pears down instead.

I had used up my firecrackers, my whip had snapped in two, and my voice was cracking. Meanwhile, the birds had turned defiant. When I shooed them off the branches, they would caw and wheel malevolently in the air like evil spirits from a witch's castle in some fairy tale, stubbornly waiting for me to relax my guard so that they could swoop down again. One day I did succeed in wounding one with my slingshot, and I tethered it by the leg in the hope that its cawing and flapping would deter the others, but to no avail. I kept carrying fallen fruit back to my hut and gorging on it.

Alarming bare spots were appearing on the heavily laden branches. What would I say to Brigade Chief Yang?

The job had turned out to be a hot potato instead of the reading holiday that I had expected. An outside laborer who herded sheep nearby told me that this happened every year. "You're in trouble even though you did your best," he said. "Your job is no picnic!"

One day Brigade Chief Yang came for a spot check. He was livid at the sight of the fallen fruit strewn under the trees and the flocks of crows circling overhead. Scolding me for negligence, he dismissed me from my duties and ordered me to fetch my bedroll and return to the brigade. Crestfallen, I obeyed, grateful that the dreaded wheat harvest at Tortoise Shell Peak was finished for the year, and I had been spared.

The autumn apple harvest was hectic, but at least we had plenty of apples to eat. Brigade Chief Yang distributed the rotten windfalls to us during breaks, and we also pilfered the unblemished apples whenever we could, gobbling them down while we picked the fruit on high branches, or sat resting under the trees, or carried heavy baskets. The Malan region was home to dozens of varieties of apples, and I tasted them all: early and late ripening, yellow, black, red, purple, and mottled, crisp, mealy, sour, sweet, or winy, and even ones that tasted like meat, persimmon, or banana. I ate them until my teeth ached and acid burbled up from my stomach into my throat.

It was the fall of 1969, a year marked by Sino-Soviet border clashes, and Lin Biao had just released his General Order No. 1, which mobilized the nation to prepare for war. Everyone, including the cadres in our remote labor camp, was frantically digging air-raid shelters and tunnels. Political purges in the cities forced many people out into the hinterlands, and numerous cadres were sent to rural May 7 Cadre Schools[1] for reeducation through labor. In this period of heightened tension the camp administrators regarded us as a risk to state security and took extra precautions against possible charges of lack of vigilance.

One November morning Instructor Lu summoned the entire brigade

[1] Named after a famous directive issued by Mao on May 7, 1966, stipulating that cadres spend time in special schools in the countryside to engage in manual labor and political study.

into the courtyard to announce that he had received orders from headquarters to evacuate Camp Willow immediately. Before we set out, there was a thorough inspection, which netted an array of ropes, knives, and other forbidden items, along with my private cache of foreign novels. Then we loaded our luggage onto horse carts, lined up in work groups headed by our leaders, and began our heavily guarded march to Camp May First, which was near headquarters.

Mystified, we wondered whether the transfer was routine or some kind of clampdown. A rumor buzzed through the camp that we were being transferred because the entire labor reeducation system was slated for abolition. We huddled in the cave dwellings at Camp May First, speculating about our fate.

"Do you really think they're going to send us all home?" my bunkmate Chen Kejian commented icily. "Dream on, men! They're not going to let us go that easily."

One evening at dusk, when the crescent moon had risen early in the west, the ground was frozen solid, and the air was so cold and dry that it hurt to breathe, we were summoned out into the yard for one of Instructor Lu's tongue-lashings. He began by admonishing us not to become complacent.

"If any one of you imagines that you've hit rock bottom once you've landed in labor reeducation, so you might as well do as you please, you're sorely mistaken!" he warned.

Pointing to a group of prisoners standing on the platform, he announced that they had been slapped with extended or harsher sentences. They were living proof that the "government" (cadres like him were fond of equating themselves with the government) could reconsider our sentences if we broke the rules or committed new crimes. Then he kicked off a new campaign, during which we would be rewarded for informing on others and confessing our own additional crimes.

"Reactionaries are swarming the earth these days," he told us. "And some of them are standing right here before you. Don't forget that there's going to be a crackdown on all you enemies of the people if war breaks out between China and the Soviet social-imperialists. Your only salvation is to make a clean breast of things and turn over a new leaf. If you're planning to put up a fight, you'll soon find out that you're beating your heads against a brick wall."

His harangue, delivered as always in the hackneyed wording of the official documents he constantly read aloud to us, failed to produce the desired effect of striking fear into our hearts. In fact nothing he said made any impression on us.

Next, a couple of brigade chiefs dragged a new prisoner onto the platform. Dressed in black cotton from head to toe, he was tall, with a big nose, curly hair, and a recalcitrant demeanor. His name was Gao Bin, and he was a member of an underground Christian church who had been sentenced to three years for proselytizing. Instructor Lu, who had no understanding of the concept of religious freedom, labeled him a cultist. He charged him with refusing to come clean, flouting the law, shirking manual labor, and being an "arrogant reactionary" in general. Then, announcing that he had orders from headquarters to bind Gao with a rope for all to see, he brought out a long, slender rope specially designed for torturing disobedient prisoners.

"The rope punishment is not all there is to it," he blustered. "This will be entered into his permanent dossier." Brandishing the rope at us, he explained that it symbolized the authority of the law and was called the rope of the law.

"Down with cultists!" the audience screamed. "Confess your crimes!"

Gao Bin was standing in silence on the platform. One of the brigade chiefs stripped off his padded jacket, leaving him clad only in his undershirt in the sub-zero weather. I shivered at the sight. The two brigade chiefs looped the rope around his neck and knotted it, then brought both ends down and bound his arms and wrists. Next, they yanked his arms behind him, threaded both ends of the rope back through the knot at his neck, and drew the rope up behind him as taut as a wound-up clock spring. They shoved him down into an airplane position, with his wrists high in the air behind his back and his head below his crotch. The audience kept shouting for him to confess.

I had seen this type of punishment before and knew that most people would have been begging for mercy by then, but Gao never said a word. As the brigade chiefs tightened the rope, my shoulders twitched and my head bowed in an involuntary empathetic response. The audience took up a chant from Mao's "little red book": "Everything reactionary is the same; if you don't hit it, it won't fall. This is also like sweeping the floor; as a rule, where the broom does not reach, the dust will not vanish of itself."[2]

Egged on by the disagreeable chant, the brigade chiefs pulled the rope so tight that it ripped Gao's undershirt. I noticed beads of sweat on his brow and steam coming from his nostrils. Then his breath became labored, and he collapsed on the platform.

---

[2] *Quotations from Chairman Mao Tse-tung* (Beijing: Foreign Languages Press, 1967), pp. 10–11.

30

Stolen Treats

MAYBE THE WINTER of 1969–70 was unusually harsh, or perhaps Camp May First's location deep in the ravine made it colder than Camp Willow. Whatever the reason, I always felt chilled to the bone during my time there. If I could have downed my morning corn gruel while it was still hot, I might have been able to warm myself up, but this rarely happened because we were not allowed to fetch our own breakfasts from the kitchen. Instead, the cooks ladled our rations into buckets, one for each work group. Then the prisoners on breakfast duty toted the buckets out to us and placed them in the open air in the center of our circle, where they sat while each of us was called upon to shout out some drivel from Chairman Mao, such as "Fight selfishness and criticize revisionism" or "A change in worldview is a basic change." By this time our gruel was cold. After gulping it down with a shudder, I would trudge listlessly to my shift.

At our work site, the cattle sheds near the mouth of a nearby ravine, we shoveled manure onto carts, which we then hauled into the ravine and emptied onto the rice paddies. The frozen manure resisted our strenuous efforts to smash it with pickaxes, yielding only small icy chips, and the congealed mud road was pitted with ridges that made for rough going even with an empty cart, to say nothing of a full one. My hands, which throbbed from the impact of the pickax against the rock-hard manure, began to crack and bleed.

Although we were engaged in productive labor, it was largely a punitive measure, designed to break our spirits and test our willingness to reform. Most prisoners, eager to demonstrate good behavior, accepted the challenge of conquering the enormous piles of manure. Our work site took on the appearance of a battlefield or a grand engineering project. When pickaxes were inadequate, we drilled holes in the manure heaps with rock drills and pried them apart with crowbars. When even that was impossible, we thawed them with flames until they collapsed in big chunks. Once we had chipped away the hard surface layers, we could finally fill our carts.

Pulling a cart presented another set of challenges. The men had races with their loaded carts on the way to the fields, letting their legs run away with them on the downhill stretches. With three men to each cart, I had to keep up with the others, leaving me so drenched in sweat that my shirt would freeze in the piercing wind as we plodded back to the cattle sheds afterward.

With few opportunities to bathe, do laundry, or change our clothes, we were plagued with lice. Whenever we had a moment off on a sunny day, we loved to strip off our shirts, unbuckle our pants, and catch the insects that lurked in the seams of our clothes. It was easy to pop the torpid, engorged bugs with our thumbnails, although the process left us splattered with blood. Yet we could never exterminate the lice completely, because their population regenerated from the swarms of tiny nits they left behind. The only way to destroy these was to scorch our clothes over the stove in the barracks, but there was little point in damaging our belongings in this way because the entire cycle would soon begin anew.

Eventually the brigade chief gave me a solo assignment riding on a horse-drawn manure cart to unload its contents onto some distant fields. Once we had arrived, the driver lifted the shafts to tilt the carriage back, while I raked the contents onto the fields as quickly as I could. After this brief exertion I hopped onto the back of the cart and the driver took his seat in front. On the way back to the cattle sheds I belted out plaintive tunes from *Two*

Hundred Famous Songs from Foreign Lands. "The steppe is vast, and the road is long," I sang, and "Along the icy Volga, a troika makes its way." The driver, a hardened criminal, never said a word to me. He seemed oblivious of my singing, and my songs faded quickly away into the impenetrable silence of the vast ravine.

Once I had demonstrated that I would not run away on solo assignments, the brigade chief favored me with another, even better job, standing guard on the hillside to prevent prisoners from trying to escape as they went by with their carts. In this role I was indispensable to the brigade chief, for whom security was paramount; his main task was to return at the end of the workday with the same number of convicts that he had set out with in the morning. As I stood ramrod straight on the hillside, scrutinizing the passing carts, I found the occasional leisure moment to enjoy the scenery. I gazed at the odd-shaped clouds scudding across the sky and squinted, watery-eyed, at the distant, undulating mountains. By the time the workday ended at dusk, I was frozen and my stomach was rumbling.

In the spring of 1970 we were transferred again, this time to Camp Stone Pit, the farthest camp from headquarters. When the weather warmed up, I saw the black-garbed Christian sunning himself in the yard. He had been in solitary confinement throughout our stay at Camp May First, but Instructor Lu seemed to have finally decided that he might as well free him to recover his strength so that he could do his share of field labor. But the Christian, defiant to the end, adamantly refused to lift a finger when he was forcibly marched out to the work site. His arms were too severely bruised to be of any use, and his hands were puffy and swollen. His filthy, matted hair stuck to his head in clumps.

I had never seen him say a word to anyone; he remained tight-lipped whenever his group read Mao's quotations aloud or sang revolutionary songs. I got no response when I tried to greet him, as he ignored everyone equally. Some of the young hoodlums in his group bullied him for fun, seemingly with the nod of the brigade chief. Picking up pebbles, they aimed them at him, but he held still and protected his head with his arms instead of dodging or protesting. If they spit in his face, he let the spittle dribble down his cheeks rather than wipe it off. He stood his ground stubbornly, still as a statue, shielded only by his stoicism and evidently preferring death to submission. Powerless against his passive resistance tactics, the cadres resigned themselves to treating him as if he were a deaf-mute or a quadriplegic.

I lacked his desperate courage. I had developed an ordinary prisoner's mentality, constantly pursuing small creature comforts and counting the days until my release. Obsessed with avoiding hunger and fatigue, all I aspired to was an extra morsel of food, a light day's work, or warm clothing, any one of which was enough to make me ecstatic. Gradually I had stopped caring how degraded my existence was.

Camp Stone Pit, which was in a relatively wide section of the ravine, was endowed with slightly better natural resources than the other camps. In addition to agriculture, it boasted a brewery, a vegetable oil press, and a small brick and tile kiln. That summer I was assigned to fire bricks, along with two other veterans of the brickyard, Chen Kejian and Zheng Tianyou. The three of us were thus spared laboring in the brutal summer harvest.

The brigade chief let us live above the kiln so that we could work around the clock, and we were entirely on our own. The kiln was in a wilderness area, where the cadres rarely checked on us, and every evening we cooked for ourselves down in the tunnel. Back in the detention center, my cellmate Number Six had described a variety of potato dishes from Malan Farms, but I had never sampled any of them. This was our big chance to steal and eat them to our hearts' content.

Chen Kejian, the boldest of the three of us, was a former maximum security prisoner who had been culled for this job because of his kiln-operating expertise. Recognizing the unique opportunity, he sneaked into the potato cellar at night and stole half a sack of potatoes. Zheng Tianyou, also a clever thief, was an excellent chef, so Chen Kejian and I stoked the fire and left the cooking to him.

Zheng Tianyou had two unforgettable recipes for potatoes. One was called potato balls. Shredding the potatoes on a grater he had improvised by boring holes in the bottom of a tin can, he mixed them with chopped scallions and other seasonings and then shaped the mixture into balls, which he served in spicy broth. The other dish he made was glutinous potato pancakes. First he boiled, peeled, and mashed the potatoes; then he beat them until they were doughy and elastic. They were delicious mixed with sugar or dipped in sauce and had the mouth feel of glutinous rice cakes.

Zheng Tianyou went out on foraging expeditions in the daytime to gather ingredients for our evening snacks. We were so desperate for food that we ate indiscriminately, even at the risk of food poisoning. Once Zheng Tianyou killed a snake, and we had snake-meat soup. Another time he exhumed a diseased dead pig that had been buried at the pigsty, and we feasted on red-cooked pork,[*] which tasted spoiled despite the heavy seasoning.

In the fall of 1970 we were transferred back to Camp Willow again. Hoping to cadge an extra bite of food now and then, I volunteered to serve as one of the three water bearers for the kitchen. The spring was nearby, and the path was in decent condition, so that the work, while still heavy, was much easier than it had been in the orchard. Occasionally we also had to carry lunch to the field-workers, but we were usually free to relax or wander around the yard as long as the kitchen was adequately supplied with water.

From the standpoint of nutrition, the advantage of working in the kitchen was obvious. As we sprinted back and forth between the kitchen and the spring, the cooks and vegetable choppers let us sample their food. Even better, we were excused from political study. Because we had to produce three meals a day, every day, for the entire brigade, our labor was not limited to an eight-hour shift, and we had no days off. As soon as one meal was over with, we started work on the next, resting only if we finished ahead of time. Our supervisor had to accept our protests that we had no time for political study. He was a slacker, who had been demoted to this job because of his poor performance at the Xi'an Security Bureau, and he spent most of his time out food shopping for the cadres' meals anyway, so we were relatively free of his supervision.

Three kinds of cadres were assigned by the government to Malan Farms: internal transfers within the public security system, retired army men, and graduates of agricultural and animal husbandry schools. They were relegated to that godforsaken place either because they were inept at

[*] Pork braised in soy sauce.

pulling strings or because they had shortcomings of their own. They were well aware that no other job would give lowly cadres like them such power to lord it over people.

The cadres left their families at home when they came to those disease-ridden, barren mountains and lived as bachelors except for occasional furloughs. A woman was a sight for sore eyes for cadres and prisoners alike, so the cadres' office put out the welcome mat for any attractive wives who came to visit. Fu Xiangrong's wife, a pretty young bus conductor, charmed everyone like an actress entertaining soldiers in the field. During her visits, camp discipline slackened while the cadres hovered around her, drawing her into card parties. A natural comedian, she kept everyone laughing with her antics. The head of Camp Willow, an old uneducated army man named Mr. Qiao who was well liked for his candor, sighed that her voice was "music to the ears" and that her gait was "dancing."

The forests in the Malan mountains all belonged to local tree farms, and their regulations stipulated that no one, individual or collective, was allowed to chop them down. The labor camp administrators openly flouted this rule, availing themselves of their prime location in the woodlands and the abundant free manpower at their disposal. They often took teams of men and horses deep into the mountains to harvest wood for their private use, and their underlings followed suit. As far as they were concerned, if they were going to work in such a hellhole, with no fringe benefits, they should pad their income by accumulating a private supply of lumber.

When a brigade chief spotted a tree he coveted, he would send some convicts to chop it down secretly and transport it back to camp. Then he would enlist others to hew it into boards and make it into furniture, which he would send home on the next outbound truck. Lumber was supposed to be declared when exiting the mountain pass, but finished furniture was exempt from this rule. Most of the peasant cadres from the central Shaanxi plains who served as brigade chiefs at Malan Farms took home huge wooden trunks and cabinets to recompense themselves for their labors.

Our supervisor had found a huge lacquer tree in a distant ravine, and he had prevailed upon some prisoners to cut it down for him and chop it into boards. He needed a team of brawny men to lug it out to the road, load it onto a cart, and smuggle it back to camp for him. He chose me as one of the team members, asking me to carry along a batch of steamed corn buns to distribute to the other men as a reward for their efforts. Although each of the damp two-hundred-pound boards was so heavy that I could barely walk on level ground with one strapped onto my back, we hauled the entire load of them up from the bottom of the ravine to the main road. This was the most arduous job I did during my entire three years in the camps and was probably the cause of the back trouble I developed years later.

Soon after I had helped my supervisor steal lumber, I was almost subjected to the rope torture because I pilfered ten pounds of apples.

One fall day, during our after-lunch break, a couple of other water bearers and I went for a stroll in the apple orchard near the main yard, where we found a few apples still clinging to the trees. In search of more, we walked deeper into the orchards, and in Orchard Two I discovered an abandoned basket half filled with late-ripening China Glories. They were crisp and sweet, with streaky purple skins. Tucking my sweatshirt into my trousers, I stuffed it with apples and zipped up my front zipper, but the sweatshirt was still lumpy. As I lumbered back down the mountain, I had the bad luck to see Brigade Chief Zhang approaching me on the way up to the orchards with his group. Flustered, I scurried into a potato cellar by the road, but I dropped an apple near the opening, and it was spotted by a sharp-eyed young straggler in the group. Brigade Chief Zhang saw him scoop it up and caught on immediately. Walking straight to the mouth of the cellar, he shouted at me and ordered some convicts to go inside and drag me out.

He took me back to headquarters, where he weighed my apples. There were ten pounds. Then he called Brigade Chief Yang so that they could conduct a joint interrogation, during which I insisted that I had picked up all the apples from the roadside. Brigade Chief Zhang did not believe me.

"So," he scolded, "you just assumed they were yours for the taking and helped yourself! A likely story! It's still inexcusable! As long as the apples were removed from an orchard, they count as stolen."

Taking out the rope as a threat, he dropped it near my feet and demanded that I confess the truth. I clung to my story, mentioning that there had been a prisoner cutting grass nearby who could serve as a witness. Brigade Chief Zhang summoned him immediately and asked him if he had seen me stealing apples, but he claimed that he had only seen me pass by. Having failed to get the testimony he wanted, Brigade Chief Zhang put my apples into a basket and made me stand at the gate to the yard holding it as punishment. Then he went to tell my supervisor what I had done.

Brigade Chief Zhang was a nasty man, who loved to find fault with people and had been suspicious of me all along. This time I had unfortunately given him some leverage over me, and he probably would have tortured me if I had still been an orchard worker. Luckily, however, I had transferred to the kitchen and was no longer under his jurisdiction. He was powerless to punish me; only my supervisor could do that.

After I had stood at the gate as an example to the other prisoners for a couple of hours, my supervisor strolled down from headquarters. I was still dreading the rope torture. To my surprise, he just told me to run and fetch some water. Then he carried my basket of apples into the kitchen and handed them out to the kitchen staff as a treat.

31

Release

I WAS SCHEDULED FOR release in 1971, but as the long-awaited day grew near, my anxiety level rose. I feared that I would never be truly free of the labor camp system. Most urban prisoners like me faced unemployment after their release and were forcibly retained in the camps as resettled workers. If I had been a peasant, I would simply have returned to my commune and could not have stayed at Malan Farms even if I had applied to do so. I knew that I could avoid further incarceration only by obtaining, in advance, a residence transfer permit authorizing me to move to the countryside. Otherwise I would be sent to the Copper River Great Leap Forward Coal Mines, a nearby holding tank for ex-prisoners from Malan Farms. While I was still working at the brickyard, I had heard from veterans of this facility that the treatment there made the brickyard seem humane. To have suffered so much, only to end up almost exactly where I had started was unbearable. I resolved that I would go anywhere, even to some hardship post, as long as it was outside the labor camp system.

Soon after my arrival at Malan Farms, when I realized the necessity of making postrelease arrangements, I had reluctantly written to my parents asking for help. Zhengguan had to serve as messenger since he was the only member of my family young enough to have preserved some freedom of movement throughout the Cultural Revolution. Both my grandparents had passed away, Father was locked up in a cow pen, Mother and my sisters were sent to the countryside, and I was imprisoned. Zhengguan seemed entirely grown up by then; he had completed two years of his three-year factory apprenticeship and was poised for promotion to full-fledged novice worker status.

On one of his visits to Malan Farms he brought me Father's reply. Father refused my request for help, saying that he had given up hope in me and would from now on lend no credence to my empty promises. Rebuking me for ignoring his advice over the years, he speculated that I had probably not changed my ways, even after three years of labor reeducation. There was no point in his going to all the trouble to get me transferred back from Malan Farms, he said, because I was likely to disgrace myself soon again. He urged me to stay on in the camp system as a resettled worker, despite the hard life, because it would be safer for me to remain out in the wilderness under police surveillance than to return to the city without a job. He and Mother were not callous, he maintained, or unconcerned about my future. The problem was that they lacked the necessary power and connections to help me in such a topsy-turvy world. Reminding me that I had only myself to blame for my plight, he concluded by offering the small comfort that I would be allowed to come home for visits on holidays and that he and Mother would be content just to know that I was safe and sound.

Although Father's letter sounded heartless, it was in fact completely realistic and left me little room for argument. I asked Zhengguan to try to talk Mother into bringing him around to my position. Meanwhile, I sent Father a letter threatening that unless he saved me from the coal mines, I would run away with some hoodlums I had befriended in the labor camp. I emphasized that I would rather risk future reimprisonment as an escapee than go docilely to my fate as a miner.

In the summer of 1971 Zhengguan came to bring me the exciting news that there was some hope of my finding permanent residence in the countryside on the outskirts of Xi'an. He assured me that Father's letter had been merely angry bluster and that all the while he had been busily using his contacts at work to get me established as a resident of Gaoqiao Commune, in Chang'an County, a mere fifteen miles from town.

The waterworks had resumed normal operations, and Father had been reinstated. Now he was a deputy chief engineer, in charge of surveying water sources along the Feng River. He had met some rural cadres and had asked some acquaintances to help arrange my transfer. Nowadays, Zhengguan informed me, people were resorting to the back door to bring their offspring back from rural banishment. This meant that one had to wine and dine the local cadres, greasing palms as necessary, to get what one wanted. Father and he had braved the blazing summer heat to ride their bicycles to Chang'an County several times on my behalf, Zhengguan added.

Knowing that back-scratching had never been Father's strong point, I could imagine how uncomfortable this had been for him. Zhengguan described how Father had mustered awkward grins for the rural cadres, clumsily supplied and lit their cigarettes, arranged banquets for them, and helped them obtain coupons or letters authorizing the purchase of scarce manufactured goods. Father had always buried his nose in purely professional activities, completely neglecting to network with other people. When not attending to technical matters at work, he sat at home, drinking in solitude. If my problems had not forced his hand, he would never have had anything to do with these petty local cadres. I pictured him stumbling over the unfamiliar polite phrases and pressing liquor on everyone, drinker or not. I knew that such red-carpet treatment of guests would irk Mother, who had to pay the bill, to say nothing of doing all the cooking. She deeply resented it when Father invited people over for meals, especially if the guests were peasants.

In late August Mother came to the camp for a brief visit, during which she complained nonstop about how much the family had sacrificed for the sake of my residence transfer permit.

"You good-for-nothing! What sins did I commit in my last incarnation to deserve a son like you?" she moaned. Mother always launched into her scolding sessions with this refrain. "You're the eldest of my four children," she continued, "and the others have grown up without a hitch.

Why are you always such a nuisance? It must be Nanny's fault. She spoiled you when you were little. And I should never have sent you to Silent Garden to live with your grandfather and ruin your mind reading all those crazy books."

Her endless nattering imparted a homey atmosphere to the crude cave that the labor camp provided for visiting relatives. But as she grumbled, she opened a concealed pocket, took out an official document, and handed it to me. "Here's your residence transfer permit. Open it now, and make sure it looks all right."

This had been the real purpose of her visit. Accepting the precious document, I scrutinized it carefully. It was a certificate from Gaoqiao Commune in Chang'an County, granting me permission to establish residence there, and it was stamped with an official vermilion seal. With a sigh of relief, I assured Mother that it looked fine and should ensure my return back to Greater Xi'an. Then Mother submitted the document in person to Instructor Lu, extracting an oral promise from him to release me on these terms.

While the brigade was out in the fields after breakfast on the morning of September 18, Instructor Lu shouted down to me from his headquarters on the cliff that I should go up to his office with my luggage to complete my exit paperwork. I had finally served my entire sentence, down to the last moment, as specified by the draconian penal code of the day. As the depressing gates of the compound swung shut behind me for the last time, I looked back and caught a glimpse of the black-garbed Christian prisoner, who was being punished again. He was sitting under the eves of the jailhouse, tight-lipped as always, with bits of straw bedding in his matted hair. His hands, apparently paralyzed by the rope torture, rested woodenly on his knees.

It was a clear autumn day, and the forest was peaceful. I turned my gaze away from the hellish vista behind me, hoping never to see it again.

Instructor Lu had subjected my luggage to a final inspection before completing my exit paperwork, but I had prepared in advance by burning all the letters and notes I had saved during my entire three-year sentence. What a shame that I could not keep a single word! As soon as Instructor Lu returned my residence transfer permit to me, I followed Mother's example and carefully tucked it into my innermost pocket, knowing that it was my ticket back to the realm of the living. On the way down to general headquarters, I located my trusty mulberry wood carrying pole in its usual hiding place in the grass by the road and hung my luggage on it. Swinging it rhythmically back and forth, I strode down the hill to the bus stop.

32

Homecoming

WHEN I RETURNED to Xi'an in late September 1971, people were gossiping in secret about the Lin Biao debacle,[1] although they had to feign ignorance in public because the news was still classified. I heard about it from my old girlfriend the music teacher, who added that she had seen a big truck full of handcuffed People's Liberation Army officers whiz past the South Gate one morning a few days ago. I was stunned and delighted by the news. A crack had appeared in the monolith. If even Mao's right-hand man was plotting treason, how many real supporters could he have left? Beefed-up militia units patrolled the streets, which were deserted after nine in the evening. Occasionally a police motorcycle roared by, startling me in the autumn night.

My parents forbade me to go out alone, lest I bump into Officer Hua. Without proper residence registration in the Xi'an area, the transfer permit that had secured my release from Malan Farms was useless. Eventually the police would nab me when they came knocking at the door for a rou-

---

[1] Lin Biao, Mao's heir apparent, died in a mysterious plane crash over Mongolia, allegedly on his way to defect to the Soviet Union after plotting a failed coup d'état.

tine inspection, and Officer Hua could give me a hard time if he wanted to, now that I had a criminal record. I had been planning to flit around town, visiting Zhao Yi and my other friends, but I had to obey my parents because I was under their roof. They were too apprehensive even to let me go to trite Albanian movies[2] without my little brother. Once I ran into the pretty music teacher at the end of a movie, and she tried to make a date with me, but I had to decline because I was house-bound.

However, I did go alone to the Sanzhao Crematorium to pay my respects before my grandparents' cinerary urns. I was heavy-hearted over my failure to bring Grandfather the eight-treasure rice pudding he had asked for on his deathbed. The vaulted columbarium was lined with rows of niches, each containing an urn. I located my grandparents by number and put a pack of Grandmother's favorite Qianmen brand cigarettes in front of her remains. In Grandfather's niche I placed a pack of sandalwood incense. Then I lit two sticks of incense and went outside to burn a pile of paper offerings for each of them.

Looking down from the heights outside the southeast corner of the city wall on that brilliant autumn day, I discerned the distant outlines of the enclosed compound of the Number Two Brickyard and the lofty roof of the Shaanxi Normal University Library. Although my former classmates had graduated by then, they had been denied good work assignments. Their noisy rebellion had backfired on them, and the three-in-one revolutionary committees[3] formed during the Cultural Revolution had banished them to military farms. Later, when the political climate relaxed somewhat, the college had given them lackluster work assignments, relegating many of them to the hinterlands. My swaggering uniformed class monitor, who had risen to be a rebel leader, had later been jailed during a surprise crackdown and was still being held on vague charges.

---

[2] The only foreign films permitted at the time.

[3] Comprised of the revolutionary masses, local military officers, and revolutionary cadres. See Roderick MacFarquhar and John K. Fairbank, eds., *The Cambridge History of China:* Vol. 15, *The People's Republic, Part 2: Revolutions Within the Chinese Revolution 1966–1982* (Cambridge, U.K.: Cambridge University Press, 1991), p. 162.

I switched my gaze from Shaanxi Normal University to the high walls of the brickyard. It was the autumn harvest season, and the fields outside the walls were a dry, withered patchwork of green and brown. During the mass evacuations of the cities in response to Lin Biao's General Order No. 1, the resettled workers at the brickyard had been forcibly removed to the countryside. As Ermao had predicted, many of them were glad to avail themselves of the opportunity to escape the system. But even the old-timers who had married and settled in the area had been evicted. This included Li Zhimin, meaning that all his efforts to climb to the top at the brickyard had been for nothing. In order to secure official residence in nearby Chang'an County, he had married into a peasant family living in the foothills of the Zhongnan Mountains. Mao Zhiyi had been unable to obtain permanent residence in the mountainous area to which he had been sent, so he had brought his residence permit back to the brickyard and asked the authorities to help formalize his return to Xi'an. Instead, they had imprisoned him on nebulous charges of troublemaking. Ermao was probably thriving, having settled in Hancheng County and married a local woman. Changhai had defied his orders to move to the countryside and had disappeared into his old hardscrabble neighborhood; the police would probably round him up before long. Pimple Ma's story was heartrending: After seducing a young urban woman on a farm, he had been slapped with a twenty-year sentence for fraud, racketeering, and sabotaging the campaign to send educated youth to the countryside. He had been transferred to labor reform at a brickmaking facility reputed to be even more draconian than the Number Two Brickyard.

Mother pronounced me lucky to have received a comparatively light sentence early in the Cultural Revolution. She maintained that if I had continued to mingle with such shady characters at the brickyard instead of being whisked away to the relative security of Malan Farms, I probably would have received a much harsher prison sentence and would still be serving time. Perhaps she was right. Luck plays a huge role in the grand scheme of things. Who knows what the police might have done?

Deprived of grain ration tickets, I was reduced to mooching off my parents again. We all were eager for me to move to Gaoqiao Commune so that I could start to take care of myself. One Sunday Father invited Mr.

Zhang, the man who had obtained my transfer permit to the commune, to come over and discuss the next step in the process. Mother had to cook a special meal in his honor, even though she hated having company because Father always took advantage of the situation to get drunk. All his drinking buddies were persona non grata as far as she was concerned.

She especially disliked Mr. Li, whom Father had invited for moral support that Sunday. An experienced electrician from the waterworks, he was a bibulous glutton and a smooth talker, whom Father relied upon to create the right atmosphere by filling in the polite phrases that he could not bring himself to utter. Mr. Li had taken charge of public relations at the waterworks branch on the western outskirts of town during the recent leveling campaigns of the Cultural Revolution, when certain workers assumed the cadres' responsibilities. Zhengguan said that he had been a frequent visitor ever since Father had started hobnobbing with various rural cadres in his efforts to resettle me and that he had in fact helped Father get acquainted with the right people.

Mr. Li had introduced Father to Mr. Zhang, a top administrator at the Sand and Stone Management Station by the Feng River. He had connections in all the right places and was willing to do Father a favor because he thought that Father's urban connections might be useful to him. Indeed, Father had arranged for him to buy some rationed high-quality pig fodder for his private use at a factory on the western outskirts of town. Soon afterward, Mr. Li told me, Mr. Zhang had made the arrangements with the commune for my transfer permit, and he, Mr. Li, had personally ridden his bicycle from the center of town out to the commune to pick it up. Taking along some fancy cigarettes, he had gone with Mr. Zhang to extract the permit from the commune's copy clerk. While Mr. Li had lit cigarettes for the clerk, Mr. Zhang had coaxed the permit out of him with a skillful combination of small talk, humor, and coercion.

Father had not realized that this precious slip of paper would not entitle me to move to Gaoqiao Commune. He broached the subject during Mr. Zhang's Sunday visit, once everyone's tongue had been loosened by liquor. Mr. Zhang explained that there was still a major hurdle: The local peasants themselves had to approve my application since I would be moving into their production team, which was the official unit that owned the land, delivered the state's quota of grain, and distributed all work points[4] and rations. The commune administration's powers in this situation were confined to the registration and safekeeping of permits approved by the peasants. The commune clerk could issue a certificate under the table, but neither he nor Mr. Zhang had the power to make the production team accept me.

Mr. Zhang explained to Father that the only way to gain an initial entrée with the head of the production team was to present the team with a significant gift. It was customary in such circumstances to arrange for the purchase of a truck, a lathe, or a quantity of steel, items normally controlled by the state. But Father had no access to such things and lacked the power to make these arrangements. Besides, he was also trying to help Shuci transfer back to the city from a commune in faraway Long County. Family background was the obstacle in her case, making Father feel guilty, especially when he saw her sulking around the house during her visits home. As soon as he had gotten me transferred back from Malan Farms, he and Mr. Li had turned their attention to finding the right contacts to pursue on her behalf. Even if Father had been able to get the farm equipment that Mr. Zhang had mentioned, my sister took precedence over me. Father had after all obtained my release from the labor camp system. I was an adult, and I needed to take responsibility for my own life from then on.

As Father and Mr. Li refilled their cups throughout that Sunday afternoon, Mr. Zhang refrained from getting drunk. Realizing that Father was not in a position to arrange major purchases for the production team, he hinted that there was another way to obtain my residence permit, although he was afraid we might find it out of the question. When Mr. Li pressed him for details, he suggested that I marry into the team by finding a local bride whose family wanted the groom to move in with them.[5] He added that although this type of arrangement sounded ignominious, it was actually common in the countryside.

[4] Peasants in this period were not paid for their labor in cash. Instead, they were reimbursed at the end of each year in work points, a distribution of the production team's net income based on the team's official assessment of the value of the labor contributed by each peasant.

[5] The opposite arrangement is the norm in China.

Zhengguan (left) and the author in Xi'an in September 1971. This is the photograph that was given to Mr. Zhang.

"If Zhengguo does become a peasant," he continued, "he's going to have to marry a peasant woman sooner or later, so he might as well kill two birds with one stone."

Father, in his drunken haze, missed the point until Mr. Li explained it to him again. Then he called Mother out of the kitchen to discuss the matter, while I sat there writhing.

As I watched Father dejectedly lift his cup, I suddenly noticed how much he had aged. Although he was only around fifty, he was balding on top and had lost so many teeth that his cheeks had caved in. Back in the early 1960s, I recalled, he had loved to do tricks for us with his Ping-Pong ball and to show off on his bicycle, riding it up the steps outside our house and hopping it across the high threshold of our doorway. The past decade had clearly taken its toll on his health.

Mr. Zhang elaborated on his plan. His neighbor, he said, was a recent widow in her twenties who had two children, a plot of land ten yards wide, a new tile house, plenty of grain, and two fat pigs but needed a man around the house. He made it sound as if she were looking for a hired hand. Then he wavered, claiming that she was not necessarily the right match for me and that he had just mentioned her as an example. There were other villagers who were better suited to me, he said, such as the only daughter of one of his relatives, who had returned to the commune as a teacher after her high school graduation. Apparently her parents were looking for a man who would move into their household. Asking Father for my photograph, he offered to find me a few matchmakers in the village. As I did not have any recent pictures of myself alone, Mother gave him one of Zhengguan and me, taken at a studio a few days earlier.

I felt vaguely humiliated as I handed the photograph to Mr. Li. Noticing how youthful my face looked, I was overcome with the sense of being mocked and buffeted by fate. Something in me bridled at the sight of Mr. Zhang's tucking the photograph into his bag, even though he had been so instrumental in getting me out of the labor camp. I sensed that he was cynical and shrewd and that he was helping me only so that he could use Father. He was reserved and condescending toward me, as if I were not an independent adult. I wondered what kind of people would be pawing over my photograph in the near future and finding fault with it.

Two weeks later Mr. Zhang returned to get more fodder coupons from Father but did not bring up the subject of my marriage. Later Mr. Li told me that Mr. Zhang had tried to convince a few families to take me in but that they had rejected his proposal out of hand as soon as they learned that I had been a political prisoner. Even the widow next door to him, who was older than I was, had shown no interest in me.

Displaying astuteness that belied his coarse veneer, Mr. Zhang simply dropped the knotty problem of my marriage and turned to the subject of my employment. I should find a job in Xi'an, he recommended, while I was waiting for an opportunity in the countryside. Handing me a letter of introduction, he instructed me to take it to a military clothing factory outside the South Gate, where a production team from Gaoqiao Commune was working on contract to build a road. He informed me that he had already put in a good word for me with the foreman, who had agreed to hire me as a temporary laborer.

By the 1970s the system of residence permits and grain ration tickets had become totally oppressive. Just a dozen years earlier a vagrant from the countryside, like Grandfather's gardener Mr. Su, had been able to support himself by doing odd jobs in the city. There had been a labor marketplace in the streets in those days, and the unemployed could find work simply by standing in a certain location in the early morning. If this type of marketplace had still existed, I would have been able to find some menial job, such as mixing concrete, hauling bricks, or pulling carts. But nowadays even such humble employment had to be arranged through the neighborhood committees, and an urban residence permit was required. Jobs spurned by urban dwellers were now contracted out cheaply to rural production teams that came to town looking for work. City people referred to them as laborers, drawing a sharp line between them and the workers formally hired by the state or the communes. They were denied the guarantees of the state hiring system and regarded as second-class citizens.

These laborers were paid in commune work points, never receiving a penny in cash. The urban factories dealt solely with the production team as a unit, depositing funds in the team's bank account when the project was finished, and the laborers were not remunerated at all until work points were distributed. To make matters worse, they even had to bring their own bedrolls to the flimsy sheds in which they lived at the work sites.

After I had been hired, I moved into the laborers' shed with the bedroll that I had brought back from Malan Farms. Like everyone else at the site, I would not be paid until the end of the year and had to defray all my own costs. The laborers operated a kitchen in one of the sheds, to which everyone had to contribute sacks of cornmeal from home in exchange for a commensurate number of food coupons. My parents had to procure my contribution for me at special grain shops or on the black market. They even had to foot the bill for my shovel. Since I still wasn't supporting myself, I wondered why I had taken such a backbreaking job. Was it to get out of my parents' way? Was it to experience the discrimination against peasants in the city firsthand before I officially became a peasant myself? Or was it just to have a place to go?

My brother and sisters were kind to me during this period. In fact no one in our family ever cut off relations with me, even though I had been designated a criminal reactionary element. Zhengguan was poorly paid, but sometimes he gave me money for cigarettes. Shuci, who was in the countryside, had set aside some grain and sold it for a hundred pounds' worth of grain ration tickets, which she had given to Mother to help feed me now that I was at home without a residence permit or ration tickets of my own. When Shuzhi, who was working in Datong, Shanxi Province, received a generous distribution of potatoes from the farm at her work unit, she wrote and offered to send us some, and I wrote back to decline her offer. Twenty years later she photocopied my letter and sent it to me. Here is an excerpt:

> Dear Shuzhi,
>
> Thanks for your letter. Don't bother to send the potatoes. It would be a nuisance for you to mail them, to say nothing of the expense. Anyway, we've got enough grain for now, so don't worry.
>
> I've found a job paving a road at Factory No. 3538 on the southern outskirts of town. I've been there for almost a month now, working ten hours every day except Sunday. The work is harder than anything I did in the labor camps—shoveling concrete into carts, which I then have to haul—but I can handle it. I'm eating peasant food now, and it's pretty awful, but it's enough to keep me going. This may be the best I can hope for in life. Now at least I'm in the city, but things will probably get worse after I move to the countryside. We get paid every six months, so I plan to work at least until the end of the year. I'm not sure I like the life of a peasant contract laborer at an urban factory, but I'll have to deal with it somehow. I'm regarding the experience as a dress rehearsal for becoming a real peasant later on, so I'd better find out if I can take it. Most of all, I want to reassure Mother and Father that I've changed my ways. I've given them such a hard time all my life, and this is the only solace I can offer them.
>
> Love,
> Guozi
> October 31, 1971

33

Adopted Son

As the new year's holiday approached, the peasant laborers went home, and work halted at the site. I found myself freeloading off my parents again. At Mother's behest, I made several fruitless trips on Father's bicycle to ask for my wages at the office of the production team, Team Number Four of the Wuxifang Brigade in Gaoqiao Commune.*

One sunny day in late January I tracked down the foreman, Niu Dinghan, but got the same old story: He was still waiting for the factory to deposit the funds in the team's account. I had my doubts, but he was the boss, so I bit my tongue and pushed my bicycle homeward.

On my way home I saw some team members working in a fallow field outside the village, and one of them called out my name. It turned out to be Xuanmin, a friend of mine from the construction site. He and his father were making adobe bricks; he loaded wet earth into the molds while

---

*Team Number Four was one of the twelve production teams subsumed under the Wuxifang Brigade, which in turn was one of the eight brigades in Gaoqiao Commune, in Chang'an County near Xi'an. Team Number Four roughly coincided with the eastern half of Xinwang Village.

his father tamped it down. As I approached, the peasants set down their tools to chat, and I distributed cigarettes to one and all. I told them that I had come to ask Dinghan for my wages.

"You'll be lucky if you get paid by next year at this time," quipped Xuanmin's father, Guodong, who was a wisecracker.

I mentioned that I was looking for a place to settle. At this, Guodong perked up his ears and asked me if I could buy lumber or a lathe, the items Mr. Zhang had said I would need. Guodong sounded as though he knew exactly how to go about getting me a residence permit in exchange for such gifts. I pointed out that if I had been that powerful, I would never have joined their team as a contract laborer, nor would I have ridden so far on my bicycle to collect my paltry wages.

"I can see that you're pretty bad off," Guodong replied. A bighearted fellow, he made a more realistic suggestion. "You should marry into a local family or find a childless old man to adopt you as his son. If a peasant household wants to take you in, the team will approve it, and the cadres will have to go along with their decision."

"Marriage on those terms is out of the question," I told him. "But maybe I could let someone adopt me."

Guodong turned to the other peasants in the field and asked them if they thought his next-door neighbor Li Baoyu might be interested in adopting me. As I distributed another round of cigarettes to all, they gave Guodong the go-ahead. Then Guodong told me about Li Baoyu, who was fifty-six years old, a confirmed bachelor, and the head of the Poor and Lower-Middle Peasants' Association. He had always been a pauper—both before and after the Communist takeover—and still lived in a decrepit old earthen house that shared a wall with Guodong's.

Glancing at the sun setting in the west, Guodong dismissed his fellow workers for the day and offered to take me to meet Li Baoyu. I felt that I had nothing to lose. I was too desperate to move out of my parents' house to give the matter any serious thought.

Li Baoyu lived in an earthen hovel, a typical residence of the central Shaanxi plains. True to their name, such dwellings were built almost entirely of rammed earth, except for the wall that was topped by the eaves, which was made mostly of adobe but had a few rows of real bricks along

Xinwang Village in the mid-1990s, showing the traditional houses with porticoes in the upper-left and upper-right corners.

its base. The roof slanted steeply, and the interior was dark and cramped. Li Baoyu cooked and slept in the same room, with his *kang* at one end and his stove at the other. The walls and ceiling were black with soot; cobwebs dangled in the corners; and clay jars, basins, and pots lined the wall. I breathed a sigh of dismay at the sight of such abject poverty.

Li Baoyu showed an interest in me as soon as he heard that I was from the city and that my father knew Mr. Zhang. Guodong called Niu Ding-han, and the two of them summoned Niu Shiquan, the deputy chief of the production team. After hammering out the conditions I would have to meet, they resolved to go together to see Mr. Zhang that afternoon about clinching the deal. It was two o'clock in the afternoon by then, lunchtime in the village, and my prospects looked good: Guodong and Dinghan had smooth-talked Li Baoyu into the adoption. He lit his stove and boiled me a big bowl of noodles, throwing in some red-cooked pork left over from the Lantern Festival, which he took out of a niche in the adobe wall. Too hungry to mind the obvious flecks of soot on the meat, I wolfed it all down.

Li Baoyu's ramshackle house was the impetus for the deal. Like many other team members, he could not afford a tile roof, using instead sticky alkaline mud from the flats of the Feng River that dried into a hard layer when mixed with wheat straw. Every summer he, like other peasants, added a thick new coating of this mixture to his roof in preparation for the soaking autumnal rains and furious winter blizzards to come. But his roof was beyond repair by then. It leaked like a sieve during the rainy season, and he had to put jars and basins all over his floor and *kang* to collect the water. Everyone was afraid that his whole house would collapse in a heavy rainstorm. He was always trying to save enough to buy a tiled roof but could never seem to manage it.

Guodong and the production team leadership had their own reasons for wanting Li Baoyu to repair his dilapidated hovel. The Wuxifang Brigade was located on barren land near the river, and the state's allotment of chemical fertilizer was entirely inadequate. The peasants added their own supplies of manure, but they also used the rotten earthen walls of demolished houses; the older the house and the smellier its walls, the richer it was as a source of compost. Every spring the team targeted a few houses for demolition, took the old walls as compost, and sent some of its stronger laborers to help the villagers build new homes out of fresh adobe bricks. This year Guodong and Li Baoyu's duplex hovel was scheduled to benefit from this customary barter of labor for fertilizer. Guodong and his son, Xuanmin, were ready to foot the bill of the new construction with the money they had earned hauling carts in town, but Li Baoyu's poverty was holding up the works.

At this point I had suddenly appeared on the scene. As soon as the villagers heard that Father was a well-paid engineer at the municipal waterworks, they seized the opportunity to ask my family to finance Li Baoyu's new house in exchange for the adoption.

I was twenty-eight years old that year. If I had graduated from college on schedule, received a job assignment in a state enterprise, and gotten married at the normal age, I would have been a father by then. But through a cruel twist of fate I was still a drain on my parents, and now I had to ask an old pauper to adopt me.

The wheat fields ahead were shrouded in darkness as I pedaled homeward. I had already agreed to let Mr. Zhang bring Li Baoyu and the production team leaders into town to meet my parents in a few days, but I was starting to have second thoughts. I had made these plans on my own, without consulting my parents. When I got home, I would have to present them with a fait accompli. Mother would surely scold me, as always.

"You good-for-nothing, you're a disgrace to the family!" I imagined her saying.

She would be entirely justified this time. I really was a disgrace to the family, a terrible disgrace.

34

Reincarnation as a Peasant

ON THE APPOINTED day Mr. Zhang came over with Guodong, Li Baoyu, and Niu Shiquan. My parents agreed to supply Li Baoyu with new tiles for building a kitchen and a two-room annex on his house, in return for which I would be granted official residence status in Production Team Number Four as of April 1, 1972. After existing in limbo since my discharge from the labor camp in September of the previous year, I was relieved to have a place to call home. My parents, however, were ashamed to have stooped to such a transaction, and I knew that they were going to find it awkward to explain to people in the future.

Mr. Li stayed for a drink after the others had left. "It's a good thing you don't have to worry about Guozi anymore," he said reassuringly, noting Father's embarrassment. "Now you can concentrate on getting your daughter transferred back to town. Anyhow, with the way the world is today, people will understand. We've been socked with too many political campaigns, and we all have shameful family secrets."

Father sat sipping his liquor in glum silence. Although Mr. Li had managed to console him for the moment, he could not dispel Father's deep-seated anguish. It was so private that no one, not even his son, could fully empathize.

The idea of relocating me to the countryside had actually occurred to Father before. After my expulsion from college, he had toyed with a plan to settle me with an old classmate of his who lived in a village. In fact I had often had a paranoid suspicion that Father wanted to get rid of me because I was such a disappointing eldest son.

I remembered from my childhood that Nanny used to claim that Father had written a will instructing her to raise me in her village in the event of his death. Soon after the Communist takeover of Xi'an, Grandmother, Father, and Third Uncle had become heroin addicts. Grandmother pawned everything she could find to support her habit, and Third Uncle's wife divorced him. One dark afternoon Father swallowed an entire bottle of sleeping pills, hoping to escape his overwhelming debts and personal agony through suicide. I'll never forget how Mother rushed into the room in a panic, saying that Father had taken more than twenty sleeping pills and had passed out on the bed, his tongue stiffening. She whisked Nanny out the door to look for a doctor, and we managed to get Father to the hospital just in time. A few days later he was released, and life returned to normal.

I overheard Nanny telling people that Mother had found Father's will near his bed while he had been hospitalized. According to Nanny, the will authorized Mother to take my two sisters with her if she remarried but stipulated that since I was a son, I had to perpetuate the family name. It went on to request that the Kang family entrust me to Nanny, who would take me back to the countryside, raise me properly, and make sure that I got a good education.

For years afterward Nanny was moved to tears whenever she mentioned Father's will, as if her weighty responsibilities for me had not been merely hypothetical. In her opinion, I would have been much better off with her than if I had followed Mother into some stranger's home. She was firmly convinced that she was the only person on earth who could take proper care of me, and her tears were actually a sign of gratitude to Father for putting her in charge of my future in his will, which in fact had been nothing more than an irresponsible suicide note. Long after the incident had blown over and Father had returned to work, she kept harping on that obsolete will. When I went to pay a New Year's call on her during my stint at the brickyard many years later, she commented to me regretfully that she would have begged Father to let her adopt me long ago if she had known that my family's elevated class status was going to cause me so much trouble. In her view, I might have avoided expulsion from college if I had been shielded by her poor peasant status.

I don't know if Father's will actually stipulated that Nanny raise me in the event of his death or if this was just her wishful thinking. Either way, her tale seemed to prophesy my adoption by Li Baoyu, with the significant difference that the present proceedings had been initiated by me rather than by Father. An adoption by Nanny would have been more emotionally acceptable to my parents. Unfortunately life can be cruel and rarely plays out in storybook fashion. My path had now become intertwined with Li Baoyu's. His needs and mine were complementary: He had never managed to marry or to afford a decent house, while I was desperate for refuge in the countryside.

My entry into Team Number Four was a major event for all the team members, and Li Baoyu was obliged to treat everyone involved to a banquet, which also served as my formal adoption ceremony. Carrying the same bedroll I had used at Shaanxi Normal University, the Number Two Brickyard, and Malan Farms, I arrived at the village on the afternoon of the day before the ceremony. Li Baoyu's dilapidated mud hut had been demolished, and the plot was piled with rubble, which the villagers were carting out to the wheat fields as compost. Dirt was swirling in the air, filling it with a farmyard stench. As Deputy Chief Shiquan worked with the villagers to shovel the rubble into handcarts, he kept heartily praising its fertile odor and exhorting everyone to work harder.

Li Baoyu had set up temporary residence in a thatched shack in the brigade's firewood storage area, which is where my formal adoption ceremony, headed by the brigade leadership, was held at noon on April 1. Mr. Zhang and all the brigade and team leaders, along with some of the village elders, attended the banquet in a festive mood. Father and Mr. Li had also come specially for the ceremony.

"May I have your attention?" announced Niu Dinghan when the guests had enjoyed their fill of noodles and liquor, and Guodong had handed out cigarettes. "Everyone who has eaten here today is a witness. Li Baoyu's adoption of a son is hereby formalized. Does anyone have any objections?" Seeing that there were none, he continued: "All right then, Team Number Four has unanimously approved the adoption."

The guests, their faces flushed with liquor, sat back to belch and digest their food. Meanwhile, a group of peasants, mostly women, had gathered on the sidelines to gawk at me and Father. Neglecting their afternoon meal preparations, they buzzed and pointed at us, trying to size us up.

After the banquet the team accountant, Niu Rangdao, filled in my residence permit and asked me to complete some paperwork. Apologetically he told me that in order to obtain the commune's approval of the permit, I would now have to change my surname to Li. I assured him that this formality was fine with me, as Mr. Zhang had prepared me for it ahead of time. What objections could I possibly have at this point? I had given my parents so many headaches over the years that nothing could probably offend them anymore. And if they could accept this situation, why couldn't I? Right then it occurred to me that it might be a good thing to change my name. Settling down in the countryside with a brand-new class status would be better than sponging off my parents. Even if my life was tough from now on, my family would be spared any further suffering on my account. Changing my name seemed like a small price to pay.

"While you're at it," I said after a moment's thought, "go ahead and change my given name too. Since it's springtime now, let's put it down as Chunlai."[1]

We finished filling out the paperwork, which specified the obligations of each party. Li Baoyu was responsible for finding me a wife, and I was to support him in his old age and take care of his funeral. He and I each kept a copy. Li Chunlai, or Chunlai for short, became my official name. But the villagers had a complex traditional system of addressing one another according to age and position. Since Li Baoyu was a few years older than Father, I was to call him Uncle, as if he were Father's elder brother, and now that I was a fellow villager, his position determined how the other vil-

---

[1] Literally, "spring arrival."

lagers addressed me. Some called me Big Brother Chunlai, while to others I was Young Uncle Chunlai or even Grandpa Chunlai.

At first I didn't seem to hear people when they addressed me as Chunlai. After all, I hadn't drunk an amnesia potion.[2] I couldn't just shed my past like a severed umbilical cord, and my new name grated on my ears at first. But the villagers' attitude was very different from mine. They took my settlement in the village very seriously and treated my adoptive relationship with Li Baoyu according to their ancient customs. I had gone through the motions of the adoption just to get a residence permit, but in their eyes the agreement was a bona fide contract, and I was a genuine member of their community.

Very few people understood my past, and nobody paid it much attention. Once I had my new name, it was as if I had been reincarnated in Team Number Four with a completely clean slate. Nobody seemed to care that I was a reactionary or to show any curiosity about my expulsion from college and incarceration in the labor camps. Neither did anyone seem to think it was important that I'd been to college and was highly literate.

Now I was a "new man," according to the jargon I'd learned in the labor camps. The challenge that lay before me was how to be that "new man," or how to become an acceptable peasant and to get along with the villagers as if I had always been one of them.

[2] According to Chinese folk belief, a special potion is administered to all new arrivals in hell after death, so that they can be reborn into their next incarnation without any memories of the previous one.

35

My Adoptive Father

THE TEAM SENT laborers to begin construction on our new house in the spring of 1972, as soon as they had finished carting away the old walls. I helped them set up the beams, install the roof, build the walls and coat them with mud, and construct the *kang* and stove. I hauled bricks, adobe, and tiles, and rolling up my trousers and going barefoot, I mixed batches of mud and carried it to the site one shovelful at a time.

The work tired me out, but I could always find a second wind. My real problem was that I had no way to replenish my depleted savings. Ashamed to ask my parents for anything more, since they had paid for the new tiles, I resolved to make the most of the little I had. I donated my own cigarettes to the villagers who were building our house and refrained from purchasing nails or any other supplies unless absolutely necessary. Li Baoyu was penniless too, so he recycled everything he could from his old house, although he had to buy some cheap rafters.

The new house was nothing special. It was distinguished only by its gleaming red machine-made roof tiles, which outshone everyone else's gray handmade ones. The villagers sighed over the high-quality tiles, at the

Our new tile-roofed house more than twenty years later, in 1994.

same time clucking that factories nowadays could never match the standard of their pre–Cultural Revolution output.

We stacked a few dozen leftover tiles under the eaves. But we still had no wall facing the street, so we were vulnerable to trespassers. The first was Kuanrang, known as something of an opportunist in the village, who asked Li Baoyu if he could "borrow" the tiles to repair the arch over his gate. Li Baoyu refused, insisting that he still needed them. Kuanrang was followed by a continuous procession of other villagers, all with similarly earnest requests.

The villagers never expected Li Baoyu, a crusty old bachelor, to share his tiles willingly. Yet this did not stop them from asking. It was my first experience with such poverty, and I was learning some new lessons about human nature. Apparently, people could coexist only if everyone was equally destitute, and a stroke of good luck could be a nuisance in disguise. Now Li Baoyu, the proud owner of the only machine-made tile house in Xinwang Village, had to deal with his covetous neighbors.

Since I was not very good at hoarding material possessions and could not withstand pestering, I would simply have given the tiles away. But Li Baoyu was the head of the household, and after so many years in a mud hovel he felt completely within his rights to refuse. He moved the leftover tiles indoors, stacking them against the plank beside his *kang*. This was the sort of behavior that had earned him the derision of the villagers, who called him a bald old skinflint behind his back.

Li Baoyu had a chronic scalp infection, which he had kept hidden under a white sheepskin headscarf for as long as anyone could remember. No matter how hot the weather, he never took off the scarf; it was a defensive covering, like the shell of a tortoise. Prolonged bachelor life had made him suspicious and vaguely hostile. He tended to avoid confronting people directly on his own, but he was always ready to plunge into a village brawl.

"Chunlai," commented Guodong one day as we worked in the fields, "even though your uncle is classified as a poor peasant now, he used to be a landlord's henchman."

I was mystified, just as I had been by the villagers' association of baldness with miserliness.

Guodong explained that Li Baoyu had moved to Xinwang Village from Wugong County before the Communist takeover and had worked as a hired hand for a local landlord, who had treated him almost like an honorary member of the family. Li Baoyu had "loafed and stuffed his face," doing more housework than fieldwork, occasionally taking the landlord's children to a neighboring village to see an opera, or running errands for the women of the house. The family had tolerated his cantankerousness and had even let him get away with talking back to the head cook. He had faithfully backed his master up in quarrels with others but never seemed eager to lay a hand on anyone.

"Baoyu only pretends to be tough during a brawl," Guodong concluded. "He's not really aggressive—just an average henchman."

He had been entitled to receive the landlord's property when it was redistributed by the Communists, but the struggle sessions against the landlord had scared him away to his old home in Wugong County. All the property had been claimed by the time he returned to the village. If his niece hadn't pulled some strings for him, he would never have gotten his mud hovel with its generous plot of land. He had always been the poorest inhabitant of the village, a distinction that eminently qualified him for membership in the Poor and Lower-Middle Peasants' Association.

He was apathetic and irresponsible, the kind of person the villagers called a slug. It was the same to him whether he worked for the landlord or for the commune. He completely lacked entrepreneurial skills and the incentive that private property would have provided. As long as some "master"—whether a landlord or the Communists—gave him work and food, he was content to be passive. Villages all over China were rife with indifferent peasants like him.

The Poor and Lower-Middle Peasants' Association was supposedly a grassroots organization to represent the peasants in their dealings with the cadres, but actually it had no power. Recognizing Li Baoyu's usefulness as a puppet, the leadership installed him as chairman of the association. He was not greedy or dishonest, even if he was often stingy and mulish. Also, his house was the only one in the village unprotected by the privacy of a wall, a unique qualification for taking charge of collective property; he could not pilfer because he would have nowhere to hide the loot. Overall, he had been chosen for his harmlessness, even though he was a man of below-average intelligence, practically the village idiot, who might have been the butt of many a joke. Still, people refrained from taunting him openly.

Guodong and the other villagers loved to chuckle over the story of the time that Li Baoyu had slept with a woman during the famine after the Great Leap Forward. In Chang'an County, which was spared the famine's worst ravages, a bachelor could lure an itinerant female beggar onto his *kang* with a bowl of rice. Guodong recounted Li Baoyu's tale for us during our breaks in the field.

"One day at lunchtime," he began, "a middle-aged female beggar with a Hebei accent came to our village. Her clothes were in decent condition, and she had an educated manner of speaking. Xuanmin's mother gave her a bowl of noodle soup, and some of the peasants tried to find out her story while they shared their meal in the village square. A plan was hatched to make her Li Baoyu's common-law wife.

"She was ushered to Li Baoyu's hovel and onto his *kang* with less ceremony than registering at a hotel. Guodong set off a string of firecrackers from the co-op in Li Baoyu's doorway, while Shuanzhu loaned him his newlywed quilt for a simulated wedding night. Shiquan, who was team chief at the time, invited some cadres to Li Baoyu's house for dinner, and formal arrangements were made at the table.

"Yinzui, our team chief now, was still young in those days. He stationed some boys outside Li Baoyu's window to eavesdrop that night. At first they heard nothing out of the ordinary. Li Baoyu got on and off the *kang* a few times, like thunder without rain. Then the woman complained that Li Baoyu's scarf was smelly and asked him to take it off. When the couple had stripped naked, the boys heard the woman grumbling that Li Baoyu was impotent. After that they listened in vain for the sound of a man and a woman having sex.

"The next morning after breakfast the woman asked Li Baoyu to take her to a bathhouse in town and told him that they would sleep better that night if he took a bath too. Li Baoyu bought the bathhouse tickets, and they took separate baths in the men's and women's sections, but when he came out of the men's section, she had slipped away for good."

Li Baoyu and I settled into a routine. We had two rooms, each with its own door and *kang*, so that we could go about our own business with little need to interact except when we both were in the kitchen. Everything seemed new, like a fresh start on life. Li Baoyu hoped to build up a nest egg with the help of my earning power. Then he wanted me to bring home a wife who would bear children to carry on his family name. Buoyed up by his good luck, he seemed to bounce to and from the fields or the village square.

"He's so happy that sparks of joy are coming out of his ugly old onion nose," said Guodong.

Li Baoyu, who usually worked alone in the cotton fields, made his own hours. Since he got home before I did, he had a simple breakfast waiting for me each day when I got back from the morning shift. No one had any flour during the springtime gap between the old harvest and the new, and the villagers breakfasted on bland corn gruel, which they livened up with heavy cornmeal noodles liberally seasoned with salt, vinegar, hot peppers, and garlic.

Our village farmland, which was typical of the central Shaanxi plains, was dedicated to meeting the state quotas and orders for wheat and cotton. We had no room to grow vegetables, except for a few plots of scallions and chives. Because vegetables were so scarce, no one could afford to be particular, and most people subsisted on the homemade pickles the women made from wild herbs or old discarded cabbage leaves from the marketplace in town, which they kept in vats and doled out at each meal. But Li Baoyu and I had no such vat and no pickles. Instead, we bought onions in nearby Xianyang because they had a long shelf life, and we sprinkled them on our gruel occasionally for variety.

We cooked lunch together during our long midday break. As I stoked the fire and fanned it with the bellows, he deftly rolled out noodle dough and sliced it with a cleaver. He was so quick that he could finish this task by the time I brought the water to a boil. We usually had noodle soup, without any vegetables. Once in a while the team gave us a few chives or scallions, which I would chop and sauté briefly in a few drops of oil, shrinking them pitifully. Still, they made an attractive green garnish for the white noodles, and the oil added a hint of fragrance.

Dinner, the last meal of the day in the village, was more casual; people simply grabbed a steamed bun or a bowl of leftover gruel. In the evenings we took our logbooks to the accountant to record the day's work points. After exchanging the latest gossip, we went home to sleep.

My first year passed quickly. Despite fluctuations in the food supply, I was free of the fear of starvation that had obsessed me in the labor camps. Food, like fuel for an engine, was simply an energy source for my toil in the fields. By keeping the engine stoked, I could earn more work points, which I could convert into more grain. Then, with more to eat, I could work even harder. It was a never-ending spiral.

36

A City Slicker in the Countryside

PRODUCTION TEAM Number Four was so poverty-stricken that many of the men could not afford traditional marriages. The village was full of blended families, and there were plenty of other adopted children besides me. Some of the older bachelors had scraped together enough money late in life to marry widows with children. Shiquan, for example, had acquired a couple of stepsons in this way. Shili, our village carpenter, had married the widow of a criminal landlord element, adopting her daughter and two sons. Our accountant, Rangdao, who lived next door to me, had been adopted from a relative's family. And Yinzui was actually the grandnephew of his adoptive father, who had taken him in because he was afraid that his own son, Dinghan, was not reliable enough to support him in his old age. Dinghan had been away in the labor camps at the time and had returned unmarried. Recently, however, he had found himself a woman from Gansu who had run away from her husband, and she had a son and a daughter. Given these haphazard family arrangements, you had to be careful about whom you called a bastard.

I was different from the other outsiders, all of whom were peasants. Their farming skills and customs were easily transferable to their new location, and they fitted right in once they had taken the surname Niu.[1] I was the only city slicker from Xi'an. Even my style of farming annoyed the locals.

Although the old peasants were illiterate, they agreed with Confucius that "a craftsman who wishes to practice his craft well must first sharpen his tools."[2] They believed that every farmer needed a complete, well-maintained array of tools. Shovels and pickaxes had to be nicely mounted on lightweight handles, while hoe and sickle blades required constant sharpening. All I had brought was a single shovel, so I was constantly borrowing other people's tools, and they resented it deeply. I had joined the team solely for my own personal gain, they carped, and had little to offer the collective.

When it came to handling tools, the old peasants were as strict as martial arts masters. They took it upon themselves to correct sloppy young people, including me. Since I am so tall, I had attached an unusually long handle to my shovel so that I would not have to stoop over too much. The old peasants found my posture slovenly and inefficient.

"Come on, bend over and put some strength into it," one of them urged me. "You're still young and strong. Don't complain to us old folks about your back!"

They poked fun at me too. I held my shovel gingerly, they gibed, "like a doctor taking a patient's pulse," and I clasped the handle of my pickax to my breast "like a nursing baby" when I leaned on it to rest.

Li Baoyu's poorly maintained set of farming tools also got me into their bad books. I liked his pickax, which had a nice heft, but its handle was loose. Every time it fell off, I had to stop working and go hunt for a peg.

Some of my critics, like Rangdao's father, meant well. He was a kindly man and a semiliterate lay Buddhist who could puzzle out bits of the sutras. But I also had malicious detractors like Shikai, a man with sunken cheeks and a monkey face, who thrived on making insinuating, derisive comments. I was his favorite target. As a newcomer in the village I was reluctant to offend my elders, so instead of talking back to him, I just let him have his say while I went about my work.

---

[1] The surname of most of the local villagers.

[2] *Confucius: The Analects*, trans. D. C. Lau (London: Penguin, 1979), p. 133.

Basking in the spring sunshine one day, I let my eyes wander over the vast fields. My surroundings seemed totally alien. I was keenly aware that I was not one of those youths who had been sent to the countryside temporarily, for "reeducation" by the peasants and that I was not being graded on "behavior." There was no point in feigning enthusiasm. Nothing would get me a job in the city. I was stuck in this village forever, no matter what. As defiant as ever, I intended to do things my own way, regardless of what people said. I figured that as long as I did not make a complete mess of things in the fields, I had done my job. While I sincerely respected the old peasants for preserving their high standards, I had no desire to model myself on them. I did not consider myself of their ilk, resonating with Confucius's sentiment that he was "not as good [at farming] as an old farmer."[3] I was simply not cut out to be a peasant.

Every household in the village had a handcart except ours. When it came time to haul dirt, I first had to scurry from door to door to borrow a cart. The other peasants had already completed a round trip with their cartloads before I even arrived at the field. Still, I liked this job for the same reasons that I had enjoyed carrying water before. Although the work was tiring, I had some measure of independence, which was vastly preferable to laboring under the old peasants' noses.

When the wheat began to ripen, the cadres started biking around the fields in their straw hats. Xuanmin said they were making an estimate of the summer output, on which they would base the projected local contribution of grain to the state. Once the estimate was complete, the loudspeakers of the public broadcast system proclaimed from atop the village electric poles that the summer harvest had begun. "Make hay while the sun shines," they called shrilly. Throughout the harvest season they blared out a steady stream of noisy announcements, progress reports, and summonses to official meetings, interspersed with revolutionary songs and model operas in the local dialect, all intended to inspire our toil under the hot sun.

I had come to rely rather heavily on Xuanmin, a wiry, suntanned little man who called me Uncle Chunlai, whenever I encountered one of my fre-

[3] Ibid., p. 119.

quent problems. Since we were neighbors, he often brought his food over to my house so that we could eat together, and I always treated him to a cigarette after our meal. On the eve of the harvest he and I sharpened our sickles together by the pale moonlight. Li Baoyu's was rusty and dull because he had not harvested wheat in many years. At daybreak the next morning the bell called us to the fields, and I went out with all the other men. But when I got there, I realized that I had no idea how to harvest wheat.

Yinzui had the men spread out in a line across the field for the moving harvest. This was new to me, so I stood back and watched at first. The men advanced in their line across the fields, grabbing the wheat stalks with one hand and lopping them off with their sickles as they went. Their stance was wide-legged and crouched, as if they were riding horseback, and they grasped the stalks like reins. The wheat fell neatly behind them in even swaths. Some men were faster than others, but no one ever stopped to rest, and their rhythmical movements were roughly synchronized.

I tried my hand at it but quickly had to admit defeat. Noticing my awkward gait and clumsy sickle strokes, Yinzui was afraid I would slash my own leg. Meanwhile, the other men rejected me from their team, fearing that my inefficiency would cost them work points. I was immediately banished to the women's team.

The women stooped over the wheat and cut their bundles one at a time, a more forgiving but also much slower technique. I could not hunch my back for extended periods of time, so I had to squat or kneel on a bundle of wheat as I worked, even though this method was most inefficient.

Feeling light-headed in the noonday sun, I stood up to stretch from time to time. If I looked back at the wheat stubble behind me, the distance I had covered seemed pitifully short in comparison to the endless expanse that lay ahead. The women had left me far behind. I wished I could catch up with them, but I simply was not up to it. My eyes smarted with sweat from my brow, and my hands and arms were scratched and swollen. The women slogged silently and steadily ahead, as the wheat fell continuously in their wake. From my vantage point, they were a faraway row of hunched backs in brightly colored shirts, spotted here and there with sweat and dried salt crystals.

After I had finally reached the end of my row, I turned back to bind my harvest into bundles. But when I went to load them onto my cart, I found that some were too sloppy or too big, so I had to undo them and tie them up properly. My incompetence affected me alone this time, since work points on the women's field were assigned to us individually. Even though my whole body ached by the end of the day, I had earned fewer work points than usual. At the accountant's office that evening Yinzui and several other people made disparaging remarks about my measly output.

There was nothing I could say in my own defense. I was a substandard peasant.

When the harvest was done, we tilled the fields again, and a team of men was selected to plant corn before the scorching heat of summer arrived, while the rest of us threshed wheat. Soon green corn was sprouting up between the wheat stubble, and we had to hoe the hard, dried earth. The hoes we used for this job were massive, but not as romantic as the "silver" ones used to "till the Five Ridges that touch the sky" in Chairman Mao's poetic hyperbole.[4] The oversize blade, at the end of its gooseneck, was wider than my two feet placed side by side, and I had to wield it like a pickax to break up the clods of dirt. The villagers had a ditty that said it all:

Heave that heavy hoe on its big long handle.
Get your butt in the air, and keep your head down!

I did not have the knack for hoeing either. Each time I brought the hoe down, I narrowly missed gashing the corn sprouts or my own feet. The peasants forged quickly ahead, leaving me behind to fret about my slow progress. As I tried to keep up with them, I stopped from time to time to stretch my aching back. Guodong was proceeding at a steady pace ahead of me, switching his hoe skillfully from one hand to the other, his upper body swaying in time with the strokes of his hoe.

"You'll be able to skip ahead if you find an old grave," he told me. This was a village saying, but it was unfortunately outdated. With the increased population nowadays, most of the grave sites had been razed to create more arable land. All the old wells had been plugged up too, leaving an

---

[4] From Mao's 1958 poem "Farewell to the God of Plague."

unrelieved expanse of corn stretching toward the horizon like a brimming green lake. Every row had to be hoed all the way to the end.

We were perfectly capable of finishing our morning assignment early, but if we went back ahead of time, the chief would rebuke us and slap us with a heavier load the next day. So when we finished a couple of rows, we retreated to a shady spot to chat and smoke. Because of me, people always brought the conversation around to Xi'an. Despite its proximity, many of the villagers had never been there, and to them, it was a strange fairy-tale world. With the characteristic prejudice of country folk toward cities and their inhabitants, they loved to tease me about urban life.

"Chunlai"—Rangdao baited me one day as he buttoned his pants after urinating—"you city slickers pride yourselves on your cleanliness, but I think you're dirtier than we are. You have your toilets and kitchens under the same roof. I'll bet those high-rise apartments reek in the summer!"

I contended that we had flush toilets and running water. The others echoed Rangdao, arguing that flush toilets did not work. They knew, they said, because the public toilets in town stank of urine.

"I like the country better," Rangdao continued. "Out here the whole field is one big toilet. You can pull down your pants and go anywhere you want, and the wind will clear the air. No wonder you city people need to use so much perfume, with your toilets right in your bedrooms!"

This elicited loud guffaws.

"Yes," I replied. "It is more convenient to do it in the field, but most people don't want to donate their shit to the team, so they hold it in until they can get home and add it to their own manure piles. And what about your outhouses? They're connected to the pigsties, and the pigs are waiting inside to lick the crap right off your butt! Once I heard about a city girl who was so scared by a pig in a village outhouse that she fell into the pit."

Our banter was interrupted at this point by Kuanrang, who had a story to tell.

"Once I went into Xi'an on business," he said, "and needed to go to the bathroom around the West Gate, but I can't read, so I couldn't find a public toilet. I started to feel like I was going to do it in my pants. Then I found a garbage heap by the city wall, and there was nobody in sight, so I pulled down my pants and moved my bowels right there. Just as I was finishing, I saw a man approaching in the distance. I was so scared that I pulled up my pants without wiping myself! By then he was so close that I was afraid he'd be able to guess what I'd been doing, so I covered my pile with my straw hat. Wondering why I looked so nervous, he walked right up to me and asked me suspiciously what was under the hat. I suddenly remembered that city folk liked to keep orioles as pets and said that I had one under my hat. I told him that if he would hold the hat down while I ran and got a cloth sack, I would sell the bird to him cheap. He fell for it, and I left him standing there while I made my getaway."

No one even tittered. His tale had obviously been rehashed many times.

Then the discussion turned to eating habits, and everyone wanted to weigh in on the superiority of country life.

"Chunlai," someone said to me, "when you city folks cook a meal, you try to feed a whole family on a tiny little tin pot of noodles. How can you fill up on that?"

"They buy their food in stores"—someone else chipped in—"and it's rationed too tightly, so their stomachs have shrunk and they're not as strong as we are."

"And that's why they're so stingy too," a third person added. "They don't mean it when they invite you to a meal. They usually don't ask you if you've eaten yet[5] until you're on your way out the door."

"Although city folk have refined grain"—a fourth person chimed in—"it's been sitting around in the government's granaries for years. We live on the coarse stuff, but we never get sick because we eat the new crop while it's fresh. We don't have to run to the hospital all the time the way city people do."

Finally, Shuanzhu, who was fond of dirty jokes, brought our conversation to a climax. He poked Laishui, the village simpleton, who was dozing against a tree trunk. Laishui woke up and sniffed hard, sucking in the mucus that had been trickling out of his nose. He was everyone's favorite laughingstock.

"Laishui," Shuanzhu asked, "what's so good about the skirts the city girls wear in the summer?"

[5] A traditional greeting in China.

"I don't know," mumbled Laishui drowsily. "I've never seen them."

"Everyone says skirts are cooler," continued Shuanzhu. "But I could never figure out why until one day when I was in town. Would you believe that the girls are naked under their skirts? The cool wind can blow right onto their private parts. I've seen this with my own eyes on a bus."

As we pricked up our ears for more juicy details, we heard the cry of a popsicle vendor from the road. This was a rare occurrence in the countryside, and his cry of "Sweet, cool, creamy popsicles" whetted everyone's appetite. Our throats were parched from chattering for so long in the blazing heat. Nobody cared anymore what Shuanzhu had seen under the ladies' skirts.

Just then Yinzui arrived at the field with a hoe on his shoulder, and everyone started begging him to buy a round of popsicles with team funds. Kuanrang pressed the point that they were creamy and only a dime each. Yinzui refused, saying that there was no precedent and that he thought the other villagers might object. Squatting, he puffed on his cigarette and scratched his head. Then he glanced at me.

"Here's what we're going to do," he announced to the group. "I'll make a bet with Chunlai in the name of the production team. If he loses, the popsicles are his treat, and if he wins, the team will foot the bill."

With all eyes upon me, I asked him to tell me the terms of the bet. He said that Team Number Three had just buried someone in our old graveyard north of the village, on the boundary with Xianyang. He would send someone to put a sprig of willow in the new grave this afternoon, and I would have to retrieve the sprig at midnight in order to win the bet. He added that the team office had a carton of Baocheng cigarettes left over from the last time they had hired some well diggers, which he would throw in for good measure. Then he threw down the gauntlet to the others. They all seemed terrified of graveyards at night, however, and not one of them stepped forward.

"I'll do it," I told Yinzui, without hesitating. "Go ahead and send somebody to buy the popsicles."

Yinzui sent Rangdao, instructing him to pay out of the team's kitty.

"Chunlai," he said to me, "if you lose, you'll have to reimburse the team tomorrow, plus a carton of Baocheng cigarettes.

"No problem," I assured him. "I can afford it."

37

A Skillful Mechanic

INZUI WOKE ME up at midnight, and armed with a peach-wood stick that Xuanmin had given me as a talisman against evil, I set out through the north gate of the village. He had warned me that Yinzui had stationed villagers along the way to scare me, but I was not afraid of ghosts or the dark and remained undaunted. Thanks to his tip, I was not surprised when clods of earth rained down on me from both sides as I passed the peach orchard, and I shielded myself with my straw hat. Singing loudly to keep my spirits up, I soon arrived at the graveyard. My eyes had adjusted well to the darkness by that time, and there was plenty of starlight, although there was no moon. By the light of a match, I grabbed the willow sprig and then squatted calmly and moved my bowels on the new grave to prove that I had been there. Prize in hand, I marched triumphantly home.

I let Yinzui keep a few packs of the cigarettes he awarded me and handed out the rest to the other peasants the next day in the fields. Yinzui was a poor loser, however, and my victory rankled him. One day during lunch break, when the villagers were eating outside on their doorsteps, he offered a reward of cigarettes to anyone in the village who could best me in a wrestling match. Nobody seemed eager to step forward, however, despite the bait.

After a while Shiquan's second son, Fangmin, hesitantly accepted the challenge. His name, which meant "Liberate the People," indicated that he had been born in 1949, the year of the Communist takeover. He was a burly young man, much stronger than I was, who had been trying to pick fights with me during our breaks in the fields. His belligerence reminded me of the hazing that certain bullies had inflicted on me when I was the new kid in my elementary school class.

I was glad to see him step forward. This is my chance to teach him a lesson, I thought. The people of Xinwang Village don't know much about me yet. I may be a city boy, but I've done time in the labor camps, and I've rubbed elbows with the dregs of society. I wasn't born yesterday! I've got a few wrestling tricks up my sleeve.

I agreed to the match on the condition that we did not follow the village custom of starting in a locked embrace, which I regarded as an awkward, childish contest of brute strength, no better than arm wrestling. Since he had no practice in playing by the normal rules, Fangmin's brawn was of little use. I had him running in circles; then I bluffed a few times, causing him to falter, and nimbly dodged all his blows. Finally, I tripped him and knocked him down. After I had trounced him twice, he retreated to the sidelines in humiliation, while his irate father grumbled that Yinzui was "pitting the masses against the masses."*

With time, I won the loyalty of the young village bachelors, who used my house as a club where they gathered to smoke and talk. Eventually I mollified all my enemies, even Fangmin, and Shikai's son, Xingshan. The latter, taking his cue from his father, had also been bullying me. Completely unprovoked, he hurled insults at me while we were working in the fields.

"You're so tall you could fuck a goddamn donkey!" he scoffed one day. "I'll bet you wouldn't even need a ladder to eat camel shit!"

I was dying to have it out with Xingshan but had not found the appropriate moment. As my position improved in the village, I eventually managed to disarm him by peaceful means instead. He started to come over to

---

*A popular quotation from Chairman Mao.

my side after I won both bets with Yinzui. Not one to hold a grudge, I showered him with cigarettes, and he came around to my house after every meal looking for a smoke. I dropped him a hint about the hard time his father was giving me in the fields, and he actually intervened the next time he saw Shikai carping at me. After that Shikai stayed out of my way, and I could get my work done in peace.

By the time we had done our second round of hoeing, the heat of high summer had set in. The air was still, and a few puffy clouds drifted by overhead. With no prospect of rain, the team had to resort to antidrought measures. Mechanized irrigation pumps chugged around the clock to keep the fields flooded with well water. One day our pump motor burned out. Since motors were rationed in those days, we were faced with having it overhauled at a repair shop, which took weeks. Frantic with worry, Yinzui asked me to take it into Xi'an and have it fixed quickly. To his surprise, I replied that I was capable of doing the job myself. When he looked skeptical, I revealed that before I left Xi'an, I had done a month's apprenticeship at a Muslim-owned electrical repair shop near the Bell Tower.

Back during the spring, before my move, I had girded myself for peasant life by acquiring two practical skills that might keep me in pocket money in the countryside: I asked one of Father's colleagues, Mr. Xu, to teach me how to repair clocks, and I also let his friend Mr. Li find me the apprenticeship in motor repair at the Bell Tower Electrical Repair. During my month there I practiced the gamut of basic procedures under the supervision of the shop electricians. I began with the crudest task, setting fire to the broken motors on the sidewalk in front of the retail department to burn away the thin layer of insulation on the coils. Then I learned to remove the old copper wire, clean out the grooves, and painstakingly install new coils. The amount of time and specialized equipment required for these procedures made them seem arcane to the rural customers. In fact, however, the technique itself was simpler than it looked, although it proved much more physically taxing than I had expected. After a morning of laying wire, my fingers were throbbing with pain.

Once the wires were in place, the next step was to put all the coils in order and install new paper insulation. Then we could connect the circuits, plug the motor in, and give it a trial run. If it passed the instrument tests, we varnished the new coils, baked them dry, and remounted the motor in its housing. Then we returned it to the farm it had come from, where it was set to work pumping water around the clock again.

I had had no occasion to show off my skills in the countryside, and I was eager to do so now that the opportunity had finally presented itself. Wait until I've fixed the team's motor, I gloated privately. Then we'll see if people still call me useless.

Yinzui balked at the idea, fearing that the cost of the parts would go to waste if I failed. He finally decided dubiously to let me give it a try, but on the condition that I assume responsibility for any damages.

"Don't worry," I assured him. "I know what I'm doing."

I extracted the burned-out wires, copied all the specifications, withdrew some cash from the team kitty, and headed for Xi'an to buy the parts. Yinzui gave me only a day's turnaround time. The fields were drying up, he stressed, and we would lose the corn crop unless I hurried.

This was my first business trip for the team. I received ten work points a day plus a one-yuan supplement, in addition to all my transportation expenses. I set out early in the morning, hiked three miles to the bus stop, rode to the Bell Tower, and bought everything I needed right away at the shop where I had worked. Glad that I had gotten my first independent job, my former teachers helped me prepare my tools, cut insulation paper to size, and install new coils. Mr. Tie gave me a repair manual, with the warning that the last step in connecting the wires was highly critical and required great care.

After months of exile in the countryside, the city seemed entirely alien. I had not seen an office or a telephone in months. The phone on the desk at the repair shop caught my eye, and I grabbed it with trembling hands and dialed my old flame Manli. I had dreamed of doing this for a long time and could not believe my ears when I heard the sound of the phone connecting on the other end.

38

An Old Flame

MY LAST ENCOUNTER with Manli had been in 1971, on an autumn day soon after my return from Malan Farms. I had spotted her in a shopping line on the sidewalk in Xi'an. "Guozi!" She hailed me from afar, her eyes lighting up. Then she rushed to my side and grabbed me by the arm.

We spent the rest of the day ambling around town, while I brought her up-to-date on my recent misfortunes. She listened, thrilled, interjecting curious questions now and then. When I was done, she remarked wryly that I seemed unchanged and still looked like a student.

"I don't think they succeeded in straightening you out in the labor camps," she teased.

Although I had first met her back in my middle school days, through her elder sister, who was my classmate, my relationship with her dated only from the spring before my arrest. In those days she had worn her hair in a single long pigtail arranged fetchingly over her chest, and a skimpy black Chinese tunic that barely covered her midriff. She deliberately modeled herself on the glamorous ladies of the Nationalist period, like Phoenix, the star of *Thunderstorm*, Cao Yu's hit play from the 1930s.

At a party one evening someone proposed an odd theory about her name, claiming that it was often used in movies and fiction for seductive ladies who turned out to be Nationalist spies. To my surprise, she found this suggestion gratifying. She conducted herself self-consciously, as if always onstage. Her clothes were risqué, and she seemed oblivious of the perils of keeping bad company.

The mention of female spies in the movies brought a famous thriller to mind. "Miss Ahlan, let's dance a rumba," I suggested, imitating the male lead, and she wriggled and batted her eyelashes at me in response. When I asked her to take off her tunic, she complied with a slow imitation of a striptease, eventually flinging the tunic aside to reveal her tight chemise.

Snubbing the men close at hand, she eventually allowed her sister and brother-in-law to arrange a marriage for her with a Uighur wrestling champion in faraway Yili, on the border of Xinjiang and the Soviet Union. I speculated that she was attracted by her husband's stardom or that she wanted a change of scene. At any rate, believing that she had left Xi'an, I was surprised to bump into her that day in 1971.

She spoke noncommittally about her marriage, saying merely that it meant little to her. She had sent her little blond son to live with her husband, whom she visited only once a year. As we parted, she invited me to call her for a weekend date if I had time and gave me her work phone number and address. Painfully aware of my lowly status as a recent returnee from the labor camps, I was shielding myself from rejection by keeping my distance from people. I asked her if she wasn't afraid of tainting her reputation by associating with the likes of me.

"You're underestimating me!" she protested. "I'm glad to have you as a friend, and I don't care what anybody thinks." The vehement loyalty in her voice moved me deeply.

I lost touch with her over the following winter. As a member of the peasant construction team I lacked a private mailing address and access to a telephone, to say nothing of the energy for dating. Her job, she told me, was classified work in a tightly sequestered defense research institute on the southern outskirts of Xi'an, and bus transportation into town was highly inconvenient.

When I finally found my way to a telephone during my apprenticeship at the Bell Tower Electrical Repair early in the spring of 1972, I called her right away. Delighted to hear from me, she arranged for us to meet at the Bell Tower bus stop.

If I had not taken the initiative, we probably would never have met again after our chance encounter in the street. But I had been desperately lonely and obsessed with the thought of her. As a pariah in the city I craved the comfort of a girlfriend. Yet I could not help imagining what my parents, ever pragmatic, would have said.

"You've sunk so low you ought to be ashamed of yourself!" Their voices rang in my ears. "How can you go gallivanting around on dates? Your friends are all a bunch of useless nobodies."

I had chosen to pursue Manli that spring despite the knowledge that she and I had no future together. My experiences as a lovelorn youth had taught me that I would have to fend for myself in matters of the heart and must not let any opportunities slip through my fingers.

I stood at the bus stop watching buses come and go until she finally appeared. The weather was chilly, and we had no place for a private rendezvous, so we went to a restaurant instead of aimlessly pounding the pavements. In those days I could not even afford a bowl of noodle soup for myself, to say nothing of treating a date. Sensing this, she tactfully slipped me a large banknote on the way in so that I could pay for our meal. I was embarrassed but accepted her gentle reassurances.

After we were seated in a quiet corner, I told her about my impending move to Xinwang Village. As always, she came across as a free spirit, with her head in the clouds, and interrupted me with the whimsical request that I include her in my memoirs if I ever wrote them someday. I should be sure to mention how nice she had been to me when I was down and out, she insisted. I agreed absentmindedly to her seemingly irrelevant request.

The last time I saw her before my move to the countryside was on a balmy day later that spring, when we sat together on the steps of the public library. I was apprehensive about moving, but she was bubbling with excitement and asked me to let her know as soon as I had settled in so that she could visit me and satisfy her curiosity about my house and my *kang*.

I wrote to her when the new house was built, and she turned up one Sunday soon thereafter. Li Baoyu had gone shopping for the day in Xianyang, and I was at the mill grinding flour when Xuanmin came running in to say that my little sister had arrived for a visit. Surprised, I hurried home and found Manli there with a string of crullers that she had carried for me all the way from the bus stop. She was busily handing these greasy treats out to Xuanmin's little brother and three little sisters, while their mother stood there watching delightedly. My sister was adorable, she pronounced, and looked exactly like me!

I gratefully reminded myself that Manli's false claim would spare me endless questioning by the nosy villagers later. When the crullers were gone, she and I shooed away a gaggle of begging children and went inside the house. Since our yard had no front gate, anyone could come in without warning. I locked the door and closed the curtains over the translucent paper windows. The only furniture in the room was the *kang*, so we lay down on it together, started to whisper, and soon found ourselves locked in an embrace.

Since I had never been alone with her before, we had never been able to touch each other. This time she had traveled a long way for a tryst at my place, yet I had no real privacy even in my own house. More villagers would be stopping by to gawk as soon as the workday ended, and when Li Baoyu returned from his shopping trip, we would be separated from him by only a thin room divider.

Now I was finally in bed with her, and there was not a moment to be lost. Yet I found myself inexplicably paralyzed, as if with writer's block. Maybe prolonged celibacy causes one to grow rusty. I simply could not seem to get started. Manli, who had also lived alone for a long time, lay in my arms passively, until she eventually pulled off her clothes in deference to my wishes. Like huge beached fish, we lay pale and stiff in the harsh light of day.

Just as my repressed passions were rising, someone shouted from outside, "Chunlai, my grandson wants a cruller." I recognized the voice of Shiquan's wife, an obnoxious old lady with bound feet, who was always coming around to borrow things. Like a candle that dissolves into a pud-

dle of wax in a hot oven, my pleasurable urge melted away instantly. Manli
shrank from our embrace, her mood spoiled too.

"Bug off!" I cursed our unwelcome visitor under my breath.

"Chunlai," the old lady called again, but I kept quiet. Then she turned
away, hushing her crying grandson.

Thus the act of love that I had rehearsed so many times in my fantasies ended in awkwardness. Manli avoided my ardent gaze after that.
Glancing down at the damp spots on our naked bodies, we both were
suddenly overcome with embarrassment. She wiped herself off deftly,
balled up the used toilet paper and stuffed it into her purse, and pulled
on her clothes.

We wandered into the kitchen, making small talk to assuage our disappointment. Sitting down at the stove to cook me a meal, she tossed her
wad of toilet paper into the fire, causing it to flare up and illuminate her
flushed cheeks. We bantered a bit. I accused her of destroying top secret
documents, and she replied with a pout that she was burning the garbage
of my desire.

Now I was in Xi'an, repairing the team's pump motor, and I had
reached her on the telephone. She agreed to take the afternoon off work
and meet me at the Bell Tower bus stop.

Feeling as though I had been suffering a sexual dry spell as severe as the
drought in the team's cornfields, I could not wait to see her again. The disappointment of our last encounter had inflamed my desire further, but it
had also worried me. Had neglect caused me to lose sexual functioning? It
was much easier to make sweet talk than it was to perform the act of love.
My body did not seem to obey my wishes unless my surroundings were
optimal. I vowed to make the most of this unique opportunity. I had to
find a place where we would not be disturbed.

The weather was so sultry that the slightest activity was enough to
drench me in sweat. When Manli finally stepped off her bus, we boarded
another one to the Dongguan section of town and then walked to the
Guanyin Cave in Silent Garden.

At the foot of the east wall of the garden, beyond the wisteria trellis
and the artificial mountain, there was a broad sunken area accessible by a

few stone steps. It was full of fruit trees—peach, pear, crab apples, and walnuts—which I had often climbed to harvest as a youth. On the west side of this sunken area, nestled in the earthen rim, was a large brick cave where I used to eat watermelon to cool off in the summertime. We called it the Guanyin Cave because it had housed a large, valuable Six Dynasties[1] bronze statue of the Bodhisattva Guanyin, which had been carted away to an uncertain fate by the Red Guards. Now Third Uncle, who was alone in the world, was living there. When he was released from the cow pens and evicted from his home during the Cultural Revolution, he had found employment as a construction worker. He had moved into the abandoned cave, holing up there every night like a lone bear at the end of each grueling day.

I found the key in its hiding place outside the door and turned it in the lock. Taking Manli's hand in the cool, dim cave, I led her to the bed. After a while my eyes adjusted to the darkness. She lay passively, as if under assault, her closed eyes curtained shyly under her long eyelashes, and she rebuffed my caresses with her hand, as a playful kitten would defend itself with its claws. She kept moaning and frowning. Her attitude deflated me, sapping my ability to act. Making love is nothing like writing essays; there is no ingenious way to begin! Afraid to waste any more time, I stepped up my advances, rubbing and squeezing her more insistently. She continued to balk, arousing me further, but eventually she yielded, allowing me to reach the climax I had dreamed of for so long. Once it was over with, she relaxed, her face brightened, and her long eyelashes fluttered open over her wide, doll-like eyes. I poked fun at her fondly. Should I include what we had just done in my future memoirs? I asked. In place of an answer, she pummeled me with her fists. Then she lay back in my arms and sighed. She was terrified of getting pregnant, she said. I must not do this to her again.

That night I returned to the village and stayed up all night fixing the motor. Soon the pumps were whirring again. Looking at the flooded cornfields, I leaned against a shady tree and composed a parody of a pas-

[1] 220–589 C.E.

toral poem. Actually I craved the city and felt nothing but indifference for the new socialist countryside. Here is the poem:

The waterwheel whirs;
The canals meander along.
I watch the sky as the birds fly away
And lean on a tree while the cicadas sing.
I'll make do with muddy water
To wash my feet,[2]
And use my elbow for a pillow in my hut.[3]
Do I see a pretty girl approaching across the fields?[4]

[2] "If the blue water is clear, it is fit to wash my chin-strap. If the blue water is muddy, it is only fit to wash my feet." See *Mencius*, trans. D. C. Lau (London: Penguin, 1970), p. 121.

[3] The Master said, "In the eating of coarse rice and the drinking of water, the using of one's elbow for a pillow, joy is to be found." See *Confucius: The Analects*, trans. D. C. Lau (London: Penguin, 1979), p. 88.

[4] An allusion to Ode Number 94 in the "Airs of Zheng" section of the ancient classic, *The Book of Songs*, trans. Arthur Waley (New York: Grove Press, 1996).

39

Clock Repairman

I FIXED A FEW more motors after that, some from our team and some from neighboring villages, making several trips into Xi'an for parts. While I passed my days in this pleasant commute between town and country, the corn shot skyward, sprouting tassels around its ripening ears. Peasants all along the Feng River hung up their hoes and entered the so-called slack season. With plenty of rain, there was no need for irrigation. On the north side of the village the green fields billowed into the distance for as far as the eye could see, engulfing all human habitation like an ocean at high tide.

Unlike townspeople, peasants did not have regular breaks from work on Sundays or holidays and were allowed to rest only during inclement weather. They had very little leisure time, a problem mainly attributable to the wasteful commune system, although it was exacerbated by the peasants' own work ethic. Guodong said that there had been a natural rhythm of work and leisure back in the old days before collectivization, with more slack days than busy ones in the year. Work always had a purpose then: to meet the seasonal demands of agriculture. Because people were farming their own land, no one was inclined to make a show of doing unnecessary fieldwork. Those with an entrepreneurial bent had sidelines to supplement their incomes, hiring themselves out as laborers or producing handicrafts. Traditional holidays, local fairs, and family celebrations created natural intervals of rest in the relentless year-round march of agricultural chores. My dim childhood memories of visits to Nanny's parents' village corroborated Guodong's description. Before collectivization, pastoral pleasures had enlivened the tedium of country life.

Lamentably, many colorful customs had been banned by the Communists, and now, with the mass campaign to emulate Mao's model commune of Dazhai, peasants were actively discouraged from engaging in lucrative sidelines. Everyone, from the poor and lower-middle peasants to the former landlords, was obliged to toil like a beast of burden in the fields day in and day out. And work was performed for its own sake, often unnecessarily. Now people were eating out of the collective pot and jealously eyeing one another's rice bowls. Anyone who seemed to be shirking would be accused of freeloading or taking advantage of the collective. As they dragged one another down into this quagmire of overwork, peasants forgot about leisure time.

The problem was aggravated by their desperation to earn work points, which they needed for essentials like grain and cotton and for the cash remainder distributed at the end of the year. Unfortunately they had no concept of the basic arithmetic of their situation. It was almost impossible for the production team to increase its income. The state set the price it paid for agricultural products at an artificially low level, and the production team's output was stagnant, while farming costs grew. As the number of work points earned by team members rose, the value of a day's work declined, like a serving of an overly diluted kettle of porridge. Unaware that their complicity in the system was causing the devaluation of their own labor, the impoverished peasants trailed their team chief around, begging for assignments whenever the weather permitted, and he felt obliged to create make-work jobs for them.

A rift appeared between Li Baoyu and me. He was disappointed with what he perceived as my shirking, and I heard rumors that he was complaining about me. He would have preferred to have adopted a big, strapping breadwinner like Xuanmin or Fangmin. His criticism was not completely unfounded. I was not as hardworking as some of the other young men. Even so, I was not lazy. It was just that I valued my leisure, an attitude that set me apart from Li Baoyu and everyone else.

I longed for rainy days. When I heard rain in the night and realized that I could stay home the next day, a delicious torpor spread over my limbs. Lulled by the soothing patter of raindrops, I slumbered past dawn, skipping breakfast. My hidden fatigue seemed to swell like rising bread: The more I slept, the more tired I was and the more I needed to sleep. Over and over I opened my eyes drowsily, then shut them and dozed off again, unable to escape the clutches of the sleep demon. When I finally got out of bed, fully rested, I felt like a new man.

One rainy day I took out my set of clock repair tools and practiced my skills on an old alarm clock.

These instruments had been a gift from Mr. Xu, an unskilled laborer at the municipal waterworks, who had met Father when the two of them had been imprisoned together. They would never have become acquainted without such a coincidence, Mr. Xu had pointed out to me, since Father was "Senior Engineer Kang," and he was merely a temporary laborer. He had served in the Guomindang army and, thanks to his rudimentary education, had been hired as a propaganda worker in the People's Liberation Army after the Communist takeover. Soon afterward, however, he was convicted of some crime, perhaps merely former service in the enemy army, and packed off to the labor camps for several years. During the famines after the Great Leap Forward, he was allowed to return to his wife's house in Xi'an and found a job in the maintenance department of the waterworks. Then, during the Cultural Revolution, he was locked up with Father. Upon their release, Father was reinstated, but Mr. Xu was laid off and had to sit idly at home.

He often dropped by to see Father, probably fishing for opportunities to get his old job back. He was severely myopic but never wore glasses; instead, he craned his neck to see better, blinking and squinting drolly. His clothes were so grubby that I had not even deigned to talk with him the first couple of times he stopped by. But it turned out that I had misjudged him. When Father told him about my plans to move to the countryside, he showed unusual concern for me, suggesting that Father make arrangements for me to learn some useful skills. If Father did not consider such work too lowly, he offered, he would teach me how to be an itinerant clock repairman like himself. In fact Father did look down his nose at such employment, but Mr. Xu persisted so earnestly that he eventually consented one day over a cup of wine. The next morning Mr. Xu came over to pick me up, and I hopped astride Father's bicycle and accompanied him on his rounds in the countryside.

The city and the countryside are linked by a road, but where the pavement ends and the road dwindles into a dirt path through the fields, a different universe begins. We entered a village at lunchtime, when all the peasants were eating outside on their stoops. Mr. Xu had arrived with empty pockets, but he knew he would fill them that day.

"Clock repair!" chanted Mr. Xu. "Get your clock movements cleaned, hairsprings replaced, pinions sharpened, springs mended."

I followed him somewhat uncomfortably, observing how he hawked his services at the top of his lungs as he wended his way through the back streets of the village. But no one brought out any broken clocks. Just as we were mounting our bicycles to leave, a villager approached with a round desk clock, which he said had stopped years ago. It was grimy and rusty, and the rooster on the end of the second hand, which was supposed to peck at the grains of rice on the face to mark the passing seconds, was standing stock-still. Mr. Xu claimed that he could get the rooster moving again right away. After haggling briefly, he and the villager agreed on a price, and the villager brought out a small table where Mr. Xu could do his work.

Mr. Xu rapidly dismantled the clock, dropping the gears into a bowl, and had me wipe everything off with gasoline while he demonstrated the entire overhaul procedure for me. He sharpened the pinion on an oilstone, adjusted the hairsprings, and then cleaned and replaced all the parts. There was nothing serious wrong with the clock, he said, and it would keep good time now. Seeing the rooster pecking its way around the clock face again, the satisfied owner paid Mr. Xu one yuan.

Peasants, who still told time by the sun, had no need of clocks. Sometimes couples purchased them after their weddings, but they eventually got clogged with soot and were abandoned as junk. There was no place to have a clock repaired in the countryside, and no peasant would make a special trip into town for such a purpose. Unless an itinerant repairman came to the village, the castaway clocks would be melted down for scrap metal. There were countless such clocks in the countryside, Mr. Xu believed, a source of endless business. All I needed was the patience to search for them. I should not consider myself above announcing my services with a loud, recognizable cry or taking the time to persuade potential customers to part with their money. I followed him for a good part of the day, during which time we fixed six or seven timepieces, netting a dozen yuan. Then he took me to a restaurant for dinner and stuffed a few yuan into my hand.

On rainy days that autumn, when I had snoozed to my heart's content, I practiced repairing clocks. Once I had confidence in my ability to take them apart and reassemble them, I started repairing them for people gratis. Soon I had fixed all the clocks in the village. Word got out, and a steady stream of peasants from neighboring villages brought me all kinds of broken clocks, providing a valuable opportunity for practice. I clung to my mantra: I remembered how I had dismantled each clock and reassembled it the same way in reverse, just as I memorized the route to a new destination so as to retrace my steps on the way home. After repairing a clock, I kept it for a few days' monitoring, making adjustments as necessary. I often had as many as seven or eight clocks in my house, and the scene that I awoke to on rainy days was an assortment of clocks all around the room, their second hands ticking in pleasant harmony, offset by the languorous pitter-patter of the rain outside.

Zhengguan, who had by then been promoted to the position of lathe operator, bought me a new set of clock repair tools, which I supplemented with some standard replacement parts. One overcast day late that fall I sneaked out of the village on my first solo clock-repairing expedition. Hampered by the lack of a bicycle, I could do business only in villages within walking distance. I followed Mr. Xu's example, entering a village at lunchtime, and shouting, "Clock repair," as loud as I dared. To my surprise I attracted my first customers and earned a few yuan.

A full day's work on the commune was recorded in the account books as ten work points, which were supposedly worth seventy-five cents. At the yearly reckoning, however, after various deductions, I netted much less in cash. Compared with this paltry sum, the windfall I had discovered seemed too good to be true, a fairy-tale stroke of good fortune. In the midst of the campaign to "Learn from Dazhai" and "Cut off capitalist tails,"[1] I knew that I would be severely punished if I were found out. Therefore I was exceedingly circumspect, sneaking out only at opportune moments and only if I was desperate for money to buy cigarettes.

At the yearly reckoning, I had logged 171 workdays, for which I netted 128 yuan and 25 cents.[2] Li Baoyu had almost nothing to show for a full year's toil, after the capital he had borrowed to build a house had been deducted from his pay. He and I had pooled our finances, with him as the head of household and me as his dependent, so I turned my income over to him in exchange for a symbolic 10 yuan. With misplaced sympathy, some people commented that I had gotten the short end of the stick. But I paid them no heed. Li Baoyu was so underpaid that he often had to trade his basic ration of grain for a bit of cash. I felt sorry for him and refused to dicker with him over money.

Instead, I planned to line my pockets through my clock repair business and made the most of the lull in farm work at the end of the year. Having just received their pay, the peasants had some cash to spare, so this was my opportunity. I went out early and returned late, traveling far and wide to ply my trade. After a while I grew bolder, staying out overnight and making my way along the dirt road toward Xi'an. When I reached the beginning of the paved road, I took my earnings into town and splurged on a meal to celebrate the Chinese New Year.

Eventually I was discovered. When I returned from Xi'an, Xuanmin alerted me that tongues were wagging about my clock repair business. Fortunately, however, class struggle in our village was much milder than Communist propaganda would have one believe, especially during the slack season. I went on my guard after Xuanmin's warning, but the team leaders never got around to questioning me. They had disappeared on a gambling spree, and no one knew where they were, not even their children, who searched for them in vain at mealtimes with bowls of food.

[1] Eradicate private enterprise.

[2] About $330 today.

The villagers had a saying, "At the turn of the year, even the old beasts of burden take a break." The animals, tethered outdoors, basked in the sun and wallowed in clouds of dust on the ground. Oxen munched dried corn-cobs, white spittle dribbling from their mouths as they chewed their cuds. The stillness was punctured at random by the raucous braying of bored donkeys. All living things were at rest, and people were minding their own business.

Reports of my career as an itinerant tinker spread far and wide, and strange, amusing tales of my exploits found their way to my ears. People spoke of a tall, odd-looking fellow who sneaked out of the village and hawked his services along the roads. I was inexperienced, they said, and there was talk of one short winter afternoon when the clock I had fixed stopped again right away, and I had to turn around and come back again to redo my work. By the time I finished the job, the peasants were lighting their lanterns and serving dinner. They had kindly offered me a steaming bowl of corn porridge, which I accepted with frozen, grimy hands that were shivering too hard to hold chopsticks. . . .

Spring came, and the weather warmed up. Whenever I got on the road, a throng of mischievous children would follow me, taunting:

Here comes Chunlai, get your clocks repaired and keys made!
Here comes Chunlai, get your clocks repaired and keys made!
Here comes Chunlai. . . .

40

A Fleeting Idyll

THE ADOBE BRICK *kang* was central to family life in rural North China. An integral feature of the architecture of every house, it often occupied most of the available living space and was bonded firmly to the interior walls with wheat straw paste. It was indispensable in the peasant formula for domestic bliss: "All a man needs is an ox and some land, wife and kids on the *kang*, and life will be grand." At night it served as a bed, but during waking hours it provided a warm, multipurpose surface, dining room, living room, and pantry rolled into one. People used it for serving meals to guests and for gossiping and playing cards on rainy days. They even stored prized sacks of grain in its far corners. But these functions were useless to me, undesirable bachelor that I was. Moreover, I hated sleeping on the thing. As far as I was concerned, it was a monstrous eyesore and a waste of space, and I was dying to get rid of it.

And so I demolished my *kang* after only one year of use, heaping the rubble in the yard. With money I had earned repairing motors I bought myself a single bed and placed it in the corner of my room. Instantly my cramped quarters seemed much larger. Then I made an old wooden storage crate into a bedside table by covering it with brown wrapping paper

Li Baoyu's kang, *occupied in 1994 by another villager.*

and gluing smooth plastic sheeting onto the lid. I also brought a desk and chair from my parents' house and put them by the window. A few finishing touches—writing materials and photo frames on the desk, posters and a calendar on the walls—transformed my rustic little burrow into a gentleman farmer's study.

My life in the countryside had settled into a pattern by then, and my early feelings of alienation had worn off. Occasional ostracism notwithstanding, I had finally established a foothold. The young men had befriended me first, followed by the women. The team leaders had gotten used to me and had come to accept my incorrigible sluggishness. They gave me undemanding tasks whenever they could, such as sending me to represent the team on routine brigade-wide business. This enabled me to broaden my social network, and I had friends on each of the twelve teams in the brigade.

Now, for the first time since my childhood in Silent Garden, I had a place to call my own. For years I had lacked privacy, moving from my college dormitory to prison, the labor camps, and the construction workers' shed. I squeezed in time for some reading, borrowing the latest books from people in town. I even managed to obtain several translated foreign works, restricted-circulation reference materials intended only for high officials and specialists, who were supposed to write critiques. Some were from the Soviet Union, like Kochetov's *What Is It You Want?*[*] and the Byelorussian writer Andrey Zamyakin's *Snowy Winter*; others were American, including Erich Segal's *Love Story* and William Shirer's *The Rise and Fall of the Third Reich.* These books rekindled my interest in the outside world, transporting my mind far beyond my rustic surroundings. Abandoning my hasty vow to forgo the study of foreign languages, I resuscitated my Russian and translated some Lermontov and Gorky on rainy days and in the evenings, by the light of my kerosene lantern. Mother had been right to say that I had a short memory for pain.

Li Baoyu and the other villagers all accused me—wrongly, I thought—of having done irreparable damage to the house. The opinionated peasants clustered around the debris pile in our open front yard.

"They just built that *kang* a year ago. What a waste of adobe bricks!"

"Chunlai has a lot of gall, tearing down a perfectly good *kang* for no reason. Where's he going to sleep when winter comes?"

"City folk like beds better. But his bed won't be big enough for a wife and kids."

"Yeah, it's a single bed. I'll bet he's not even planning to get married."

The night after I demolished the *kang*, Li Baoyu had stormed out of the house instead of cooking dinner, locking the door behind him, and had stayed out until bedtime. Then he had spent the next day in bed with his door closed, refusing to answer me when I called him.

This was not the first time he had registered a protest against my behavior by peevishly refusing to cook or sulking behind closed doors, sometimes for days on end. During the year or so that I had lived with him, he had accrued a list of grudges against me. Besides my laziness, he resented my frequent junkets into town, especially because I never brought him back any gifts as a token of my respect. One of my worst offenses was inviting over urban students who had been exiled to the countryside for manual labor. Calling them a bunch of chicken thieves, he claimed that

---

[*] Vsevolod Kochetov (1912–1973) was a Stalinist writer who opposed the liberalizing trends under Khrushchev and Brezhnev. The Chinese Communist Party welcomed his novels as an antidote to Soviet revisionism.

they might come back and steal us blind. Another of my peccadilloes was keeping the cash I had earned as a repairman instead of turning it over to him. Moreover, he thought me an irresponsible householder because I let the village women borrow vinegar and scallions without paying us back. He even objected to my whistling and singing in my room and would start to simmer whenever I belted out the love tunes from my *Two Hundred Famous Songs from Foreign Lands* behind my closed door.

Such slights, he believed, undermined his authority over me. He insisted that I accord him the respect due a patriarch, although his behavior did not command it. He avoided direct confrontation, expecting me to read his mind, but I refused to play along and pretended not to notice his irritation until he spoke up. He would accumulate a series of petty grudges until he finally reached the bursting point, when he would fly off the handle. Even then, however, he did not rebuke me to my face. Instead, he would burst out of the house and curse as the village women did, without mentioning any names. Once, when I was singing in my room, he rushed out into the street, yelling, "All this caterwauling is driving me crazy!" Nobody knew what he was ranting about until Xuanmin pointed to my room.

I had borrowed a red china vase from my parents, put it on my makeshift bedside table, and filled it with red and white wildflowers. The local peasants did not grow flowers, nor did they appreciate them. In fact certain wildflowers were subject to strange taboos. For example, there was a trumpet-shaped variety they called broken rice bowl, claiming that if you picked one, you would shatter your bowl. Then there was the yellow baldpate blossom, which was supposed to make your hair fall out if you touched its pollen. And there was another sort that looked like a purplish gray butterfly wing, which went by the macabre name ghastly butterfly.

Li Baoyu went on the warpath when he caught me jinxing the house with a bouquet of baldpate blossoms one day, and he unleashed all his bottled-up anger at me for dismantling the *kang*. Out into the street he went.

"That motherfucker!" he screamed. "How dare he dig up the fucking *kang*? He almost brought the house down! At least he should have gotten a double bed. That fucking single bed is as narrow as a casket. Only a prick could fit on that thing! What an asshole! That bastard has no plans to get married and settle down here. What the hell have I done to deserve this? I opened my doors to him, and he walked all over me! I've produced a fuck-ing monster!"

This was his idiom; expletives hurtled from his lips like machine-gun fire. His hopes for a life of ease in his new house now dashed, he wanted to kick me out of his house. Unfortunately I was not simply a guest, and he could not evict me on a whim. I was as firmly embedded in the village as a nail hammered into a log.

I understood why he wanted me to bring home a wife. We two bache-lors had been huddled over a single pot for a year, and we were heartily sick of it. A relatively feeble old man, forced into a life of thrift by his lack of earning power, he was used to subsisting on meager fare and claimed that a mere handful of fresh boiled noodles would keep him going all day long. My arrival had changed everything. He had adopted me in the hope that my future wife would cook for him too, but I had let him down, and I was eating him out of house and home for nothing. Before adopting me, he had raised cash by setting aside some of his grain ration for sale on the black market; now even that was impossible. Guodong had told me that one of the features of Li Baoyu's personality was that he "could not stand to take a loss," and I clearly represented a loss to him.

With festering resentment, he went to the team leaders before the sum-mer harvest to request permission to disown me.

"You created this nuisance," Yinzui chided him, "and now you're toss-ing it to us team leaders like a hot potato so that you can have your new house all to yourself. I never thought it was a good idea to adopt Chunlai in the first place. Maybe Guodong and my uncle Dinghan can step in, if you'll listen to them. I wash my hands of you! I'm sure you've heard the saying 'It's hard to get rid of an unwelcome guest.' I think you'll just have to try to make the best of things for now."

Li Baoyu was stuck with me, but the breach between us continued to widen, and he finally proposed that we take turns in the kitchen. I had been dying to do this for a long time but had known that he would have to propose it. Now I finally had the freedom to eat whatever I wanted to. I had become a decent cook by then and could roll out dough and bake buns. On Sundays I would add a couple of stir-fried dishes and invite Xuanmin over for dinner.

But the new arrangement was a nuisance too. I had to wait when Li Baoyu cooked first, and I knew he was waiting to use the kitchen while I was cooking. We had more spats. Sometimes, in a fit of pique, he locked the kitchen to prevent me from cooking, hoping to make things so uncomfortable for me that I would decide to leave the village. I had to cadge my meals wherever I could. I went to Guodong's house or to nearby villages where some of my urban student acquaintances were exiled or even to my parents' house in the city.

I was embarking on the life of a wanderer.

41

Back in the Cooler

O NE SPRING DAY in 1974 I took a bus to the Huaqing Hot Springs* in Lintong with a couple of fellows from another village. On our way home that afternoon we noticed a throng of people on the main street of town and squeezed in to see what was happening. The center of attention was an altercation between a short townsman, apparently a rural cadre, and a pair of peasants with a cartload of ripe apricots. The cadre, who had a white shirt tucked neatly into his trousers and a wide leather belt around his paunchy middle, was giving the apricot vendor a tongue-lashing, ignoring his miserable entreaties. Several onlookers were asking one of the peasants to weigh their net shopping bags of apricots, while his associate was scurrying around, trying to stop the ruffians in the crowd from pilfering fruit during the momentary chaos. We elbowed our way to the front just in time to witness the cadre grab the vendor's scale, ruthlessly snap its arm in two, and command him to pull his cart to the Market Management Authority right away.

*Eighth-century playground of the Tang dynasty emperor Xuanzong and his concubines.

Some of the onlookers began to jeer, demanding to buy out the vendor's apricots at five cents a pound.

"Twenty-five cents a pound is really a gyp!"

"This guy's a ruthless scalper!"

"Now's our chance to snap up a bargain."

Drowning out the vendor's pleas with their clamor, they formed a line and waited for the cadre to give them permission to buy the apricots at a reduced price.

No one came forward to defend the peasant vendor.

I quickly assessed the situation. With the nation in the throes of the campaign to emulate Mao's model commune of Dazhai, peasants were strictly forbidden to sell their produce privately. The cadre, who was from the Market Management Authority, had ultimate jurisdiction over the vendor's apricots.

As a resident of Xinwang Village I had been sent to town to sell the team's melons a few times, and the Market Management Authority cadres had always ridden roughshod over me. They had bought my melons for a song, heaping abuse on me all the while. I detested them, along with all the bargain-hunting townspeople, and empathized with the apricot vendor. The cadres might forbid a person to sell apricots, but what right did they have to break his scales? What an outrageous bully! My blood started to boil.

I stepped forward and grabbed the cadre. Towering over him, I snarled that he was oppressing the peasants. Both peasants took heart and toughened up a bit. Then I grabbed the cadre's collar from behind and dragged him into the street, followed by the jeering crowd.

"Take him to the police station," someone shouted.

The cadre weakened, his protests taking on a defensive, supplicating tone, while I went into a frenzy. I gave him a kick in the rear end, and he fell to his knees.

"He's assaulting a Market Management Authority cadre in broad daylight!" someone called out.

"That brute has a lot of nerve, kicking a cadre like that!"

"Let's get him! What a bully!"

A group of workers surged forward and seized me by the arms. The cadre scrambled to his feet, clutched my collar, and wrapped himself around my neck like a millstone. I had not expected my efforts to boomerang, but they had. The crowd had turned on me in an instant. My companions tried in vain to intervene, but we were outnumbered, and all of us were hustled off to the police station.

The voice of experience told me that I was in serious trouble. It was much more difficult to leave a police station than to enter one. I knew that the authorities would start by asking me to identify myself, so while they had their tête-à-tête, I asked the peasants to back up my claim to be a student who had been sent to do manual labor in their commune. They supplied me with a false name to use and corroborated my story with the police at first.

They were intimidated by the police, however, and started to hem and haw after a while. Watching the police abuse me, they decided that they wanted nothing more to do with me. Meanwhile, the authorities remained united and quickly arrived at a conclusion: I had viciously assaulted a good, innocent cadre and would be detained for further investigation. The entire cartload of apricots would be confiscated by the Market Management Authority. The police frisked us, without finding any IDs. Just before sundown they released the peasants and shooed my two companions out of the police station.

The police made a phone call to verify the name and address I had given them and found out that there was no such person. When questioned further, I invented a new false identity, which they quickly exposed as well. Infuriated, they shoved my head down and made me squat in the corner. I was so famished by then that I kept foraging in my pocket linings for old stale bread crumbs. Waves of panic washed over me. They would deal harshly with me once they found out about my bad record. Night was falling, and the police station was emptying out. Three officers were deciding my fate in the next room. I strained to hear what they were saying, but they were just out of earshot. Finally they emerged, and one of them ordered the other two to escort me to the county detention center. Dirt swirled in the air as we made our way along the road in the failing light. I spent the whole time looking for a chance to escape, but sandwiched tightly between two guards, I never got one.

I had heard of this detention center. Every county seat had one. Managed by the civil administration, it was a holding tank for vagrants: run-away wives and youths, travelers without proper ID, and beggars. No matter whether they had broken the law or not, displaced persons could be rounded up and tossed into its filthy cells. Then the authorities would find out their addresses and see that they were escorted back to where they belonged. Since identifying the vagrants was a protracted process, some languished behind bars for a long time.

The official line had it that such detention facilities were social welfare institutions, sheltering and feeding homeless vagrants for their own protection. In fact they were oppressive institutions, designed to remove unsightly riffraff from the city streets. They treated their needy charges like trash, locking them up without due process. Moreover, because they were not formal penal institutions, they were scruffier than actual prisons.

The cell door was opened for me, and I was shoved inside. A few other inmates were seated on the bare bunk in the gloom. I was worn out, and my head was splitting. Squeezing into an empty space on the bunk, I lay down and went right to sleep but found myself tossing and turning all night, tormented by strange itching and prickling sensations. I was being devoured by insects, ubiquitous in Chinese jail cells. Unable to stand the torture any longer, I finally rose with the sun and massaged saliva into the itchy red welts all over me. As the sky brightened, I saw that the peeling walls were spattered with blood, smashed bedbugs, and dead lice. There were also yellowish smears of snot that reminded me of "flying white" calligraphy with its characteristic dry, streaky brushstrokes.

The cell door was kept unlocked in the daytime, so that we could go in and out freely to fetch water, use the toilet, or walk in the yard. I had four cellmates. One was a raggedy peasant beggar, who mixed dry bread crumbs from his cloth sack with boiling water in his enamel mug and supped in silence. The second was a well-dressed young man with a large knapsack who had been arrested in a hotel while trying to elope with his girlfriend. She stopped by during the day to sit with him and nibble on food from the knapsack. There was also a burly fellow with an out-of-town accent who slept on the floor to avoid the bedbugs. His story was that he had been arrested in the middle of the night, when he had fallen asleep drunk in the bus station. He still had a bottle of beer, which he sipped while he scratched furiously at the insect bites all over his body. Finally, there was a clever-looking boy of twelve or thirteen who sat in the corner; he said he had run away from his abusive stepmother.

Breakfast was a fist-size dark steamed bun and a bowl of salty corn gruel boiled with celery leaves. The gruel was scorched, and I could not stomach the medicinal overtones of celery, so I gave mine to the boy, who washed the bowl and brought me back some hot water after he had eaten it. Mashing the bun with hot water in my mouth, I felt as though I were mixing cement but somehow managed to choke down the whole thing.

My questioners displayed boundless patience throughout my interrogations. Rather than try to browbeat me into confessing my true identity, they gave me plenty of time to think matters over in my cell. The state had plenty of food for vagrants like me, they said. I could keep enjoying their scrumptious celery leaf gruel until I told them my real name and address.

While serving time at the Number Two Brickyard, I had heard of people who had, through constant vigilance, managed to find ways to slip out of this facility. I lacked their resourcefulness, however, and on the third day I decided to confess, driven by the combination of bedbug bites, horrendous food, and worries about the gossip that my absence must be generating back in the village.

I told the truth at my next interrogation. Everything was verified with a quick phone call, and all I had to do was wait.

The next day the Market Management Authority sent some representatives to escort me to the center of town, where I was to be the object of a struggle session. When we arrived at the Market Management Authority, I staged a small sit-in at the office, complaining that I was so weak and dizzy with hunger that I would faint in the hot sun during the struggle session. They gave me a couple of white steamed buns, which I wolfed down while they prepped me for the struggle session. As long as I confessed willingly, they promised, I would receive lenient treatment. At the session, I had to wear a sign on my chest for the first time in my life. LI CHUNLAI: ASSAULTED A MARKET MANAGEMENT AUTHORITY CADRE, it read. The session itself was anticlimactic. The leaders of the Market Management Authority read a description of the incident, the cadre gave his version, and there were a few speeches. I had indeed kicked the cadre, but there was not too much more to say about it. The main purpose of the session was to hold me up for public humiliation in order to strengthen the deadlock grip of the Market Management Authority over the local market.

Still, I was on tenterhooks throughout the session. I knew that I had a criminal record. If they discovered it, they might charge me with a serious crime such as class revenge or sabotaging official regulation of the marketplace. Then I would really be in trouble.

Fortunately my fears were not realized—in fact, quite the contrary. Three days after the struggle session the Wuxifang Brigade sent the militia chief and his assistant to pick me up. They told me that this was the first time that something like this had ever happened in the brigade and that the news that I had committed a crime in Lintong had spread like wildfire as soon as the detention center telephoned. To my surprise, my escorts added that they thought I had performed a great service, avenging us peasants by slugging a "motherfucking" cadre. They rewarded me with a restaurant feast of pork stewed in soy sauce with dumplings. When I got back to the village, everyone there patted me on the back except Li Baoyu. He seemed to feel that I had disgraced him and stormed out of the house as soon as I arrived. With the new incident as an excuse, he put in another request for permission to disown me, claiming that he could not live with me any longer.

After the summer harvest the team leaders caved in to Li Baoyu's demands and gave us our distributions of the new crop separately. Li Baoyu took over the kitchen, while I had to make do with a small burner in my room.

In midsummer the county government came to the team to recruit laborers to build the Shibian Valley Reservoir. Yinzui and Shiquan put my name down right away and came over to tell me the news. I had just returned from the fields and was in my room, sorting my new distribution of wheat.

"This is a great job offer," Yinzui assured me. "The team will continue to credit you with all your work points, and we'll throw in half a pound of grain plus forty cents a day. Your earnings at the reservoir will be on top of that. Lots of people here are dying to go, but I chose you because Li Baoyu has disowned you and you have no place to cook. You'll be living and eating at the reservoir from now on. There's plenty of work to do there, so you might as well plan on staying there for a few years. And since you're an educated young man, they might even keep you on as a permanent worker if you make a good impression on them."

Eager to distance myself as far as possible from the village, I accepted the job on the spot.

自述

42

The Forbidden Radio

SHIBIAN VALLEY, in the Zhongnan Mountains, was the site of a huge dam construction project. The crew from our commune was assigned to retrieve the debris from the daily dynamite blasting and to haul it, one cartload at a time, up to the top of the dam to be used as filler. The construction project was run in quasi-military fashion, with the various commune crews pitching camp at the foot of the mountain. We lived in makeshift grass sheds, while the leaders occupied the only building in the area.

The walls and boulders along the arduous path from the sheds up to the work site bore splashy red slogans: "The foolish old man moves mountains,"* and "Struggle against heaven and earth." As we trudged up the mountainside, we were bombarded with earsplitting propaganda broadcasts from the speakers atop the headquarters building. Like it or

---

*A reference to an ancient story, held up as a model by Mao, about an old man whom people mistakenly called foolish because of his admirable conviction that he and his descendants could move mountains, piece by piece.

not, we heard strident pep talks, production statistics, and encomiums of the latest labor heroes, along with songs and bits of doggerel. Here is an example, which still grates on my ear today:

Oh, Shibian Valley, the educated youth adore you,
And devote themselves to you, body and soul.
Oh, Shibian Valley, the poor and lower-middle peasants yearn to transform you,
And dare to wrest from you endless water and electricity.

Such verse was intended be inspiring, but we were put off by its phoniness. Our daily slog up the bumpy mountain road seemed anything but heroic. In teams of three, we dragged cartloads of rubble to the top of the dam, where our haul was subjected to a strict weigh-in. We received no work points unless we fulfilled the daily quota. It was too dangerous to work during the afternoon blasting sessions, so our foreman, Lao Wang, roused us for work in the middle of the night instead. Groggily we plodded up the dark mountainside until we were drenched in sweat and wide awake. By the time the sun rose over the mountain, we had already clocked several hours of toil under the floodlights.

When I studied history as a child, I had been unable to imagine the corvée labor used by ancient Chinese emperors to build roads and canals. But now I felt a bond with those laborers of old. Despite their ostensible iconoclasm, the Communists had perpetuated many traditions of ancient Chinese despotism, including the use of unremunerated conscript labor for large-scale engineering projects.

We rested from lunchtime until evening. If I needed pocket money, I went out to repair clocks in nearby villages. Otherwise I read books in the shed or prowled around camp with a pack of young urban malcontents who had been exiled to our commune, looking for girls to pick up. The shy girls nervously quickened their paces as they passed us, but the more sophisticated ones stopped and flirted for a moment. The toughest ones shook us off with insults.

It was the autumn of 1974. When harvesttime came, all the peasants went home to help. I had no desire to return to Xinwang Village, and a skeleton staff was needed at the construction site during the interim, so

Lao Wang kept me as dormitory watchman. With only a few odd jobs to do around camp, I had plenty of time to study.

I had been teaching myself English, although I had never spoken it with anyone. I owned a copy of the latest English-conversation textbook, *English 900*, a gift from Shuzhi. But with no one to pronounce the words for me, I had to sound them out according to the phonetic transcriptions in my dictionary. I had heard English spoken by only three people in my entire life. The first was Professor Liu, my former cellmate, who had taught me vocabulary words from the English translation of *Quotations from Chairman Mao*. The second was Shuzhi, an English major at the Foreign Languages Institute, who had gone on to become an English teacher in a small-town high school. She had taught me the international phonetic system. Finally there was Father, who had been formally educated in English before the Communist takeover. His command of the language was excellent despite years of disuse, and from time to time he had read passages aloud to me very beautifully.

While my high school had offered Russian, I had hoped to learn English too. Many of the literary classics I had read were translated from the English, so I knew that it would open up new worlds in reading for me. Shuzhi told me that English teaching was a promising field. In a few years, she said, village schools were going to be starting English programs, and more teachers would be needed. She encouraged me to work on my English so that I would be ready when the time came.

Given my firsthand experience of rural life, I thought that village schoolteacher was an appropriate calling for me. Unfortunately there were no job openings, nor was I a desirable candidate. Some people got these teaching jobs by pulling strings, even if they themselves had not even finished middle school. No matter how poorly educated they were, they met the basic job requirement of fundamental literacy in Chinese, their native language. But teaching English was different. Even the son of a commune party secretary could not teach a language that he did not know. As I pored over my English book, I dreamed of the day when village schools would face a teacher shortage. Then we'd see if they'd have me!

I remembered some advice Father had once given me. He had been sipping his liquor one day while I was studying my English and had suddenly snatched up my book and read a passage aloud.

"English is the world language," he had said. "Learn it well. You have a long life ahead of you, and someday you might have an opportunity to go abroad. You'll always be a misfit in China, so I hope you'll find a way to get yourself out of here." The liquor had clearly loosened his tongue. Pouring me a glass, he continued calmly, placing his hand on my shoulder. "China is in the throes of a grandiose social experiment, a gambit with people's lives and the nation's future, and we're the sacrificial lambs, but you might escape someday. Keep working on your English."

I downed the glass of fiery liquor he had poured for me. The scalding in my throat and the rare moment of father-son intimacy are vividly etched in my memory to this day. He had hinted at a whole new world for me. The soul of discretion when sober, he would never have incited me to any impropriety. But liquor transformed him completely. It had been his drunken recommendation of *The Water Margin* that had gotten me hooked on reading, although he had later tried to put a damper on my enthusiasm. I also traced my fascination with writing to his gift of the blank diary, which he had later ripped to shreds.

Taking Father's advice to heart, I decided that I needed an eight-tube transistor radio capable of picking up foreign shortwave broadcasts. Such items were novelties in the early 1970s and still very costly. The sort of radio that I wanted usually carried a two-hundred-yuan price tag. Unable to afford such extravagance, I stared longingly at the glass display cases in the shops, always turning away empty-handed. In the summer of 1973 I exhausted my entire earnings from repairing motors on the purchase of a used radio for forty-five yuan in a consignment shop.

Years before, I had listened to banned "enemy stations" at Pimple Ma's house. The reception had been crackly, and we had known we were taking a grave risk, but he and I had loved the Chinese-language broadcasts from the Voice of America, and from Moscow and Taiwan. His old-fashioned five-tube radio had been nowhere near as sensitive as my newly purchased little transistor set. When I lay down on my bed now in the dead of night and inserted my special earphones, all I had to do was twirl the dial and the "enemy stations" streamed right into my ears.

I never missed the nightly news and editorials on the Voice of America. When they were finished, I scanned the airwaves for other stations, like the BBC from London or NHK from Japan. Once in a while I hit upon the faint signal of a "Red Star Station." These programs, which were beamed from secret locations inside China, attacked Mao, his associates, and his Cultural Revolution; I found them highly cathartic. As they were riddled with static, I had to strain my ears to catch the precious fragments of authentic news. I treasured my transistor radio, my invisible link between the confines of my earthen hut and the wide world beyond. With a flick of its magical dials, I could hear people authoritatively voicing sentiments that no one I knew would dare voice in the light of day.

In China my whole being was in a constant state of craving. In the camps I had craved food, and at times I had craved female company, but what I craved the most was freedom of knowledge and expression. I was always intensely curious about everything that our repressive government forbade us to know and eager to express the ideas that we were forced to keep to ourselves.

The Voice of America also had English lessons, which, fortunately for me, used *English 900*. I was elated at the discovery that I could follow along in my book; this was the fourth time I had heard English spoken, and it was the first time I had ever heard a native speaker.

My addiction to shortwave radio was accompanied by a growing sense of paranoia. I was obsessed with an old movie I had seen titled *Steady Signal*, set during the period of the Chinese Communist underground struggle against the Nationalists in Shanghai. The hero of the movie is a Communist agent who reports to his superiors by wireless radio under cover of darkness every night, while the Nationalists try to trace his broadcasts. I kept replaying the climax of the movie in my mind, when the Nationalists, using a car outfitted with high-tech tracing gadgetry, finally locate the Communist and arrest him. Every night as I tuned in to my favorite "enemy stations," I would panic at the slightest rustling or the sound of a dog barking outside, imagining that a similar police car had arrived at Xinwang Village and was headed for my door.

My paranoia was not entirely unfounded. In fact the Xi'an Security Bureau had had me under surveillance for some time. The first person to tip me off about this was my old girlfriend the attractive music teacher. Although my parents tried to stand in the way of my relationship with her when I was living with them after my release from Malan Farms, I had resumed contact with her once I was on my own in the countryside. She had all the latest underground books, so my excursions into town usually included a stop at her house to borrow a few and catch up on the news.

Early in the summer of 1973, when I had just torn down my *kang* to make room for my rustic study, she sent me a message via a mutual friend. I was to come see her as soon as possible. She had urgent news that she needed to deliver in person, and I was not to look for her at her school but to meet her instead at a prearranged spot in town.

As we stood together on the noisy street corner, she peered nervously around, then warned me that a couple of plainclothesmen from the Security Bureau had questioned her twice about me, trying to wheedle and threaten her into informing them about what I did during my visits to Xi'an, whom I contacted, what reactionary things I had said to her, and why I wanted to learn English. She assured me that she had dodged most of their questions, claiming that our parents, who were friends, had introduced us to each other. To my great surprise, she told me that they had asked her about my relationship with Manli, which she believed had probably touched off the entire ominous investigation.

I soon received a similar report from Manli, who had also been interrogated by plainclothesmen. Her palpable anxiety belied her previous bravado about associating with me. Even though I had warned her that my bad reputation might rub off on her, I had never really expected this to happen. We decided to stop seeing each other and parted hastily. That was the last I ever saw of her.

What had I done to deserve this? Had someone squealed on me? Had I associated with suspicious characters? Was it because I had changed my name? Or bought the radio?

Hongjun, a friend of mine from Team Number Three, also began to distance herself from me. A relative newcomer to the village, she and her mother, a former small-town restaurant accountant with a landlord family background, had fled to our area from Sichuan to escape deadly persecution during the Cultural Revolution. Her mother, a tall, beautiful woman, had been married off to a hunchbacked local bachelor soon after her arrival. When I met Hongjun, her new stepfather had already promised her to an army man from a neighboring village in exchange for a dowry, and they were scheduled to marry as soon as the serviceman received his discharge.

Hongjun and I became friends while working shoulder to shoulder on the construction site in Xi'an. She was cute and petite, with narrow, crescent moon–shaped slits for eyes and a tantalizing gaze. She always addressed me respectfully as Elder Brother Chunlai. She and I were uncomfortable in the countryside for similar reasons: We were the only city people for miles around, and both of us were regarded as freeloaders. Her solution to this problem was to spend as much time as possible on the construction crew in Xi'an. When I came to town, I took her to shops and the movies or to see the music teacher. Occasionally I asked her to borrow a book from the music teacher and bring it to me on her next visit to the countryside.

Hongjun had been the one to relay the music teacher's urgent summons to me. But why was she avoiding me now?

One autumn afternoon I ran into her at Yinzui's house. Choosing a moment when no one was looking, she slipped me a note and scurried away. The note instructed me to meet her beside a well outside the village so that she could transmit a secret message. I went to the field and slipped behind the tall green curtain of cornstalks. She arrived, looking skittish, and told me that a commune cadre had appeared at her house two days before. He had ushered her out of the south gate of the village into a waiting jeep, which had whisked her to the commune office. There, some plainclothesmen from the Security Bureau had peppered her with questions about her relationship with me and asked her to spy on me and report the things I said, whom I was associating with, and whether I was part of some conspiracy. They tried to tempt her by offering to see to it that the commune leaders gave her priority for any good work opportunities that might come up. She assured me that she had refused to cooperate with them, claiming that she did not know me well enough to provide them with any special insight. But they had insisted that she think the matter over and had left her their telephone number, saying that they would be back to talk to her again. She had been looking for an opportunity to warn me ever since and had followed me into Yinzui's house. Moved by the risk she had taken on my behalf, I told her to stay away from me from then on. As the cornstalks gleamed in the setting sun, she gazed up at me affectionately, eyes glowing soft as moonlight.

I stopped going into the city, quit making rounds to fix clocks, and kept my friends at arm's length. Skulking in my hut like a wild animal in its lair, I waited jumpily for disaster to strike. Whenever I heard a car in the night, I sprang out of bed in a daze in case I had to flee over the back wall.

I figured that the Security Bureau had questioned a number of people about me and that these three women friends had been the only ones concerned enough about my safety to take the risk of warning me. The investigation apparently reached its peak between the spring and late fall of 1973. After I went to the Shibian Valley Reservoir the following year, I heard nothing more about it and went off my guard.

During a visit home from Shibian Valley in August 1974, I had a particularly heartbreaking run-in with Father. I had tuned in to the English lesson on the Voice of America one afternoon while he was at work and plugged his outdoor antenna into my radio for better reception. Unfortunately I forgot to replace it. Noticing my oversight as soon as he walked in the door, he lost his temper before I could offer any explanation. I had a lot of nerve, he fulminated, listening to shortwave radio in his house in broad daylight! I protested innocence, but he pointed to the antenna and called me a liar. It was up to me if I wanted to go back to jail, he snapped, but I should go back home to Xinwang Village to listen to enemy stations instead of jeopardizing the whole family. Then he went berserk. Before I could even unplug his antenna, he had grabbed my radio and hurled it to the floor, cracking its plastic exterior. I was nothing but a jinx on the family, he railed. Wasn't it enough for me that I had ruined my own life? Did I have to ruin my brother's life while I was at it, and bring the whole family down with me? Addressing me for the first time as Li Chunlai, he ordered me to leave the house and never to darken his doorway again.

I picked up the broken radio and left, unable to hold back my tears. Devastated by the violence of his outburst, I resolved never to go home again.

43

Father's Death

O N OCTOBER 20, 1974, Lao Wang, my boss at the reservoir, brought me an unexpected visitor just as I was climbing into bed. In the dimly lit shack I barely recognized Zhengguan.

"Guozi," he announced flatly, "Father is dead. It's time for you to come home now."

I sat woodenly on the bus with him, in a state of shocked denial. It had been two months since Father had smashed my radio and driven me out of the house, and I had not been back since. Now I was tormented by the knowledge that we had parted for all time on such terms. And all I had done to bring about such a tragedy was to listen to the shortwave radio! In the China of the day absolute trivia was blown up out of all proportion.

Two weeks earlier Zhengguan had come to tell me that all was forgiven at home. I was welcome to visit now, he said. Father was even saving some canned tidbits, a gift from a visiting relative, in case I happened to show up. My willful resolve to stay away was shaken, but I kept postponing my trip because of rain, never dreaming that Father would pass away before the weather cleared up.

He had collapsed at home on the morning of the fateful day. Upset by an incident at the office the previous afternoon, he had risen slightly later than usual, swallowed his morning tea, and then sat down with a glass of liquor instead of going to work. After the first sip on an empty stomach, he had crumpled in his chair. Zhengguan and Shuci had rushed him to the hospital, where he died of a cerebral hemorrhage that afternoon. The doctor said that he would have been a paraplegic had he survived. He left no will. The glass of liquor he had dropped to the floor was his final imprint on this life.

In the period preceding his burial, his company made a show of unprecedented compassion. All his colleagues and superiors eulogized him, regardless of the calumny they had stuffed into his dossier during his lifetime. In particular, they praised him for winning the company's lawsuit against the foreign contractors in the early years of the Communist regime.

I was not moved in the least by their fine-sounding words, which rang false to my ears, just like the charges they had fabricated against him a few years earlier. As long as a deceased employee was not an outright criminal, it was company practice to treat him or her with more dignity in death than in life and to stay involved with the bereaved family until the funeral was over with. The leaders, who usually kept aloof, were suddenly approachable. Meanwhile, the deceased was reduced to the role of a bargaining chip that the family played to extract a generous condolence stipend.

My relatives urged Mother to cash in on this opportunity to have the company arrange for Shuci's transfer back to the city and to get enough money to cover the costs of my wedding. I was thirty years old, long past the age of majority, but to my chagrin I found myself treated as an orphaned dependent. My role was limited to keeping vigil while the adults haggled with the company.

During a family caucus after we brought Father's cinerary urn back from the crematorium, the subject of my marriage came up for the first time. My parents had never discussed this matter with me, not because they had forgotten about it but because they feared it was hopeless. The problem had been aggravated by my move to Xinwang Village; now it was no longer clear whether I belonged in the country or the city. My parents had hoped to arrange for my transfer back to the city if the political maelstrom blew over, but after Father's death my relatives agreed unanimously that I would be a headache for Mother, who was about to retire alone. Decreeing that I should settle permanently in the countryside with a peasant wife, they

The Kang family, 1974. From left to right, back row: Shuci, Zhengguan, the author, and Shuzhi. Front row: Mother, Shuzhi's daughter Naidong, and Father.

offered to hire a matchmaker and to allocate Father's entire condolence stipend of five hundred yuan to my wedding needs. Eager to wash their hands of me, they warned me that I had better not reject their proposal; otherwise Mother would sock the money away for Zhengguan's wedding.

In my village it was customary for parents to arrange their children's marriages early rather than take the risk of waiting too long, and girls were usually spoken for by the age of twenty. When a teenage couple was betrothed, the boy's family paid the girl's family a bride price, after which the girl was formally considered to have switched families even though she still lived at home. From then on the boy's family helped support the girl financially. These payments amounted to a form of marriage insurance. The longer the engagement period, and the more the boy's family contributed, the less likely it was that the girl's family would back out. There was no place for me in such a hard-nosed marketplace. My age alone was enough to disqualify me, to say nothing of my other shortcomings.

When I first moved to the village, there was only one eligible young woman left. Her name was Fendan, and she was already twenty-one. Her advanced age notwithstanding, there was nothing wrong with her. Quite the contrary, her problem was that she and her mother both seemed to believe that her brains and good looks entitled them to set their sights impossibly high. Her mother had spurned one suitor after another; no one seemed good enough for her daughter.

After Li Baoyu and I got our new house, when he was still optimistic about family life with me, he expected to arrange my marriage. He strode the village streets cheerfully, as if he had hit the jackpot. As the village cotton technician he was in charge of the girls who sprayed the cotton plants with insecticide. Fendan was his best worker. Every night he stopped by her house to log her hours, lingering awhile afterward to mingle with her family. He got along well with her mother, who helped him cook steamed dumplings and noodles to offer guests every New Year. Whenever he was bedridden, Fendan came over and made him hot sour noodle soup, which she served him on his *kang*.

One day when I got home from work, I found my door ajar. Fendan was sitting on my *kang* leafing through my photo album. She had taken it out of the cloth bundle I kept on my bed, and I caught her in the act of stuffing it hastily back in when I entered the room. As she greeted me, I noticed how pretty she looked when she was blushing. It was the perfect opportunity to sit down alongside her, so I showed her the pictures of my parents, sisters, and brother, telling her a little about each one of them. In true peasant style, she naively inquired how much each of them earned.

"How come there's no picture of your other sister?" she asked out of the blue, when we had finished the album.

"What other sister?" I asked, momentarily confused.

"The one who visited you with the string of crullers."

Her eyes were keen, I reflected, and she was watching me. Forced to confess that Manli was a friend from Xi'an, I explained that she had only been joking when she had claimed to be my sister, although Xuanmin's mother had taken her at face value.

"No wonder she didn't look like you," Fendan said, eyeing me quizzically.

I decided to toss her a tidbit of information to dispel her curiosity. "She has a son already," I told her.

"She looks so young, you'd never know," she muttered. Laying my photo album on the *kang*, she left.

Li Baoyu spent more and more time at Fendan's house in the evenings, and sometimes I went with him. He chatted up Fendan's parents and brother, while I joked with Fendan's sister on the parents' *kang*, never taking my eyes off Fendan, as she sat quietly over her embroidery. Her sister, whose name was Xiandan, was a vivacious girl of about eighteen, who loved to laugh and was not the least bit shy. She regarded city people as monsters, a different species, just as Chinese people in general regarded foreigners. This was all right with me. At least I was exempt from the normal social expectations, giving me leeway to tease her and horse around a bit. When things got too wild and I had her in stitches, her mother would rush over with an amused smile on her face and pretend to chide us. Brandishing her small whisk broom, she would make a show of rapping me with it lightly, then use it to smooth out the checkered homespun bedcover that we had mussed.

Our team grew half an acre of melons each year, which we sold to raise money for chemical fertilizer and everyday expenses. About the time that the corn was reaching its full height, the melons were picked and distributed to the commune members to sell. We were paid in work points, but we were responsible for turning in at least the wholesale price, even if it meant making up the difference out of our own pockets. This was the only time that the commune encouraged us to go out and do business for profit, but the risk was entirely ours. If we had the bad luck to run into any cadres from the Market Management Authority, they would make us turn over our stock at a cut price, meaning that our hardhearted commune leaders would squeeze the difference out of us when we got back.

Li Baoyu used one melon-selling expedition as an occasion to throw me and Fendan into each other's arms. He arranged for two cartloads to go to Xi'an together one day, one managed by Xuanmin and me and the other by Fendan and her father. They thought it best to follow me, since Xi'an was my home turf. I took them to a bustling, relatively safe neighborhood, where our sales proceeded without major mishap. At one point some troublemakers tried to harass us, but I got rid of them.

"Chunlai is a real champ," Fendan's father kept telling her. "Let's come with him again next time."

Then one of my fellow water bearers from Malan Farms happened by. An unemployed man-about-town, he pitched in and helped us for the rest of the afternoon. Standing beside us, he called to passersby whom he knew to buy our melons. Thanks to him, we sold all of them at a profit that day.

On our way back, Xuanmin and Fendan's father pulled the carts in front, while Fendan and I walked behind, giving us the chance to become better acquainted. She asked me if I was ever going to be transferred back to the city. I did not know, I told her. Then she inquired whether I might find a respectable job as a worker, and I replied that I thought it unlikely. It dawned on me that she was simply a gold digger. She had no desire whatsoever to settle down with me and Li Baoyu. In fact she had her eye on my house in the city and was probing to see whether I met her snobby standards in general. Suddenly disillusioned, I decided to stave her off with a full disclosure of my background. I had done time in the labor camps for reactionary ideas, I cautioned her, and would not be able to obtain a Xi'an residence permit unless I was rehabilitated.

Thus I was not surprised when Li Baoyu's hopes were dashed to the ground late that fall. When he sent Guodong to sound out Fendan's family, he discovered that she had snubbed me for a young man from a neighboring village, a cook in a big state-run factory cafeteria.

All the desirable girls in the village thought that workers, no matter how lowly, made better husbands than peasants. One of their ditties explained why:

Marry a worker,
And cruise on the back of his bike.
Marry a peasant,
And spend your days yoked to his cart.

With Fendan engaged, all the young women in our village were spoken for. Only young teenage girls were left. One solution would have been to shell out a dowry for one of them and then wait until she reached a marriageable age. This was no more feasible for me than it had been for Du Mu.* As my relationship with Li Baoyu deteriorated, very few, if any, of the villagers saw me as a viable prospect.

One day at lunchtime a female beggar from Gansu appeared in the village. She was in her twenties, plump and rosy-cheeked, with a baby at her breast, and said she had run away from her husband. She sat down on the rock in front of Guodong's house, clearly hoping that someone would offer her shelter for the night. Guodong, a born matchmaker, took her in and tried to talk me into marrying her. I knew that he meant well and that the villagers would not look askance at such a marriage since it was their custom. But I refused flatly, feeling that I was not doomed to eternal bachelorhood yet. Still, I felt vaguely ashamed. The folk wisdom, based on experience, was that there were never enough women to go around. Sure enough, the young mother I had spurned was snapped up by a man a few years my junior, and the three of them became a happy little family.

In the winter of 1974 my interlude at the reservoir came to an end, and I returned to Xinwang Village. With no kitchen access, I had to cook on a coal briquette stove in my room. I kept my chopsticks in an empty toothpaste box tacked to the wall, an emblem of my forlorn bachelor existence. I tried to fix my transistor radio, but it would no longer receive shortwave broadcasts, and I had to make do with the official stations. I decided to forgo my study of English, as well as my clock-repairing expeditions. Although I had no direct indication that I was under police surveillance, I could not be certain that I was not.

Years later, when things had taken a turn for the better, several acquaintances disclosed that the police had indeed been trailing me during that period. One false step, and I would have found myself behind bars.

One such person was my friend Fucheng from a neighboring village, who was a fairly well-read, independent thinker, a rare soul mate for me out in the boondocks. One spring night when I was hunched over my translation of a long Lermontov poem, he came to the door. Since he

*Ninth-century poet who betrothed himself to a preteen girl but waited too long to come back and marry her, losing her to another man.

lived a few miles away, I was surprised to see him so late at night, but he told me he had decided to drop in while visiting a relative in the neighborhood. We exchanged a few brief, awkward words, and then he left, looking rattled. The old chestnut about unexpected visitors' being a bad omen came to mind.

Many years later, after I had been transferred back to the city, he came to see me and sheepishly disclosed the truth about that odd visit. That day the Security Bureau had summoned him to the commune office for an interrogation about his relationship with me, striking terror into his heart because he was from a landlord family. They had strong-armed him into snooping at my house that night, warning him sternly not to let me know what he was up to. He had left in such a hurry because there had been a police car waiting outside. He begged my forgiveness, which I granted, fully understanding his trepidation at the time.

The police had also tried to enlist Mother's neighbor and good friend Granny Li, who had always been kind to me. During this period she suddenly started urging me to stay in the countryside and behave prudently. She seemed to have something on the tip of her tongue, and my suspicions were aroused. Years later she finally found the courage to reveal that the Security Bureau had questioned her several times about me, threatening her with dire consequences if she told me or anyone in my family about the investigation.

A third person whom the police had approached was my old middle school classmate Liu Hongshen, head of a neighborhood factory. He had always helped me with urban errands I did for our village, like purchasing bearings or steel. But he shunned me during this period and seemed reluctant to help me anymore. I assumed that I had asked too much of him, that he had simply had enough. Later he told me how Security Bureau agents had arranged to meet him at a teahouse, where they had plied him with fine cigarettes and asked him to infiltrate my circle of friends. They had left him a contact phone number and the address of a secret meeting place where he could report his findings. He had been petrified but had not done their bidding.

Years later Dinghan and Yinzui disclosed that the Security Bureau had been spying on me in the village too.

"Chunlai," Dinghan confessed one night when we were drinking together, "the Security Bureau was out to get you that year. When I was the foreman of our contract labor crew in Xi'an, the police came in a jeep and made me go to the station with them. They treated me like some kind of hick, railing at me and shining a blinding light into my eyes, as if that would scare me to death. They asked me why I'd welcomed you into the village, who your friends were, and lots of other things. I'd never seen you doing anything bad, and I didn't feel like lying, so I didn't let them squeeze anything out of me. But they didn't give up easily. The whole thing took hours! I decided to play it safe, in case you really were a counterrevolutionary, so I didn't tell you what was going on."

Yinzui drained his glass and then launched into his story.

"The police kept coming here. They parked their jeep outside the village and walked to my house. One time, when you were in the fields, they made me take them to your house to snoop through your books and all those papers filled with your scribbling. They asked me a lot of questions, but I played dumb. Then there was another time when their troublemaking actually turned out to be a good thing for the team! Do you remember when we had those burned-out motors, and you were going to fix them here, but later we decided to send you into town to do it?"

I told him that I remembered well. I had stayed with one of the master repairmen I knew, who had been very hospitable and had even taken me to a nice restaurant.

"He was a stool pigeon," said Yinzui. "His assignment was to spy on you. The police took the motors to his house in their car. They wanted you to go there, so they could keep an eye on you. He took you to dinner on their expense account, and they paid for the repair job too. They were trailing you then, and they would have arrested you if they had uncovered any clues at all."

I sipped my liquor in horror, striving to remember the details of my stay in that fellow's house, but my mind kept going blank. Somehow, the incident seemed even more terrifying with hindsight.

Everyone in my family thought that my prolonged bachelorhood was attracting this unwanted police attention and that it would stop if I settled down with a wife in the countryside and quit associating with random people. Not knowing what else to do, I redoubled my efforts to find a bride, hoping that my family was right.

I decided to follow the example of other unmarriageable rural bachelors I knew, men with physical handicaps, or landlord's sons. They often found wives on the cheap—and they were much prettier than the local girls anyway—by scouring the impoverished backcountries of Sichuan, Gansu, northern Shaanxi, and Shang-Luo Prefecture. Penniless hillbilly girls could not afford to be picky. All they asked was to move to the fertile plains, where they would be able to fill their bellies.

Once an acquaintance tried to set me up with a relative from Sichuan, and I sent her family the bride price and requisite grain ration tickets. But on her way to my village she thought better of marrying such a dismal prospect and turned around and went home again. Another friend brought a young lady from the Shaanxi backcountry to my house, but she shook her head and walked out as soon as she saw my room with its makeshift stove and the toothpaste box chopstick holder on the wall.

I reached the end of my tether that winter. I reminded myself of what Grandfather would have said: I had hit rock bottom and had "nowhere to go but up." I prayed to the Bodhisattva Guanyin for protection. Maybe things would take a turn for the better, if I could just evade the dragnet this time.

44

My Wife

ONE EVENING AFTER the Chinese New Year in 1975, Fifth Aunt introduced me to a truck driver named Mr. Yin, who delivered the mail in the rugged Shaanxi backcountry of Shang-Luo Prefecture. He said there was a woman on his route, named Zhuyin, who traded him walnuts, chestnuts, and other mountain products for white sugar and manufactured goods from Xi'an. She was clever and pretty, he told me, and had confided to him recently that she was looking for a husband from the city. He offered to take me with him in his mail truck to meet her. In those days I was hauling carts with the peasant contractors, and I didn't even have a decent set of clothes. But I made a date with Mr. Yin anyway and spruced myself up a bit. Borrowing Zhengguan's coat and uniform, I got a haircut and shave and went to the main post office, where I boarded Mr. Yin's truck headed for the hills.

Mountain peach trees in full bloom cloaked the ridges in brilliant crimson. We drove through the Qinling Mountains, Shang County, and the county seat of Danfeng. Toward midafternoon we stopped near a grove of willows, behind which we saw a house with a porch. A young woman came out to greet us, invited us to sit down, and called Zhuyin. An attractive

woman, her thin lips pursed shrewdly, emerged from the grove and saun-
tered over to us with a bent willow branch in her hand. She greeted us,
stole a glance at me, then turned and went into the house.

The woman on the porch, who turned out to be Zhuyin's sister-in-law,
sat down right away and started trying to find out all about me. I had no
desire to obtain a bride under false pretenses and believed in being perfectly frank from the start so that the other party could back out right
away if necessary. Without mincing any words, I confessed that although
I was originally from the city, I had settled permanently in the countryside and had served time as a political prisoner in labor reeducation.
Then she and Mr. Yin went inside to talk things over. As soon as they
came back out again, I could see that the family was not going to give its
consent. Mr. Yin had to continue his postal rounds, so he suggested that
I spend the night there and made arrangements to pick me up on the road
to Xi'an the next morning.

After he left, Zhuyin opened up a bit. She invited me to visit some relatives with her, and we climbed a ridge behind her house and headed to the
right, along a ravine. As we walked, she explained that she was in no hurry
to get married since she was still young and her family did not want her to
leave the area. Her sister-in-law, in particular, said that if she was going to
leave, she should find a husband who did not have to grow his own food.

"Just so you and Mr. Yin won't have come all this way for nothing," she
said, eyeing me earnestly as we stood together atop a knoll, "I'm going to
try to fix you up with my cousin's daughter." She added that the daughter
was twenty-three, the legal marriageable age, and that we could get married
that year if we liked each other.

Night was falling, but still we wended our way across hill after hill,
finally arriving at an inhabited gulch, where we crossed a creek on step-
ping-stones and entered a house constructed on stilts. By that time the
kerosene lamps were lit. The family seemed to be expecting us and soon
served dinner, a huge bowl of boiled lumps of dough in oversalted broth.
Realizing that this was a sincere expression of backcountry hospitality, I
somehow managed to choke it all down.

The eligible woman, whose name was Xiuqin, was bundled up in a
puffy quilted jacket, so I couldn't see much of her in the dim lamplight

except for the rosy blush on her cheeks. She was taller and sturdier than Zhuyin, but I didn't think that she was as pretty. Xiuqin's father was an exceedingly gaunt man, his face deeply etched with the creases of lifelong suffering, who impressed me from the start as a sensible fellow. He offered me some homemade persimmon wine, over which I told him my tale, how I had started out at Shaanxi Normal University and ended up in Xinwang Village. I was as explicit as I had been earlier that day, to forestall any misunderstandings. He was glad to hear that I had been to college and said that even if I had blundered politically, my education was sure to stand me in good stead someday. Zhuyin told me afterward that their whole family had liked me. If I had no objections, Xiuqin could go with me in Mr. Yin's truck to meet my family in Xi'an.

When the time came for Xiuqin to board the truck the next morning, however, I was getting cold feet. I had come to the hinterlands to find a wife, but now I was confronted with the disconcerting prospect of marrying beneath my station. My hesitation annoyed Mr. Yin, who simply couldn't figure out what was bothering me. It hadn't been easy to bring me all the way up there, he reminded me, and Fifth Aunt and Uncle had entrusted him to find a match for me, so he couldn't return empty-handed. Insisting that he should decide who rode in his truck, he invited Xiuqin to climb in.

When we arrived at my house, Fifth Aunt and Uncle were waiting for us there. They liked Xiuqin on sight. Mother was busy cooking a meal for Mr. Yin, so Fifth Aunt sat down with Xiuqin, took her by the hand, and started to question her, while Fifth Uncle stood by, sizing her up.

"She's tall and strong and looks like a good worker," he commented, taking me aside. "She'll make a great farm wife."

After Mr. Yin left, Fifth Aunt told Mother to invite Xiuqin to stay with us for a few days, and she and Fifth Uncle kept trying to talk me into the marriage. I was a peasant now, she reminded me, and I was thirty-one years old, so it was high time I settled down. Meanwhile, Fifth Uncle instructed Mother to go to the bank and withdraw the five hundred yuan that the waterworks had given her in compensation for Father's death. He thought she should seize the opportunity to get me married off that spring.

One unseasonably hot early April afternoon not long after Mr. Yin had

taken Xiuqin home, he brought her back to Xi'an again. This time she had
come to marry me. She was equipped with two trunks, a stack of lumber
for building a kitchen, and the documents she would need to get a marriage license, and she had her sister and Zhuyin in tow.

Fifth Aunt was overjoyed that matters were proceeding so smoothly, but
I was still unenthusiastic. I wondered why Xiuqin and her family seemed
so desperate to get her married off and out of the village. What was she
running away from? I'd been introduced to many prospective brides, and
all of them had objected to my "reactionary" history. Why didn't Xiuqin
and her parents seem to mind? With my head in the clouds, I watched the
preparations for my wedding as if they were for someone else's.

The details were too much for Mother, so Fifth Aunt took charge. She
bustled around ostentatiously, taking Xiuqin shopping for clothes, bedding, and furniture, setting the wedding date, inviting relatives, and
preparing gifts. Mother lacked the patience to deal with family occasions
and tended to grumble at everyone when she was overloaded with things
to do. She scowled her way through all the wedding preparations and kept
accusing me of being a good-for-nothing son. It was my fault that she had
to entertain all these hillbillies, she complained. Besides, she said, I was
such a disgrace that she had never been able to hold her head up in front
of the neighbors, and it was shameful that I could not yet stand on my
own two feet at my age. If the waterworks hadn't given her the five hundred yuan when Father died, she claimed, she wouldn't even have had the
funds for my wedding.

On April 20, 1975, Mother treated a couple of tables full of indifferent relatives to a restaurant banquet, and we had a rather spiritless wedding
ceremony.

After a few days, when I felt as if I could not bear another moment in
our cramped compound, the time came for me to take Xiuqin back with
me to Xinwang Village. Now Mother could finally wash her hands of me.
Her farewell injunctions to me were to stay on the farm now that I was a
married man and to quit coming back to town all the time and disturbing
her peace of mind. Fifth Aunt came over to say good-bye too. She echoed
Mother's sentiments, and as if entrusting a wayward son to Xiuqin, she
entreated her to make sure I behaved myself as a peasant should.

It was harvesttime in Xinwang Village, so we toiled throughout our honeymoon. But after sweating for our work points in the wheat fields all day, we frolicked in bed at night instead of sleeping. Despite our exhaustion, we got out of bed every morning as soon as we heard the bell summoning us to the fields. My limbs were stiff, like the spokes of a stubborn umbrella. After a month of this I was reduced to mere skin and bones, but I still had a spring in my step. Xiuqin, however, was not feeling well, and we could not tell whether her malaise was caused by the unfamiliar locale or the workload. Then she became nauseated and feverish, and we soon confirmed that she was pregnant.

The next few years passed in a blur. We were so busy eking out our hand-to-mouth existence that I never had time to go into town to pester Mother. My nagging suspicions about Xiuqin and her family were completely drowned out by the rigors of peasant life. Before I knew it, we were an old married couple with two children, and Xiuqin's father had passed away.

One cold winter's night when our children were sound asleep, she decided to tell me her whole life story, revealing for the first time how her father had brought ruin upon their entire family, and how, as a consequence, she had despaired of ever finding a husband.

In the manner of an oral historian, I jotted down everything she said that night. Her tale, which filled a dozen pages in my diary, follows:

Fang Xiuqin's Story

Before the Communist takeover, Pa was a penniless man, the youngest of five brothers, with only a two-room thatched hut to his name. He had to keep on the move all the time to escape being drafted by the Guomindang. He was a guerrilla with the Communist Eighth Route Army, but then the Guomindang took him prisoner. After they let him out, he kept doing underground work for the Eighth Route Army. He'd been to middle school, so the other villagers looked up to him. He also performed in the local flower drum opera.

Ma came from a rich peasant family. Her pa was a scholar, who sat in the house studying all the time and never worked in the fields. During a famine one year he sold Ma, who was only six years old, to another family as a child bride. But at the age of sixteen Ma eloped with Pa, and they came back to our village, Ginkgo Gulch, and got married.

My parents got the landlord's mansion during Land Reform, and Pa was appointed head of the township.[1] During the big steel-smelting campaign in the Great Leap Forward of 1958, Pa was transferred to the Iron Valley Station Steel Mill, where he ran the financial office. We were regarded as one of the most revolutionary families in the village in those days, and everyone tried to butter us up. I was the teacher's pet in elementary school; he called me the whiz kid. For a time there was a campaign to make everyone go to the mess hall for communal meals instead of eating at home, and we all gorged ourselves happily, but then the portions shrank, and the mess hall closed down. In 1960 the steel mill closed too, and Pa came back to the village.

After that came the famine, and people were starving to death. We heard rumblings that Defense Minister Peng Dehuai opposed Chairman Mao and that there was going to be a coup in the Party Central Committee. Encouraged by this news, Pa and some people he knew hatched a plot to take over the post office and the township government, cut the telephone lines, break into the Iron Valley Station granary, and give the grain to the people. They planned to act on the second day of the second month of the lunar calendar because that was when the "dragon would rear its head," so it was supposed to be a lucky day for a peasant rebellion.

But Pa's blabbing wrecked his life and put our whole family under a cloud of suspicion. On a shopping trip to town on the twenty-ninth of the first month, he stopped by a friend's house to try to convince him to join their rebellion. The friend ran to the police and squealed as soon as Pa set out for home, and they sent some plainclothesmen out to intercept him. Somehow he slipped into the woods, and they organized a manhunt, but they couldn't find him. I'll never forget how more than twenty fully armed policemen surrounded our house that night. They accused Pa of counterrevolutionary conspiracy and grilled Ma about where his hideout was. But she just stood there and wailed helplessly because Pa had kept her completely in the dark all along.

---

[1] In general, the lower one's class status, the better treatment one was accorded.

Since Pa had taken to the hills, nobody told the rest of his band that their secret was out. On the second day of the second month they went to the mountaintop where they had planned to meet, but the People's Liberation Army got there first and arrested them all. One of them, a woman, tried to escape into the woods, but they shot her in the back as she ran away. I heard that the bullet came out in front through her breast, which exploded and splattered the hillside with blood. After a week of hiding in the mountains, Pa had to come out and confess. Six months later he was sentenced to eight years' hard labor as a counterrevolutionary and sent to Malan Farms to serve his time.

I was only in fourth grade, but I had to bear the stigma of being a counterrevolutionary. My teacher started to give me a hard time, and the other children called me names whenever they saw me. Not daring show my face at school anymore, I dropped out. I had a one-year-old sister and a four-year-old brother, and Grandma had her hands full with the baby-sitting and cooking. Ma had to start taking me to the fields with her, so she told me to gather firewood while she worked.

Our private plot[2] was too much for Ma to handle all alone, and she needed help from our relatives, but they had to come in secret so that the commune cadres wouldn't catch them and yell at them. Once a cadre caught Zhuyin's brother helping us. "Who told you to help a counterrevolutionary family?" he hollered. "What's your class status? You don't give a damn about class struggle, do you? Get the hell out of here right now! I'm warning you, don't let me catch you trying this again." After that our relatives started sneaking over to help at night, but even then Ma was worried, so she made me stand watch at the edge of the field.

Iron Valley Station had a fair on the eighth day of the fourth month every year. Pa always used to take me and buy me a bowl of buckwheat noodles. When fair time came around that year, I threw a tantrum. I envied the other children I saw going down the mountain to the fair with their pas, but Ma wouldn't let me go. She could barely make ends meet, and Pa was gone, so there was nobody to take me. Besides, I was ten years old, and

---

[2] In the early 1960s, after the famine resulting from the Great Leap Forward, peasants were granted small private plots to supplement their food supplies.

she needed my help. My jobs were to gather all the firewood for the household and to go up into the mountains with a basket on my back to get grass and holly leaves for pig fodder.

Production team members were paid in grain according to how many work points they earned, but our family didn't have enough breadwinners. So Ma took me into the fields when I was twelve, even though I could earn only three points for a full day's work. When a famine came, everybody got busy clearing new farmland, the men pushing boulders aside while the women followed behind felling trees. Ma's partner was the landlord's wife, and mine was their daughter. Rocks kept tumbling down from above and bruising my hands and feet. The team chief wouldn't let me rest, even when my bare hands froze during the blizzards of winter. Ma never let me go home either. I cried the whole time I was working my fingers to the bone, and all for a paltry three work points.

All year round we lived on pickled sweet potato leaves, which Ma soaked in big vats. Every morning at daybreak we warmed some and downed them with cornmeal mush. Then we went into the fields and slogged until midday, when I was about to keel over. I watched everybody else go straight home, but Ma made me help her gather firewood and grass along the way.

I earned three work points a day until I was fifteen. Then Ma took somebody's advice that she should marry me off early. She'd get the bride price, and a son-in-law would be an extra pair of hands to help around the house. Matchmakers started visiting us in the evenings, but Ma couldn't make up her mind. I was against the idea anyway, and she couldn't force me into it. She was an ignorant, fatalistic woman who wasted all her money on incense and firecrackers for the gods. Completely illiterate, she couldn't even recognize paper banknotes, so I'd been managing our family finances from the time I was little. Now that my brother and sister were growing up, I felt obliged to stay and help Ma take care of them. Our family disaster had robbed me of my only opportunity for schooling, and I just couldn't let the same thing happen to my brother and sister. No matter what, I was determined to help Ma put them through school.

In those days, raising pigs and selling firewood were the only ways for mountain folk to earn money. Ma and I hiked up into the mountains to chop down oak trees, which we sawed up and hauled out in baskets on our backs and then sold by the main road at the entrance to our gulch. It was a six-mile journey, and the most that I could carry at one time was fifty pounds.

One day I made three trips, with a full load of wood each time, and earned more than two yuan, which I used to replenish our supply of salt and kerosene. But I overdid it that day, and blood started streaming out from between my legs. I was too young to know where the blood was coming from or how dangerous bleeding was, and I didn't even have any clean paper, so I just splashed myself with cold river water. Another time, when wood was selling for a good price, I spent a whole day chopping wood in the mountains. I gashed my hand carelessly with the ax, but I had to take care of myself, since I was alone. Luckily I remembered an old folk remedy and stanched the bleeding with a handful of dirt.

We were deep in debt. Ma earned six work points a day, and together with my three, that made a measly total of nine. The cash value of a full day's work for an able-bodied laborer was less than twenty cents, but Ma and I made barely half that much. We slaved all year round, never missing a day, but at the end of the year we still owed the team seventy or eighty yuan. The team didn't have the money to pay its members anyway, so it just kept careful records instead. Then, when the time came to allot work points, the team left it up to the members to haggle it out, and the members who were supposed to be getting paid had to collect their pay themselves from the people who owed the team money. Every year my family sold a fat pig, which we had raised on leaves and grass. Since we had these pigs, our credit was good, but the cash we made selling them always got swallowed up by team members who were collecting their pay.

When the Cultural Revolution began, everybody else joined the Red Guards, but the landlord's daughter and I weren't considered eligible. Our family was still living in the landlord's mansion, and his family lived next door to us. The Red Guards raided their house first. The landlord had been dead for a while, so they hauled his first wife out for a struggle session. They hung her on a big tree outside our house overnight, and the next morning we found her dead body still hanging there.

Next they ransacked our house, claiming we had concealed weapons.

They turned everything upside down, and even ripped up our private plot with pickaxes, without finding anything. Insisting that we must have a cache of weapons somewhere, they dragged Ma to a struggle session and tried to bully her into revealing where it was. They hustled me along to watch, and I crouched in the corner with tears rolling down my cheeks.

Later the People's Liberation Army was stationed in our village to run a study group, and there was a campaign to reassign people's class status. For no good reason, they switched ours from lower-middle peasants to upper-middle peasants. Once a soldier stopped Ma when she was on her way home from the fields and bawled her out. "Are you the wife of Fang Xiangwu, the counterrevolutionary?" he demanded. When Ma admitted that she was, he poked her in the face and hurled insults at her for a couple of hours, while a crowd of villagers gathered around to watch. That night Grandma cooked our dinner of cornmeal mush mixed with sweet potatoes, but all of us were crying too hard to eat it.

I turned to the portrait of Chairman Mao on our wall. "Chairman Mao," I sobbed, "didn't you say that the People's Liberation Army was the people's own army? Why was this soldier so mean to Ma? She never did anything wrong. Why should we pay for Pa's sins? Isn't it enough that he's doing time in the labor camps, or are you trying to wipe out our whole family? Tell me, Chairman Mao, whose policy is this?"

Grandma was a fearless old soul. After we'd closed our door for the night, she'd point her finger at Mao's portrait and give him a piece of her mind. "Mao"—she cursed under her breath—"you old bastard! Just look at that huge mole on your chin. You're such a butcher! It's your fault that my daughter has to slave all day in the mountains just like a man. You've robbed the people of their food and driven so many to their deaths! The world would be a better place without you. Mao, you old fiend, I'd like to stab your carcass to death with a needle." Whipping herself into a fury, she slapped Mao's mouth with her shoe and jabbed her sewing needle into the mole on his chin.

There was a poor peasant in our team who had two sons. The elder one had a limp and a prickly temper, and we all called him Roughneck. Nobody wanted to marry him, so he was still a bachelor even though he was thirty-something. His family sent a matchmaker around to see the landlord's family, and the landlord's concubine started scheming. She liked Roughneck because he was a tough guy from a poor peasant family, and she wanted a son-in-law who could protect her a bit. So she gave her daughter Dengwa to him in marriage.

I had started to think about finding a husband too, now that I was almost seventeen, but all the go-betweens who came to our house were just trying to take advantage of us and get something for nothing. Since Pa was a counterrevolutionary, they all matched me up with louts like Roughneck. But I was different from Dengwa. I wasn't the kind of girl to let people push me around. I wanted to marry for love, not just to gain a protector, and I turned down all the suitors I didn't like. But the ones I did like snubbed me because I wasn't from a good family.

Roughneck had a brother named Shuangxi who was cast from a different mold. A gentle fellow with a high school diploma, he was the village elementary school teacher. Almost all the girls liked him. I did too, but he was several years older than I was, so he thought of me as a child and never noticed me. I had to keep my crush on him a secret.

I got so frustrated with all the matchmaking that I fell seriously ill. It started with a high fever the first night, and the next day my legs were so achy that I couldn't get out of bed. Ma couldn't afford a doctor, so I lay in bed for three months without any medicine. All she could do was kowtow to the gods, make offerings of incense and lucky strips of yellow paper, and pray. When my uncle came to visit and saw that my legs were paralyzed, he took me home with him. Somehow he finally managed to cure me with a combination of acupuncture, hot broth made of herbs he'd gathered in the mountains, and a few other folk remedies.

My pay was eventually raised to four work points a day, but the team always assigned Ma and me to work in the farthest mountains. Even our private plot was on a mountain peak. She and I had to lug in all the manure we needed on our backs, basket by basket, and haul out all the sweet potatoes we gathered the same way. One year the team had a bumper crop of turnips, and we received a huge handout in the field, but then Ma and I had to tote them home ourselves on our backs. The basket rubbed a sore spot in the skin over my tailbone, so I flung it to the ground in agony. Ma picked up a big turnip and hit me with it. I ran to the edge of a cliff and threatened to jump unless she quit making me work so hard. We were utterly miserable, but we just had to keep slogging. When I couldn't stand it any longer, I'd sit on the mountainside and wail, and Ma would try to comfort me with the promise that things would get better when Pa came home from the camps.

He did come home in 1969, and things did improve once we had three breadwinners. There were no political campaigns for almost two years, and people left us alone. But all too soon another campaign began, and a work team came to our village and discovered that Pa had escaped official labeling as a criminal counterrevolutionary element. They reviewed his dossier at the Shang-Luo Prefecture office and held a brigade-wide meeting at the end of 1970 to publicize his updated status.

From then until the day he died, Pa never enjoyed a day of peace. I hated watching what they did to him at struggle sessions. The cadres chose two of us family members and made us escort him onto the stage. We couldn't refuse, or we'd be in the same boat as he was. We had to stand on either side of him and twist his elbows behind his back, and then we had to take him onstage when the cadre told us to. They hung a placard around his neck and made him stand with his head shoved down so low that his waist was bent at a ninety-degree angle. Then the village toughs came prancing out and beat him up. Pa kept saying that he'd been better off in the labor camps and would rather have had a longer sentence than come home to this. "They're trying to do me in," he'd mutter. "I'm not long for this world."

Our village was such a hellhole I decided to stop looking for a husband there and try to find a way out. In 1972 my cousin from Heyang County brought his tractor to our village to pick up a load of wood, and I rode with him to Xi'an for the first time in my life. We ate in restaurants, went shopping, and walked in the parks. For a hillbilly girl like me, that three-day trip to Xi'an was like a visit to heaven. My cousin bought me a bunch of strange-looking greenish yellow things called bananas, but I'd never seen them before, so I just held them in my hand, not knowing how to eat them. He and I drove by high school and college campuses, and I found out that city girls my age didn't have to work and that their parents supported them through school. I was terribly envious of them, strolling along the boulevards in their skirts, sucking on their popsicles.

These new sights whetted my appetite for city life; I had to find a way to move there. First I got a job at the commune's construction site; then I found work building a reservoir thirty miles from home. It took me a whole day to walk there with my bedding and food on my back. The female workers all shared a tent, which helped me to get to know people, and I started to look for ways to move to Xi'an.

We got plenty of work points for our labor, along with a grain subsidy. By selling my leftover steamed buns to fellow workers, I managed to save up enough money for several visits to Xi'an, where I was introduced to various prospective husbands and their families. Except for one who was a worker, all were peasants who lived on the outskirts of the city. But every one of them had to look for a hillbilly wife because of some shortcoming that made him ineligible for a city woman.

I searched high and low but never found the right man. I went to Xi'an so often that the villagers started to prattle about my being involved in some kind of racket there, and the cadres singled me out for criticism at a brigade-wide meeting. Discouraged, I decided to quit wasting my money on useless trips to Xi'an and to try my luck in the county seat of Danfeng instead. Someone introduced me to a tall, fair-complexioned young temporary worker in the cement factory there, and we hit it off right away. The next evening we got together on the Danfeng River bridge, and then he took me to see his house, a big new one with three rooms, where we had a nice, long chat. As we parted, he said he liked me, and would make up his mind after he'd talked with his family. I'd known better than to mention Pa's crime, so I was terrified that his parents would ask around and find out about it. That's just what happened, and he jilted me.

It started to dawn on me that I might never find a decent man. When the Chinese New Year came around, everyone else was merrymaking while I sat alone at home with my tears. From then on I refused all offers of matchmaking. I wished I could be adopted by somebody with good class status, so that I could get rid of the awful stigma of the counterrevolutionary label. But who would want to adopt a great big girl like me? Every night I sobbed into my pillow.

In 1974 we were caught again in the throes of a merciless campaign for class struggle. Pa was hauled out to a dozen struggle sessions, big and small. The first few times the rest of us family members sat and brooded at home instead of going. Then the work team came over and yelled at us and forced me to write a self-critical essay. After that I didn't dare stay away from the struggle sessions. I watched Pa stand onstage, enduring the piercing, icy stares of the other villagers. I couldn't stop the tears from rolling down my cheeks, but I was afraid to make a sound, so sometimes I had to run outside into a cornfield to cry.

On the day of one of the struggle sessions the work team, along with a gang of villagers, burst into our house, carrying scales and sacks. Without any explanation, they opened our storage bins and started to scoop out all our wheat. All we could do was stand by and watch helplessly as they made off with two hundred pounds, the entire harvest from our private plot, claiming that we didn't deserve to have so much land. This supply was supposed to feed our family for the next six months. After they'd finished plundering us, they finally let Pa come home from the struggle session.

Thinking that I'd better find a husband no matter what, just as a survival tactic, I left for Xi'an again. As Ma was seeing me off, she warned me that if I was too picky to settle on anyone this time, I wouldn't be welcome at home anymore. Eventually I found a prospective husband, but I didn't really like him. The son of a peasant from the outskirts of the city, he was short and ugly, and his ma seemed mean. On our engagement day she gave me a long list of burdensome requirements her daughter-in-law would have to meet. I wanted to back out, but I was afraid of what Ma would say, so I agreed in a daze and accepted a betrothal gift of clothing and shoes.

I went home to think the matter over. The more I thought, the more I regretted my decision, so I wrapped up the clothes and asked someone to return them to the go-between in Xi'an who had originally introduced us. He started sending me worried letters, pressing me to come to Xi'an to see him. I desperately needed to find a more suitable match, so that I could break off this engagement.

Right around then Zhuyin happened to mention that she knew a mail truck driver named Mr. Yin who could probably find me an eligible peasant from the Xi'an area, and she offered to ask for his help. Soon afterward she came to ask my advice. Mr. Yin had found a potential husband for *her*, a man from the city whose entire family worked in Xi'an, although he himself had settled in rural Chang'an County. The problem was that she didn't think he was a good enough match for her because he lacked a proper job.

"Tell Mr. Yin to bring him up here for a visit," I told her. "If he seems all right, you should accept his proposal. Then, once you're taken care of, you'll be able to rescue me." Zhuyin asked me to go help her look you over when you came, but I sent my sister instead, and I put in my usual afternoon's work in the fields that day.

After she'd seen you, my sister came home to give me a report. "Zhuyin doesn't want that fellow from the city because he was a political prisoner," she told me. "But he's really good-looking! Actually, he looks a lot like the head of our geological prospecting team." Then Zhuyin brought you over to our house. "I brought him here for you," she told me. "If you decide you want him, you can take the mail truck out of here tomorrow."

You were sitting in the lamplight, and I was peeking at you from the shadows. Zhuyin wanted to help Mr. Yin complete his mission, so she kept whispering nice things about you in my ear. As I sat there watching you and listening to her, I started to fall in love. Then you and Pa sat down together, and you got his blessing, especially since you'd been to college and had some book learning. Finally we met face-to-face in the light, and you know what happened next.

45

A Woman Is the Heart of a Home

Cocks crowed in the night as our rosy-cheeked son and daughter slumbered soundly on the warm *kang*. Xiuqin went on with her story, disclosing many things for the first time.

Fang Xiuqin's Story (Continued)

On one of my husband-hunting expeditions in Xi'an, I stayed with a family of highway construction workers for a few days. I had their apartment to myself while they were at work, and I sat staring out the window at the endless stream of bicycles passing by on the boulevard below. Young couples often rode in tandem on one bike, with the man in front and the woman clasping him from behind, her cheek pressed against his back and her skirt whooshing in the wind. I hated the wretched mountain gully that I came from. I had never so much as laid hands on a bicycle in my entire life! The first bike I ever rode was yours, the day you took me to see your house in Xinwang Village. It was hard for me to balance, so you told me to lean forward and put my arms around your waist, but I was afraid to make body contact. So I leaned backward instead, with my legs sticking out stiffly, and I was so wobbly that I kept tipping the bike over.

I had a few second thoughts when we got to your place. Your yard was bare, you didn't even have a gate, your room was tiny and cramped, and you had an old toothpaste box on the wall with only one pair of chopsticks in it. I took some comfort in the idea that at least we'd be on our own, and I wouldn't have a mother-in-law to boss me around or your brother and sisters to deal with. But I kept worrying about whether you were actually considered a criminal, so I went and asked your team chief, who assured me that you weren't. Once I had restored my peace of mind, I made my way home.

When I got there, I found out that the brigade leaders had snatched Pa for an interrogation as soon as I was gone. They were mad because I had left without permission, and they were sure that Pa had sent me on some counterrevolutionary errand in Xi'an. They tried to squeeze a confession out of him, but there was nothing he could say, so they bound him with rope. As soon as I got home, I went straight to the work team and told them they didn't have any right to persecute my pa like that. I did not mince my words. I said that I'd been looking for a husband and demanded to see their evidence that I'd been on a counterrevolutionary errand. Until that moment I'd been shilly-shallying about marrying you. But when I saw what a mess things were at home, I decided I'd better get out of there and move in with you as soon as I could. I wasn't going to do any better, I figured, so I might as well take the plunge.

First I had to get a letter from the brigade office, which I was supposed to take to the Iron Valley Station Commune office to get the certificate I needed for the marriage license. But the brigade office refused to issue the letter unless I "came clean" about my visits to Xi'an. I stomped into the brigade secretary's office and asked him to tell me what they suspected me of doing in Xi'an. Everybody gave me the runaround for a few days, but I finally got the letter, along with my certificate from the commune office. But the work team thought I had a "bad attitude" and couldn't bear to let me go scot-free. So they went and asked the commune secretary not to release me unless I made a full confession.

The next day a couple of militiamen from the commune came and asked me if I'd gotten my certificate. Unaware of the mischief the work team had been up to behind my back, I admitted that I had. They asked me to show it to them, but when I obeyed, they confiscated it and turned to leave. When I demanded an explanation, they told me to "go ask the commune secretary." He said he had given it to his clerk, but when I asked the clerk, he refused to give it back without the commune secretary's permission. The two of them had a great time passing the buck back and forth all the way until nightfall, yelling at me and making me grovel.

I spent the night at a nearby relative's house and went back to the office the next morning. The secretary put me off until noon, and then he went to a meeting. I started to tail the clerk around instead. He ducked into his room, then stuck his head out the door and beckoned to me. I went inside. He was sitting on his bed, which was hung with a mosquito net, and he had a charcoal fire crackling in his brazier. Suddenly he started sweet-talking me.

"I have a question that I can't ask you in the office," he said, inviting me to sit down beside him. I cowered in the doorway. The look on his face was a giveaway that the question was going to be lecherous.

"Why are you in such a hurry to get married?" he asked. "Did you let him knock you up?"

I would normally have protested against such shameless slander, but at that moment I had to take whatever he dished out.

"Nonsense," I told him primly. "That's not it at all."

He was leering at me now. He stood up and took a step toward me.

"I don't believe you. Let me take a peek under your jacket."

I refused, cringing in the doorway.

"Undo your belt," he said. "I won't believe you unless you let me feel your belly."

I finally exploded. "You're just taking advantage of me. Why don't you go ask the people in my village what kind of person I am? They'll tell you I don't let anybody push me around. Come on, let's go see what the secretary thinks about all this."

He suddenly turned hostile. "All right," he replied, waving his finger in my face. "Forget it for now. Get the hell out of here. And if you go around bad-mouthing me, I'll make sure you're stuck in this commune forever."

When the secretary returned, I went back to ask him for the certificate but got a tongue-lashing instead.

"I won't give it to you, even if you pester me all night. You're the daughter of a counterrevolutionary. If I release you, you'll probably go to Xi'an to have the verdict against your father overturned."

Meanwhile, the clerk stood and gloated on the sidelines, smirking and puffing on his cigarette. I realized that I was beating my head against a brick wall, so I walked out and went home with a heavy heart. A couple of days later my brother-in-law went to our brigade branch secretary for help. Luckily he took pity on me and managed to extract my certificate from the commune secretary's clutches. The very next day I took the postal truck to Xi'an, and then you and I went to your commune office and got our marriage licenses.

I could tell that at least half the peasants in your village were not pleased to see you settle down to start a family there. For them, all it meant was less land to go around and more mouths to feed. They saw us as freeloaders and begrudged us everything. Our neighbor Rangdao groused the loudest. He had hoped you would move away so that he could expand into your plot of land, but that wasn't about to happen now that you were a family man.

Right after we got married, Rangdao talked the team leadership into sending you back to the reservoir on business. While you were gone, some malicious villagers came over and tried to worm themselves into my confidence. Pretending to be looking out for my interests, they did their best to talk me into leaving you and going back to live with my parents. One person cautioned me that a soft city boy like you would never make a good husband and blamed you for starting a sloppy fad among the local young men, shuffling around in slippers. Somebody else insinuated that you were lazy and told me that you lolled around on Sundays, stuffing your face, even indulging yourself with store-bought eggs. The villagers produced eggs strictly as a cash sideline, and nobody ate them, not even the young, the old, or invalids. And you were a big strong man, who had never been sick a day in his life! But what Yinzui said scared me the most. He said the cops had come to snoop about you and were ready to hustle you away in handcuffs at the slightest excuse.

As for your Uncle Li Baoyu—he's really not worthy of the title, so I'll just call him your old man—it would have been no trouble to cook for him if he had just treated me decently, but he didn't. Guodong and some other friends of ours urged him to welcome me into his household. But I hadn't received any grain yet, since I'd arrived just before the summer harvest, so he refused to take me in because he was afraid I'd cut into his supply. To make matters worse, he wouldn't even let me use his kitchen, so I had to go out under the eaves and make do with your coal briquette stove. At my wits' end, I had Guodong send a messenger to the reservoir to ask you to come home.

I couldn't wait to build a kitchen and a wall in front of the house so that we could live in peace. I hauled dirt into the yard whenever I had a moment, creating a huge mound by the time you got back from the reservoir. Thanks to the help of Guodong and some of your friends from other villages, we managed to get everything built before the summer harvest. The yard was more secure, and the nosy neighbors had to quit wandering in.

Before long, my residence permit was transferred to your commune, and I received my share after the summer harvest. But the villagers wrangled with us like hungry ghosts over every pathetic scrap that came our way, and we had no money or status to protect us. The way they saw it, you were an outsider to start with, and now your new hillbilly wife had waltzed into town just in time for a handout. Of course they resented us! After we got our grain, Xingshan's dad and Kuanrang kept grumbling about how certain people hadn't even been here when there was work to be done but had turned up just in time for the grain distribution. I knew I had to show them right from the start that I meant business.

"I'm a member of this team, just like everyone else," I announced. "I deserve my share of the harvest. If you disagree, then tell me so to my face, and we can go ask the leaders what they think."

My first year here was an uphill struggle. The villagers gave me a hard time out in the fields. I bore their abuse in silence if I could, but sometimes I had to strike back. After our daughter, Xiaojia, was born in my second year here, people realized they weren't going to be able to scare me away and started to leave us alone.

You're from a rich family, and moving to the countryside was a step down in the world for you, so all you wanted was to get back to the city. I tried to reason with you about building a life here, but you weren't interested. "I'll kill myself if I'm still stuck out here in the sticks when I'm forty," you ranted. You were just letting off steam, without considering how your blathering made me feel. You and I are really different. I had always been miserably poor, and even though we weren't well off in the early days of our marriage, I was still better fed than I had ever been. Although you didn't even want to try to improve our lot in the countryside, I had my heart set on showing all the people who looked down on me a thing or two. Our future looked dim. Nobody knew if you would ever be rehabilitated and transferred back to town, and I didn't think it was a safe bet. Now that I had cast my lot with a peasant, I had to make the best of things.

I realized right away that I needed to produce a son. You didn't want to be saddled with children yet, so you bought me some birth control pills in town. I told you I was taking them, but I was fibbing. I had tossed them directly into the trash. I was twenty-three, and I knew that I would miss my chance to fulfill myself as a woman if I let you make all the decisions.

Unfortunately our first child was a daughter, Xiaojia. The official policy was not to give her a residence permit unless I got an IUD, so I complied. But as soon as her permit was issued, I bribed someone to remove the device.[1] I had my life planned out, even though I didn't talk to you about it. I never wasted my breath arguing with you. I figured that I'd never get anything done if I always had to get your permission first. My plan was to hurry up and have some kids, and I did it; I had our son, Xiaozhuang, a year later. You wanted me to abort him, but I refused. Just think, if I had obeyed you, we wouldn't have Xiaozhuang now! I had two children in the space of three years. As the saying goes, "One son and one daughter is heaven on earth." People stopped bullying me. In fact the other women were dying of jealousy.

When we were first married, we fought all the time. We were so different from each other that we never seemed to agree. I knew I couldn't change you, but I refused to let things slide, the way you did. Finally, I decided to do all the chores myself to avoid constant power struggles with

[1] In the early days of Chinese Communist birth control policy, some rural areas were rather haphazard in their enforcement. The strict one-child policy began in 1979.

you. In the meantime you kept disappearing into town for days on end, either on team errands or just on jaunts of your own.

Whenever you were away, people whispered in my ear. "He's on a lark in town, leaving you to do all the work at home. You fool! Why don't you go with him and live it up at his mom's house next time?"

"I like it here just fine," I would reply blandly. "I don't need to go into town and freeload off his family."

I knew that if I wanted anything done right, I'd have to do it myself. You were so careless that I even had to take over men's chores, like grinding flour at the mill. If I let you do it, you were too lazy to salvage the bran, so you wasted it and came home with a measly little bag of refined white flour. We were broke in those days and couldn't afford to waste a scrap. I always brought home a lot more flour than you did, even though it wasn't white anymore. Our buns were so heavily flecked with bran that the neighbors made fun of my scrimping.

Since I was good at raising pigs, I decided to raise one, like most of the other villagers. As usual, you couldn't be bothered, so I went to the market alone to buy my piglet. Too bad we didn't have enough wheat to give the poor little creature any decent mash. I had nothing more to feed it than a few watered-down handfuls of ground-up hay mixed with bran. Fortunately it was hardy and managed to grow pretty big anyway, but its belly skin still hung slack from malnutrition. It failed inspection at the state-run cooperative, which refused to buy it, so I sold it to a peasant for eighty yuan. This was the first money I'd earned in Xinwang Village. I used it to buy an old cart so that we'd finally have one of our own.

Chairman Mao died in 1976. First came the Tangshan earthquake,[2] and I took Xiaojia to sleep with me in a cornstalk shed in front of the house in case there were any aftershocks. You just slept inside, completely unfazed. So I was the first to hear the outdoor loudspeakers announcing

[2] The Tangshan earthquake, which directly preceded Mao's death, measured approximately eight on the Richter scale and killed more than two hundred thousand people. Its epicenter was about one hundred miles east of Beijing, but significant damage occurred as far away as Beijing, and even residents of Xi'an felt the aftershocks. According to Chinese folk belief, the earthquake was interpreted as a harbinger of the emperor's (Mao's) demise.

Mao's death and blaring out all the dirges, and I ran inside to tell you. Knowing better than to let our feelings show in public, we celebrated behind closed doors after dark. I'll bet people all over China were whooping it up under the covers in their beds that night! You told me this meant that you'd be able to go back to the city. Now that old Mao was dead, you were sure things were going to loosen up.

WHILE XIUQIN PAUSED to stoke the *kang*, I lit a cigarette, took a drag, and lay down again. Li Baoyu had breathed his last on this *kang*, I recalled. Soon before Mao's death, Kuanrang had replaced Li Baoyu as head of the Poor and Lower- Middle Peasants' Association. This had been a big blow to the old man, who fretted that the demotion would cost him work points. Then Mao died, and the old man went to the village memorial hall to pay his respects to his "savior." Grief and weariness took their toll, and he had simply shriveled up like a frostbitten leaf by the time the nationwide mourning ceremonies were finished.

Then he was struck with an even bigger blow: The team chopped down his three elm trees on the pretext that his plot of land was seven feet wider than the regulation size and that the trees, which were in the contested area, were team property. Li Baoyu remained tight-lipped as he watched them do their work, but he was seething inside. After they had carted away the lumber, only three forlorn stumps and a layer of damp sawdust remained. The stumps oozed bubbly sap, as if they were beheaded men who had been buried up to the neck in our yard. Li Baoyu stormed into his room and spent several days sulking in bed. After that he caught one upper respiratory infection after another and had a relapse of his chronic bronchitis. Mao's death seemed to have sapped the life out of the poor old man; he had succumbed both physically and mentally and dragged his feet all winter. On warm days he would come outside and sun himself for hours on a pile of cornstalks in the yard. Looking at his droopy head wrapped in its headscarf, I wondered what was going through his mind.

He fell silent, too lethargic even to curse people anymore.

He and I had long since divided our assets, yet he was still supposedly my adoptive father, and the villagers were watching us with a critical eye.

Every time his health took a turn for the worse, I had to rush to the clinic to arrange for costly medical treatments, while Xiuqin waited on him in bed. The villagers kept horning in on our business, stopping by continuously with unsolicited advice and expressions of feigned concern.

Although he had suffered from bronchitis for decades, he had never been examined in a major hospital, and we could not afford to take him to one. During one communal outdoor meal Dinghan commented that Li Baoyu was coughing up bloody phlegm and speculated that his lungs were riddled with lesions. Kuanrang predicted that he might not live much beyond New Year's and certainly would not make it until the spring harvest. Just before New Year's Fendan's mother called on us and discreetly pointed out to Xiuqin that she had better start to make funeral preparations.

That year I received the fewest work points ever and no cash distribution. When I visited Mother, she scrounged up a few pounds of star anise and Sichuan pepper through some connections of hers and gave them to me to resell at a profit to the peasants. These tightly rationed spices, traditionally used for stewing pork at New Year's, had been a special seasonal dispensation to city residents. The peasants ate pork only once a year, and this was the time for it. My rare spices were in great demand. Xiuqin wrapped them into tiny packets of half an ounce or one ounce each, which I sold at the market for about thirty yuan. Xiuqin used this sum to beg or borrow a few cloth ration tickets and bought some cheap black and white cloth to stitch together a burial suit for Li Baoyu and mourning outfits for us.

Once the crusty old bachelor had breathed his last, his house and plot of land would be ours. Certain villagers begrudged us such a generous inheritance and tried to make life difficult for us. Li Baoyu had no valuable possessions, except perhaps his leather jacket and anastigmatic glasses. The villagers claimed that the lenses of these glasses were made of a precious crystal that could cure pinkeye or cool you off in the summer. Kuanrang and a few others started to ask Xiuqin about the glasses while Li Baoyu was still on his deathbed. Her response was to tiptoe into Li Baoyu's room to hide them, and she took a peek at him while she was picking them up from the chest by his *kang*. Too weak to utter a word, he kept his gaze riveted on the glasses, sending shivers down her spine.

He died at breakfasttime one morning during New Year's vacation, when the villagers were idle. Bored peasants love to attend weddings and funerals, and they flocked to our house to witness his death and to see how I comported myself. They seemed to be hoping that some lapse of mine in my role as adopted son would prove that I did not deserve to inherit his property.

According to village custom, as soon as the deceased had breathed his last, his children were supposed to bathe his head and feet and dress him in his burial suit. The crowd was waiting to see how well I discharged my duties. Li Baoyu had concealed his scalp under his filthy sheepskin headscarf until the bitter end. I removed it with my own hands, exposing his bald scalp to the light of day for the first—and the last—time. The skin was reddish, like the newly formed membrane under a scab. As I wiped it with a warm cloth, I could tell that it was too delicate to withstand vigorous scrubbing. Once the ritual bathing was complete, a couple of villagers helped me dress him in the burial suit that Xiuqin had made. Then his corpse was ready to be placed in the mourning hall.

My efforts got the nod from the village elders, and the tense, oppressive atmosphere dissipated.

The villagers could not wait to find out what hidden treasures the old miser had left behind. Led by Yinzui, they started ransacking his possessions for unexpected booty, starting with his *kang* and mat. I had enlisted the help of my friend Siji from Team Number Eight, a legendary "cool cat" whose scowl was enough to scare anyone into submission. He sprang into action and zeroed in quickly on a little earthenware pot under a pile of rags in a niche in the wall, inside which he found the forty yuan the old man had just received on his annual New Year's payday. He handed the money to Xiuqin, who used it to send someone out to buy cigarettes and liquor for the guests.

The ramshackle chest beside Li Baoyu's *kang* was still locked, and the villagers were dying to know what was inside. We had no key, so Yinzui asked some people to take it outside and pry it open. Then he extracted its contents: a few bundles of cotton, which he gave to Xiuqin, and some old clothes, rags, and new sheepskin headscarves. He let the villagers squabble over the few items we did not want. Finally, he pulled out some fruit candy that Li Baoyu had bought for the New Year but had never had a chance to eat and handed it out to the children, as if we were celebrating a Chinese wedding.

Xiuqin and I made a division of labor; she took charge of domestic problems, leaving me to deal with the world outside. I dug the grave and borrowed money for the coffin, while she took care of Xiaojia and dealt with the big shots who came to call. Gently but firmly, she haggled with them over the financial arrangements surrounding Li Baoyu's death. Displeased to see us inherit the house, they tried to squeeze us for a fancy funeral to provide entertainment for the villagers. They even requested that we hire the commune movie projection team to come and show a film, along with a band of traditional musicians to send Li Baoyu off in style. While they pretended that their motive was to honor Li Baoyu, their real aim was to milk us dry. We knew that peasants, with their perverse sense of social justice, believed in social leveling. We consented to all reasonable requests, but Xiuqin vetoed the excessive ones.

Some people saw Li Baoyu's death as an opportunity to try to borrow money from us, and Xiuqin rebuffed all of them. Taking offense, the more prickly individuals started bad-mouthing us in the village. I knew that boors like them might make it impossible for us to bury the old man unless we capitulated to their demands. In self-defense against their monstrous behavior, I mobilized a vigilante team, some tough city boys who had been resettled in nearby villages. They strutted in and out of my house, wielding clubs and ready for action. This calmed things down, and we finally laid Li Baoyu to rest without incident.

In the spring of 1977 Xiuqin and I came into our own. Now that Chairman Mao had disappeared from the scene, spiriting away Li Baoyu along with him, we felt as if a heavy sluice gate had opened, unleashing a welcome springtime torrent. I took over Li Baoyu's job of recording work points and was even put in charge of recording the labors of the team chief and the accountant. As my status in the village rose, it became easier for us to get things done. We built the gates in our front and back yards and planted some trees.

Xiuqin loved to raise chickens. She had wanted to try it for ages, but the old man had hated them. Irritated by their scrabbling and defecating, he had always ferociously shooed away any stray chickens that wandered in from the neighbors' houses. Anyway, it had been out of the question to raise chickens before we installed our gates; they would have run away or been stolen. But now that our yard was secure, Xiuqin could start her brood. When I was in the field recording work points every day, she carried Xiaojia around while she fastened the gate and fed the chicks. The chicks' yellow down turned white, their feathers sprouted, their legs lengthened, their necks acquired curves, and their tails tilted up. The young roosters sported red cockscombs, while the hens grew voluptuous. When summer came, they scurried around the yard, looking for food, the bolder ones surrounding Xiaojia and pecking at the noodles in her bowl. Once a chick grabbed one end of a noodle in its beak, while Xiaojia hung on to the other end with her chopsticks, the two of them locked in a tug-of-war. That winter the hens started to lay eggs, and by the following spring Xiuqin finally had an established brood. Like the other village women, she began to tote baskets full of eggs to market.

XIUQIN HAD FINISHED stoking the *kang* and sat down again, and I asked her if she had anything to add to her tale.

"A peasant proverb says, 'A woman is the heart of a home,'" she concluded. "Just as a shoe is bolstered by its shoe last, a house needs a woman's touch. You two men lived here for years, but it was always a barebones bachelor pad. If you hadn't married me and brought me here, who knows where you would have ended up! Both your mom and aunt were glad to see you saddled with a wife and kids. Once you had to stop running around in town, the police lost interest in you. Otherwise you might have been arrested when Mao died."

Even though the Gang of Four was "smashed" right after Mao died, the Central Committee mounted a campaign to criticize Deng Xiaop-

---

[3] Deng Xiaoping (1904–1997) served as secretary-general of the Communist Party but was purged during the Cultural Revolution and then reinstated briefly as deputy premier until he was purged again after Zhou Enlai's death in 1976. He reemerged into power in the late 1970s and was China's most powerful leader until his death. Always associated with looser government control of the economy (without political liberalization), he eventually laid the groundwork for the resurgence of Chinese capitalism.

ing,[3] and kept him out of power. Hua Guofeng[4] perpetuated Mao's policies, so there were no substantive social changes to celebrate. I was deeply disappointed.

Xiuqin's family was still enduring semistarvation, and we were still suffering in Xinwang Village too. She was concealing her father's troubles from me; all I knew was that he had been ailing for a long time. Later she revealed that although he was desperately ill, the cadres had rousted him from his sickbed to go work in the fields. On one visit home she had found him lying on a pile of straw outside the house, vomiting continuously. At the sight of her he had burst into tears, wailing that he was not long for this world. She had taken him to a big hospital in Xi'an, where he had been diagnosed with advanced stomach cancer. It was too late to save him, and he had passed away at home soon afterward.

I had started to listen to the English-language instructional broadcasts on the official Shaanxi radio station. The villagers all scoffed that I was learning "foreign tongue twisters." Xiuqin shared their opinion, although she was intrigued by the sight of me muttering gibberish in my corner. While I was intoning my vocabulary words, she was teaching Xiaojia to say, "Down with English!" Xiaojia raised her tiny fist and shouted something that sounded like "Down with," but could not pronounce the rest.

---

[4] Hua Guofeng, a protégé of Mao's, chaired the Communist Party from 1976 to 1981, when he was replaced by Deng Xiaoping.

46

Thaw

I HAD DROPPED MY study of English when the police were keeping tabs on me in 1974, and the simple conversational skills I had learned from the Voice of America had grown exceedingly rusty by the time I started afresh in January 1978.

This time I used *Basic College English*, a new two-volume textbook produced by the Western Languages department of Beijing University for "worker-peasant-soldier" students.[1] The book had been a present from Chaoying, a bright, lovely young woman student from Xi'an who had recently been sent to our village. With her honeyed tongue, she blended seamlessly with the young peasants and followed their example in addressing me as Big Brother Chunlai. A few months before, she had made an unsuccessful attempt at the 1977 college entrance examinations, the first that had been offered in a decade. She inquired why I had not tried them myself, and I explained that I belonged in graduate school, as I had been

---

[1] When Chinese colleges and universities were reopened after ten years' closure during the Cultural Revolution, many of the first students were older workers, peasants, and soldiers who were chosen more for their political reliability than for their academic promise.

to college already. When she went off to her New Year's holiday in Xi'an, she brought back the new textbook, saying that she had waited in line an entire morning for it at the New China Bookstore near the Bell Tower. She intended to use it herself but found that she did not know enough English to make any headway on her own. She asked me to study the material and then help her along.

"You said you wanted to take the graduate school entrance exams, didn't you?" she prodded. "English is one of the requirements, so you need this book more than I do. You can have it." The warmth in her big eyes rekindled my long-suppressed thirst for knowledge.

This was a life-altering windfall for me, after years of dull submission to peasant norms. My eyes swam when I first glanced at the printed pages, as if eons had passed since I had tried to decipher the English alphabet. Three years of marriage and the birth of two children had lulled me imperceptibly into contentment with the peasant ideal of "wife and kids warm and snug on the *kang*."

My wife disapproved of my studies and lacked respect for books. One day in the kitchen I found that she had covered a jar of red pepper with my copy of *The Songs of Chu*, smearing the book with red grease. A historical precedent for her behavior sprang to my mind. Back in the Han dynasty a famous scholar named Yang Xiong had written a scholarly analysis of *The Book of Changes*; another scholar, Liu Xin, had scoffed that the only use the reading public would have for such an obscure treatise would be as a lid for soy sauce jars. Now I had seen one of my own books suffer a similar fate!

Another time, when I was cleaning house, I found my long-forgotten volume of Hegel's *Philosophy of History* under the bed. As I dusted its torn cover, I recalled how it had ended up there one night a couple of years before. I had wanted to read, while my wife had wanted to sleep. Every time she switched the light off, I had grabbed the pull string and switched it on again. The string had finally snapped, and she had shoved the book under the bed. Such minor squabbles notwithstanding, we enjoyed an excellent sex life. Once the lights were out, we whiled away the nights in pleasure, making up for the extra years we both had lost to celibacy.

I noticed with alarm that everyday married life had eroded my commitment to literature, which had withstood all previous attempts at coercion—whether from my parents or the penal system. The passage of time is relentless, and zeal cools easily with age! If I continued to molder like this, I fretted, my motivation to study would be entirely gone by the time I had another opportunity to attend school. Aware that I had little time before school opened in the fall, I buckled right down to the new English textbook, designing a schedule for myself to ensure that I finished both volumes in time.

Since foreign-language instruction was still subservient to politics in China, *Basic College English* presented a highly stilted version of "Chinese English" and contained a great deal of peculiar vocabulary and political jargon unknown to native speakers. It focused exclusively on Chinese current events, with lessons like "Learn from Lei Feng," "In Agriculture, Learn from Dazhai," and "Criticize Lin Biao and Confucius" instead of authentic English texts. Its aim was to train students to translate *People's Daily* or Chinese Communist Party decrees, which was all they needed to know in order to pass English examinations or to become English teachers in China. Nonetheless, the book did provide phonetic transcriptions of all vocabulary words, as well as clear grammar explanations and plenty of exercises, which made it an acceptable starting point for a person in my situation.

In the spring of 1978 the thaw began in earnest. As the first college students to matriculate since the Cultural Revolution stepped into their classrooms, the government turned its attention to education and began to accord better treatment to intellectuals. With the sense that my time had come, I reflected on the peasant belief that children should be given vulgar names for good luck. Perhaps, I ruminated, my name Chunlai boded well for that spring. After all, my wedding and the births of both of my children had occurred in the springtime, so maybe I was due for another round of good fortune now.

Indeed, I did receive two exciting job offers that spring. First, our commune asked me to train elementary and middle school teachers in Classical Chinese. They were middle-aged men and women whose Classical Chinese was shockingly poor. Then the commune middle school hired me to groom students for the college entrance examination. One of the perks of the job was an office where I had access to the latest magazines and newspapers. I expected this school to keep me on as a regular teacher, but to my surprise I was dismissed as soon as the brief cram course was over. When I got back to the village, I discovered that I had lost my enviable job recording work points. I applied to the commune education cadre for another teaching position, but he, evidently put off by my bad record, merely hemmed and hawed.

From then on I devoted all my spare time to studying English, even sounding out vocabulary words during breaks in the fields. I was the laughingstock of the village. By August I had completed both volumes of the textbook on schedule. Now I had clear goals in mind: In the fall of 1978 all county-run middle schools were supposed to start offering English classes, and I hoped to land a job in one of them while there was still a shortage of professional English teachers. My backup plan was to take the graduate school entrance examination and reapply to graduate school.

Let the stodgy old peasants fuss all they wanted about the fine points of using farm tools. We would soon be parting ways!

Hearing that the county bureau of education was hiring substitute English teachers for the fall, I went to take the examination. After I had filled in a short application form, a woman examiner gave me a simple oral quiz, then asked me to read aloud from a text titled "Hypocritical Confucius" in my copy of *Basic College English*. I passed the test and got a job at Fanchuan Middle School that fall.

Unlike my colleagues at the commune middle school, all the other teachers at Fanchuan Middle School were fully credentialed. The school offered a refreshing view after the dreary environs of Xinwang Village; it looked out on the Zhongnan Mountains, rice paddies, and fields lined with persimmon trees heavily laden with green fruit. Starting that September, I taught seventh-grade beginning English, using a brand-new textbook. I had to rehearse for each class as nervously as an actor before a performance, keeping one step ahead of my students by practicing the new vocabulary words along with the tapes every night.

Times were changing, and people were starting to think more freely. No longer was I despised, as I had been for the past decade. The principal, a good man, was willing to overlook my history and sometimes even gave me preferential treatment over the fully credentialed teachers.

Substitute teachers were grossly underpaid. To make matters worse, as a commune member I was subject to a rule requiring me to hand over most of my pay to compensate for the work points I should have earned during my absence. The pittance I had left over was not enough for me to buy food in the teachers' cafeteria. Like the peasant students who lived in the dormitories, I economized by returning from my weekly visits home with a sackful of steamed buns and pickled vegetables fried with hot green peppers.

I scanned all the latest periodicals avidly, watching for an opportunity to apply for rehabilitation. When the moment came, I knew I had to move quickly because in China such opportunities were ephemeral. I was an expert at writing confessional essays; now I had to master the art of writing appeals. I bought a box of carbon paper and started working furiously. Toward the end of 1978 I sent appeals to all the authorities I could think of: the Chinese department and Communist Party Committee at Shaanxi Normal University, the Xi'an Security Bureau, the Shaanxi Security Court and Security Department, the Xi'an Municipal Committee, the Shaanxi Provincial Committee, and even the Central Committee of the Chinese Communist Party. I also wrote up my entire tale of woe and submitted it to the *Guangming Daily*. I resolved not to take no for an answer.

The response was astonishingly swift. On the afternoon of December 30 I entered the forbidding gates of the Xi'an Security Bureau and proceeded to an office where a cadre named Inspector Zhou read me my rehabilitation verdict. Afterward he presented me with a copy, a document bearing an official seal and a red-lettered heading, "Rehabilitation Verdict in the Kang Zhengguo Case." The first portion of the document outlined my history in neutral fashion, completely devoid of the libel that had been slung at me in the past. The second portion was the formal decision:

> Reexamination of Kang Zhengguo's case has determined that he was motivated solely by enthusiasm for literature to write a letter to the Moscow University Library to borrow a book. His letter contained no evidence of malfeasance, and it was a mistake for the Security Bureau to charge him with reactionary scheming to collude with the enemy, to detain him, and to sentence him to labor reeducation. He

is hereby granted rehabilitation, a cleared reputation, the restoration of his former position, and full back pay. Furthermore, his dossier should be cleaned out and its contents destroyed in accordance with the regulations.

Xi'an Security Bureau
December 27, 1978

Now that I was no longer a criminal reactionary, I could return to the world of the living. Even so, I still had to wend my way through a morass of aggravating red tape. The "restoration of my former position" was a reference to my unwanted job as a resettled worker at the Number Two Brickyard. I had taken the qualifying examination to become an accredited, full-time English teacher in Xi'an. What I needed now was a Xi'an residence permit. I applied to have my permit transferred back to my mother's address in Kaitong Lane, and this time my request was finally granted—after fourteen years' banishment—in January 1979. The hateful residence permit system had tormented me for years. Deprivation of the right to register in my own home had forced me into one painful decision after another. Now, along with the general improvement in my situation, came the restoration of my birth name. I sloughed off the name Li Chunlai like a cicada skin; it would be forgotten by everyone except the peasants of Xinwang Village.

However, my wife and children were still registered as peasants. I had requested that the Security Bureau transfer them along with me, but to my surprise it had refused. The clerk offered a simple explanation: If my wife and children had come with me from the city in the first place, the bureau would have been obliged to transfer them back along with me. But my problem was of my own making and had nothing to do with the bureau. In other words, because I had gotten married after I had moved to the countryside, and my wife was of peasant stock, she would have to retain her peasant status. I countered that I would not have moved to the countryside, nor would I have married there, if I had not been sent to the labor camps. The clerk contended that even so, it had been my choice to marry a peasant and have children in the countryside. He added that many urban state employees married peasant women and that the bureau could not transfer all these women just because their husbands had city residence permits. Without such strict caps, peasants would swarm into the cities, causing disastrous overcrowding. As far as the children went, he continued, the law stipulated that their legal residence was with their mother. Like her, they would be peasants forever. I knew that further entreaties would fall on deaf ears. Official policies were always uniformly applied in such cases, and special consideration was granted to no one.

With mixed feelings of relief and distress, I left the Security Bureau, glancing back at the solemn emblem of the People's Republic of China over the main gate. Before this interview I had not understood that my rehabilitation would be incomplete or that the repercussions of my earlier transfer to the countryside would be so far-reaching. Although I was now Kang Zhengguo again, I was not free of my alter ego. Li Chunlai was still the name of my wife's husband and my children's father.

The back pay mentioned in my rehabilitation verdict was a reference to the thirty yuan per month that I had received at the brickyard. I was entitled to ten years of restitution altogether, from the day I had first been detained until the day I was hired at Fanchuan Middle School. But this generous sum was still subject to some disturbing deductions: I had to recompense the state for the expense of imprisoning me and the commune for the amount it had paid me for my labor. I had no idea how much my imprisonment had cost the state, nor had I been aware that I would be held responsible for this sum. My commune brigade generated an official statement of my earnings and transferred the debt to the Security Bureau so that it could make the deduction. I still have the statement it issued, logging all my workdays from 1972 to 1976:

Year	Workdays	Daily Rate	Yearly Pay
1972	171.3	0.75 yuan	128.48 yuan
1973	272.2	0.75 yuan	204.15 yuan
1974	214.1	0.75 yuan	160.58 yuan
1975	270.1	0.63 yuan	170.16 yuan
1976	334.1	0.75 yuan	250.58 yuan
Grand total			913.95 yuan

Five years of a man's life cannot be called a short time. I, a strapping young man, had sweated from dawn to dusk for five whole years and had nothing to show for it but a mere 913 yuan and 95 cents.[2] With an average yearly income of 182 yuan and 61 cents, my monthly pay had only amounted to 15 yuan and 22 cents. And Team Number Four was a relatively wealthy team. Had I spent those five years toiling in my wife's impoverished mountain gulch, I would have garnered no more than 200 yuan. This was why I was adamant about leaving the countryside and dead set against resigning myself to a lifetime as a peasant. It was also the underlying reason why fine peasant girls like Fendan and Zhuyin had spurned me and why so many peasant girls wanted to marry workers. The residence permit system had created two castes in China, consigning the majority of the population to an existence below the poverty line, excluded from any government welfare or benefits. As the rural chapter of my life illustrated, the policy of banishing students and cadres to the countryside amounted to officially declaring the place a trash dump for unwanted urban dregs of society.

I had one stroke of good fortune after another in the spring of 1979. In January my residence permit was transferred back to the city. In March the Number Two Brickyard gave me 1,900 yuan in back pay. In April the Xi'an Education Bureau granted my certification to teach English. In the same month the Communist Party Committee at Shaanxi Normal University reopened my case and rehabilitated me. Rescinding my expulsion, it conceded that it had been a mistake to confiscate my private diaries and absolved me of "disseminating reactionary ideas." In recognition of the year and a half that I had been enrolled there, it retroactively granted me an associate degree. In May I was hired at Xi'an Number Ninety-one Middle School. Fanchuan Middle School wanted me to stay on, but anxious to return to the city, I declined.

I knew that teaching middle school English was only a stopgap for me. I was not a professional English teacher. I could be hired to fill a tempo-

---

[2] About $2,300 today.

rary shortage, but I would be discarded as a mere amateur once the labor force of qualified teachers had replenished itself. I needed to return to my original field. The graduate schools had just reopened, so I registered for the June examination in classical Chinese literature. Under extreme time pressure I made a hasty decision to fall back on what I had taught myself about classical poetry as a boy, which meant majoring in the literature of the Tang and Song dynasties. One is not granted many fresh starts in life. I knew that this was no time to be picky.

In August I received my acceptance letter from the Chinese department of Shaanxi Normal University. How many times over the past decade had I dreamed of returning to that campus and stepping into a classroom again! Each time I had awoken and lain disconsolate on my pillow. Now that farfetched dream had come true.

My best friends at Number Ninety-one Middle School were two young women teachers named Xu Meiling and Zhu Yali, who lived in my dormitory. Together we whiled away many an afternoon playing badminton. They naively regarded all my past disgrace and suffering as a badge of honor, like something out of a fairy tale. When it came time for me to go to graduate school, they presented me with a beautiful thick blank diary, complete with color illustrations, like the one Father had given me long ago. Despite living in a political pressure cooker, the Chinese people had retained their basic sincerity. Still, their heads had been stuffed so full of empty political jargon that it was all they had at their disposal to express themselves. As an example, I include here the sentimental inscription Meiling and Yali penned on the frontispiece of the diary:

Hearing your life story of dashed hopes,
We admire your bravery.
Our acquaintance was brief, our parting reluctant,
Our friendship unforgettable.
The mountain road is rugged and steep,
An arduous climb lies ahead.
Accept our heartfelt wishes of good luck,
Devote your knowledge to our country.

Goethe's *Faust* concludes: "The Woman-Soul leadeth us upward and on!"[3] Meiling and Yali's gift emboldened me to resume my habit of keeping diaries. Here is the entry I wrote on my first day back at Shaanxi Normal University:

> Fifteen years have passed. Fifteen years of silence, during which I haven't dared speak, write, or even think. Now it's time to free myself from fear. I believe that the Chinese people will not permit such horror—when a man cannot even keep a personal diary—to repeat itself. If such dreadful abuses should ever plague the nation again, I absolutely refuse to burn my diaries out of cowardice, as I did fifteen years ago. Instead, I'll read them aloud in the courtroom and maintain the courage of my convictions. Starting today, I plan to resume my habit of keeping a diary, an honest record of my thoughts.

Now, with more than two decades of hindsight, this passage strikes me as bookish and naive: unduly optimistic about China and overconfident of my own capacity for political defiance. Like many other newly rehabilitated intellectuals in those days, I swaggered around as if I were Lermontov's "hero of our time."[4] Eventually, however, I came to understand what a blunder this was.

While congratulating me on my rehabilitation, some of my old middle school classmates commented that I had not changed much and did not seem to have learned my lesson. Once, over drinks with a few of them, I got into an argument with one, now an army officer. We parted in anger, our faces flushed and our necks bulging. As he was leaving, he announced to all present, "Mark my words, everybody. Kang Zhengguo has not mended his ways. He'll be back to his old tricks again before long!"

When it came time for me to leave the middle school for Shaanxi Normal University, our personnel officer called me into her office and gave me

---

[3] *Faust: A Tragedy by Johann Wolfgang von Goethe. The Second Part*, trans. Bayard Taylor (Boston: Houghton, Mifflin, and Co., 1871), p. 314.

[4] Mikhail Lermontov published one novel, *A Hero of Our Time*, in 1840.

a folder, sealed with a strip of paper bearing an official stamp. She told me it was my dossier, but it was surprisingly thin and seemed to contain only a couple of slips of paper. Its injurious contents had been expunged! I remembered how ominously fat it had looked on the two occasions when I had glimpsed it before: the day my political instructor had turned me over to my neighborhood police officer and the time when the guards from the detention center in Xi'an had escorted me to the He Family Temple. I had been obsessed with bitter speculations about all the confessional essays and betrayals that dossier had contained and had had constant visions of its going up in flames or mysteriously disappearing. Now, by some miracle, it had been cleansed, like one's digestive tract after a purgative, and contained only my résumé and a few documents pertaining to my rehabilitation. Noticing its lightness in my hand, I felt a huge weight lift from my shoulders.

The personnel cadre asked me to save her a trip to the post office by delivering the dossier to her counterpart at Shaanxi Normal University. She wished me well as I turned to leave.

"The party trusts you, Comrade Kang Zhengguo," she said. "Good luck, and good-bye!"

Carrying my slim dossier, my residence permit, and my ration tickets, I said good-bye to Xu Meiling and Zhu Yali and the rest of my colleagues, hopped onto my bicycle, and rode off to Shaanxi Normal University.

47

A Recurring Nightmare

M Y NARRATIVE OUGHT to conclude with my return to Shaanxi Normal University in 1979, which placed me squarely on the road to becoming a tenured professor. Wasn't a career in literature what I had wanted all along, ever since I had begun to train myself in the classics as a child in Silent Garden? My "reactionary crime" had consisted of nothing more than a preference for scholarship over politics. I had chosen to return to graduate school to study Tang and Song poetry, an apolitical subject that would lead to a life of placid scholarship. The chief lesson of my fourteen years of persecution was to stay out of the way of the police. I wish I could end my story here. Most of my friends who had been rehabilitated, such as Li Zhimin, Zhao Yi, and Mr. Xu, managed to live out the rest of their days undisturbed.

Li Zhimin was hired as an administrator at his alma mater. He had been successfully "thought-reformed" at the brickyard and had ended up as a master of political chicanery. He had thanked the party profusely for granting him a new life and had been rewarded with party membership and a promotion at work.

Shortly after my wedding Zhao Yi had been clapped onto death row for "viciously attacking the Cultural Revolution," but Mao had died in the nick of time. In an abrupt turnaround characteristic of those topsy-turvy days, Zhao had been spared execution and honored as a man of his convictions instead. He had been reinstated into the party, and he and his family had entered a deluxe apartment complex for retired high-ranking officials, many of whom had held posts in the provincial party committee. When I went to visit him in 1982, I was shocked to hear him cast a Maoist spin on current events. He had become a hard-liner, railing against contemporary trends toward Westernization and "bourgeois liberalism" and ignorantly attacking my interest in Western literary theory. I reflected sadly that he and I had nothing in common anymore, and never went to see him again. His health was poor, and after a series of hospitalizations he probably "went to join Marx," remaining a diehard true believer to the last.

Mr. Xu, formerly classified as an unemployed vagrant, was now elevated to the status of retired veteran army officer, and he and his family had moved into a lavish retirement community. Once he came to visit me and boasted about the chauffeured limousine he had at his disposal. He had become a toady, with a portrait of Deng Xiaoping in his living room, before which he stood morning and evening to offer his thanks for granting him good fortune in his old age. He tried to convince me to share his idolization of Deng, reminding me that without his reforms I would still be tilling the fields in Xinwang Village. I objected that I had been innocent all along and would never have ended up in the countryside at all were it not for the trumped-up charges against me. I should have become a college professor years ago. Was I supposed to thank people for ceasing to persecute me? Mr. Xu was miffed, and I saw him out the door disdainfully. We never met again.

The course of action that these three friends had chosen was also open to me. I could have swallowed my pride and obsequiously accepted favors from the party, becoming a docile professor with my nose buried in my books. This would have been a happy ending for my tale.

But perhaps I was doomed by my nature to clash forever with the Chinese state. I enjoyed only a brief respite in graduate school before falling into disgrace again for crossing the line into political heterodoxy. I was one of the first to feel the chill of the campaign to eradicate "spiritual pollution" in 1983. I was denied my master's degree and had to slink away from Shaanxi Normal University empty-handed again.

My graduating class at Shaanxi Normal University was the first one since the Cultural Revolution, and its members were as precious as first-born sons. Various universities snapped up all my classmates, while I alone was blacklisted and unemployed. Eventually I settled for a highly undesirable assistant professorship at a community college known as Xi'an Radio and Television College. In the winter of 1984 I was hired by the Social Sciences Division at Xi'an Jiaotong University to teach the rudiments of literature to vocational students. I had finally snagged a university position, although it was second-rate, and tantamount to leaving my field.

At Jiaotong University I was swept up in the protest movement surrounding the Beijing Massacre,* a horrifying reminder of the Chinese state's continuing political repressiveness and brutality toward its citizens despite its policy of economic liberalization. After my participation in the protests the Security Bureau subjected me to an unpleasant six-month investigation, which reopened my old psychological wounds.

In 1994 I had a stroke of good fortune. A major university in the United States hired me as a Chinese-language instructor, and I took refuge there with my wife and children. Once there I imagined myself safe from the menacing Security Bureau. Overwhelmed with relief, I penned an essay titled "Sound Sleep":

> I was locked up for a few years during the Cultural Revolution for "reactionary thought crimes." For years afterwards I was tormented by a recurring nightmare that I was back in prison again, flitting around like a caged bird behind the same forbidding walls. I would awake bathed in sweat and find myself still anxiously counting the days until my release. I was not free of this nightmare until I had emigrated from China and settled on the far shore of a vast ocean.

Little did I know that my nightmare would return to haunt me.

*On June 4, 1989, the Chinese government used military force to crush prodemocracy protests in Tiananmen Square, Beijing, resulting in thousands of civilian deaths and injuries. The violent suppression of innocent demonstrators sparked protests across China and around the world.

48

You Can't Go Home Again

AFTER SEVERAL PEACEFUL years in America, I decided to return to China for a visit in 2000. My first destination was an academic conference in Nanjing. Then I planned to visit Mother in Xi'an and to help my brother and sisters transfer my father's and grandparents' ashes to a new burial site. At first the ashes had been at the Sanzhao Crematorium, but when I acquired a small burial plot in Xinwang Village after Li Baoyu's death, we had decided to move them to a site beside him. We had split the cost of a tombstone and felt satisfied that we had finally laid our forebears properly to rest. Twice a year, on the Qingming Festival in the spring and on the first day of the tenth month of the lunar calendar, Xiuqin and I had gone to sweep the graves and make the customary offerings. After I moved to America, I heard about a new burial option in China: Certain villages were operating attractive private memorial parks where city people could purchase high-priced permanent plots. My siblings, who disliked going to Xinwang Village to tend the graves, had bought a plot in one of these parks and were waiting for me to come back and help them with the reinterment.

I was attending the conference in Nanjing in order to satisfy a personal, rather unimportant academic ambition. By the year 2000, almost twenty years after my graduation, I had never presented a paper at an academic conference in my homeland, even though I had produced several scholarly tomes. This, I had always thought, was a regrettable gap in my curriculum vitae.

It was not that my present job in the United States required me to fill this gap. As a Chinese-language instructor all I had to do was to teach American students the basics of vernacular Mandarin. Because I was not on the tenure track, I had no need to publish or attend conferences in my field. All my fellow language instructors simply relaxed during their free time; none of them bothered to strive for academic recognition in China. I could have chosen to devote myself to pursuing the "American dream," as they did, but the pull of my old habits was irresistible, and I was determined to make my mark in the "small world" of Chinese academe. Taking the invitation to present a paper in Nanjing as an opportunity to do this, I got right down to work.

On May 10, 2000, I went to Kennedy Airport to fly to Shanghai. The flight was canceled because of mechanical problems, and I had to spend the night in a hotel. I entered my room, closed the curtains on the picture window, and lay down in the dark, dreading my passage through Chinese customs the next day. Once I drifted off to sleep, my old nightmare suddenly assaulted me again. After almost six years in America, I had imagined myself free to dream in peace, like an American. But now I lay agitated in the dark, feeling as though thousands of newly hatched snakes were slithering around in my bed.

First I mulled over the bad news I had heard regarding a friend of mine in Xi'an, who had been questioned by the national Security Bureau. One day he had been summoned to his boss's office, where he had found three unfamiliar men who had identified themselves sternly as national security agents. They had mentioned me, calling me a "diehard reactionary," and asked him for information about my activities in America. They wanted to know what I had mailed to him and what contact he had had with me recently. He had tried to sidestep their questions, but they had persisted, warning him that they would either come back for a followup or ask him to meet them somewhere. They had also left a telephone number that he was supposed to call to report any news he had of me. He had been unco-operative, and they had left in a huff.

My friend in Xi'an had not reported this incident to me directly. Another friend named Xiao Xian, a fellow Tiananmen protester from my days at Jiaotong University, had told me about it on the long-distance telephone. I had planned to go to his home in Huizhou on this trip to China, to visit him and another protester named Zhang Yi. Unable to go into all the details on the phone, Xiao Xian had explained simply that the authorities got edgy as the June 4 anniversary of the Beijing Massacre approached each year. They probably remembered having investigated me for my role in the protests and felt compelled to keep an eye on me even though I had left the country. He thought they must have heard of my upcoming visit to Xi'an and had started snooping around for hearsay. He assured me that the investigation was probably routine and not a cause for worry.

I had to tell my wife.

"I knew this would happen," she said. "Don't bother trying to figure out who leaked the news that you were coming. You have only yourself to blame. I warned you not to blab about your trip, but you've done as much PR work as a congressman from the White House before a state visit! The trouble is, interactions between people are complicated in Xi'an, and your friends are a motley bunch."

She had never been comfortable with the idea of my visiting China again, and Xiao Xian's news only added to her worries. Now she had an excuse to urge me to call Northwest Airlines to cancel my trip. When I refused to cave in, she drew an invidious comparison between me and old Mr. Zhang, a member of our local Chinese church.

"If you want to visit China, you'd better learn to keep your mouth shut about the Communists. Or else you should take your cue from Mr. Zhang. His mother, who's in her nineties, still lives in China, but he hasn't been back to see her in over a decade. He follows his conscience and goes around speaking out against the Communists, but he knows he can't go home again. Now he's a man with some backbone! He's chosen the lonely road in his battle, not like you and your literary buddies, with all your fancy ideas, who go back all the time just to live it up. Now Mr. Zhang . . ." Allowing herself to get carried away, she exaggerated until my trip to China sounded almost criminal, a sure recipe for disaster, and she kept hammering at me until the moment of my departure.

The morning after my restless night in the hotel at Kennedy Airport, my plane took off and soared through the brilliant blue airspace above the clouds until the stewardess finally announced our descent into Shanghai Hongqiao Airport. Emerging from my reverie, I tried to focus on my imminent arrival in China. My suitcase was loaded with books and periodicals for my friends, especially Mao Zhiyi, although I had not been able to bring everything I had planned to bring. I had tried to pack a few copies of his favorite reading matter, the prodemocracy émigré journal *Beijing Spring*, but my wife had confiscated them, forbidding me to smuggle banned reading material into China.

Mao Zhiyi was my dear old friend from the brickyard who had been arrested for trying to escape to Hong Kong in his youth and had suffered decades of persecution afterward. Like many of my other friends, he had now retired, after finally having been rehabilitated and granted the status of an official state employee. His fight was over. Despite the terrible price he had paid for his youthful quest for freedom, he had, sad to say, never managed to set foot outside China.

He had written me a series of long, plaintive letters after my move to America, their weighty envelopes plastered with brightly colored commemorative stamps and so tightly sealed that I had to open them painstakingly with a letter opener. As I am a rather emotional man, I would sink into fond reveries about his friendship while contemplating the elaborate precautions he had taken against censorship. I tried to comply with his frequent requests for news from the free world or for reading material unavailable in China. Like any thinking Chinese person, he was hungry for the truth. In fact I gladly kept several of my old friends regularly supplied with reading material, believing it my moral obligation to further the cause of freedom. Although my wife objected to the expense of the postage, I persisted in sending the packages behind her back.

As an escapee from behind the bamboo curtain I sympathized with Mao Zhiyi and understood the risk he was taking in corresponding with me. With a sigh, I imagined how he must have agonized over dropping each of his missives into the mailbox. He had taken extra measures to ward off the censors, but they had high technology at their disposal these days, and I worried that he might have outsmarted himself. What if the Security Bureau knew how to read people's letters simply by passing them unopened under some special, new kind of light?

Instead of the issues of *Beijing Spring* that my wife had confiscated, I had brought Vaclav Havel's *Letters to Olga* and—to satisfy Mao Zhiyi's request for the most "reactionary" book I could think of—my copy of Pu Ning's *Red in Tooth and Claw: Twenty-six Years in Communist Chinese Prisons*. The author had presented it to me personally when I visited him in Taipei, but I was willing to part with it for Mao Zhiyi's sake.

Night was falling outside the aircraft, and the pilot had switched on the wing lights. Shanghai was directly beneath us. The plane primed for landing and gave an almost human shudder before its wheels touched the runway. With a sigh of relief I entered the terminal, but I was overcome with apprehension as I made my way toward Chinese customs. Taking a deep breath to calm my nerves, I got into line, mentally preparing myself to be denied entry or to be singled out for special scrutiny. In recent years I had seen many reports in foreign newspapers of Chinese dissidents who had been detained at the border on the way into their homeland. I stood at the crossroads, ready to try my luck.

But my entry was smooth; the immigration officer returned my documents to me through the window after a cursory check. I was in China! As I sped along the boulevards of Shanghai in a taxi, I was sorry I had left my copies of *Beijing Spring* at home. If only I had stood up against my wife!

自述

49

A Small World

PROFESSOR HONG SHENG and his colleagues had made elaborate arrangements for the conference, which was entitled "Gender Issues in Ming and Qing Literature." It was being held at the five-star Mandarin Garden Hotel, where I went directly from the train station on the night of my arrival in Nanjing. After six quiet years in the small town of New Haven, Connecticut, I felt like a country bumpkin in such lavish surroundings. I had never seen such ostentation at American scholarly conferences. In China, the booming economy had stimulated a surge in conspicuous consumption. With China's entry into the age of globalization, the Chinese now sought to conform to international standards or even to outdo the foreigners at their own game. The results often struck me as excessive.

Professor Mu, Professor Hong Sheng's mentor, delivered an eloquent opening address, couched in the pompous blend of official jargon and scholarly erudition typical of China's new generation of academic administrators. Nostalgically, he reminded us that this site by the Qinhuai River had been chosen for the conference because it was steeped in literary history. Nanjing had been the capital during the medieval Six Dynasties period, and the famous scholars and beauties of the Ming and Qing had also flourished here. A local chauvinist, Professor Mu was utterly smitten with the fake Meixiang Building[1] across the river and kept advertising it to us and recommending that we tour it during our stay.

Professor Hong Sheng had arranged an extravagant opening banquet for us that night. In a restaurant overlooking the river, we sampled the delicacies of Suzhou cuisine as an introduction to the sensory world of Ming and Qing literature. After the meal I joined some friends on a sightseeing boat. The water was polluted, and the ancient buildings had been torn down and replaced with mass-produced replicas topped with garish, flashing neon lights. Music blared out from the dance halls facing the river.

I thought of the well-turned, flowery phrases of Zhu Ziqing's famous 1923 essay "Splashing Oars and Lantern Light on the Qinhuai River," but alas, there was no gentle splashing of oars on the river that night. Unlike the Venetians, who had preserved their gondolas, Chinese entrepreneurs had spoiled the picturesque scenery with noisy tour boats sporting gaudy Mickey Mouse and Donald Duck figureheads on their prows. In the glare of the neon lights, we seemed to have bought tickets to a stage set rather than a historical site. The entire area was a tawdry cultural hodgepodge, perpetrated in the name of developing the tourist industry. After this experience, I lost interest in visiting the other historic landmarks in Nanjing, in case they had suffered a similar fate.

Our hosts held a grand farewell banquet on the last night of the conference. Some young scholars at my table, their tongues loosened by alcohol, started to complain about Professor Huo, my old master's thesis adviser at Shaanxi Normal University.

Apparently, even though he had been victimized during the Cultural Revolution, he had turned around and browbeaten his subordinates when his position was restored later. He had also clung to the position of departmental Ph.D. adviser until well beyond the advanced age of eighty, when he had finally passed it on to his son, a mediocre scholar. My indignant, slightly inebriated young tablemates resolved to publish an exposé of

[1] The Meixiang Building was the residence of the renowned Ming dynasty courtesan Li Xiangjun, but the replica that stands on its site today is merely a tourist trap.

his corruption on the Internet. One of them warned, "If there's ever another Cultural Revolution, the faculty and students in his department will get their revenge."

Since I was on a return trip from America, most of the people who addressed me were interested in finding ways to get there. Few of them were aware of my past or had read my publications carefully. I felt like a wallflower as I listened to the locals debating the conflicts in their little world, and I gradually drifted into a hazy, inebriated reminiscence about my conflicted, love/hate relationship with Professor Huo twenty years before.

IT WAS 1979, and I had gone back to Shaanxi Normal University mainly in order to show my former detractors there a thing or two. My friends and relatives tried to dissuade me, but I dreamed of gloating, "Here I am again!" like the Tang poet Liu Yuxi upon his return to the capital from exile, and of succeeding where I had failed before. Also, Shaanxi Normal University was the best option in Xi'an, where I had to stay because my wife and children were still registered in the nearby countryside, and my wife needed my help with the farming.

The same party bureaucrats were still in charge of the Chinese department at Shaanxi Normal, and they objected to the return of a controversial figure like me. However, admissions were based on merit, and I had done well on the entrance examination. When Professor Huo decided to accept me as one of his five students that year, the departmental leadership did not dare stand in his way. I was thirty-five years old, the cutoff age for a first-year graduate student. Professor Huo had granted me my last chance to further my education.

I was deeply grateful to him when I began my studies in the fall, but I soon discovered what an inferior scholar he was. While browsing in the library stacks one day, I found an old collection of his essays and learned that he was a hack writer, who had made his name as an attack dog for the party. His only academic accomplishment was popularizing classical literature for lay readers; he had a unique gift for translating ancient poetry into modern verse that approached the power of the original. He furthered his reputation by compiling dictionaries of poetry and organizing poetry reading groups.

All five of us finished our theses in the fall of 1981 and were scheduled to receive our degrees once we had passed our thesis defenses. Mine dealt with the life and works of the late Tang poet Han Wo,[2] focusing on his erotic collection *The Perfumed Cosmetic Case*. I had discussed my selection of this topic briefly with Professor Huo, who had shown a lack of interest in, even an aversion to the taboo subject of erotic poetry. I had gone ahead and written the thesis entirely on my own, ignoring his disapproval. He had left me alone, apparently having decided that it would be best to give me enough rope and let me hang myself.

Our thesis defenses were scheduled according to the chronological order of the authors we had researched, which put mine last. I waited for two full days, while all the other students passed their defenses, but my name was never called. Realizing that I had been passed over, I went to Professor Huo's house to confront him.

With feigned resignation, he informed me that the thesis defense committee had decided to reject my thesis on the ground that it was misguided and showed me the committee's write-up. Here is a sampling of the most arbitrary accusations:

This thesis takes an unwholesome ideological stance. Its attempt to prove that *The Perfumed Cosmetic Case* was authored by Han Wo contradicts ancient Chinese scholarly opinion. It reads eroticism into Han Wo's poetry and draws unsubstantiated conclusions about erotic poetry in general. Its analyses of Han Wo's works are thinly disguised appreciations of erotic poetry. It even promotes eroticism (pp. 57, 59) and the bourgeois theory of human nature[3] (p. 64), and contains subtitles like "Sleeping Alone and Insomnia: The Anguish of Sex." It irresponsibly advocates licentiousness (p. 70) and the

[2] 844–923.

[3] In contrast with the Maoist view that there is no such thing as human nature in general, because one's nature is determined by one's social class; disparate social classes therefore have few, if any, "human" traits in common.

"lust of the mind" (pp. 71, 86) and affirms erotic poetry as a genre (p. 80) with the claim that it is "an illegitimate expression of a legitimate desire of the literati."

For these reasons, the committee hereby finds this thesis unacceptable.

Thesis Defense Committee for Graduate Studies in Tang and Song Literature

September 9, 1981

Faced with this diatribe, peppered as it was with leftover Cultural Revolution jargon, I could not find anything to say to Professor Huo. Now I finally understood that the downfall of the Gang of Four had brought China only limited freedom of speech. With surprise, I realized how many taboos remained in academic research and how naive my first new diary entry had been. Broaching the forbidden was tantamount to "advocating" or "appreciating" it; that was the prevailing logic, and Professor Huo subscribed to it. To make matters worse, my thesis defense happened to coincide with the campaign against bourgeois liberalism in Bai Hua's screenplay for the film *Bitter Love*. The brand-new thaw had reverted to a deep freeze. This was the moment that Professor Huo and the departmental leadership had been waiting for; now I would get my comeuppance. "Promoting eroticism" was morally suspect, but the charge of advocating "the bourgeois theory of human nature" raised the stakes to a higher, ideological plane, and I found it truly alarming. In those days "human nature" and "humanism" were still unmentionables, dismissed as "reactionary bourgeois" concepts. Advocacy of such notions was simply indefensible.

"I warned you to watch your step politically," Professor Huo reprimanded me. "You shouldn't have ignored me. Zhengguo, academics and politics are deeply intertwined, as I've been trying to teach you all along. You have only yourself to blame for what's happened. I wish I'd never taken you on as my student! Your mistake reflects badly on me, and now my hands are tied. Let me remind you once more: You're the one who wanted to write this thesis about erotic poetry. I never backed you, and I wash my hands of you completely."

Then he recited a litany of my offenses against him, none of which had anything to do with my thesis. We had had a number of petty squabbles, most of them on occasions when I had been disloyal or had failed to take his side against his enemies. Throughout his harangue I was engulfed with wave after wave of nausea, as though I had swallowed a fly along with my rice. When he was finished, he sat down in an armchair beside me. Like a salesman negotiating a deal, he covered his mouth with his hand and whispered into my ear.

"Zhengguo, the department has already made its decision. It's still confidential, but I'll give you a heads-up. Since you didn't pass your thesis defense, you're going to be asked to leave, meaning that you won't be assigned a job along with the other graduates, and you'll have to go back to middle school teaching. I've got an idea for you. Your wife and kids are still in the countryside, aren't they? It's such a nuisance to commute. Why don't you just get a job teaching in your own village? Then you'll be able to take care of your family and tend to your crops."

His phony smile barely masked the pleasure he took in seeing me writhe. As he fixed his bleary, cynical eyes on me, I suspected that a nasty scheme lurked behind every furrow of his brow.

I rose to leave, thanking him for informing me of the committee's decision but letting him know that I was determined not to let the matter rest. I planned to appeal to the higher authorities.

The departmental party branch secretary gave a lecture about my case to the undergraduate seniors, who were embarking on their theses, as a warning that research was still subservient to politics. Once again I was notorious, and my fate was the talk of the campus.

But times had changed, and the department's smear campaign was only partially successful. I appealed to the university-wide party branch. Meanwhile, the graduate students from outside my department petitioned the Graduate Studies Office on my behalf, maintaining that I had been treated unfairly and demanding intervention from above. My department ultimately had to compromise. Instead of sending me back where I had come from, as Professor Huo had hoped it would, it gave me another chance, an assignment to write another thesis and to submit it for defense the following year.

I agreed, this time choosing to write about Du Fu, China's greatest poet. In the summer of 1982 my second thesis, entitled "A Study of Du Fu's Object Poetry,"[4] passed with flying colors, and I finally received my diploma.

Nonetheless, my departmental party branch refused to allow the thesis defense committee to grant me my master's degree, claiming that my second thesis was merely a fulfillment of my graduation requirements. Anxious to start earning a living, I made a pragmatic decision to take my diploma and leave.

Years later, after I had found a steady job, I wrote a series of letters to the National Degree Certification Committee in Beijing. We haggled for five years, until Shaanxi Normal University finally granted me my master's degree retroactively in 1987.

---

[4] "Object poetry" uses the device of describing objects from nature to express the poet's feelings.

50

"Aim Your Guns Here"

I LAY SPRAWLED ON my bed in the air-conditioned guesthouse at Nanjing Normal University, taking shelter from the sweltering summer heat and the hubbub of the city. My head reeled every time I ventured into the crush of humanity and gridlock on the streets outside. Six years of American creature comforts had spoiled me without my noticing. I had contracted a sore throat soon after my arrival, and I started to cough up phlegm again for the first time in years. Professor Hong Sheng said that he had seen many returning émigrés with similar symptoms; life abroad had weakened their resistance, while the air quality in China had deteriorated.

China had certainly modernized since my departure in 1994. In those days one still had to go to the post office to make international long-distance phone calls. But now I could use my international phone card to dial abroad from the comfort of my hotel room. I called my wife. After reporting that it was cool and rainy in New Haven and that she and my daughter were using the heat at night, she mentioned that I had received a letter from my old friend in Xi'an, Mr. Huang. She had not opened it but suspected that it might be important. I agreed, remembering that he was a terrible correspondent, who had not written to me in years. Guessing that he might need some research materials from America, I called him right away. He was delighted to hear that I was in Nanjing but claimed—somewhat evasively, I thought—that there had been no particular reason for his letter other than to confirm my impending visit to Xi'an. I remembered the story Xiao Xian had told me about him on the telephone.

It was too soon, however, for me to go back to Xi'an. I had to wait until after the Security Bureau's annual paranoid crackdown before the anniversary of the Beijing Massacre on June 4 and then take a circuitous route: first, south to Huizhou, to visit Xiao Xian and Zhang Yi, then west to Chengdu, where I would stay with Zhengguan and take a tour of Tibet to kill time until it was safe to proceed to my ultimate destination.

I RECALLED THE early days of my friendship with Xiao Xian and Zhang Yi, back in the late 1980s, when I was teaching at Jiaotong University. As new graduates of the university they had been retained as cadres there, one as a dean of employment for graduating seniors, the other as a political instructor. In my college days more than twenty years earlier such people would have been members of the campus thought police and would have had nothing in common with me. But in the heady days of the post-Mao thaw under Hu Yaobang,[1] there were plenty of liberal, innovative young political cadres like Zhang and Xiao. When the university established its new School of Management, they both quit their jobs to pursue fashionable M.B.A. degrees. As graduate students they cotranslated Orwell's *Animal Farm* and liked to ask my opinion of their work.

In 1986, at the crest of the thaw, Zhang and Xiao organized a lecture series for students, in which I spoke about Existentialism and contemporary Western thought in general. In that same year the Communist Youth League invited me to give a lecture on the "Sexual Revolution in America." I addressed a standing-room-only audience in the largest auditorium on campus. Zhang and Xiao also founded an evening reading group, in which

[1] General secretary of the Chinese Communist Party from 1981 to 1987.

we compared political systems such as communism and totalitarianism with complete candor.

Freedom is ephemeral in China, however. When Hu Yaobang was unseated in 1987, the lively intellectual milieu that he had fostered was condemned as bourgeois liberalism.

As I was a low-ranking lecturer in those days, all my family got from the housing office was a tiny two-room apartment in a shoddy building dating from the 1970s. The cagelike kitchen was so cramped that my wife had to turn sideways so that I could squeeze past her to get myself a snack while she was cooking. The bathroom was the size of a clothes wardrobe, with no room to turn around, which precluded any activity other than squatting directly over the toilet.[2] We even had to saw off part of our newly bought dresser to move it into the apartment through the narrow hallway. My wife and I slept in the larger of the two rooms, which also served as our dining and living room and was the natural spot for our prized new color television.

With my wife and children glued to the television every evening after dinner, there was nowhere for me to work, so I went to the Chinese department office, which was in the School of Mechanical Engineering Building on the northwest corner of the campus. The building was nicely heated during the winter and shaded by massive plane trees in the summer. Beyond the outer room of the department office, where each of us had a desk, there was an inner storage room with some leftover space, which I took over, even setting up a cot to sleep on. Since my apartment was so small, I felt justified in my assumption of squatter's rights.

I spent most of my decade at Jiaotong University in that "office," unless I was in the classroom or at home having a meal. It lacked the comforts of home, but at least it was my own space. I holed up in there until the spring of 1989, finishing a book about feminist literary criticism in the West. My male friends, either young and single, like Xiao and Zhang, or married men on the outs with their wives, often stopped by for bull sessions lasting until all hours of the night.

In April 1989 Hu Yaobang passed away. In Xi'an, as in Beijing and all

[2] Sunken into the floor, Chinese style.

over the country, students rose up to mourn him.[3] I remained aloof at first. I had always shunned public mourning ceremonies and had never felt the slightest love and esteem for any Communist leader, not even for Zhou Enlai or Hu Yaobang. The deaths of such men meant no more to me than the death of any stranger; I grieved only for people close to me. I also disliked movements to petition the regime for reform, which were based on the Communist Party's charade of being a benevolent parent. I was put off by television news clips of three students kneeling for hours with their petition in front of the Great Hall of the People.

In fact I was alarmed by everything I saw on the news. Recent experience had demonstrated that the current regime was just as capricious as its predecessors. I knew that the Communist Party had not changed its stripes. I had lost hope in the highly touted political reforms when my jubilant rehabilitation had been followed by a decade of disillusionment. And the crackdown on the Beijing Democracy Wall in 1979 had proved me right.[4] The Chinese people still had twin daggers hanging over their heads; they could still be charged with crimes of thought or speech. I knew better than to plunge rashly into the student movement.

I had personal reasons for lying low during the Tiananmen protests. When I was newly hired at Jiaotong University in 1984, the head of the Social Sciences Division had called me into his office for a candid conversation. He had seen my dossier, he said, and knew that I had suffered on account of my politics. He had some well-meaning advice for me, which he hoped I would take in the spirit it was given, since he too had been persecuted, as a rightist in 1957. First he asked my age, and I replied that I was forty. He reminded me that as a mature middle-aged man I had a responsibility to my wife and children, who were still in the countryside. I really could not afford to make any more mistakes, he cautioned me. I needed to settle down and do a good job at the university, so that my

---

[3] Hu's death sparked the Tiananmen protests; the students regarded him as a symbol of clean government and liberalizing trends. See Zhang Liang, Andrew Nathan, and Perry Link, *The Tiananmen Papers* (New York: Public Affairs Press, 2002).

[4] For a brief period democracy activists were allowed to post their views on a wall on Xidan Street in Beijing.

family could be transferred to Xi'an and my children could attend the university-run elementary school. He was aware that I had been tossed around for half my life, but China had now embarked on a period of peace and stability. He wished me luck from then on and hoped that I would continue to teach at this prestigious institution until my retirement.

In 1985 my wife and children finally obtained Xi'an residence permits. My wife found a temporary job at the university day care center, and my children enrolled in the elementary school. I was doing my utmost to be promoted to a full professorship so that we could qualify for decent housing.

When the Tiananmen protests began, Mother cautioned me against losing my head. I was not a student anymore, she pointed out, and my behavior affected other people more than it had in the past. Now I had dependents, whose welfare—my wife's temporary job, my children's entitlement to attend the university-affiliated elementary school, and even the roof over our heads—hinged entirely on my career. She was afraid that she would have to support my family if I ran afoul of the Security Bureau again. She reminded me that I had been a financial drain on her for more than a decade but that she had at least had a job in those days. Now that she had retired on a meager pension, I could not expect her to assume the added burden of my wife and children.

I was bedridden in my office with sciatica that April, but I too was swept up in the mounting furor. Zhang Yi had just returned from a trip to Beijing University, bringing the latest news. He told us about the speech by Chen Ziming[5] at the Sanjiaodi poster area and gave us a mimeographed transcript of the text, which moved me to tears. Zhang had also marched arm in arm with the protesters on April 27, chanting slogans and crashing one police barricade after another. He was a passionate youth, whose face and eyes shone with infectious excitement. Weakened by my sciatica, I kept struggling to stand up from my sickbed. If only my useless legs would allow me to take to the streets with the students!

[5] Chen Ziming, a middle-aged prodemocracy activist, was arrested in the crackdown after June 4, 1989, and imprisoned for thirteen years on charges of counterrevolutionary activities. See http://www.ifex.org/fr/content/view/full/17668.

I started to pay attention to the big-character posters and soap box orations on campus. Rebellion was in the air, as it had been during the Cultural Revolution, but this time was different: By openly demanding political reform, the protesters were going for the jugular of the Communist regime. The official media had never before carried such objective reports on an antigovernment movement. The live television coverage of events on Tiananmen Square, in particular, created nationwide sympathy for the demonstrators, and I found myself glued to the television set.

My wife reported my growing restlessness to Mother, who forced me to move in with her. This was ostensibly so that she could nurse me, but actually so that she could keep me under "house arrest." She clung to the stance she had maintained since 1949, believing it pointless to get involved in grassroots anti-Communist movements, and was even glad that my legs were too weak to carry me into the streets.

Soon after I had moved to Mother's house, Zhang and Xiao came to visit. They were on their way to negotiate with the provincial leadership and wanted me to sign their petition and write an article for their mimeographed newsletter. Other visitors followed, despite Mother's attempts to keep them away, and they whipped me up to the point where I made my excuses to Mother and returned to the campus. Once there I joined a city-wide protest march on May 17 in solidarity with the fasting students in Beijing. I hobbled along with the rest of the demonstrators, leaning on my bicycle for support and riding it for occasional relief. Somehow I managed to complete the entire march past Xincheng Square and through the heart of the city. That night, despite an excruciating backache, I felt deeply satisfied.

Even though I had been persecuted as a "reactionary" for so long, this was the first time that I had ever dared protest openly. I knew, better than any of my youthful compatriots, that an isolated individual was powerless against the Communists. But now they had been exposed as the true reactionaries. Realizing that there was strength in numbers, I boldly shouted, "Down with official corruption," along with the rest of the demonstrators.

With the exception of the diehard party committee at our university, everyone else—even top administrators—actively supported the fasting students at Tiananmen. When martial law was imposed in Beijing on May

20, an old friend of mine, Professor An Da, came to campus to encourage the students to rebel. Afterward he dropped by my office.

"Things have gone farther than anyone ever thought they would," he asserted. "The Communist Party machinery is paralyzed from top to bottom. If the people of Beijing can hang tough, this might be the end of the Communists. We older intellectuals must do everything we can to help."

I was skeptical, but I had to admit that the on-campus developments were heartening. The students had basically seized power, and the PA system blared out the Voice of America all day long. My young colleagues and I huddled around the foreign stations on my shortwave radio, hoping for good news.

We had been raised on Communist slogans like "The people's government is for the people" and "The People's Liberation Army is the sons and brothers of the people," and we had absorbed these ideas as if by osmosis. When we saw the Beijing students blocking the army's entry into the city with respectful salutes and heard that they had begged for the patronage of veteran Communists, we naively counted on the backing of the more benevolent Communist leaders and even imagined that the troops might revolt or that the government would yield. The campus was percolating with bizarre, encouraging rumors. This mood lasted through June 3, when a delegation of Jiaotong University students went to nearby factories to incite the workers to strike. I lent my bicycle to them for this purpose. Even as we watched Zhao Ziyang[6] tearfully exhorting the students to leave Tiananmen Square on the eve of the massacre, we were still praying for a miracle.

Instead, the tanks crushed our illusions. At dawn on June 4 China Radio announced that the army had "pacified a counterrevolutionary riot" during the night. I tuned in to the Voice of America and the Taiwan radio station for the details. Unable to go back to sleep, I got up and explored the campus on my bicycle. The student-controlled PA system was spreading the news of the bloodbath, protest posters were fluttering, and students were gathering on the playing fields to march into town. In prepa-

---

[6] General secretary of the Communist Party at the time, whose sympathy for the students resulted in his ouster, followed by house arrest until his death in 2005.

ration to join them, I ran home and put on a white headband; then I wrote AIM YOUR GUNS HERE on a piece of paper and had my wife pin it to my chest. She also sympathized with the students. Ordinarily exceedingly thrifty, she had donated ten yuan when they knocked on our door with their collection box. On the morning after the massacre she displayed unusual open-mindedness, disregarding her pact with Mother to keep me under control.

In fact, I mused as I lined up with the marchers, despite my reputation as a reactionary, this was the first time that I had ever been in a situation worthy of sticking my neck out in public. My heart was heavy with grief, and my eyes smarted with tears as I listened to the strains of "L'Internationale" on the PA system. You must go through with this, I told myself. I had never before given such careful thought to the possible consequences of my actions, and I was fully prepared to risk arrest.

Most of the marchers were students, and I was by far the eldest of the few faculty members present, who led the procession. As we marched through faculty housing, my tall stature and the provocative sign on my chest caught people's eyes. Bystanders kept flashing me the V signal and snapping photos of me.

The student broadcast reported that a number of Jiaotong University students had perished on Tiananmen Square. When we returned from the march that afternoon, I lay down to rest. Xiao Xian, utterly distraught, burst into my room. He had shaved his head. Seventeen Jiaotong University students had been crushed to death by tanks while protecting the statue of the Goddess of Freedom and Democracy,[7] he told me, sobbing. Then Zhang Yi came in, also with shaved head, and the three of us consoled one another, beside ourselves with grief. They reported that the army was poised to occupy our campus and asked me to write an appeal to students and faculty to resist the imposition of martial law.

The following morning, June 5, I drafted a protest poster and then headed for the store to buy paper and a calligraphy brush. On the way I ran into my colleague Li Ming and a few other young faculty members,

---

[7] Created by the students, this was a large papier-mâché statue that somewhat resembled the Statue of Liberty. It was ultimately destroyed by the army.

who helped me finish making the poster. We took it to the department office, where we read it aloud and collected faculty signatures. Then we posted it on the notice board at the campus gates. I gave the draft text to Zhang and Xiao, who made copies and distributed them widely.

NOW IT WAS the year 2000, and more than a decade had slipped by since these events. Xiao and Zhang met my plane in Shenzhen Airport, just south of Guangzhou. While I had been in America, they had become business tycoons, and Xiao now had a black Lexus instead of a bicycle. We drove to the Huizhou Hotel, which was on a small island in the center of West Lake, with a magnificent view of water and mountains. The grounds were lush with exotic southern foliage, and aquatic birds flitted past my window. My hosts told me that this hotel was exclusively for official guests of the municipal party committee and that Xiao had pulled a few strings to get me a room here.

That night I phoned my wife. "You've only been back in China for a few days," she teased, "and the official corruption is rubbing off on you already!"

Having spent the entire plane flight reminiscing about the Tiananmen protests, I could not wait to broach the subject with my old friends. I found them unreceptive, however. They took a dim view of the student leaders who had fled into exile, as if the freedom and success they enjoyed abroad were a sellout of their ideals and of their comrades who had stayed and suffered in China. I tried to disabuse them of their prejudices, but to no avail.

Xiao was a slave to his insistent cell phone, making it virtually impossible to have a meaningful conversation with him. He had no time of his own, even when drinking with me and Zhang in a restaurant, and seemed weary. Endless expense account dinners, with their constant toasts, had ruined his appetite and frayed his nerves. He had climbed to his company's board of directors and built a sizable stock portfolio, but at the cost of his personal life. He cherished the memory of the reading group at Jiaotong University and longed to translate Orwell again. But now he barely had the time for his brief reunion with me. His world of product development and marketing was unimaginable to me, an ivory tower academic from New Haven. The Tiananmen protests had left an indelible mark on his memory, but that was all. He had too much else on his mind to wallow in the past.

He asked me if I still remembered Li Ming, and I replied that I certainly did. The extra signatures that Li had garnered for my protest poster had shielded me somewhat during the police investigations in the aftermath of the massacre.

AFTER WE HAD hung up our poster, we heard news that Deng Xiaoping had suddenly died and that Premier Li Peng had been wounded in an assassination attempt. That afternoon firecrackers were popping all over campus to celebrate Deng's death. But we soon discovered that these "news reports" were baseless rumors. In fact students from Jiaotong University had not been run over by tanks, Deng Xiaoping was alive and well, and Li Peng had not been wounded. No army units had defected to the demonstrators' side, nor had any senior commander come forward to oppose the draconian measures against the protestors. Quite the contrary, it was this group of veteran Communists, from whom the people had expected benevolence, who had decided to fire on the students.

Events continued their downward spiral. After the students had left for the summer on June 6, the campus turned into a ghost town. One of my students suggested as she departed that I could hide out at her house in the Hebei countryside if necessary and left me her address. The campus was stripped of its big-character posters, and the army took over China Television, which it used as a platform for dire warnings to the public. People were being arrested in droves. As I lay on my sickbed in the Mechanical Engineering Building, the screaming sirens of passing police cars kept jolting me into jumping up and putting on my shoes in case I had to run for my life. Feeding on my paranoia, my hateful old nightmare returned to haunt me. We had a night watchman who made rounds through all the corridors at night, testing each laboratory door to make sure it was locked. The crunching of his heavy leather shoes on the terrazzo floors and the rattling of the laboratory doors invaded my dreams and woke me up. My back was so stiff that I could barely roll over; I kneaded it with my hand to soothe myself back to sleep.

Colleges all over China had to reopen a month early that fall for special Communist indoctrination sessions and investigations, which were led in our department by Secretary Zhao, the head of our party branch. Using a photograph in his possession, he ran a probe of everyone who had signed my protest poster. Some of the more cowardly signatories recanted, blaming me as the instigator. Fortunately Secretary Zhao was a mature, level-headed man, survivor of many political campaigns. Fully aware of the vagueness and capriciousness of party policy, he tried to be fair. He gave me the impression that the investigation was an unpleasant duty for him and that all he required from me was a modicum of cooperation. He chose to drop charges against Li Ming and the other signatories. As the ringleader I felt obliged to assume complete responsibility for the poster. Nonetheless, I followed Li Ming's counsel and maintained that I had forgotten who the other signatories were, while insisting that all had signed of their own free will.

I had antagonized the higher-ups in the university party committee with my AIM YOUR GUNS HERE sign, and they felt the need to investigate me further. One day that fall a friend of mine from the administration anxiously brought me word of a malevolent conversation he had overheard between a couple of cadres in the hallway. "That tall guy from the Social Sciences Division who gave the lecture on sexual liberation is totally outrageous," one of them had commented. "He had a sign on his chest to goad the troops into shooting him!"

I had to answer to a special on-campus case unit from the Security Bureau. There was enough evidence to arrest me, its agents threatened, hinting darkly that they had a videotape of my participation in the June 4 march as well as photographs of my poster. To save my own skin, I was supposed to confess and inform against my coconspirators. On subsequent occasions they switched from arm-twisting to wheedling, summoning me to a secret room, where they plied me with fancy tea and cigarettes and asked me to identify handwriting samples. They even left me a contact phone number. I told them truthfully that I was not involved with the student movement and did not know any of its organizers. I admitted writing the poster, but that was all. These interrogations stretched into December.

Just as I was getting out of bed in my office on December 26, the morning after Nicolae Ceauşescu's execution in Romania, two investigators turned up to sound me out about the reaction to the Romanian situation on campus. They seemed tense and hostile, as if afraid that the upheaval in Romania would set off a chain reaction dooming the Ceauşescus of China. As usual, I played dumb. "I'm sorry," I insisted blandly, "but I have nothing concrete to report." Even so, I could not resist adding that I had been delighted to hear that Ceauşescu and his wife had gotten what they deserved and that my colleagues, who probably shared my opinion, must be gleefully spreading the news. The investigators left in defeat and never came back.

I ASKED XIAO if he remembered how we had set off a string of firecrackers when we heard the rumors of Deng Xiaoping's death, but he was unresponsive. Changing the subject, he told me that Li Ming was now a district head in Shenzhen. Then he dialed him on the telephone and handed it to me. Li Ming sounded surprised to hear my voice. He invited me to go out to dinner with him the next day at a restaurant on a tree farm under his jurisdiction.

The following evening I rode through the woods in Li Ming's Toyota SUV. We made a series of turns, passed through several heavily guarded iron gates and a few hills lush with tropical growth, and came to a stop outside a small building in a clearing. There we were greeted by the head of the tree farm and his staff, who took us for a scenic stroll around the grounds before escorting us inside for a sumptuous banquet. We were treated to endless rounds of liquor and one platter after another of unfamiliar, intimidating delicacies, such as deep-fried sparrows, braised lizards, and various wild herbs.

After the meal Li Ming sought my advice about overseas study opportunities for his teenage son, whom he had brought along. I knew that well-heeled Chinese parents all wished to send their children abroad. Europe and America were the preferred destinations; second choices were New

Zealand and Australia. Money was no object to such families, who were concerned only with placing their offspring in prestigious schools. Li Ming also implied that prominent Chinese settled their children abroad in order to provide themselves with an escape route from the vagaries of domestic politics.

I remembered the farewell toast he and I had drunk on the eve of his bitter departure from Jiaotong University. Designated next in line for the chairmanship of the department, he had thrown away his future by impulsively signing my poster in a moment of indignation. He had started all over again in Shenzhen as a lowly government clerk, whose main job was to fetch water and newspapers, and had clawed his way up to the rank of district head. Like Xiao Xian, he had many unspeakable private burdens, about which I could only speculate.

I simply could not engage my friends in a conversation about the Tiananmen protests. Muddled with the spirits I had drunk, I leaned back in my easy chair. Did they find the subject unduly depressing? What did I hope to gain by discussing it with them? How many people in China, with its bizarre juxtapositions of glory and corruption, had managed to remain idealistic in these hard-nosed times? Everyone insisted that China had changed beyond my understanding during my prolonged absence and that I should suspend all judgment for the time being.

After the banquet Xiao Xian drove me and Zhang Yi to a new hotel, the resort at Qilin Hill, which had been built in anticipation of a visit by Deng Xiaoping that may never have taken place. Now it was reserved for guests of the Shenzhen party committee; money alone could not guarantee you a room here. It was composed of villas scattered in the woods, overlooking a serpentine lake. Gardeners were toiling over the neatly manicured grounds, which were peaceful in the gathering dusk. Exhausted from the drive, Xiao lay down and fell asleep on the bed.

Zhang Yi, who remained wide awake, was the only one of my former acquaintances who still seemed passionate. After marrying a Christian woman from Hong Kong, he had converted to Christianity. To draw on a hackneyed Communist slogan, this new worldview had completely transformed him. Once his friend was asleep, he seized the moment to proclaim his ardent religious faith to me before I returned to America.

Although I did not share his conviction, I was delighted by his earnestness. In a nation where everything was false—from the political rights guaranteed by the Constitution to the hymens of young women who resorted to hymenoplasty to conceal their lost virginity—true religious faith like his was a force for good and was vastly preferable to crass materialism.

As he sang the praises of God, his face lit up, just as it had in the old days. But now he was too otherworldly for me, and our conversation was somewhat discordant. Each of us was trying too hard to convert the other, and neither of us was listening. With disappointment I sensed his disdain for the weighty social problems that concerned me—official corruption, political reform, and the misery of the peasants—preferring instead to harp on the growing number of Chinese Christians in recent years. He seemed to stiffen, however, when I mentioned the persecution of the underground church. Why was he avoiding politics? Was his preoccupation with religion simply a cover for cynicism? I wanted to challenge him but held my tongue lest I appear irreverent.

Using peculiarly Christian terminology, he applauded my family's move to America and especially the news of my wife's conversion to Christianity. Unless I appreciated the special favor that God had bestowed on my family, Zhang asserted, and treasured the salvation he had granted, his blessing would be wasted on me.

The hour was late, but Zhang's evangelical zeal was indefatigable. In fact, for the entire time I was with him, from the moment he first met me at the airport, he sounded like a broken record: "Have faith in God! Have faith in God! Have faith in God!"

51

Exodus

ZHENGGUAN AND I were visiting the Potala Palace in Tibet, which was a magnificent citadel, a conglomeration of buildings from various eras piled up like toy blocks on a mountainside.

To reach the top, we had to pass through the lower palaces, climb a steep staircase, and snake through narrow passageways, dark inner chambers, and a series of corridors and courtyards. Our hands were greasy with the butterfat smeared on the banisters by Tibetan pilgrims, who brought it to deposit into the eternal lamps in front of the Buddha statues. We followed the leader of our international tour group at a brisk pace, not pausing to contribute fuel at the lamps or cash offerings at the altars. Decorating solemn Buddhist shrines with banknotes was a Tibetan Buddhist tradition, but to me the wrinkled old bills seemed an eyesore in the devout atmosphere of gilded statues, glowing lamps, droning prayers, and pilgrims prostrating themselves and inching along the floor on their hands and knees.

By noon we had arrived at the peak, where we emerged into the brilliant sunlight of the clear blue sky over the Tibetan plateau. As a tourist I was more keenly aware of the date than usual. It was June 4, the anniversary of the Beijing Massacre, and I was on the lookout for signs of unusual activity. But all seemed quiet in Lhasa. No one in our group, not even Zheng-guan, mentioned the massacre. Scanning the horizon from my observation point on the rooftop of the world, I reflected bleakly that I would not find any commemorative ceremonies in Tiananmen Square or anywhere else in China, even if I could see that far from here.

Only eleven years had passed since the butchery of 1989. But China, a land where little value was placed on human life, seemed to be in a mute, drugged stupor; it was as if these dreadful events had never taken place. I found this entirely unacceptable as a returnee from America, which, like the rest of the world, was keeping the memories alive on this notorious anniversary. Feeling the compulsion to observe the occasion in some way, I tried to satisfy myself with a silent prayer.

The story that Xiao Xian had told me on the telephone had set my nerves on edge, and I kept looking over my shoulder to make sure that no one was following me. After all, I had signed up for this tour of Tibet only to protect myself from possible charges of troublemaking during the Security Bureau's annual June crackdown.

On the morning of the first anniversary of the massacre a decade ago, when people's memories were still raw, huge, provocative posters demanding "an eye for an eye" had appeared on the wall outside the main gate of Jiaotong University. That evening I had pedaled through the city streets with a female student on the rear of my bicycle, scattering paper money for the martyrs. Afterward I described our experience in a poem: "Let's drink a toast while avoiding the dragnet, and scatter paper money by the red lantern's light."

In 1990, when Beijing was awarded the right to host the Asian Games, an unprecedented surge of chauvinism eclipsed the memory of the bloodbath. The people of Xi'an, who had turned out in droves in 1989 to cheer the protesters on and supply them with drinking water, now lined the same boulevards to root for the torch-bearing Asian Games parade.

If only everyone would boycott these games and this parade! I reflected helplessly, wishing I could tear down the welcome signs that festooned the city. Hosting the games had given the regime the means to manipulate public opinion, reversing the antigovernment mood that had followed the massacre. This discouraging trend continued over the next decade.

Zhengguan and I had started our Tibetan tour from Chengdu, where I had met the dissident intellectual Liao Yiwu in a teahouse. Although we did not know each other personally, we were familiar with each other's writings and soon found ourselves comparing notes about the Tiananmen protests. Like me, he had not participated in the original student movement. But he had stayed up until dawn on the night after the massacre, composing a long, angry poem entitled "Slaughter,"[1] which he recorded in his own voice and distributed widely. He and a group of underground poets also shot a video, *Requiem for the Dead*,[2] intending to screen it on the first anniversary of the massacre. But the Security Bureau arrested everyone involved before the video was finished. Liao was named the ringleader of a group of counterrevolutionary poets and sentenced to four years in jail. When he was released in 1994, his life was in a shambles, his wife, job, and residence permit gone. From then on he had lived a hand-to-mouth existence by playing the flute or cashing in his paltry royalties.

Liao's story illustrates some of the terror tactics used by the butchers of June 4 to muzzle the Chinese people. No wonder the massacre seems almost forgotten in China today!

I had fared much better than Liao because my protests had been confined to the Jiaotong University campus and because I had cooperated with the subsequent investigations. While some of my colleagues were imprisoned or barred from teaching, I had received a mere slap on the wrist, a denial of my promotion from instructor to professor.

Jiaotong University was basically a technology school. The Social Sciences Division, which included my department, was a revamped version of the former department of Marxism-Leninism. Humanities electives had been added and staffed with rejects like me from Chinese literature departments. Courses such as mine in Chinese literature were considered mere embellishments at Jiaotong University, not to be mentioned in the same breath as the political curriculum. I had no illusions about this pecking order. Even if I had avoided involvement in the Tiananmen "distur-

[1] A translation by Michael Day can be found at http://www.sino.uni-heidelberg.de/dachs/leiden/poetry/liaoyiwu_slaughter.html.

[2] See http://www.sino.uni-heidelberg.de/dachs/leiden/poetry/liaoyiwu_intro.html.

bances," I would not have been able to compete for promotion with my colleagues who taught politics. As with many other things in China, the number of promotions was limited, and people squabbled bitterly over their allocation.

Still, my wife nagged me constantly. "We won't get decent housing unless you're promoted."

"Then we'll have to make do with what we have," I replied. "Anyway, I still have my office."

"You never make a fuss when you're supposed to," she countered. "But you always stick your neck out when everybody else has the good sense to lie low. You're just pigheaded! If you're not going to do anything about this, then I'll go see your department chairman."

To avoid the embarrassment her threatened visit might bring, I made a reluctant appeal to the dean of faculty.

Fortunately, I had recently published my first monograph—*A Study of Classical Chinese Poetry on Women and by Women*—a revision of my rejected master's thesis on erotic poetry. It had been difficult to find an editor daring enough to accept it, but I had found one, a young woman scholar from Henan. Arming myself with a copy, I went to see the dean of faculty and made the case for my promotion as forcefully as I could. He seemed receptive, so I presented the book to him. To my surprise, he examined its flashy silver cover dubiously, inquiring if it was a romance novel. When I explained that it was a scholarly monograph, written with the latest in Western methodology, he dismissed it as having little "economic value."

I returned home in defeat and tossed the book onto a chair. All the satisfaction I had derived from its publication had evaporated. My wife resorted to gratuitous sarcasm as an outlet for her frustration.

"Didn't you say your book was groundbreaking? I was expecting our house to be crammed with reporters! How come nobody has noticed it, even though it was published so long ago?"

She was right. The book had failed to elicit the response I had anticipated. Nothing I could say would enable her to share my sweet sense of accomplishment. She had always belittled my scholarly work. Even Mother, who had been to college, subscribed to the prevalent opinion— born of decades of political pressure—that the humanities were worth less than other, more practical fields. My mother and my wife had joined forces to lament that I had chosen the wrong type of writing, berating me for my failure to make money like the best-selling author Jia Pingwa.

Accusing my wife of shortsightedness, I retorted that she should keep her mouth shut when she was obviously out of her depth. She fired back with her old gripe that we were the poorest family in the department because I had holed up in my office all these years instead of moonlighting to bring in extra money. Her embittered rebuke reminded me of the endless dressings-down Mother used to give Father for drinking.

With no prospects at Jiaotong University, I decided to look for a new job. First I applied to a few schools in Xi'an; then I expanded my search to some of the new colleges in the Special Economic Zones[3] around Guangzhou and Hainan. All proved fruitless, however. Potential employers rejected me as soon as they discovered that I had taken part in the Tiananmen "disturbances." I seemed to be sinking back into my old vicious circle, ruining my chances of staying anywhere very long with my inability to "make a good showing" politically. I had taught docilely for almost a decade since my graduation, painstakingly repairing the damage I had done with my unorthodox thesis, but now my participation in the "disturbances" had set me back anew.

"Why not just sit tight?" my department chair counseled me blandly. "I don't think you're very marketable anymore, at your age and with your history. You'd be better off staying here. In a couple of years, when some of the people ahead of you have gotten their promotions and things have loosened up a bit, you'll probably get yours."

I retreated to my office, where I flopped down on my cot and riffled through a few English magazines. A color photograph of the United States caught my eye. It was a suburban house with a lawn. Golden leaves were floating down from the trees by the street, and a man with a leaf blower was swirling them into a big pile. How lovely! I sighed, drifting off into a daydream. If only I could find sanctuary in such a peaceful land! Then I could shut my door and while away my days in scholarship, stepping outside to work in my yard like the man in the picture whenever I

[3] Established in 1980 to promote foreign trade.

needed a break. I could stop worrying about whether the party bureaucrats approved of every step I took, leave the shame of my Chinese life behind me, and venture into a new, American one.

Laozi said, "Frank speech is not always pretty."[4] He also said, "Opposition is the movement of the Dao."[5] I am incapable of saying what people want to hear. In fact I regard it as my personal mission to speak the opposite. In this sense I resonate personally with Laozi's suggestion that opposition is the motive force in the search for truth. Opposition entails reversal or return and is by nature reactive. I am a reactionary in this sense, and this concept has informed my behavior all my life. It is far more than mere political dissent.

In the summer of 1990 Zhang Yi and Xiao Xian got their M.B.A.'s and headed south to work in Huizhou. The students who had marched with me during the Tiananmen protests also graduated and reported to their first jobs. Several of them asked me to write in their yearbooks before they departed, and I remember composing a long poem for the young woman who had scattered paper money from the back of my bicycle. It began like this:

What is the classroom?
A meat grinder.
All kinds of meat
Must be minced for dumplings.

Once the students were gone, I went away for a few weeks' vacation. When I returned I found a letter from America in my jam-packed mailbox. I did not know anyone in America, I thought, puzzled. I picked up the envelope and scrutinized the neat Chinese handwriting; it was indeed addressed to me. It turned out to be from someone who knew my research. After skimming it once, I reread it, trying to picture its author. It began: "Your servant has read your masterpiece, *A Study of Classical Chinese Poetry on Women and by Women*. . . ." Such antiquated, self-effacing diction conjured up the image of

[4] Chapter 81.
[5] Chapter 40.

an elderly gentleman, well versed in the epistolary art. He introduced himself as Professor Chang, from Yale University and extolled my book at length. He went on to say that he hoped to assign it to students in a course on women poets of the Ming and Qing and was writing to find out how he could purchase it. I wrote back to him right away with the address of my editor and publisher and set off for the post office to mail the letter.

I thought of the cataclysmic results of the only other letter I had ever sent to a foreign country, to Moscow University in 1967. Decades later, mailing this second letter abroad awakened a sense of déjà vu. Both letters had to do with a book, and both were addressed to a famous university abroad. Just as I had in 1967, I strode up to the window at the post office and asked how much postage I needed. This time I was relatively unafraid. In fact, as I affixed the stamps, I felt a vague stirring of optimism. I could not quite put my finger on it, as it was extremely faint, like a whiff of spring in the dead of winter.

I dropped the letter into the slot, mulling the vagaries of fate. Come what may, it was always a good sign to receive fan mail. Then I went home and told my wife about the letter, as leverage against her belittlement of my scholarly work. As long as what I wrote had real merit, I pointed out, it would be noticed sooner or later.

Eventually I received a reply, and Professor Chang and I struck up a professional correspondence. In the summer of 1991 the Yale University East Asian Languages and Literatures department sent me an announcement of upcoming conferences and invited me to participate in one on "Women and Literature in Ming-Qing China" in 1993, all expenses paid. What a rare opportunity for an unknown scholar like me! If I wanted to present a paper, I had to send a title and abstract as soon as possible. I happened to be studying *Random Notes from Xiqing*[6] at the time, so I dashed off a title about marginalized scholars and ill-starred women writers and sent it off to Yale.

The publication of my book had apparently set off a fortunate chain of events, which had acquired a momentum of their own. As it turned out,

---

[6] Memoir of the eighteenth-century scholar Shi Zhenlin, in which the works of the peasant poetess He Shuangqing are preserved. See Paul S. Ropp, *Banished Immortal: Searching for Shuangqing, China's Peasant Woman Poet* (Ann Arbor: University of Michigan Press, 2001).

I had not spent so many desk-bound years for nothing. Now it was finally time for me to reap the benefits, although I would have to clear a number of hurdles first.

I received regular updates from the conference organizers. In the summer of 1992 the official agenda and invitation arrived in the mail. I knew that endless layers of red tape lay ahead of me, and all would be lost if I hit a snag at any stage of the way. In order to apply for a business travel passport, I needed a signed, sealed certificate from each level of the university party bureaucracy. But the Office of Academic Research, which had the ultimate say over my application, balked over my role in the Tiananmen "disturbances." It decided to conduct a full-scale investigation and to require me to write a self-critical essay.

The investigation lasted six months, by the end of which I was so exasperated that I could barely restrain myself from lashing out at the authorities. When I completed my conference paper in late 1992, the Office of Academic Research asked a well-known old professor in my department to verify that it did not leak state secrets or depart from the official party line. Fortunately the old professor was supportive, and my paper was entirely apolitical, so he endorsed it and even went on record with the comment that it was a model of "historical materialism." In the spring of 1993, after leaving no stone unturned, the Office of Academic Research finally gave me the go-ahead.

By the time I completed the next step, obtaining the approval of the university's Office of Scholarly Foreign Exchange, I had no time to lose. I got my passport in early May, but I still had to submit it to the appropriate authorities in Beijing to get my visa, and the conference was in late June. I finally had my documents in order by early June, just in time. I was certain that the organizers at Yale could not imagine a government on earth that placed such roadblocks in the way of foreign travel. It was lucky that they had allowed two years of lead time for the conference.

These headaches galvanized my determination to leave China. When the day came to go to the airport, I checked in my new luggage and went through the exit formalities without a hitch. But as I strode toward the departure gate, I kept looking back over my shoulder, fearing that someone might try to catch me before I could board the plane.

At last we were airborne, and my spirits soared as the plane hurtled through the sky.

My lifelong quest for freedom had focused on two deep wishes. The first was for the emptying of my detested dossier, which would grant me a new lease on life. This wish came true on the day when I transferred from Number Ninety-one Middle School to Shaanxi Normal University. I still remember how elated I felt when I picked up the dossier and noticed its lightness, rejoicing like the Monkey King when he crawled out from under the Mountain of the Five Elements.[7] The second was the wish to leave China for a land—any land—where I would be free of the Communist Party, its personnel cadres, and the Security Bureau. Now this too had come to pass. I was being borne away on the wind from Beijing, with its vulgar display of Mao's embalmed corpse in its mausoleum. In stunned disbelief I stared out at the wing as the plane hummed steadily east, toward the sun. Over the Pacific it emerged from the darkness shrouding the Eastern Hemisphere into the daylight of the Western Hemisphere, and the sky kept brightening as we flew.

We landed at Kennedy Airport in the afternoon. I sailed through customs, exited the waiting area, and arrived in New Haven by nightfall.

Professor Chang gave a reception on the eve of the conference. Our host and hostess, Professor Chang and spouse, were waiting in the doorway to greet the conference participants as we arrived and climbed the steps from the road to the house. As soon as we shook hands and introduced ourselves, I discovered that the elderly gentleman of my imagination was in fact a middle-aged woman scholar. She had soft, curly hair, tastefully adorned with a bow, and a kind, bodhisattva-like smile. She lavished praise on me for being the first to send in my paper, commenting that it had been excellent. She added that even though the conference organizers had pressed contributors for their papers, some people procrastinated until the last minute. I replied that I had never had the honor

---

[7] In the classic novel *Journey to the West*, the mischievous Monkey King was imprisoned by the Buddha under the Mountain of the Five Elements as punishment for causing havoc in heaven. Five centuries later he was freed by the Tang dynasty priest Xuanzang to assist him on his pilgrimage to India.

of participating in an academic conference in my field and had reacted to her invitation like an elementary school pupil taking a test, terrified that some oversight might disqualify me entirely. I needed a head start to compensate for my handicaps, I added, and was pleased that I was not behind schedule. Professor Chang smiled graciously. Then her husband offered us some red wine. Grape wine was a brand-new taste experience for me, and its tartness made my lips pucker. It bore no resemblance to the familiar flavor of Chinese liquor. This was the first of many eye-opening experiences during my trip.

I had brought much more luggage than I needed for this short conference. But I had decided beforehand to try to stay in America by any means possible and was laden with toiletries, winter clothes, writing paper, and reference books. I had long cherished the hope to escape from China, but this was the first time a plausible destination had ever presented itself.

Everyone close to me had egged me on. My wife reminded me that the university was planning to put its housing up for sale to faculty, but we had no savings. Her job in the day care center placed her squarely on the gossip circuit, and there was plenty of hearsay about Jiaotong University professors who had wrung money out of their trips to America. Even if I could not stay there forever, she said, at least I had to find a temporary job in New York. A few thousand dollars would convert into tens of thousands of Chinese yuan, enough to buy housing.

But it was not as easy to stay in America as we had imagined. When the conference ended, I spent a few days poking around in New York. First I looked up a friend, a graduate student in the Bronx, but my arrival seemed to bring a jinx: It coincided with the loss of his part-time job, making my visit exceedingly awkward. And I was appalled by his ramshackle, high-crime neighborhood, with graffiti scrawled all over the buildings. I left in a hurry to stay with another friend, who was struggling to subsist as a poor immigrant in Queens. Her tale of woe extinguished my resolve to linger in America. Having seen the price that people paid for their freedom, I realized that I was not cut out for the life of an illegal immigrant. I decided to return to China right away.

My wife stomped off into the bedroom as soon as I entered the apartment with my suitcase. She refused to speak to me for days on end, claiming that worry about our inability to afford our university housing kept her awake at night. I tried to assure her that we would find the money somehow when the time came.

Although I had given my solemn word that I would return, my colleagues seemed surprised, and somewhat disappointed, to see me. "How come you're back already?" people asked, which I found both irksome and amusing. Apparently, people were betting that I would defect to America, and I had let them down.

A friend told me that our departmental party secretary had been delighted to hear of my return, pronouncing me "a true patriot." I burst out laughing when I heard this and assured my friend that I did not deserve such praise. I had never imagined that Mencius's statement that the doings of a gentleman are "above the understanding of the ordinary man"[8] would ever apply to me. The title "patriot" should be reserved for people who love the party. It is an inaccurate description of me, a perpetual misfit in China. I had never found the Communists' attempts to pigeonhole me with their jargon to be apt—whether positive or negative.

Professor Chang also lauded my decision to return to China. She was a law-abiding citizen, and she did not want to see a scholar whom Yale had vouched for disappear in New York as an illegal immigrant. In her view, I was not so desperate back home that I had to find a job in a Chinese restaurant in America, and such a course of action would destroy my academic career. Unwillingness to worry her and to give scholars from China a bad name factored heavily in my decision to go home.

It turned out to be the right choice. I had made a good impression on the East Asian Languages and Literatures department at Yale, and the following year it offered me a job teaching Chinese.

The offer came by fax in April 1994. It emphasized that this was a language teaching job rather than a professorship and that I needed to be sure I was willing to devote myself to this relatively lowly career path before I took the position. I accepted with alacrity, and the department responded with a formal letter of appointment. The job title was senior lector, and

[8] *Mencius*, trans. D. C. Lau (London: Penguin, 1970), p. 176.

the term of hire was three years, from July 1, 1994, to June 30, 1997. I also received the application documents for my HI visa, which would make me employable in America.

This time I needed a passport for private travel. My department and university agreed to issue the necessary certificates, as long as I complied with a new university rule requiring me to resign from my job first. If I transferred to a new job overseas, my family could not continue to enjoy the perquisites of my association with the university. My resignation would mean the termination of my health care coverage as well as my family's right to occupy university housing and send our children to the university-run schools. In short, we were being evicted. I notified Yale of the problem, requesting permission to bring my family to America, and the department sent the paperwork for my wife and children's visas right away.

My wife had second thoughts when she heard that I would have to give up my job and housing. I had been a member of the workforce for almost thirty years, beginning in the spring of 1965 at the Number Two Brickyard, and was entitled to retirement benefits. People close to me said that it was unfair of Jiaotong University to kick me out, negating all my previous service. But I did not want to dwell on my losses and was ready to cross the point of no return. I wanted only to obtain passports for my whole family as quickly as possible. Since I had always hated the socialist system, I should not harbor any illusions about its "superiority" or expect to enjoy any of its benefits. This sacrifice was the price of my freedom. I submitted my resignation resolutely and followed through right away with the rest of the formalities for my departure from the university.

In May my whole family was cut loose from Jiaotong University. I received my terminal paycheck, my wife quit her job at the day care center, and my children withdrew from school in the middle of the semester. We set to work emptying our apartment, which the university required us to vacate before I could have the certificates for my passport application.

We sold whatever belongings we could, saving the best for Mother and other relatives, and borrowed money for our travel expenses. On June 10, 1994, we boarded a train from Xi'an to Beijing, planning to get our visas and leave directly from there. We had reduced our possessions to the contents of three trunks and three suitcases, all half full of my books. I had brought my diaries and treasured photo albums, and my children had their pet silkworms, which were on the verge of spinning their cocoons. They lay in their cardboard box, their heads waggling dumbly on their roly-poly translucent bodies.

My mother, brother, and sisters saw us off at the station. As we sat on the train waiting for it to depart, we gazed at them longingly through the window. The train's horn gave a mournful blast. The women and children were bawling, and Zhengguan and I had tears in our eyes. Then the train pulled out of the station, quickly gathering speed, and my family and hometown quickly faded from view.

The next morning we went to the American Embassy to apply for our visas. Word had it that the Americans were callous and might turn us away on a whim. If this happened, we would be expected to give up and go home, our time and money simply wasted.

We, however, no longer had a home. If the Americans denied us our visas, we would end up as street people in Beijing. As we joined the long line outside the American Embassy on Xiushui Street, I resolved to stop at nothing to obtain our visas.

After a few hours' wait we were finally called to the window. The woman clerk inside leafed through our papers, asked a few gentle questions, and then went into the office to consult with her colleagues. She came out with the news that I could take my wife and sixteen-year-old son to America, but my eighteen-year-old daughter had to stay in China. When I asked for an explanation, she said that my daughter was old enough to live independently of her parents. Moreover, the Americans were concerned that she would attend college in the United States and stay there afterward. The implication was that she was being kept behind as a hostage.

There was a long line behind us, and I could see that I had little bargaining power. It is not my nature to beg. I retorted adamantly that I would not go to Yale unless all four of us could have visas, and I reminded the clerk that Yale had provided all the necessary INS documents, intending for us to go as a family. Keeping my family together and educating my children were my priorities as a parent, I insisted, and it would be inhuman to abandon my daughter at such a tender age. Without her, I added, I would not want to go to paradise, much less to America. At any rate, we could not go back where we came from, so we were ready to put up a fight. I still had my letter of invitation from Yale, along with Yale's clout to back me up.

Taken aback, the clerk ducked into the office for more advice and came out with a compromise solution. She told me to leave our passports with her and come back again another day.

As soon as we got back to our room, I called Professor Chang, who mobilized the department secretary to contact the embassy and send more supporting documents right away. Thanks to their efforts, we found visas attached to all four of our passports when we returned to the embassy.

We boarded our plane for America on July 7. For the second time I savored the relief of flying out of Beijing. But this time was different. The first trip had been merely a blithe trial run. Secure in the knowledge that I would probably be back, I had been in a happy-go-lucky mood. Now my elation quickly turned to gloom. Exiling myself and my family was a serious matter. I was fifty years old, an age at which I should be reaping the rewards of a lifetime of work, with my family well established and a foundation laid for my retirement. But here I was dragging my wife and children along with me to start a new life from scratch in a foreign land. And even though I had a job waiting for me, we were practically destitute.

Then I noticed my wife and children, first-time fliers, staring out the window at the bizarre cumulus formations. They were broadening their horizons already. My spirits lifted like cloud cover cleared by the wind, and I felt myself rising to the challenges ahead. I remained in a bittersweet mood for the rest of the flight. After endless rounds of beverages, the plane finally approached New York in the afternoon, circling over the Statue of Liberty.

We breezed through customs at Kennedy Airport and were met at the exit by Professor Chang and her husband, who drove us to a second-floor apartment on Orange Street in New Haven. At last we had a place to call our own. I felt as safe as a freshwater eel in its mud hole; once it has slithered inside, no one can yank it out by the tail. When night fell and the curtains were drawn, I watched my wife and children dozing in bed in the soft lamplight. Inspired by the peace of the moment, I rose to my feet, palms pressed together in silent thanks to my guardian angel, the great and merciful Bodhisattva Guanyin.

52

My Nightmare Comes True

AFTER ZHENGGUAN AND I returned from Tibet, he convinced me to treat my lingering cough at some aromatherapy steam baths in a massage parlor in Chengdu. I soon found myself baking in hot steam laced with refreshing Chinese medicinal herbs. From the neck down I was encapsulated in a pod, like a cello in its case, standing in a row of identical pods under a strip of lights. Zhengguan's head protruded from the pod on my left, and an attendant was proffering him a cold drink and mopping his brow.

"How are you holding up?" Zhengguan asked me.

"Fine, as long as it doesn't get any hotter!" I replied, glancing at the thermometer in front of me. With the reading at forty-two degrees Celsius, I was overheated and faint, and my heart was racing.

I was leery of massage parlors, but Zhengguan insisted that this one was respectable. It was not that I was being stuffy. Rather, I had serious misgivings, having read reports in the papers about the police using masseuses, and cocktail waitresses in nightclubs, to frame dissidents on charges of patronizing prostitutes. Dogged by paranoia from the moment I set foot in China, I kept my distance from such establishments.

After we started to wilt in the steam pods, we dived into cool showers and then followed the attendant through winding corridors into a spacious massage therapy room. Paunchy half-naked men, their skin hanging in folds, were sprawled on the massage tables like a colony of seals lolling on coastal headlands. Clad in identical baggy pants, they lay with their feet thrust languorously into their masseuses' faces. Zhengguan and I lay down and joined them.

As I sipped my cool drink, I remembered a close call I had when looking for a barbershop on my first morning in Shanghai a month earlier. First I walked down West Nanjing Road, but the state-run establishments were not open yet. Then I turned off into the back streets, where I saw plenty of signs for little "hair salons." When I stepped inside one of them, I was greeted by some girls who looked like migrant workers. None was particularly attractive, and all were dolled up in the latest outlandish styles, including cumbersome platform sandals mounted on huge soles that looked like thick wedges of cake. After a moment's hesitation I said I needed a haircut. They replied that the barber would be there soon, invited me to sit down, and offered me a massage while I was waiting. They gathered around so that I could choose among them, and a short, fat one sidled up to me, crooning an invitation to step into a back room for her services. I noticed in the mirror that I looked like an unshaved migrant worker, clearly not a local. With the uncomfortable realization that I had stumbled into a brothel, I panicked and backed out the door, mumbling, "No, no."

I did not relax until I had collapsed onto a reclining chair in a state-run barbershop. The male barber had wet my skin with a steaming washcloth and given me a gentle shave and was now scrubbing my scalp with his fingernails. Such pleasures were unique to China, I sighed to myself. His practiced touch, and the cool breeze of the fan in the bright morning sunlight, lulled me into a state of bliss.

The foot massage I had with Zhengguan in Chengdu, however, was entirely different. A regular customer at the massage parlor, he surrendered unselfconsciously to his masseuse. But as a first timer I was not sure I liked the elaborate pampering, despite its much-touted therapeutic effects. I was ashamed to thrust my big foot with its discolored toenails into the hand of my lovely masseuse. For a full forty-five minutes she kneaded and pounded my toes and the pressure points on my feet with her delicate fingers, inquiring solicitously all the while how it felt. Noting her furrowed brow, I kept wishing in embarrassment that the massage would soon be over.

The foot massage was followed by a back massage, which took even longer. I commented to Zhengguan that I doubted the effectiveness of these procedures, although I did not mind frittering away my money this once. Crestfallen, he snapped that I had stayed in America so long that I had turned into a bookworm.

Having taken early retirement to start his own company, he was much better off than he had been on his state salary and enjoyed a life of ease in the newly ostentatious society of post–Mao China. He worked hard for his money, which he lavished on the trappings of leisure. He even kept a new Buick parked in the lot of his apartment complex and took road trips with his family during vacations.

"What's so great about America?" he asked me smugly during our Tibetan tour. The implication was that he and his peers in China had—with comparably little effort—attained or even surpassed the middle-class living standard that we had sought when we emigrated in pursuit of our "American dream." People of his class liked to pat themselves on the back because their material lives were not inferior to those of their counterparts in the developed countries, and their cockiness was nourished by the anti-American propaganda churned out by the official media.

After the massage we drove to the night market for a snack. Over a couple of iced beers he nagged me to stop writing what he considered anti-Communist drivel. I had been away too long, he said, and my notion of China was hopelessly behind the times. Moreover, it was stupid for me to associate with overseas prodemocracy activists. They weren't paying me, and I had a good job. Why on earth would I want to incur political suspicion for nothing? I had been asking for trouble by publishing my defense of Wei Jingsheng*

---

* China's most famous prodemocracy activist, first imprisoned in 1979 for controversial essays posted on Democracy Wall in Beijing. Released eighteen years later, he was deported to the United States. See http://www.weijingsheng.org/wei/en.html.

in the Hong Kong magazine *Ming Pao Monthly* and by photocopying it and mailing it to my friends in China.

"You're not cut out for politics anyway," he commented, lighting a cigarette and handing me one out of habit.

I declined. I had quit and could not even bear the smell of secondhand smoke.

"Why don't you use the prestige of your big-name American university to set up exchanges with Chinese scholars? Then you'd get invited to come back here and give conference papers all the time. You'd be famous here, and that would show Professor Huo at Shaanxi Normal University and those people at Jiaotong University a thing or two. Besides, there are so many wonderful places to go sightseeing in China nowadays! If you'd just quit your scribbling and spend your summers here with me, we could do some traveling together. But you'd rather make life hard for yourself. Just look—even though you've been formally invited to present a paper at an international scholarly conference, you're glancing over your shoulder all the time to see if plainclothesmen are following you. You're too scared even to go out and have a little fun. China has changed, and people have a lot more leeway than they used to. As long as you don't criticize the government in public, you can earn plenty of money and live pretty comfortably. In some ways, we have more freedom here than you do in America."

I did not bother to contradict him. I had heard similar vague claims about how much life had improved in China from many people, including Zhang Yi and Xiao Xian. Except for a few marginalized intellectuals like Liao Yiwu, no one had been willing to talk about the Beijing Massacre with me, and everyone had seemed to disapprove of the overseas prodemocracy activists and their activities.

Mah-jongg was all the rage in Chengdu. The teahouses were outfitted with special tea tables that could be flipped over, revealing felt-covered undersides that doubled as gaming tables. People asserted that at any given moment more than half the citizens of Chengdu were engaged in this pastime. I was amused to discover mah-jongg dens concealed inside "senior citizens' centers" in the back alleys. The doorway of such an establishment was usually hung with blue cloth, which covered the opening like a surgical mask, and was blazoned with bold lettering: HIGH-CLASS ENTERTAIN-

MENT ONLY. NO GAMBLING. But inside, I found the familiar whooshing sound of mah-jongg tiles, and young people, not "senior citizens," raising their voices now and then in sporadic arguments. Caught up in an endless cycle of winning and losing, they raked money in and expelled it again like snakes gobbling their own tails and excreting directly into their own mouths. After having visited several cities during my month in China, I took these clandestine scenes as a metaphor for Chinese society in the post-Mao, post-Deng era; it was a large-scale producer of material, spiritual, and even human garbage, hidden behind a curtain of propaganda.

I knew that Zhengguan meant well and that his pragmatic views were shared by most people in China. Yet I replied that I could not follow his advice even if I wanted to. One's choices in life are not entirely voluntary but are dictated by one's ability. This is what Mencius meant by his distinction between "cannot" and "will not." I turned to writing in the knowledge that I was not cut out for a life of action, and I have always derived pleasure from it, although it has often backfired on me. I could have chosen a new profession when I had the opportunity to go back to graduate school after my rehabilitation, but my natural proclivities channeled me into a career in literature and teaching. Even if I had wanted to become a businessman like my brother, I would never have succeeded. Moreover, I believed that dissenting voices were essential forces of progress. The regime's vaunting of "stability" showed that its vested interests still obstructed any social change that might undermine the power structure. Despite people's insistence that things had improved, I could see that Chinese citizens were still denied many of the same basic rights they had lacked under Mao.

It was not that I did not want to keep coming back. After all, my cultural roots were in this land. Even a simple pleasure like a haircut on Nanjing Road rekindled fond memories of a lifetime of mundane Chinese delights. There had been many a forlorn evening in the sleepy town of New Haven when I sorely missed my convivial junkets to the night markets with my friends in China.

The Chengdu night market was still bustling despite the late hour, and Zhengguan and I had another round of beer. My tongue loosened by alcohol, I vented some of my frustration on him.

"Do you think that publishing a few books and teaching Chinese language at a famous American university gains me an automatic entrée into the Chinese academic community? It's not that simple. Scholars, just like businessmen, need to network and market themselves. If I hadn't hosted some Chinese visitors in America, nobody would have invited me here. But I'm just an ordinary language teacher, not well connected enough to bring people to America. Besides, I'm no good at back-scratching. I don't have as much power as you think I have, and even if I did, I wouldn't know how to use it. Anyway, there's nothing special about these academic conferences, even if the banquets sound like fun. Most of the papers are extremely run-of-the-mill. You're expected to toe the line, and nobody wants to hear controversial, cutting-edge ideas. I was the only person at this Nanjing conference who dared poke holes in some of the second-rate papers that were presented. It raised quite a flap, so I'll bet that's the last time anyone invites me here!

"I've always been a maverick. As a young man I disliked the double-dealing I saw around me, and when I got older, this feeling crystallized into anticommunism. I don't belong here, even without the threat of arrest. Let me quote a famous poem by my good friend from Yale the Taiwanese poet Zheng Chouyu:

My horse's hoofbeats are a beautiful delusion.
I'm only a sojourner,
Not here to stay.

"Come on, let's have another round of beers," I said, and we clinked glasses again. "The real reason I came was to see the people who are important to me," I concluded. "Frank conversations like this are all I need. The hell with academics and politics!"

"Guozi, are you drunk?" Zhengguan asked me, slurring his words.

"No, beer always passes right through my system. It never goes to my head."

He ordered another round, and we kept chugging beer until his wife picked us up and drove us home.

Zhengguan begged me to stay with him a few days longer, but now that

June 4 was past, it was time to go to Xi'an to help with the reinterment. On June 11, I took a train to Xi'an. A few days later I was arrested. The Security Bureau agents did not apprehend me in a massage parlor, as I had feared, but in Mother's house. Eight men in two squad cars knocked on our door early in the morning on June 15 and hauled me away, ignoring my protestations of innocence.

53

Arrested Again[1]

OTHER, RETIRED FROM a lifetime of middle school mathematics teaching, lived in a modest two-bedroom corner apartment in the Honglou Building in the Jinglong subdivision of the Dongguan section of Xi'an. Her living space was cramped, but she had augmented it somewhat by allowing her kitchen to spill over into the balcony. She had bought the apartment from her former school a mere six years before, in 1994, and it was already much the worse for wear: The doors would not shut, the paint was peeling, and the plumbing was rusty. The neighbors grumbled that the building was just the sort of shoddy construction often featured in media exposés.

Mother had visited me in America for six months in 1997, and in those days she had still been physically and intellectually active. But since then she had aged to the point where she needed a live-in aide. When I arrived

---

[1] Perry Link has published a translation of an earlier essay by Kang regarding this episode, to which the translator is indebted for certain terminology in this chapter. See Kang Zhengguo, "Arrested in China," trans., Perry Link, *The New York Review of Books*, Vol. 48, No. 14 (September 20, 2001), pp. 6–8.

in Xi'an on June 11, 2000, the aide had just gone home for a few days to help with her village harvest, and I had to attend to Mother's daily needs and push her around in her wheelchair. I was too busy to visit any of my friends, including Mao Zhiyi and old Mr. Huang from the Foreign Languages Institute. Instead, I called them and made dates to see them as soon as our aide returned. Mao said he could hardly wait to see the books and magazines I had brought him.

On June 14, as soon as I had help with Mother again, I called Mao several times but got no answer. The apartment was hot and stuffy after dinner, so I went out for a breath of fresh air. As I headed for the East Gate under the evening streetlamps, I was suddenly gripped with worry about Mao. I decided to take a taxi to his house in town but changed my mind when I saw a monstrous traffic jam inching along in that direction. Turning homeward, I passed noxious garbage heaps and flashing neon signs advertising hair salons, pedicures, and massage parlors. Saccharine pop music wafted out from behind beaded door curtains, along with occasional whiffs of women's perfume that mixed with the garbage stink.

It was late by the time I got home. I lay down and began to drift off to sleep, but just then Shuzhi called. Speaking elliptically in case the phone was bugged, she told me in dismay that Mao Zhiyi's wife had just called her with a mysterious warning that I should leave China as soon as possible. I was dumbstruck. Then Zhengguan called from Chengdu and repeated Shuzhi's message, still without providing any details. It was the middle of the night. Where was I supposed to go? Reluctant to disturb Mother, I rolled over and went back to sleep.

I was awakened by a hubbub of voices. People were calling my name. Springing out of bed, I found plainclothes Security Bureau agents swarming into the living room. I excused myself long enough to douse some cold water onto my face and then went back out to deal with them.

"What a lot of people!" I commented, looking around the room before I sat down. "I don't think I know any of you."

"It's time to introduce ourselves," replied a gaunt, beady-eyed man. He was Section Chief Liu, he told me, flashing his ID. It read, "State Security Bureau, Xi'an Branch."

"What's this about?" I asked nonchalantly.

"We're here for a returnee interview, a routine information-gathering procedure. We've got a few questions to ask you about America and hope you'll cooperate."

"Go right ahead." I glanced at the door. Agents were still pouring in, and the living room was filled to overflowing. Section Chief Liu explained that he wanted to take me somewhere more "convenient" for the interview, where we would have privacy from my mother and her aide. He instructed me to pack an overnight bag, including my identification papers, and to leave with him in the car he had waiting outside.

"Am I being detained for an interrogation?" I asked.

"That's a bit of an overstatement. This is just a returnee interview," he replied.

"What a coincidence! Here you are at the crack of dawn on our aide's first day back."

"We knew that you wouldn't be able to leave until now," Section Chief Liu said glibly, as if waiting until today had been a grand, humane gesture. After this rather prickly exchange I was ushered into his waiting Santana sedan. Despite my best efforts, my old nemesis had trapped me after all. The Security Bureau had been monitoring my every move since my arrival in Xi'an.

The sedan pulled up in front of the hotel attached to the nearby Electric Power Institute. A phalanx of eight plainclothesmen escorted me inside for breakfast, then upstairs to Room 721. I saw agents from other rooms heading downstairs for breakfast at the end of their night shift and surmised that they had been transferred here the previous evening in preparation for my arrival. In and out they marched, girding themselves for battle.

Section Chief Liu started by asking for my documents. Once he got his hands on my Chinese passport and American green card, he announced that he was going to keep them.

"Don't kid yourself," he sneered. "An American green card doesn't guarantee you any special treatment in China. We issued your passport, and we have the power to confiscate it if we need to." Pocketing my documents, he walked out of the room.

More people came in. One was a sullen lady named Inspector Wang, the division chief; another was her deputy, Inspector Huang, a corpulent man with a muffled voice. They were accompanied by a few young clerks. There was an oppressive silence in the room. The sight of their unfamiliar faces activated my "fight or flight" response, as if a gang of muggers had encircled me on the street.

Then everyone left except for an officer named Inspector Zhou and his clerk. Over breakfast earlier that morning Inspector Zhou had smilingly informed me that we had met some time ago. I said that I did not remember him. I had not been abroad very long, he replied. How quickly I forgot my friends! He gave me another chance to think, but I simply could not dredge up any memory of him. Then he explained that he had been the one to announce my rehabilitation to me in December 1978 and that he had also overseen my investigation at Jiaotong University after the Tiananmen incident. Our "old friendship" was the reason he had been assigned to my case.

He started our "chat" with a few gentle questions, while his clerk took notes. It was, no matter what he called it, an interrogation. Unwilling to talk, I announced that I would answer his questions as best I could but would not volunteer any information. He offered me a cigarette, which I declined.

"All right, then, let's get down to business," he said. He started grilling me about friends in Xi'an with whom I had corresponded. Then he went on to press me for details about overseas prodemocracy activists like Liu Binyan[2] and Hu Ping[3] and my "reactionary" article about Wei Jingsheng in *Ming Pao Monthly*. In particular, he wanted to know to whom I had mailed my article and "reactionary" periodicals like *Beijing Spring* and *China Monthly*. I refrained from mentioning people whom he did not specifically name and denied having sent anything to anyone.

A slick interrogator, he fished deftly for information through amiable small talk. My denials were pointless, he advised me, because the Security Bureau would not have summoned me without incontrovertible evidence.

---

[2] Liu Binyan (1925–2005) was a leading dissident journalist who became a permanent exile in the United States after the Beijing Massacre of 1989. See David Barboza, "Liu Binyan, a Fierce Insider Critic of China, Dies at 80," *New York Times*, December 6, 2005.

[3] Democracy activist, editor in chief of *Beijing Spring*.

He explained that the bureau's job was to block infiltration by enemies from abroad and to prevent the dissemination of printed matter that endangered state security. He also tried to assuage my fears that criminal charges against me would be pressed, claiming that this interview was simply a long-awaited opportunity for the bureau to corroborate some facts. All it wanted was the names of the people to whom I had sent foreign periodicals. My case would be wrapped up, he promised, as soon as the leads I provided had been checked out.

At the conclusion of our morning session the clerk asked me to sign the notes he had taken, endorsing them as my oral deposition. I refused, determined to stall until I found out what was up their sleeves.

When Inspector Zhou left, I plopped down on the bed, grabbed the telephone on the bedside table, and called my sisters. I told them to let Zhengguan know right away what had happened to me, so that he could notify Professor Chang at Yale. I had to get word out in case the unthinkable happened. It was imperative not to let the Security Bureau hush up my case.

Section Chief Liu and Inspector Huang took over the interrogation after lunch, dispensing with the kid-glove treatment. When I remained tight-lipped, they laid their cards on the table.

"We know you called Mao Zhiyi all day long yesterday without getting through. That's because he was here with us, informing on you," Section Chief Liu told me, widening his beady eyes. "We've got him in custody too, and he's given us a full confession. At his house we found all the letters and reading material you've sent him over the last six years. We even know what anti-Communist drivel you've brought him this time, the copy of *Red in Tooth and Claw* that the author himself gave you in Taiwan!"

They had even read my most recent letter to Mao Zhiyi. This was a mortal blow.

Then Inspector Huang zeroed in on my three-day visit to Xi'an in December 1997, when I brought Mother back from America. A skilled interrogator, he bluffed and ran rings around me, then swooped in for the kill.

"We even know all about the party that sweetie of yours at Shaanxi Normal University held to welcome you back," he suddenly revealed with a genial smile. "We have the complete guest list. There was an old classmate of yours who teaches at the Foreign Languages Institute, wasn't there?

"We left you alone then because we were waiting for you to seek us out voluntarily. And you thought you had fooled us! Then you went back to America and kept sending your reactionary periodicals. That's why we called you in."

Then he mentioned Xi Lin, one of the guests at the party that evening, and asked me what I had mailed to him.

I was shocked at how much they knew about that ordinary private party, given by my one of my friends, the bold woman editor who had published my controversial monograph about erotic poetry. She had just been transferred to Shaanxi Normal University from Henan Province. I had indeed seen Xi Lin that night, although it had been the occasion of an unfortunate altercation between us. I felt as if the Security Bureau had been following my every move with a camera and had snapped a photo of me naked. I deeply resented such an invasion of my privacy. What did such worthless snooping have to do with state security? He was flaunting this trivia just to make a show of omniscience. In a display of even worse taste, Section Chief Liu asked me derisively whether I had seen my "sweetie" during this visit.

I closed my eyes wearily. With hindsight I could see that Xi Lin's complaints had been entirely justified. I had been presumptuous to accuse him of paranoia.

Xi Lin, a professor at Shaanxi Normal University, was a creative, thoughtful scholar, from whom I had learned a great deal during our intellectual debates over the years. He and I differed sharply in scholarly outlook and temperament, however. I was rooted in my childhood reading in the Chinese classics, while he was trained in the Marxist-Leninist canon. Where I tended to be brutally frank, he was prudent, always trying to play it safe in the shifting sands of politics. I thought it unfortunate that he allowed his timidity to keep him from taking part in dissident activities. For his part, he considered me politically incompetent, a wild-eyed bookworm and a failure.

He felt marginalized in academia, however, and I was eager to help him after I emigrated to America. Yet the action I took on his behalf, submitting some of his manuscripts for publication abroad and mailing him banned periodicals, engendered bitter conflict between us.

He wrote me to say that he was being watched. The Security Bureau had been tampering with his mail from abroad and had trailed him around the clock during President Clinton's visit to Xi'an. He begged me not to endanger him by making any more indiscreet attacks on the regime in my letters or by continuing to mail him banned periodicals. I had submitted one of his manuscripts to *Beijing Spring*; after its publication I clipped it and sent it to him, but he never received it.

When we met at the party at Shaanxi Normal University, he was dismayed to learn that I had mailed him the excerpt from *Beijing Spring* and accused me of "betraying" him. Sarcastically I called him a chicken, brave enough to write an article but not to accept the consequences. After a heated argument we parted in anger.

Now I saw how much I had harmed him with my dogged, insensitive bulldozing. Section Chief Liu threatened to drag him in for interrogation along with me unless I was more forthcoming. When I refused to let him call my bluff, he picked up the telephone. I capitulated to spare Xi Lin such a rude shock and offered to take all the blame for submitting the manuscript and sending the periodicals. I stressed that there was no need for the Security Bureau to intimidate a docile citizen like Xi Lin.

"Xi Lin wrote to me a long time ago asking me to stop sending him banned reading material," I concluded. "I think he deserves praise from you."

Section Chief Liu put down the telephone and smugly had his assistant record my confession.

Then I found out why Inspector Zhou had asked me about Liu Binyan. I had given Mao Zhiyi's address to Liu so that he could send Mao some periodicals. Once again the authorities were overreacting. They wanted to know how a "criminal" like Mao had connected with such an eminent prodemocracy activist as Liu and suspected that I had acted on the bidding of some anti-Communist organization. I assured them that the truth of the situation was perfectly benign. All my actions had been motivated purely by friendship, and no organization had reimbursed me for my postal expenses.

Section Chief Liu gruffly countered that no matter what my motivation, mailing reactionary periodicals was a violation of state security law.

"Is state security so fragile that it can really be threatened by a few outspoken magazines?" I asked.

He refused to allow me to up the ante. Instead he whipped out a pamphlet entitled *Security Law of the People's Republic of China* and opened it to the article prohibiting "creating, disseminating, or circulating printed matter harmful to state security." He explained that writing reactionary articles would be considered "creating," while mailing reactionary periodicals would count as "disseminating or circulating." Now that he had presented the evidence against me, he asserted, I could not keep denying it.

With this, they concluded the afternoon session. Then they drove me to Mother's apartment, where they searched my luggage and confiscated the copy of *Red in Tooth and Claw* that I had brought for Mao Zhiyi. Their suspicions further aroused by a couple of videotapes that I had made of my travels in China, they decided to seize those too.

They returned me to my room at the hotel. Flopping down on the bed in exhaustion, I sucked Golden Throat lozenges to soothe my parched vocal cords while I tried to assess the situation calmly.

What had Mao Zhiyi done wrong? Years ago he and I had secretly listened to enemy broadcasts, for the same reason that I had written my disastrous letter to Moscow. The Chinese government, with its iron grip on the media, was entirely to blame for our desperation for knowledge. I knew I had to stand firm. Mailing the periodicals to Mao had been nothing more than a gesture of friendship. I agreed with Confucius that "a benevolent man helps others to take their stand in so far as he himself wishes to take his stand,"[4] and believed that it was my duty to satisfy my friend's desire to read. When Chinese émigrés returned to visit, they brought American ginseng or multivitamins for their friends and relatives. Why couldn't I bring an intellectual the spiritual sustenance he needed?

The Security Bureau had been duping Mao and me all along. It had allowed him to receive my mailings as if nothing were wrong, but not without first keeping a record of their contents on file to use against me

[4] *Confucius: The Analects*, trans. D. C. Lau (London: Penguin, 1979), p. 85.

the next time I visited. Its leaders knew that if they allowed me enough lee-way, I would incriminate myself.

Letters had always been my downfall. I had a lifetime of firsthand expe-rience with the censorship of the Chinese postal system. My mistake had been to imagine that the dictatorship had relaxed its grip in the post-Mao era when in fact it was as restrictive as ever, and its spy apparatus was now streamlined by the latest technology. Like a spider in its web in a dark cor-ner of the room, the Security Bureau was always lying in wait for its prey. Once again I had overstepped boundaries concerning letters and the mail, bringing my recurrent nightmare to life one more time.

Had Zhengguan spoken with Professor Chang? Xiuqin must be ruing the day she had let me go. What was being said in the foreign media? I was painfully aware that I was still a Chinese citizen and that the Security Bureau was probably gearing up to punish me harshly.

I spent the night in the hotel, and the returnee interview continued the next morning, June 16. After breakfast Section Chief Liu brought me pen and paper and ordered me to write a confession. He delivered a stern ulti-matum: I would not be released until I had demonstrated my sincere con-trition in writing.

It had been six years since I had written such a thing. Picking up the pen, I painfully squeezed the half-forgotten jargon onto the blank sheet of paper, which seemed to mock me like a fun house mirror. I remembered how Xiuqin had needled me before this visit, hoping to talk me into stay-ing home. "The Security Bureau hasn't attacked you for six years now. Do you miss them?"

I was starting to regret having come.

There was no sign of Inspector Zhou, who had been assigned the gen-tle warm-up. Now the bureau was stepping up the pressure. At noon I was fed in my room, as if to demonstrate that I was a prisoner. Section Chief Liu, eager to wrap up the case, kept coming in to press me for my confes-sion, redoubling his threats every time.

I handed one in, but it was rejected immediately. Section Chief Liu and the two division chiefs I had met before came barging into the room. Inspector Huang rebuked me for my "bad attitude," complaining that my essay lacked a title and needed to say "Confession" at the top. Inspector

Wang accused me of adopting a cold, distant tone, inappropriate for a Chinese citizen like me. I had been abroad for only six years, yet I referred to people like her as "functionaries" and called the Chinese government a "regime." She repeated Section Chief Liu's heavy-handed admonition that my confession would not be accepted unless it was genuinely remorseful.

Section Chief Liu ordered me to produce another draft right away, slating two particular passages for deletion. The first one read: "There was nothing illegal about mailing such periodicals from the place where I did it. In other countries, freedom of the press and private correspondence are protected by law." I was not in America anymore, he blustered. Having mailed the periodicals into China, I was subject to Chinese law, and my self-defense was sheer "drivel." The second passage was my charge that the Security Bureau had been covertly inspecting my mailings to Mao Zhiyi all along and that its claim to have discovered them recently had been false.

"Even if we did inspect your letters," Section Chief Liu whispered into my ear, "we did so with the full backing of the legal code. I can't stop you from believing what you will, but you are not allowed to put such accusations into writing."

I wrote another draft, without deleting the offensive passages, and it was rejected again. Hurling the sheets of paper at me, Section Chief Liu warned me that his bureau chief, who was masterminding the situation, had lost patience and would not free me until I excised both passages and apologized for jeopardizing national security.

In the late afternoon two young clerks suddenly turned up with a formal "summons" authorizing the Security Bureau to detain me for twelve more hours. This meant that I would have to spend another night there. After dinner I was suddenly moved to Room 418, where the bedside telephone had been disconnected and the young recording clerk had reappeared as my guard. Section Chief Liu came back to demand a third draft of my confession, insisting that I satisfy the bureau chief. Unless I complied promptly, he warned, my status would shift to "supervised residence." This meant that they could detain me for as long as six months, holding me responsible for the hotel bill for me and my guard. If I wanted to shell out several hundred yuan a day, they had all the time in the world.

"Can't you see it's all just a bunch of Commie bullshit?" my young guard said. "Quit nitpicking and hand in the damned thing, or I won't be able to take my Sunday off tomorrow."

Zhengguan had flown in from Chengdu that afternoon with news from America. Professor Chang had called him back to say that the president of Yale, Richard Levin, had notified the U.S. government of my plight. The White House had contacted the U.S. Embassy in Beijing, and my rescue operation had begun. Professor Chang had also asked Zhengguan to instruct me to cooperate as much as possible with the Security Bureau, to avoid exacerbating the situation.

I sank into a heavy, confused slumber, from which I was awakened by an unfamiliar clerk reading an announcement that as of that moment, four o'clock in the morning on June 17, my "summons" had expired, and I was formally in "supervised residence." He asked me to sign the announcement, but I refused, so he scribbled a note on it and informed me that it was effective whether I signed it or not.

"That's what you think," I retorted. "I never agreed to any such thing." I turned out the light and lay down again, but sleep eluded me. I was worried about the expense of "supervised residence" in such high-priced accommodations. China had become so horribly commercialized, I reflected, that even the penal system was tainted with consumerism.

In the morning Section Chief Liu prodded me for my third draft, but I had not produced one. I was too upset about the exorbitant hotel bill to write another word, I told him, and I refused to cooperate until they agreed not to bill me for my own imprisonment.

He pestered me for another draft all morning, promising that I could go home as soon as I satisfied the bureau chief. At lunchtime Zhengguan brought me some homemade Sichuanese food, a gift from his wife. Shuzhi also came, with an e-mail message from Professor Chang saying that Beijing was sending special negotiators to Xi'an to settle my case and that I should obey my captors so that they would agree to release me.

Now I had to make a painful decision: Should I capitulate? Professor Chang's instructions had been unequivocal. She had worked indefatigably ever since my arrest, and had requested help from every possible quarter.

The American authorities had done everything in their power, even eliciting a promise from the top stratum of the Chinese government, but the last step was up to me. Fearing that I might forfeit my opportunity for release if I delayed, even for a day, Zhengguan and Shuzhi advised me to stop being so headstrong.

This was not the first time in my life that I had been forced to compromise my principles. Resignedly I handed in my third draft after lunch. I had excised the objectionable passages and confessed to having violated Chinese security law. I also promised to preserve the reputation of the Security Bureau by keeping quiet about my detention after my return home. The draft was accepted right away.

My captors proceeded to assemble a meticulous paper trail, covering their three-day deprivation of my human rights with a veneer of legality. I was made to give an oral deposition about my mailings to Mao Zhiyi and Xi Lin, which I had to sign and fingerprint. Finally I had to fill out an "apology," in which I admitted to having harmed state security and promised not to mail any more reactionary printed materials. This humiliating red tape took until six o'clock in the evening, when Section Chief Liu finally announced my release from "supervised residence."

I returned to Mother's apartment in outrage, my interest in visiting completely destroyed. I had proceeded on the naive assumption that China was more democratic these days but had found myself beating my head against a brick wall. China was still a police state, and I was still doomed to writing confessions. China's petty bureaucrats had stripped me of my humanity one more time.

My detention alarmed my friends in Xi'an and forced me to terminate several relationships. Mao Zhiyi, who had been released immediately upon his confession, called to say that he still wanted to get together. Zhengguan and Shuzhi, however, were adamantly opposed to my having any more contact with him, and I never saw him again.

Someone suggested that Mao was a Security Bureau stool pigeon, who had been assisting in a frame-up operation when he asked for the periodicals in the first place. I found this explanation as farfetched as something out of a murder mystery and could not believe such evil of Mao. No matter what, I sympathized with his thirst for truth. As Mencius put it, "A gentleman can be taken in by what is reasonable."[5] Even if I had been duped, I had no reason to regret having performed a good deed.

Old Mr. Huang came to see me on the day after my release, and I told him that his name had come up during my interrogation. To my great surprise, he revealed that Security Bureau agents had questioned him in March, long before my visit. Having gotten wind that I would be in Xi'an in the summer, they had asked him to write me to find out my exact arrival date. He had balked at first, but they had forced his hand, and he had written to me in late April; that explained the letter Xiuqin had received after my departure. I asked him whether he had mentioned the Security Bureau's questioning, and he admitted that he had not dared disobey its injunction to silence. Then why hadn't he tipped me off when I had called him from Nanjing? I asked. His excuse was that he had been afraid the wires were tapped. It occurred to me that he might not have appreciated the gravity of the situation.

I had to chide him for such a grievous lapse. "I would have been spared a lot of humiliation if you had told me this while I was still in Nanjing!"

"With friends like him, who needs enemies?" declared Shuzhi angrily.

Zhengguan had a couple of amusing anecdotes for me. Some friends had called while I was in detention, and he had tested their reaction with the ominous reply "You want to speak to Kang Zhengguo? He's been arrested!" Two of them, speechless with fear, had hung up immediately. I thought he had been rather indiscreet, but he maintained that his "test" had been worthwhile. Then he told me about a professor from Jiaotong University who had called to invite me to dinner but had launched into a tirade as soon as he learned of my arrest; it was terribly irresponsible of me, he judged, to continue to associate with my friends when I knew that I had broken the law.

Section Chief Liu had kept my passport and green card as leverage, refusing to return them until he had extracted a written confession from my brother-in-law. Apparently Mao Zhiyi had implicated him unnecessarily by revealing that he had loaned Mao a copy of *China Monthly* that I had mailed from America. Then the Security Bureau had tried to confiscate my

[5] *Mencius*, trans. D. C. Lau (London: Penguin, 1970), p. 140.

brother-in-law's copies of *China Monthly*, but he claimed to have lost them. Now the bureau wanted a full confession regarding the incident.

On the morning of June 19, Zhengguan, Shuzhi, and I met Section Chief Liu at the gate of Children's Park in the pouring rain. Shuzhi handed over the confession in return for my precious documents.

Two days later Section Chief Liu and his entourage turned up at our house to get my signature on a triplicate form terminating my "supervised residence." They gave me a copy, but then Section Chief Liu asked for it back again. It would be better for him to keep it, he claimed, since I had no use for it.

The Security Bureau was obsessively paranoid. While fabricating evidence against me on the one hand, it made sure, on the other, not to leave me with anything that I might use to redress my grievances in the future. I had no choice but to let the bureau lord it over me, as I was on its turf.

I wondered if I had heard the last from the bureau. My whole family was thoroughly fed up. Afraid that a delay might mean trouble, everyone advised me to make a quick getaway. I received several phone calls from Xiuqin and a number of e-mails from Professor Chang and my American friends, all urging me to rush home.

54

Farewell to China

NXIOUS FOR ME to return home, Xiuqin called repeatedly, but I had to stay in Xi'an to help with the reinterment, regardless of the danger. The Security Bureau had probably finished with me for now, I assured her, promising to behave myself. Taking Zhengguan and Shuzhi's advice, I refrained from discussing my interrogation with anyone, canceled my plans to see old friends, and made all my important calls from pay phones to thwart eavesdropping.

I went back to Xinwang Village to collect the cinerary caskets.

Everything had changed. The main street had been realigned to run from east to west instead of from north to south. All the original dwellings, including ours with its red tile roof, had been razed and replaced with large prefab concrete houses. The villagers said they had raised money for the fine new construction by selling sand from the riverbed, averring that they could not have paid for it with their farm income, even if they supplemented it by moonlighting as workers.

Xinwang Village lay on the Feng River, which had been pristine during my time in the village. The water had been limpid, the sand immaculate, and the reed-covered banks lined with tall, leafy poplar trees that rustled in the summer breeze. But this bucolic scene was destroyed during the 1980s, when the sand was removed and sold to urban capital construction projects. After that, the gutted riverbanks collapsed in the yearly autumnal floods, killing the reeds. Then the water supply was cut off from upstream, and the riverbed dried up. Now the unsightly mud of the river bottom, scarred with deep pits where stones and sand had been carted off, was exposed.

As the urban demand for building materials continued to outstrip the supply, the villagers turned to underground exploitation. Buried beneath the fertile topsoil of the farm fields granted to the villagers by Deng Xiaoping's reforms were huge shoals of sand deposited during ancient floods. In the mid-1980s the villagers had begun selling this sand; they had depleted it entirely by the time of my visit in 2000. The flat fields were riddled with ten-yard-deep pits. This sacrifice of the ancestral farmland had sufficed to finance the villagers' new housing, but they wanted more. Many families had signed contracts permitting factories to use the pits in their fields as landfill for industrial waste. With undue optimism, the villagers expected to cover the landfill with topsoil and continue to farm the fields as usual.

Many of the people I had known were dead. One of them was Yinzui, my former team chief, a diabetic of approximately my age. My old friend Guodong's pithy assessment was that he had been "a pauper with a rich man's disease." As his condition worsened, his appetite increased, but he wasted away nonetheless. Originally a hulking, ursine man, he died a mere bag of bones. The sight of his grave in the village cemetery reminded me of some words we had exchanged in the fields years ago.

"Chunlai, you'll never get out of Xinwang Village," he had said, pointing to the cemetery. "One day you'll end up fertilizing the fields over there along with the rest of us."

"Don't be so sure," I said. "Times will change. You can't expect me to bear the stigma of being a counterrevolutionary element for the rest of my life." I paused to beat on my chest for emphasis. "I'll make a bet with you: I say there's no permanent place for me, Kang Zhengguo, in your little village." I made a point of using my birth name. His words still stinging my ears, I turned and announced to our companions in the fields, "Did you hear that? When I finally do get out of this place, I'm going to summon you as my witnesses."

"What do you want to bet?" Yinzui challenged me. He was a gambling addict, always ready for action.

"Never mind. I'll just buy you a few cartons of fancy cigarettes some-day when I strike it rich." I decided that giving him a gift outright suited me better than making a wager with him.

Now I had been gone for twenty years and had traveled farther than I had imagined in my wildest dreams. I had hoped to present Yinzui with the cigarettes on this visit, but he had been transformed into fertilizer first.

I also wanted to give Yinzui's uncle Dinghan some money. He had con-stantly tried to borrow from me when I lived in the village and resented me for being unable to oblige. Since he had helped bring me into the village and taken my side during my difficult adjustment period, he was right that I owed him something, especially now that I could afford it. I was looking forward to pleasing him, finally, on this visit.

Unfortunately he had died of stomach cancer. Before his death his common-law wife, the runaway woman from Gansu, had killed herself by swigging pesticide, and her son and daughter had returned to Gansu. Dinghan had died without a penny to his name, and his creditors were squabbling over the rights to seize and demolish his house.

Laishui, the village simpleton with the perpetually runny nose, had died too. Back in New Haven, Xiuqin had asked me to give him a hundred yuan on this trip. She said that she still owed him money for baby-sitting our son, which she had planned to pay him after we moved to Xi'an, but we had been too broke. Now that she could afford it, however, the opportu-nity had vanished. Laishui had died a bachelor, and I could not even find anyone to accept the cash on his behalf.

My old buddy Xuanmin showed me around town. First I saw Fendan's mother, who was sitting on a reed mat in front of her big new house. A spry, well-preserved lady of eighty-four, she was the oldest resident of the village and the only woman left with bound feet. Still clad in an old-fashioned homespun Chinese jacket, she told me that her sight and hearing were intact and that she was still cooking for her fourth son, who had never married. I wanted to ask about Fendan but held my tongue.

Next we went to Fangmin's house. He was out, but I saw his father, Shi-quan, my former deputy team chief. First Xuanmin took me into their backyard and shouted into a dark shed.

"Grandfather Shiquan, Uncle Chunlai is here." After a while Shiquan hobbled out, holding on to the doorframe. His swollen feet were spattered with urine, over which greenhead flies were swarming. He stared at me vacantly, without recognizing me, and muttered something inaudible. How diminished he was, I reflected, remembering how he had lorded it over us in the past. Every morning he would ring the bell and shout in the streets to roust us from our beds and assign us our jobs. Then he would brew himself a pot of tea, which he carried from one work site to the next, sipping from it while he spurred us to work harder. He was especially brutal to weaklings and cursed us if he found us taking it easy toward the end of a hard day.

"Quit jerking off and get back to work!" he would yell.

When we ignored him, he had to let us rest. Yet he never allowed us to quit early, as this might arouse the envy of the other villagers. He had us under his thumb in those days, striving to earn bogus work points from the production team. With no one to bully since the disbandment of the teams under Deng Xiaoping, he had gradually withered. The only trace of his former murderous visage was his eyebrows, which were still bushy and grasshopper-shaped, although faded from black to gray.

I thought of my old grudges against him. In particular I remembered the day he had caught me composing my pastoral poem and resting, after irrigating the cornfields. Wagging his finger at me, he approached and let out a volley of curses. I replied in kind, and he pounced on me in a fury, intending to beat me up. I gave him a shove, landing him with a plop in the wet cornfield. Maddened, he grabbed my collar with his muddy hands and dragged me off to see Yinzui, railing that I had "a lot of nerve, beating up a cadre in broad daylight." He demanded that Yinzui turn me over to the brigade for punishment. But Yinzui, always at odds with Shiquan, chuckled when he saw him so bedraggled and refused him any moral support.

Still spoiling for a fight, Shiquan brought his tiny-footed wife and both his sons to my house that evening. As they approached, I let out a blood-curdling war whoop, like the legendary ancient Chinese general Zhang Fei, and stood guard in my doorway brandishing the old red-tasseled spear Li Baoyu had used during his militia service in the days of Land Reform. I had trounced Fangmin before, so he and his brother gave up as soon as they saw my weapon. Shiquan was a typical bully; he tended to back off when faced with a show of strength. As I later established a firm footing in the village, going into town on team business and teaching his son how to fix motors, he gradually relented and started to grant me a few favors.

But I should let go of the past, I reflected as I looked at the doddering old man, and try to think of reasons to be grateful to him. No worth was attached to the life of a Chinese peasant, especially an elderly one. Shiquan was a genuine proletarian who had served the party faithfully for more than thirty years. Yet the state had no welfare benefits for him in his final years, forcing him to rely on the support of his sons. Unable to afford medical care, all he could do was mark time in misery until his death. Since he was incontinent, his daughter-in-law Lianlian kept him isolated in a dark, stinking shed in the backyard while her husband, Fangmin, was at work all day.

Lianlian rushed into the room and yelled at the old man to get back inside his shed. Intimidated, he retreated to the doorway, whereupon I pulled out a fifty-yuan note.

"This is for you, Uncle Shiquan," I said, handing it to him.

Grinning from ear to ear, Lianlian grabbed the money before Shiquan could reach out his trembling hand. Then, in a show of solicitude, she helped her father-in-law back into his shed. She might as well have been corralling livestock.

My friend Siji, who had helped me manage Li Baoyu's funeral, came over as soon as he heard I was in town. His bloodshot eyes had cleared up, but he was as swarthy as ever, and his teeth were severely tobacco-stained. He told me that life was treating him fairly well and that he was running a profitable livestock-breeding business for which he raised male pigs, sheep, dogs, and cats. He was bringing in about a thousand yuan a month.

"That makes you a wizard of animal husbandry," I quipped.

Angling for a dispensation, he began to catalog all the favors he had done for me, and I assured him I had not forgotten them. But when I offered him money, he turned up his nose at Chinese currency, asking instead for a couple of American dollar bills as a keepsake.

Guodong, his wife, and their younger son lived together in one new house, while his elder son, Xuanmin, and his wife and children lived as a nuclear family in another. They were much better off than they had been, although they still had to economize.

When I explained my mission, Guodong and Xuanmin got their pick-axes and shovels and accompanied me to the cemetery to help dig up the cinerary caskets. Thanks to the plastic bags we had wrapped them in, all three were in perfect condition. My siblings had been tending Li Baoyu's grave mound during their regular visits to the cemetery. But there would be no one to do that anymore, now that we were removing our family caskets. I made a final burned paper offering to Li Baoyu. The smoldering paper quickly turned to ashes in the scorching midday sun. Like black butterflies borne on the wind, they swirled away into the stubbly fields with their new growth of corn, and all was still.

As my car sped along the bumpy dirt road toward the asphalt highway, I watched the village and fields recede into the distance.

Good-bye forever, I whispered to myself.

I took the caskets to Mount Li Cemetery with my brother, sisters, and cousins Zhengxin and Shuren. We buried my grandparents together in one tomb, and Father in a separate one with space for Mother in the future. The tombs had stone lids engraved with the names and life spans of their occupants. Decades after their deaths we had finally laid our forebears properly to rest in their ancestral home of Lintong, facing the Wei River to the north, with green hills behind them to the south. The new graves were neatly arrayed on the hillside and surrounded by flowering trees. Standing in silence beside a few sticks of burning incense, I prayed to the Buddha for my deceased relatives.

The two burial plots had cost more than ten thousand yuan. Money could buy anything in today's mercenary China. Back in the Mao era such plots had simply not been available for purchase. Now, however, the entrepreneurial peasants had found that converting their barren hillsides into cemeteries was a lucrative business.

Before I left for home, Shuci and I took Mother out for a ride in her wheelchair. Her world had shrunk with the onset of old age; she was sick and tired of being cooped up and reacted to our offer with childlike joy. First we stopped on the street for fried crullers and soy milk, then headed south to Xingqing Park.

Entering through the east gate, we crossed a wooden bridge to the spacious Eaglewood Pavilion, a senior citizens' paradise in the early morning. The lawns and flowery lanes were filled with retirees going for walks, doing calisthenics, and practicing martial arts. Elderly urban retirees like Mother were much better off than their counterparts in the countryside, I reflected, comparing the scene with what I had just witnessed in Xinwang Village. At least they had adequate pensions and medical care, which allowed the able-bodied to pursue their interests in physical fitness.

The lake was still overflowing, with wavelets lapping at its shores, but there were more boats now, and they were more Westernized. The water was foul and green, its surface littered with plastic wrappers and empty bottles. Shuci and I chatted as we pushed the wheelchair around the lake. On a secluded path near the north gate of the park, we encouraged Mother to get out for a walk, pushing her empty wheelchair for support. She hobbled along, dragging her right leg, with its crippling bone spur in the knee, painfully behind her.

Mother and Father had graduated from the same university. She had majored in chemistry and had become a middle school teacher shortly before the Communist takeover. In my memory, she was always busy teaching, correcting papers, or doing housework. Sundays, days of rest for most people, were her hardest workdays. She rose at the crack of dawn and swept the house, front and back yards, and gate area. Then she cleaned everything from top to bottom, including the windows, the furniture, and the tea service. Nothing escaped her eye. After breakfast she did the weekly family laundry. Rain or shine, she sat on the steps under the eaves and scrubbed all our clothes on a washboard in a wooden basin. By afternoon she had our yard draped with drying laundry.

My parents never took us out for fun. Their occasional plans for family outings always seemed to be derailed by marital spats. We never went anywhere except for our afternoon visits to Silent Garden; Mother sometimes even did her laundry there.

Mother's life slipped away between her teaching and domestic chores. Keeping house was of paramount importance to her, and her standards of cleanliness were sacrosanct. When she finally retired from teaching, she was beyond retirement age, and her legs had started to fail her. Her condition deteriorated despite medical treatments, until she needed live-in help. She was so finicky that no one ever satisfied her requirements, and she had to hire a string of aides over the years.

As my brother and I were too far away to be much help, my sisters shouldered most of the burden of her care. Shuci, a patient woman, was probably the only person on earth who got along well with Mother. She said Mother's biggest problem was ennui. Obsessed with her lifelong grim routine of teaching and housework, she had neglected to develop any hobbies that might have alleviated the grinding monotony of her retirement years. Her only outlet was endless grumbling about her health and the care she received from her offspring.

Pushing her wheelchair out of the west gate of the park, I headed north along the playing field of Number Two Middle School to one of the remaining segments of the old wall of Silent Garden. Silent Garden itself was long gone. During the flurry of liberalization after Mao's death, Third Uncle had moved out of the Guanyin Cave in the garden and reoccupied Grandfather's inner sanctum. Then he and Zhengxin had started a protracted legal battle to recover the family property from the neighboring commune, which had appropriated it years ago. When they finally won their case in the mid-1980s, we got back about one and a half acres of land and a number of buildings, but Third Uncle had already died an embittered man.

Despite my strong sentimental attachment to the inherited property, I had not been interested in managing it, so my male cousins had eventually sold it to a real estate developer for an excellent price. This had happened during the years when I was an impoverished instructor at Jiaotong University, and I had used my portion of the divided proceeds to buy our color television and matching furniture. Now the site was jammed with ugly tract houses, like chicken coops, and the ground was so tightly sealed with concrete that grass could not sprout anywhere. With a cold glance toward the new housing development, I pushed Mother quickly by.

We turned left into Longqubao Street and found Number Two Middle School. During the Great Leap Forward the street had been lined with walls blazoned with propaganda murals. By now the old walled housing compounds had been demolished. The middle school had changed too. None of the buildings, including the one that my family had sold to the school, was as I remembered.

Only the sturdy old Chinese toon tree had withstood the passage of time, although it was surrounded with a new protective brick wall. No magical powers had been attributed to this tree in the supposedly super-stitious society of pre-Communist China, but now it had inexplicably become the object of mass worship. Over the past decade a steady stream of worshipers had burned incense and paper offerings at its base and fes-tooned it with red silk. But they had inadvertently set it on fire once, com-pelling the local government to build the protective wall. Now its branches still bore strips of red cloth, and I still saw incense beside the wall.

We took a taxi into town, stopped for lunch at a restaurant, and con-tinued to my last stop on this farewell trip, the old housing compound in Kaitong Lane where Mother had lived for more than forty years. The only remaining old-timer was Mrs. Wang, who still lived by the front gate. Leaving Mother to reminisce with her, I went for a stroll around the com-pound. Our house had belonged to Mother's aunt until the Real Estate Bureau confiscated the front half of the compound, making us govern-ment tenants. A few years ago the Real Estate Bureau had bulldozed the old houses and replaced them with tacky buildings. The old-fashioned courtyard was gone, and now thirty families were crammed into the space that had once held seven or eight.

Like Mother, all the original residents had moved into new apartments built by their employers and sublet their old spaces in the compound to tenants, migrant workers or entrepreneurial peasants who lacked Xi'an res-idence papers. With its new population of second-class citizens, the neighborhood had gone downhill. Still, Mother derived substantial monthly income from the rent she charged for her old three-room house in the compound. While city people, especially state employees, benefited from the collapse of the state-run system, the peasants who had flocked to the cities were constantly being fleeced.

I hastily wound up my affairs in Xi'an, said good-bye to my family, and took a train to Beijing to catch my plane for America. As everyone was worried that I would not make it onto the plane, Shuzhi went with me. She insisted on seeing me to the airport, watching me board, and waiting there until my plane had taken off.

55

Breaking the Silence

EVERYONE SCOLDED ME for my foolhardiness after I arrived safely in New Haven in July 2000. I should not have gone back to China on a Chinese passport, people said, especially while the Security Bureau was monitoring my activities. In fact Professor Chang had warned me of the danger beforehand, but I had been too eager to see my friends and attend the Nanjing conference to pay attention. Afterward she remarked sternly that I would probably have been imprisoned for a long time if the president of Yale had not mobilized his powerful contacts in the U.S. government to intervene on my behalf. Zhengguan said that he never would have asked me to help with the reinterment if he had understood the risks. He also told me that he had sought help from the American Embassy in Beijing right after my arrest but had met with polite refusal; there was no protocol for intervening in cases involving Chinese citizens.

I began to see my Chinese citizenship as a liability. Paradoxically, going home was more dangerous than staying abroad. Whose "homeland" was this? Did Chinese citizens have any rights worth mentioning? As I pondered these vexing questions, the blue cloth curtains in front of the mah-jongg parlors in Chengdu sprang to mind. The Chinese state was largely a facade that served to legitimize Communist Party repression of the Chinese people. Since 1949 millions of people had been hounded viciously for being antiparty or counterrevolutionary. This persecution, unprecedented in Chinese history, had ultimately discredited the Communists and their lofty revolution. Nowadays an epithet like "counterrevolutionary," once frightening, had lost its lethal power, like a knife blade dulled from overuse. But the regime, as oppressive as ever, had concocted new excuses for persecution; now it was guarding against "subversives" or "threats to state security." Behind the flag-waving, however, lurked a kleptocracy. As long as these usurpers were in power, I decided, I had better keep my distance. I resolved to scrap my Chinese passport; it was as useless as my old earthen *kang* had been in Xinwang Village.

I completed the formalities promptly, and at the age of fifty-six I found myself redefining my identity once again for the sake of obtaining refuge. This time my new name was Zhengguo Kang, as it appeared on my American citizenship certificate and passport. As Mencius said, "The people turn to the benevolent as water flows downwards or as animals head for the wilds. Thus the otter drives the fish to the deep; thus the hawk drives birds to the bushes. . . ."[1] Today the repressive Chinese Communist regime is driving millions of Chinese people to seek asylum in the world outside.

That fall we sold our small colonial house in downtown New Haven and bought a new one in the suburbs. Like a wild animal retreating to its lair to lick its wounds, I hoped to free myself from my old nightmares by moving to the peaceful Quinnipiac Valley, where it would be more difficult for certain people to contact me.

We had a big sunny ranch house with a lawn and flowering trees in front and a wooded yard and swimming pool in the back. Xiuqin, who had been yearning for the land, could finally do some gardening. All around the pool she placed flower pots, which she sprinkled lovingly with her watering can. I plowed a vegetable patch for her, and she had a friend bring

---

[1] *Mencius*, trans. D. C. Lau (London: Penguin, 1970), p. 122.

her Chinese seeds for cucumbers, beans, and green peppers. Every year she harvested a bounty of vegetables, with plenty of surplus for our friends.

I had a spacious study. The sliding glass door overlooked our deck, which was shaded by tall copper beech trees lush with reddish green leaves, and the blue swimming pool beyond. Xiuqin did the light yard work, leaving the heavy manual labor to me. I plowed the garden in the spring, mowed the lawn in the summer, raked the leaves in the fall, and shoveled snow in the winter. I was living the dream life that had attracted me in that American magazine at Jiaotong University long ago.

We had half an acre of land, less than a quarter of the original dimensions of Silent Garden. However, American houses were not enclosed by walls as Chinese houses were. Here the lawns were connected, divided only by trees, and wildlife roamed freely from one property to another. Sometimes wild ducks even laid their eggs in the grass beside the pool. The whole neighborhood was a shared park.

"Guozi seems destined to live in a garden," a friend in Xi'an commented when he saw the photos of our new house. "Even though the commune destroyed the Kang family garden, he has a new one in America now."

As I surveyed the scene in the hushed twilight every evening, I thought back to Silent Garden and thanked the Bodhisattva Guanyin for restoring my lost paradise. I even toyed with the idea of karma, wondering whether I was somehow reaping the benefits of Grandfather's devotion.

At Silent Garden there had been a young man named Zhao Shun, whom Grandfather had culled from one of his orphanages and supported through school. Zhao was an excellent artist and calligrapher, and Grandfather had put him to work producing sutras in the Silent Garden printshop. In the late 1970s Zhao visited Xi'an and stayed with Third Uncle for a few days. Deeply distressed by the story of Grandfather's suffering and by the sorry state of Silent Garden, he made a painting of the original property from memory for Third Uncle, which Third Uncle hung in Grandfather's inner sanctum. I inherited it after Third Uncle's death, as I was the only one in our generation who still had a sentimental attachment to Silent Garden. All my male cousins were preoccupied with disposing of Grandfather's real estate.

I took the painting to New Haven and hung it in my study, but it was unfortunately lost in a small house fire along with a bookcase full of books from China. Luckily I still had a color photograph, which enabled Zhengguan to commission an artist in Chengdu to paint a reproduction for me. I wrote a poem and asked Mr. Paul Sun, Professor Chang's father and a noted calligrapher, to inscribe it on the new painting. It read:

Lu Zhonglian[2] preferred drowning to the tyranny of Qin;
I've chosen an expatriate life in New England.
Barred from my homeland, even in dreams,
I'll have to make do with this painting.

In the spring of 2001 Mr. Sun came to deliver a sermon at our local Chinese church. I hung the framed picture in our newly decorated living room, and Xiuqin invited some of the congregation members over for a reception in his honor. After years of unspeakable oppression at the hands of the Guomindang in Taiwan, he had eventually converted to Christianity, changed his name to Paul, emigrated to America, and decided never to go home again. An exceedingly pious man, he read only the Bible and religious books and spent most of his time trying to save other people's souls. Since I was not a Christian and had no intention of becoming one, his sermon did not speak to me. However, I was deeply inspired by his courageous determination to sever his ties with his past and forge a brand-new identity. I was also moved to learn that he had prayed around the clock for me while I had been in trouble in Xi'an.

He said that God had released me from my life of suffering in China, and had granted me a new start in America. He hoped that I would join the ranks of the faithful, as Xiuqin had. Yet I could not change my secular outlook, nor could I give up my old habit of writing, so his road to salvation did not suit me.

I sought salvation through describing my trials and tribulations in writing. My purpose was not merely to complain but rather to salvage my dignity through honest revelations about myself and everyone who had

[2] An inhabitant of the state of Qi before the 221 B.C.E. unification of China under the despot First Emperor of the Qin dynasty, with whom Mao is often compared.

The painting of Silent Garden.

interacted with me, whether friend or foe. I was well aware that this was only a start and that the Chinese people would not be saved until they took action as a whole. As long as the entire nation was intoxicated, as it was today, a lone individual could accomplish little. Still, I believed that the more people who spoke out, the better.

Even though I wanted to publicize the story of my arrest in Xi'an, I held my tongue initially. I avoided the press, refrained from putting pen to paper, and even dodged my friends' questions. Nor did I follow Wei Jingsheng's exhortation to testify before the congressional hearings on human rights. I maintained my silence for almost a year.

Such cowardice was entirely out of character for me, and I found it puzzling.

There were reasons for my silence. The problem was that I had promised to preserve the Security Bureau's image by hushing up my story. Just before my release, Inspector Wang, who turned out to be a fellow graduate of Shaanxi Normal University, took me out to dinner with her underlings on the pretext that she and I were "schoolmates." They whisked me into the same Santana sedan they had used to arrest me, and off we went to a Sichuan hot pot restaurant, where I had to sit through an entire banquet with them. Apparently they felt entitled to a celebration now that they had taught me my lesson. To me their hospitality seemed farcical, after what they had put me through. Did they think that a lavish meal could make up for the psychological damage they had done? Or that I was in any mood to enter into an alliance with them, my oppressors? In the crassly materialistic society of contemporary China, I reflected, even an absurd episode like my detention seemed to require an extravagant conclusion.

Throughout the meal they kept leaning on me to keep my mouth shut about my arrest, cloaking their threats in a veneer of "humanity." Even if I did not plan to come back to Xi'an regularly to visit my aged mother, they said, it would be my duty as a son to attend her funeral, at which time they could subject me to another "returnee interview." Section Chief Liu swore to keep monitoring me even if I became an American citizen and to have me blacklisted at the Chinese Consulate in New York if I continued to "harm state security." Then I would no longer be able to get a Chinese visa.

I was certain that similar veiled threats had been used on thousands of returnees who had been "interviewed." This explained why so few of them dared speak out even after returning to the world of freedom outside.

Another reason for my reticence was the advice of my friends and family, who urged me to lie low even after my return to America. Despite their good intentions, I felt as though they were muzzling me with a velvet handkerchief. Moreover, I sensed that the officials from Yale and the U.S. government who had engineered my rescue also wanted me to keep quiet. I wondered if they had made any promises to Beijing along these lines. However, since they had done me a favor, I thought that it would be ungrateful of me to indulge myself by speaking out.

My resolve had been eroded by the knowledge that my own pigheadedness had harmed some of my friends and disappointed others. But after almost a year of silence I felt utterly miserable.

The well-meant advice of friends and family to keep quiet, even at the cost of compromising my principles, was proof of the despotic power of the Chinese Communist Party. It maintained this power not only through persecution but also through enticement. Although the Chinese Communists were glorified hijackers, given China's size it was to the advantage of people in the world outside to stay on good terms with them. My misadventure had taught me that Americans, including government officials, university administrators, and esteemed professors, were reluctant to offend the Chinese Communist regime.

This spineless reaction to enticement empowers the devil. The pedophilia scandals in the Roman Catholic Church were hushed up by the Catholics themselves, including the victims' parents, in order to preserve their public image. In a world where even the church whitewashed the news, nobodies like me had to take insults lying down.

I first breached my vow of silence in the summer of 2001, when Professor Perry Link introduced me to a reporter from *The Chronicle of Higher Education*, who interviewed me about Security Bureau harassment of overseas Chinese academics during their visits home. Then, encouraged by the eminent historian Yu Ying-shih and his wife, Monica, I wrote up my story and published it in Chinese. Perry Link translated it as "Arrested in China" for *The New York Review of Books*, and reprints appeared in numerous places. Readers all over the world learned, to their surprise, that the Chinese Security Bureau was still up to its sinister old tricks.

I spoke from a personal need to unburden myself and to make the truth known. But I had another reason. My story proves that the Chinese Communists are losing their monolithic grip on public opinion. Try as they might to muzzle the cry for freedom, pressure from abroad can be brought to bear. My advice to anyone who is detained in China is to seek outside help rather than try to plea-bargain. The story of the young woman cyberdissident known as the Stainless Steel Mouse shows how the worldwide forces of freedom and democracy can be mobilized to rescue a persecuted dissident nowadays.[3]

After my return to New Haven I stopped mailing banned reading material to my friends in China. This was not a failure of nerve. The rapid

[3] Liu Di, a former psychology major at Beijing Normal University, was arrested in 2002 and released more than a year later, just before Premier Wen Jiabao's visit to the United States. See http://www.wired.com/news/politics/0,1283,61420,00.html?tw=wn_story_related.

development of the Internet had simply rendered "snail mail" obsolete. There were almost a hundred million Chinese Internet surfers, all well equipped to exchange information instantly through e-mail, attachments, and links. This was the medium through which the petition of Dr. Jiang Yanyong[4] about the Beijing Massacre and the challenge by Jiao Guobiao[5] to the Propaganda Department were disseminated overnight throughout the Chinese-speaking world.

The censors can block some sites, but they can never block all of them. Thus they caught Du Daobin,[6] but people like Liu Xiaobo and Yu Jie[7] sprang up in his place. The Chinese Communists will never stifle the Internet. Its magic is more powerful than theirs.

---

[4] Dr. Jiang wrote two controversial letters to the Chinese government. One alleged that it was covering up the SARS epidemic. The other urged it to admit that the Beijing Massacre of 1989 had been a mistake. He was placed in military custody for forty-five days, beginning in June 2004. See http://www7.nationalacademies.org/humanrights/Chinese_Surgeon_Jiang_Yanyong_Released .html.

[5] Leading media studies professor at Beijing University, who was persecuted by the authorities and fired from his job in 2005 for an Internet article entitled "Crusade Against the Propaganda Department." See http://www.rfa.org/english/news/politics/2005/03/29/China_Media/.

[6] Cyberdissident Du Daobin was arrested for posting essays critical of the Chinese government on the Internet but got a "light" sentence in 2004 thanks to the international attention his case received. See http://pekingduck.org/archives/001335.php.

[7] Two prominent writer-activists who have been persecuted by the Chinese security police. Liu launched a solidarity campaign in support of Du Daobin. See http://www.ifex.org/en/content/ view/full/59082/.

56

Epiphany

WHEN MY WIFE and children first arrived in America in July 1994, they faced a difficult adjustment to American life. Groggy with jet lag, they holed up for days in our Orange Street apartment, sleeping and watching television. But Xiuqin soon ventured out on long walks around the neighborhood and to the local Chinese grocery store. Industrious by nature, she decided she needed a job; she was not the kind of person to let her lack of working papers and poor command of English stop her from looking for one.

On her walks she scrutinized passersby, trying her Mandarin on the ones who looked Chinese. Unfortunately they never seemed to understand her. When she came home crushed, I pointed out that they might have been Korean or Japanese. One afternoon she happened upon an old couple from Shandong who were visiting to baby-sit for their eight-month-old grandson. As they had to return to China at the end of the month, their son and his wife, who had full-time jobs in New Haven, needed a baby-sitter. By sheer coincidence, the son's wife turned out to be a Xi'an native, and she and Xiuqin cemented their relationship by comparing their neighborhoods in Xi'an. Starting on August 1, the couple delivered their baby into Xiuqin's care every morning. I could barely pronounce his English name, so I adopted the Xi'an custom of calling him Stinky Egg. Xiuqin was happy again. Disposable diapers were a novelty for her, and she enjoyed pushing the baby around in his stroller.

She netted five hundred dollars in the first month. Like other new Chinese immigrants, she multiplied by eight to convert dollars into Chinese yuan. After receiving a paltry sixty yuan a month at the day care center at Jiaotong University for so many years, this was her first taste of the high value placed on labor in America.

"The only good thing about America is the dollar," she declared, in her first verdict on American life.

Every morning she changed Stinky Egg's diaper, buckled him into his stroller, and took him to East Rock Park at the north end of our street. There she networked with other Chinese women pushing their strollers, who helped her search for a better job and expand her base of operations in New Haven.

In the fall I began teaching and our children started school. Xiuqin took Stinky Egg out every day, gradually learning her way around the city and making more Chinese women friends, some of whom could drive. No longer confined to stores within walking distance, she now had access to cheaper groceries. Her friends also took her to the local Chinese church on Sundays. At first she went out of curiosity and the desire to socialize and land a better job. But she found that the prayers spoke to her, and began to put her heart into singing the hymns. Before long she avowed her faith in God, was baptized, and joined the congregation.

She received a godsend that spring, an excellent job manufacturing surgical needles and sutures at the nearby U.S. Surgical Company. Although she had never worked in a factory before, her task was simple, requiring only the ability to sew. She loved stepping into the immaculate, climate-controlled workshop, always met her quota promptly, and snatched up every opportunity for overtime. After a year as a temporary worker she was promoted to a steady job with paid vacations, health and disability insurance, and a pension plan. At first she rode to the factory in a fellow worker's car. Then she rose to the challenge of obtaining a driver's license and learned to navigate the highways in our newly purchased used car.

Her attitude changed as she got used to American life. After a few years she had a new verdict: "Everything in America is fine except English."

English was the sole front on which she had made little progress, mainly because her menial factory job required only a minimal vocabulary. As she put it, she worked in a "United Nations," along with people from China, Vietnam, Laos, Poland, Russia, and Latin America. They spoke English on the job, but during breaks in the coffee shop they broke up into groups and lapsed into their native languages.

In China such a job would have been beyond the reach of Xiuqin, one of the dispossessed. She had low expectations after a lifetime of exploitation and was delighted with the generous treatment of American workers. The factory management valued diversity and did its best to avoid political incorrectness. It came as a surprise to her to be better off in America than she had been in her homeland, thanks to the century-old struggle of American workers, women, and people in general for their rights. Now well into her forties, this was the first time she had ever been accorded a measure of social status and personal dignity.

Like many of the other Chinese women workers in her factory, she came to prefer life in America and was content to stay here. It was enough for her to keep up with news from China through the watered-down official broadcasts on the satellite television in our living room.

Still, she had a nagging sense of obligation to certain people in China. Unreturned favors weighed on her mind like unpaid debts. She often reminded me that she could never have weathered her harrowing lifetime in China without the support of friends and family, and it would be a relief to her to visit them and bring them some cash. In October 2003 she spent her three-week vacation in China and brought me an update on developments there.

Mother's health was declining rapidly; her senility and joint problems had compelled my siblings to consign her to a nursing home in Lintong. Feisty as ever, she hated it there, remaining fixated on moving back to her apartment in Xi'an. I had sensed my brother's and sisters' exasperation with her during our long-distance telephone conversations and was anxious to hear Xiuqin's report.

"Your mother is very well cared for," Xiuqin assured me. "She has a private room with professional nurses around the clock, and your sisters visit her all the time. I took her back to her apartment for a few days, gave her a bath and a pedicure, and pushed her in her wheelchair to visit her sister and her husband, Fifth Aunt and Fifth Uncle. I gave them your best wishes. All in all, your mother is in good health and should live a long time. It's just that she resents her children for sending her to the old folks' home, so she's crotchety no matter what anybody does for her."

This news was disquieting, but I figured there was nothing I could do, and I asked Xiuqin about her village, Gingko Gulch.

"Everything was different. My sister met me at the Xi'an train station, and now there's direct bus service to Danfeng County. The narrow, winding mountain roads were gone, replaced with big straight highways and new bridges and tunnels, so it took us only three hours to get to Iron Valley Station. Then we took a motorized pedicab along the ravine to my house. The mountain paths where I used to lug my basket had been upgraded into country roads. They were still bumpy, but they were drivable. Everyone was scooting around on motorcycles and using tractors instead of human labor for heavy loads. They finally had electricity, and most people had televisions. Some even had telephones.

"The biggest change was the new policy of letting the peasants plant private orchards instead of forcing them to grow grain on terraces in the mountains.* The mountainside is covered with trees, and the only grain fields are on the flats beside the river. But people still have enough grain because the new incentive system means higher yields, and they can buy grain from the government if they need to. Also, most of the young people have moved away to find jobs, and lots of them are in the mines. So the old people, women, and children who are left don't need as much grain.

"There are new houses everywhere, and people like the new system much better than the old one. But it's hard for the peasants to build their own houses. City people, who work in the state sector, are much better off. All they have to do is let their work unit assign them to an apartment and then

---

* During the Cultural Revolution the misguided overcentralization of agriculture resulted in low farm yields and hunger in mountainous areas where the traditional cultivation of fruit trees would have been more appropriate than the forced cultivation of grain.

snap it up later at a discount. The state cares for city people the way farmers care for their livestock. But I really feel sorry for the peasants; with no official benefits, they're left out in the cold like wild animals. All they ask is not to be harassed or saddled with unfair taxes. The best government they can imagine is one that simply leaves them to till their own land in peace.

"They sweated blood for every last brick and tile of their new houses, and some even paid with their lives. About sixteen of the young people who went to work in the mines died in accidents. That makes three villagers out of every hundred in our village of five or six hundred people! Peasants' lives are worthless, and their deaths count for nothing. The ones who are still alive are killing themselves trying to make ends meet.

"Even though I'm fifty-one, the villagers were surprised at how young I look. The other women my age had married early and borne many children, who had already given them grandchildren. With their gray hair and missing teeth, they'd been ground down by hard work until they looked like old ladies."

I asked about her family.

"Life is better, but it's still tough. I come from a family of survivors. I escaped from China, and my sister and her husband got as far as the county seat. My brother's family is still stuck in Ginkgo Gulch, but his sons, who might even make it to college, are probably his ticket out of there."

Her description brought back memories. She had not returned to her village for years, not even when her parents died, because she loathed the "demons" she had had to deal with there. The vicious cadres had prohibited her family from burying her father, still waging class warfare on him even after his death.

"It's forbidden to bury counterrevolutionaries on collective land, so just keep him in your house and let him stink it up forever," the team accountant had blustered. Eventually Xiuqin's uncle and brother-in-law found the courage to inter him secretly.

I asked about her parents' graves and what all the evil cadres were up to these days.

"I burned a paper offering by my parents' graves and sat there and cried for a while. Even though the system has changed, and the days of class struggle are over, the same nasty people are still in power, lording it over everyone else and finding sneaky new ways to line their own pockets. My brother told me about a wicked local mayor, an extortionist and blackmailer, who was hacked to death in the woods by one of his desperate victims.

"Those hicks are so stupid! Now they're jealous of my family's good fortune and claim that it's because Pa's burial site has valuable feng shui. Even the mean accountant who forbade us to lay Pa to rest now wants to be buried in the luckiest site in our family plot, even though he used to call Pa a counterrevolutionary. My brother's trying to stop him. I told my brother to let him shoot off his mouth all he wants to, but to hire a lawyer and sue the pants off of him if he ever lays a finger on our family plot."

A mayor hacked to death, valuable feng shui, the accountant's burial plans: It all sounded so exotic. I did not know whether to be angry or to laugh out loud.

Xiuqin was pleased that she had been able to give cash to her uncle, who had been persecuted for his relationship with her father and whom she had found on his deathbed. She had also mailed money to the cousin who had shown her around Xi'an on his tractor and to Zhuyin's brother, who had taken the risk of helping with the farming while her father had been in the labor camps, and who died soon after her return to New Haven.

I wanted to know what had become of Zhuyin. I remembered that she had rushed into a marriage with an army man soon after my wedding. She had expected her husband to find a steady job in a state-run factory after his discharge from the service, but he had disappointed her by remaining a good-for-nothing peasant. What was worse, his chronic poor health was a severe drain on the family finances.

Xiuqin told me that even though Zhuyin was a year younger than Xiuqin, she looked like the older of the two. When Xiuqin gave her some money, she had collapsed in tears.

"What was it? Was she crying because she was grateful, or was something wrong?" I asked.

"She's a very ambitious person, and the sight of me awakened some complicated feelings."

Sometimes crying helped people to put their tangled emotions into perspective, I reflected. "What happened next?"

"Zhuyin introduced me to her husband and teenage daughter and told them that Mr. Yin had introduced you to her years ago, but she had passed you on to me instead. Her daughter sighed and blurted innocently, 'You sure did her a favor, Ma!' Her husband offered his own explanation. 'Maybe Xiuqin's a better judge of character than your ma,' he said. 'Anyway, these things are all determined by fate. Your personal destiny is yours alone, and nobody can take your place.' I tried to smooth things over by telling them that an ambitious girl like Zhuyin and a dangerous character like you would have been a mismatch. You were such a mess back then that Zhuyin would probably have left you in a few days."

Xiuqin had made a special side trip to Xinwang Village to repay people like Guodong and Xuanmin, whose kindness to me I had often remembered while writing these memoirs.

"I gave money to everyone in Xinwang Village that you asked me to. Peasants aren't calculating and picky like city folks. They seemed pleased with whatever I gave them, even if it wasn't much. Guodong and some other families sent you a homemade checkered cotton bedspread, insisting that you liked village handicrafts. As for myself, to tell the truth, I have no love lost for that village. I'm never going back there again."

Finally she told me about her visit to Mao Zhiyi and Xi Lin in Xi'an, who had capitulated to the Security Bureau; they had submitted written promises never to receive banned reading material from me again and in fact to sever relations with me forever.

"Well, the police got what they wanted," Xiuqin gloated. "They've shut you up. You and all your reactionary propaganda! What was the point of wasting so much money on postage? Your silliness cost you a lot of friendships in Xi'an, and now look at you, an outcast in a foreign land! Like it or not, nobody wants to get that stuff from you in the mail anymore. Xi Lin asked me to tell you to stop calling your friends in Xi'an because the Security Bureau has all the latest eavesdropping technology. Of course you're safe here in America, so you don't have to worry, but don't forget how dangerous it is for your Chinese friends to answer phone calls from you."

Xiuqin gave me a pathetic report on Mao Zhiyi, who had aged considerably, taken early retirement, and now lived in reduced circumstances in the same little apartment. At least his previous correspondence with me had provided him with a tiny escape valve, I mused. How could the Security Bureau be so petty as to deny him such a trivial freedom? Xiuqin's description evoked a clear mental image of my dear old friend's depression. Ever since the moment he rashly hopped a train to try to sneak across the border to Hong Kong, he had yearned for freedom like a frog looking at the sky from the bottom of a well. The Chinese Communists had wrecked his life.

Xiuqin had called on Xi Lin at Shaanxi Normal University. He had moved to a spacious, extravagantly furnished apartment and seemed fairly prosperous. He and his wife, obvious beneficiaries of Deng Xiaoping's policy of economic liberalization, had been very circumspect in their conversation with her. Xi Lin had said that I was a foolhardy person and that he was still angry at me.

I was not the least bit angry at him, however. Professed loyalty to the Communists was simply the pathway to success in China. Finally redeemed from his marginalized state, he had been promoted to full professor and thesis adviser. I saw nothing strange about his wish to keep in step with the current regime.

Xiuqin sighed and gave me some hard-nosed advice: "I think you should simply close the Chinese chapter of your life. Your sisters are taking good care of your mother, and all you need to do is stay in touch by telephone. You're going to have to phase out your friendships in Xi'an. And it's disappointing to return to the countryside. People even threw stones at Jesus when he went back to his home village, although he was hailed as a savior everyplace else. If this happened to him, ordinary people like us are just asking for trouble by returning! I had to make this trip, but I didn't like what I saw over there, so I've made up my mind never to go back. I haven't shed a single tear, and I'm not the least bit sorry. When I boarded the plane for New York in Shanghai, I was completely at peace with my decision."

A wave of homesickness washed over me, but then I came around to Xiuqin's point of view. I penned the following couplet to galvanize my will:

A wanderer doesn't look back,
An intrepid traveler mustn't return home.

"When we get old, let's arrange to be buried in America," I said.

自述

ϵ p i l o g u e

My Children

WHEN WE ARRIVED in America in 1994, my daughter, Kang Qian, and my son, Kang Zhuang, were teenagers, and we had stopped using their childhood nicknames. Their English was poor, and I was afraid they would fall behind in school because they were too old to learn it quickly.

"Don't worry," Professor Chang assured me. "Kids pick up languages in no time. Soon they'll be so Americanized that you'll be more concerned about their Chinese."

As our local public school was next to East Rock Park, in the metropolitan New Haven school district, its student body was diverse. My colleagues at Yale looked down their noses at it; it was not an exclusive suburban school. Yet I thought that it was the right place for my children, who faced a huge cultural adjustment. The atmosphere was tolerant and inclusive of the slower students. Unlike Chinese students, who lugged around huge backpacks full of books all day long, the students here owned no textbooks. Instead, the teacher kept the books and handed them out during class. My children had to borrow books from the teacher when they wanted to work at home.

I had never demanded good grades of my children. As a teacher I knew that grades were an imperfect measure of a student's ability and that competition in high school served no purpose other than to determine college admissions. In China, however, once education was released from the grip of politics in the 1980s, grades reigned supreme. When Kang Qian was at the Jiaotong University middle school, she often complained that the teachers chose their pets, as well as class officers and Communist Youth League members, on the basis of academic performance. She always felt like an outsider because she never got good grades. I remembered being ostracized for my "poor performance" in middle school. Was my daughter doomed to follow in my footsteps?

In China the teachers often made the parents of laggards stay after PTA meetings for a special long-winded "report." I don't know if the other parents reprimanded their children afterward, but I always shrugged off the teacher's needling. Far from feeling disgraced by my children's poor grades, I objected to the educational system itself, which discriminated against slow students by publicizing grades and unduly emphasizing class rank. When I finally stood up and said so at a PTA meeting one evening, the teacher and all the parents glowered at me in shock, as if I were completely crazy.

My children were not academically gifted. If I nagged them, they could get marginally respectable grades; otherwise their grades remained low. All around me I saw pushy parents tirelessly supervising their children's homework. Frankly, I had better things to do. In my opinion, the teachers were assigning too much homework if the students were incapable of finishing it on their own.

My children's mediocre transcripts followed them to New Haven, but fortunately their new school upheld a student's right to privacy and had other criteria for student assessment. Kang Qian told me that her teachers were much kinder and more encouraging than the ones in China. One American teacher brought chocolate to class and rewarded students for correct answers, as if training puppies. Another allowed her to return after lunch to complete a chemistry exam that she had been unable to finish before the bell rang at the end of the class hour. I could scarcely believe my ears. A teacher in China would be reprimanded for such "irresponsibility." But for Kang Qian, who was still struggling with English, this relaxed, respectful tone was much more effective than harshness would have been. Eventually her English improved, she was chosen for the football cheerleading squad, and she made plenty of friends. Even gregariousness, regarded as a student's shortcoming in China, was hailed as a virtue here.

As a teacher I despised grade grubbers, especially those who whined unless they ranked number one in the class. I preferred students like my daughter, who accepted their low grades without protest. More than blind fatherly love, my support of her was my household antidote to the Chinese educational system. My children grew up to be lively, resilient, and independent, and I like to think it was at least in part because they were not anxious about grades. Ultimately they thrived like plants potted in moist soil, and their latent talents blossomed.

Kang Zhuang was a poor writer in Chinese. When assigned to compose an essay in his Chinese school, he would stare dumbly at his blank sheet of paper while he gnawed on his pencil. Once I caught him doing this in front of the begonia on our windowsill. I saw that he had scrawled a few lines in his notebook.

"Oh, begonia, teach me to withstand the icy wind!" it read.

"Isn't that a bit of an exaggeration?" I asked. "How can you learn from a plant?"

"That's what the teacher told us to write. Our homework is to write an essay like 'The Pine Tree,' a model essay in our textbook comparing brave Communist Party members to evergreens in winter. Everybody is supposed to sing the praises of a plant. You can choose whatever plant you want, but all we have in our house is this begonia."

He had my sympathy. In my opinion, the assignment, rather than his lack of talent, was entirely to blame for his writer's block. I advised him not to force anything and even to hand in a blank paper if necessary.

In private, however, I lamented my children's lack of interest in literature. How different they were from me! In fact my refusal to push them was largely a rationalization; I knew such pressure would be useless. Still, I was worried about their prospects for college.

To my great surprise, Kang Zhuang turned out to have an aptitude for English. The kind of child who responded best to praise, he flourished once he was free of the harsh Chinese academic environment. During his second summer vacation in America he went to Zimbabwe for a few weeks as a member of the New Haven Middle School Students' International Delegation to Africa. When he returned, he wrote a prizewinning article for the school newspaper. He would never have had such an opportunity at the elitist Jiaotong University middle school. Perhaps American public schools were less rigorous than their Chinese counterparts and overly tolerant of laziness and ignorance. Nonetheless, there was no doubt in my mind that their nurturing atmosphere benefited average students, who were after all the majority.

When my friends in China told me how lucky I was, I replied, "It's not a big change for me. All I've done is switch from a famous university in China to one in America. My children are the lucky ones. Their new school has turned them around completely."

I was delighted that my relationship with my parents was not repeating itself in my relationship with my children. My parents had always mistrusted me as a nonconformist and a troublemaker. I could barely recall an occasion when they had ever praised or encouraged me. Instead, they had constantly echoed the admonishments of my teachers and party secretaries and tried to enforce the rules of the police state on me at home. Of course, their vigilance had been well intentioned, motivated by fear for my own good and for the safety of our family.

The politicization of Chinese society was so pervasive that even my parents were forced to cast me as a "reactionary" and write me off as a wayward son. Father and I parted forever in anger over politics. And my most recent visit to Mother in Xi'an was disrupted by my horrifying arrest. During the process of writing this book, I have often recalled my parents' constant scolding and their disappointment in me. Such remembrances still evoke feelings of remorse and indignation, tormenting me like the rasping of a rat's teeth on old furniture in the night.

Both my children eventually became American citizens. As the clerk in the American Embassy in Beijing had predicted, Kang Qian never returned to China. Since her graduation from the University of Connecticut, she has continued to live with us, driving herself to her job at a nearby company. She has plenty of friends and enjoys socializing on her days off. Sometimes she brings me along, in order to "keep me young." My children have provided me with invaluable exposure to the realities of American social life. Otherwise, given my poor English and rarefied existence as a Chinese teacher, I would have been forced to rely on mere book learning.

Without asking my permission, Kang Zhuang enlisted in the army after graduating from high school. He knew that we had not accumulated enough of a nest egg to put two children through college simultaneously. One day, after a trip to Boston for his physical, he told me of his decision. The army would pay his college tuition while he was on active duty, he said, freeing me to support Kang Qian. Three years later he came home and spent six months finishing his bachelor's degree online. Because of his experience as a supply manager in the army, he quickly landed a job as fleet manager in a big company in upstate New York.

In China his grades were worse than his sister's; in fact he was at the bottom of his class. Now, however, he never misses an opportunity to demonstrate his maturity and competence to me. He calls me almost daily to talk about his job, and I listen, make suggestions, and try to be generally supportive. Since I know little about his profession, he often lectures me as if I were his student. The tables have turned; he had to listen to me the whole time he was growing up, but now he is doing the talking.

I have truly achieved salvation. Not through writing this book, as I expected, and not through the long-awaited rehabilitation papers I received from the Chinese government but vicariously, through my children.

My parents dismissed me as a disgrace, a failure, and a good-for-nothing. With hindsight, I suspect that my decision to be adopted by a stranger fulfilled their unconscious desires.

But I have no need to worry about Kang Qian and Kang Zhuang or to struggle to rein them in, as my parents did with me. My relationship with them is free of the watchfulness, evasiveness, fear, and aggravation that poisoned my relationship with my father. This is largely because they are free to read and write anything they choose. Kang Zhuang composes short essays in English, which he loves to e-mail me for my praise. He reads in English, especially biographies of historical figures such as Jefferson and Franklin. Kang Qian still reads in Chinese, occasionally flipping through the classic *Dream of the Red Chamber* or a contemporary novel. But she refuses to read my books, which seem hardly to register on her consciousness.

Once I put one of my newly published books by her bed, hoping she would read it, and discovered later with disappointment that she had not touched it.

"Take it easy, Dad," she teased. "Writing is like an audiotape or video-tape of the author. I only read books by authors I don't know personally. I see you every day. We eat together and go for walks, and your voice and laugh are familiar. I've even listened to you clearing your throat all the time when you're writing all those books. What do I need to read them for?"

I laughed in embarrassment. Then I asked myself: Why did I still need to look to writing for closure? My daughter embodied the closure I sought.

My son was more ambitious than my fun-loving daughter. After earning his M.B.A. in 2003, he went to China to interview at some newly opened American companies there. He loved Shanghai and worked for a time in the Shanghai headquarters of an American company. Soon after his return to America the company offered him a job as regional sales manager. In late December he quit his job in upstate New York and came home to prepare to move to Shanghai.

Xiuqin tried to talk him out of going, but he refused to listen to her, so she asked me to talk to him. I could understand that she, as a mother, was worried about letting her son go so far away, but I did not want to cater to her subjective, catastrophic vision of China. Completely disgusted with what she had seen there, she was unduly worried about the lure of Chinese corruption for a young man like Kang Zhuang. Shanghai was a debauched place, she said, rife with dens of iniquity, where he would be fraternizing with sleazy officials and businessmen. He was in danger of picking up a raft of vices. Why was he giving up his nice safe job here for such a risk?

"Maybe you've been watching too many Chinese soap operas about combating corruption?" I said. "Yes, there's vice in China, but it's no more contagious than it is here. America is plagued with drugs and violence, but your son never became an addict or a murderer. He comes of good stock. If he doesn't have an inherited predisposition to immorality, he'll be safe, but if he does, it's no use worrying. You ought to trust your children as extensions of yourself. The best you can do as a Christian is to pray for him and ask God to protect him."

By "God," I meant the Bodhisattva Guanyin, the embodiment of the human proclivity for good, in which I was a firm believer. Maybe biology is destiny, but our own inclinations, combined with luck, determine how we actually fare in the world. Our goodness is rooted in our ancestral legacy and perpetuated by family relationships, ethical traditions, and personal effort. The Chinese Communists have engaged in an unprecedented fifty-year rampage against this intricate social fabric, creating a moral vacuum. Their regime, with its capricious schemes to remodel Chinese society, has turned out to be the real reactionary force. My objections, and those of countless people like me, represent the desire to restore the natural human tendency to strive for good.

I trusted that my son's rearing would bring out the best in him.

Xiuqin gradually calmed down, and Kang Zhuang got ready for his trip. I saw him off at Kennedy Airport. He was carrying his American passport, M.B.A. diploma, and newly updated résumé. Everything about him gleamed like a painting freshly applied to white canvas. Gratified, I reflected that he must have inherited some of my strengths. But his life would be much better than mine. He had more vigor and self-confidence than I had ever possessed, and he would be much safer. At the very least the Security Bureau had no dossier on him. No matter what setbacks lay ahead, it was reassuring to see him off to a flying start, like a jet plane.

Spring had arrived. Stepping onto the deck outside my study, I allowed my fatigued eyes to roam over the budding greenery in our yard. An airplane soared across the blue sky, trailing a long, gauzy ribbon of white smoke. As I watched it fade, like the diaphanous brushstrokes of the "flying white" style of calligraphy, I grew pensive, and my mind wandered to that faraway place. A piece of myself was going back there, I mused. I was an exile, but I could return vicariously through my son. He would find more constructive things to do than make money in China. There were millions of seekers there living in a moral vacuum. They were as full of youthful promise as he was, and some were more talented, but they had not had his advantages. I hoped that he would cast his lot with them and that they would carve out a new future together. And as I had at such moments throughout my life, I offered a silent prayer to the Bodhisattva Guanyin, the goddess of compassion and mercy.

TRANSLATOR'S NOTE

I would like to thank Kang Zhengguo for his enthusiastic assistance throughout the translation process. He has glossed terms, provided background information, made adaptations for the English reader, and checked the entire translation for accuracy.

I have used the Pinyin system of romanization throughout, except for a few names that may be more familiar in other spellings. References to Internet addresses in the notes to this translation are current as of the summer of 2006.

Susan Wilf

INDEX

Page numbers in *italics* refer to illustrations.

Chaoying (woman student), 336–37
Chen Duxiu, 10
Chengdu, 363, 390–96, 398, 407
Chen Kejian, 199, 210, 216
Chen Ziming, 366
China:
  air pollution in, 362
  constitution of, 93–94, 375
  customs procedures of, 351, 352, 354
  economy of, 14n, 25–27, 75, 178, 247–48, 334n, 355, 370–71, 373–74, 380, 407, 411–12, 416, 419, 436, 443
  famines in, 25–27, 51–52, 163, 178, 188, 248, 257, 272, 312–13, 314n, 315
  imperial period of, *see specific dynasties and emperors*
  industrial production of, 7, 14–15, 75–76, 118, 221, 222
  legal code of, 224, 404, 406, 408
  military of, 3–6, 97–98, 100, 183–84, 226, 272, 312, 314, 368
  moral corruption in, xi, 196–98, 275, 370, 374–75, 383, 393–94, 413, 421–22, 442
  peasantry of, xv–xvii, 12, 25–27, 47n, 68, 83, 91–92, 107, 138, 179, 184, 195, 197, 229–32, 248–49, 254, 272–76, 277, 283–85, 313, 314n, 375, 411–16, 417, 419, 432–35
  rural areas of, xiii, xv–xvii, 12, 25–27, 98–99, 222–23, 229–32, 247–48, 272–76, 277, 417, 432–35
  tourism in, 51, 355–56, 393
  urban areas of, xvi–xvii, 25–26, 92, 98, 188, 256–58, 302, 319–20, 341–42, 417, 419, 432–33
  water pollution in, 411–12
China Café, 169–70, 172
China Monthly, 400, 409–10
Chinese classical literature, 18–19, 35–36, 42, 57, 78, 84, 166, 185–86, 191, 292, 338, 340, 344, 347, 349, 356–61, 378, 402
Chinese Communist Party:
  agricultural policies of, xiv, xv–xviii, 14, 21n, 25–27, 178, 248, 249–50, 254–55, 270–71, 284, 327, 412, 432
  birth control policy of, 328n
  cadres of, 110, 129, 144, 146, 183–84, 197, 199, 209, 210, 211–18, 229, 236, 248–49, 253, 283–88, 314, 319, 339, 346, 363, 384, 414
  Central Committee of, 97, 99, 113, 313, 334–35, 340
  domestic campaigns of, 7–11, 12, 20–21, 23, 32n, 42, 43, 47–48, 53, 64, 73, 91–93, 97, 99, 100–101, 149, 177–78, 188, 192, 313, 415

economic policies of, 7, 14–15, 25–27, 52, 75–76, 118, 178, 245–46, 334n
educational policies of, 35, 292, 318, 336n, 338–40, 348–49, 437–38
leadership of, 100–101, 108–16, 334–35, 363, 364–65, 367–68, 371
martial law imposed by, 367–70, 371
membership of, xix, 11–12, 48, 49, 55–56, 96–97, 227
official jargon of, xix–xxii, 22–23, 93n, 104–5, 111, 116, 131–32, 147, 149, 177–78, 338, 358–59, 383, 386
political opposition to, xv, xix, xxiv, 103n, 178–80, 181, 189–91, 294, 313–14, 317, 349, 352, 363–81, 383, 393, 400, 408, 418, 428
propaganda of, xv, 20–21, 22, 36, 38, 51, 91, 113, 116, 156–57, 275, 290–91, 338, 348, 394, 419
repression by, xii–xiv, xviii, xix, xxiv, 22–23, 39–40, 46–47, 48, 50–51, 56, 72, 89–94, 102–3, 211–12, 253, 291, 334n, 348–49, 352, 363–81, 383, 384, 393, 394, 400, 408, 421–22, 426–28, 443
rise to power of, 3–6, 189–90, 241, 247, 260, 272, 417
socialist ideals of, xiii–xiv, 11–12, 21, 36, 40, 48, 51, 54, 69–70, 78, 89–99, 189–90, 275, 279n, 314, 378, 387, 402, 433–34
Chinese language, xx–xxi, xxii, 18, 91, 165–66, 168, 174n, 175, 351, 424, 439, 443
Chinese medicine, 169, 191–92, 196, 318, 390–91
Chinese Soviet Republic, 100
Christians, 211–12, 215–16, 224, 374–75, 424, 427, 442
Chronicle of Higher Education, 427
Chu, King of, 57
Chu Anping, xxii–xxiii
Civil War in France, The (Marx), 189–90
class struggle, 40, 48, 69–70, 74, 89–99, 101n, 104, 173–74, 177–79, 275, 314, 433–34
Clinton, Bill, 403
coal mines, 221, 222
College Russian, 78
communes, xv–xvii, 92–94, 106, 107, 137, 138, 188, 221, 222–23, 224, 228–32, 235, 248, 270–71, 274, 284, 296, 302, 338–39, 418
Communist Youth League, 23, 40, 43, 48, 53, 55, 67, 74, 97, 159, 363, 438
Complete Works of Lu Xun, The (Lu), 105
Complete Works of Zhang Taiyan, The (Zhang), 104
Comrade Wang Ruofei in Prison, 76
condolence stipends, 299–300, 310

Made in the USA
Middletown, DE
03 November 2019